Sustainability, Big Data, and Corporate Social Responsibility

Sustainability, Big Data, and Corporate Social Responsibility

Evidence from the Tourism Industry

Edited by
Mohammed El Amine Abdelli, Nadia Mansour,
Atilla Akbaba, and Enric Serradell-Lopez

CRC Press
Taylor & Francis Group
Boca Raton London New York

CRC Press is an imprint of the
Taylor & Francis Group, an **informa** business

First edition published 2022
by CRC Press
6000 Broken Sound Parkway NW, Suite 300, Boca Raton, FL 33487-2742

and by CRC Press
4 Park Square, Milton Park, Abingdon, Oxon, OX14 4RN

CRC Press is an imprint of Taylor & Francis Group, LLC

Library of Congress Cataloging-in-Publication Data
Names: Abdelli, Mohammed El Amine, editor. | Mansour, Nadia, 1984– editor. |
Akbaba, Atilla, 1969– editor. | Serradell-Lopez, Enric, editor.
Title: Sustainability, big data, and corporate social responsibility:
evidence from the tourism industry / edited by Mohammed El Amine Abdelli,
Nadia Mansour, Atilla Akbaba, and Enric Serradell-Lopez.
Description: Boca Raton: CRC Press, 2022. |
Includes bibliographical references and index.
Identifiers: LCCN 2021052590 (print) |
LCCN 2021052591 (ebook) | ISBN 9780367685508 (hardback) |
ISBN 9780367685546 (paperback) | ISBN 9781003138051 (ebook)
Subjects: LCSH: Social responsibility of business. | Big data.
Classification: LCC HD60.S884647 2022 (print) |
LCC HD60 (ebook) | DDC 658.4/08–dc23/eng/20211104
LC record available at https://lccn.loc.gov/2021052590
LC ebook record available at https://lccn.loc.gov/2021052591

ISBN: 978-0-367-68550-8 (hbk)
ISBN: 978-0-367-68554-6 (pbk)
ISBN: 978-1-003-13805-1 (ebk)

DOI: 10.1201/9781003138051

Typeset in Times
by Newgen Publishing UK

Contents

Foreword

The tourism sector in the life of societies and the general economy is growing in importance day by day. In all areas of life, a digital transformation is taking place. The digital transformation is taking place in the tourism sector as well. This digital transformation is changing the face of tourism. This book gives us a theoretical and empirical framework to link the fields of digital transformation and tourism. It is written for professionals who want to innovate in the tourism sector and promote sustainability and corporate social responsibility. The book outlines good applications of sustainability and corporate social responsibility by linking tourism with digital transformations. This book is an excellent guide for tourism professionals to explore solutions and implications of digital transformations for sustainability and corporate social responsibility. Particularly useful for destination managers, hoteliers, educators, students, investors, and tourism planners.

Professor Patrick Paul Walsh,
Director of the Centre for Sustainable Development Studies,
University College Dublin,
Senior Adviser—UN Sustainable Development Solutions Network

Preface

For many destinations worldwide, tourism is very important for its weight in GDP, and some regions are even dependent on tourism. Because of the growing strength of this industry, the question of the effect of technological innovation is becoming more and more frequent, particularly in destinations that are taking up activity or destinations, which have had setbacks because of tourism activity. In the era of digital transformation, we are seeing a significant increase in tourist bookings.

This impressive performance was partially made possible by a better knowledge of customers' preferences who now carry out a large part of their shopping journey on the internet, thus enabling firms to have relevant information to guide them in setting up their offers. Big Data is, therefore, more than ever at the service of tourism growth!

Indeed, the data collected shed very direct light on consumer behavior, making it possible to account for the existing situation and better frame the evolution scenarios, and thus streamline internal decision-making. And on the other hand, companies use Big Data to better retain and redirect their customers toward high value-added offerings, which directly impacts the competitiveness of tourism companies. Professionals believe that the personalization of offers and the targeting made possible thanks to Big Data are crucial for their business development. Also, a significant part of the tourism companies' marketing budget is now dedicated to digital.

This situation leads us to ask questions about ethics. Companies must ensure ethical data management (General Data Protection Regulation [GDPR]) that they collect for their business. Privacy and monetization of data appear to be crucial issues in this regard. Furthermore, the development of technologies associated with Big Data requires companies and individuals to define acceptable limits.

However, the entry into force of the GDPR provides a drastic framework for the collection, processing, and retention of data, at the risk of being subject to very heavy penalties.

Hence, the application and institutionalization of Corporate Social Responsibility and Sustainability in the tourism sector seem relevant, especially in destinations with vulnerable environments.

Indeed, this question answers the communication on CSR and Sustainability launched by companies faced with the risks of stricter regulation of their activities. In response to the pressing demands of markets—investors and consumers—and the activism of nongovernmental organizations affecting their reputations, strive to legitimize their actions by adopting new decision-making criteria: Ethical criteria. The company then seeks to communicate as clearly as possible the key elements of its ethical practices.

Editor Biographies

Mohammed El Amine Abdelli is a researcher at the University of Western Brittany and the Technical University of Cartagena. He is a member at Western Economics and Management Laboratory—LEGO—and a Visiting Researcher at the University of Salamanca (Spain). Mohammed El Amine's research interests focus on Big Data, Entrepreneurship, Governance, Innovation, and Sustainable Development. He is an editor of several books. He was a guest editor of several high-quality journals (Scopus) and published 15 papers between chapters and articles. He is a committee member of several international conferences in the UK, India, China, Turkey, Algeria, and Estonia. He is an editorial board member of several indexed journals (Scopus).

Nadia Mansour is an assistant professor at the Faculty of Economics and Management of Sousse—Tunisia. She is also a visiting researcher at the University of Salamanca—Spain. She holds a PhD in Management Sciences from the Higher Institute of Management of Sousse—Tunisia. Mansour's research interests focus on Banking, Macro-economic, Business Tourism, Entrepreneurship, Education, and Innovation. Mansour is a member of Interdisciplinary Research Laboratory on Changes in Economies and Enterprises—Tunisia, an academic member and ambassador of Communication Institute of Greece, a committee member of ICMHHE2020 conference, editorial board member of the 'Journal of Entrepreneurship Education,' fellow member of the Global Journals, a reviewer in the 'International Journal of Corporate Finance and Accounting (IJCFA),' and 'International Organization for Migration.' Mansour has presented various scientific papers in international (France, Morocco, USA) and national (Tunisia) conferences. In 2018, Mansour published two papers in the Global Journal of Management and Business Research: The first titled 'Prudential regulation and banking efficiency in MENA countries,' and the second 'Prudential regulation and banking risk in MENA countries.' In 2019, Mansour published a paper in Global Journal of Management and Business Research, titled 'Interaction risk banking and financial stability: MENA countries.' For 2020, she has also two book chapters accepted in IGI GLOBAL: The first titled 'Leadership and innovation on business tourism: implication of employees,' and the second 'Girls child education challenges and solutions in MENA countries: case study Tunisia.'

Atilla Akbaba is a professor at the Faculty of Tourism at İzmir Katip Çelebi University (İzmir, Turkey). He received his MSc from Florida International University and his PhD from Dokuz Eylul University with a major in Tourism Management. He teaches hospitality and tourism-related courses. His areas of specialization include service quality, organizational culture, and management of tourism businesses. He has published widely in his areas of specialization at national and international levels.

Enric Serradell-Lopez is Associate Dean and Professor at the Business Economics Department at the Universitat Oberta de Catalunya (Spain). Serradell holds a PhD in Management from the University of Barcelona. His work combines professional and academic activities. His main research lines are eLearning, corporate culture, intangibles, and product innovation and ICT applications in management, especially business games. He is the director of the Go2sim research team—Innovative tools for eLearning—that aims to analyze and design environments in which personal and professional decision-making skills can be created and adequately developed. His research has been published in academic journals and presented in recognized international conferences.

Contributors

1. **Mohammed El Amine Abdelli,** *University of Western Brittany, Brest, France*
2. **Emel Adamış,** *Bursa Uludağ University, Bursa, Turkey*
3. **Abderrahmane Nadja Afifi,** *Djillali Liabes University, Algeria*
4. **Hasan Evrim Arici,** *EU Business School Munich, Munich, Germany*
5. **Nagihan Cakmakoglu Arici,** *TR General Consulate Stuttgart, Germany*
6. **Nilgün Avci,** *Ege University, Bornova, Turkey*
7. **Ekrem Aydın,** *Artvin Coruh University, Artvin, Turkey*
8. **Tahar Lazhar Ayed,** *College of Business, Umm Al-Qura University, Mecca, KSA*
9. **Özge Çalhan,** *Univ of İzmir Katip Çelebi, İzmir, Turkey*
10. **Ouahiba Chehat,** *University of Algiers 3, Dély Ibrahim, Algeria*
11. **Samet Can Curkan,** *Ege University, Bornova, Turkey*
12. **Mohamed Fadhel Djlassi,** *Mediterranean School of Business, Tunis, Tunisia*
13. **Eren Erkiliç,** *Recep Tayyip Erdoğan University, Rize, Turkey*
14. **İlknur Eskin,** *Trakya University, Edirne, Turkey*
15. **Anissa Ben Hassine,** *ESSEC de Tunis, University of Tunis, Tunis, Tunisia*
16. **Cenk Murat Kocoglu,** *Karabuk University, Karabük, Turkey*
17. **Hasan Tahsin Kokonalioğlu,** *Kırklareli University, Kırklareli, Turkey*
18. **Hande Akyurt Kurnaz,** *Bolu Abant İzzet Baysal University, Bolu, Turkey*
19. **Nadia Mansour,** *University of Sousse, Sousse, Tunisia*
20. **Funda Ön,** *Muğla Sıtkı Koçman University, Muğla, Turkey*
21. **Omer Sarac,** *Kastamonu University, Kastamonu, Turkey*
22. **Bükre Aslan Savaşan,** *Izmir Katip Çelebi University, İzmir, Turkey*
23. **Khaled Tamzini,** *University of Sousse, Sousse, Tunisia*
24. **Sihem Touati,** *University of Algiers 3, Dély Ibrahim, Algeria*
25. **Demet Tüzünkan,** *Istanbul Kent University, Istanbul, Turkey*
26. **Ahmet Vatan,** *Istanbul Medeniyet University, Istanbul, Turkey*
27. **Senem Yazici,** *Mugla Sitki Kocman University, Muğla, Turkey*
28. **Faruk Yüksel,** *Ordu University, Ordu, Turkey*

Part I

Sustainability and Tourism Businesses

1 Innovation as a Key Driver of Sustainability in Tourism

Ekrem Aydın

CONTENTS

1.1 INTRODUCTION

According to the World Tourism Organization (WTO), tourism revenues and tourist arrivals have increased worldwide since 1950. Although this increase in tourist arrivals provides economic benefits to tourist destinations, it becomes difficult to satisfy the increasing needs and prevent damage to the natural, cultural, and social environment. Thus, to reduce the ill effects, the concept of sustainability has come to the fore in the tourism industry (Prud'homme and Raymond 2013). Considering the dependence of tourism activities on the social, cultural, and physical environment, sustainability

DOI: 10.1201/9781003138051-2

has been shown as one of the main strategies that can be used to develop the tourism industry (Ceylan 2019). In the tourism literature, researchers have conceived the concept of sustainability as *sustainable tourism development* (Andereck 2009, Kuščer et al. 2017, Nunkoo et al. 2019, Park and Kim 2016, Poudel et al. 2014, Rasoolimanesh et al. 2017, Ribaric 2015). Sustainable tourism development refers to the practice of creating an equilibrium among the economic, environmental, and social benefits of tourism development and the impact of such action on tourist destinations. Moreover, sustainable tourism development aims to improve the community's quality of life while simultaneously protecting the environment and other local elements for future generations (Rasoolimanesh et al. 2017).

While sustainability is crucial for the tourism industry, implementing this idea is still debated (Park and Kim 2016). Regarding this issue, some researchers suggest that innovation is one of the most crucial factors in supporting sustainability in the tourism industry (Booyens and Rogerson 2016, Elmo et al. 2020, Hjalager 1997, Horng et al. 2016, Marakova and Medved'ova 2016, Ribaric 2015). The long-term survival and consistent performance of tourism enterprises depend on their ability to be innovative (Elmo et al. 2020). In addition to eliminating the adverse effects of tourism on the environment and society, innovation also supports creating new ideas that will contribute to the sustainability of tourism destinations (Horng et al. 2016, Marakova and Medved'ova, 2016). Tourists prefer innovative tourist destinations over their noninnovative competitors. Therefore, innovation is the foundation of competition and sustainable tourism development (Ribaric 2015). Schumpeter's innovation theory is the starting point (Alsos et al. 2014). According to Schumpeter, innovation is the research, discovery, development, advancement, acceptance, and commercialization of new processes, products, organizational structures, and procedures. This definition is generally accepted in all sectors, including tourism (Nordin 2003).

Within this framework, this section aims to reveal the contribution of innovation to sustainable tourism development. This section consists of *Innovation in Tourism, Sustainable Tourism Development, Innovation, and Sustainable Tourism Development.* Furthermore, the relationship between social innovation, eco-innovation practices, and sustainable tourism development is explained within the section on innovation and sustainable tourism development.

1.2 INNOVATION IN TOURISM

Innovation has become almost a prerequisite for the sustainability, survival, and future growth of modern industries operating in today's highly competitive global market. As one of the different subsectors of the worldwide economy, tourism strives to expand in an intensely competitive environment. Therefore, it is not surprising that tourism companies are suggested to turn to innovations to keep up with the changing environment and gain a competitive advantage (Divisekera and Nguyen 2018). In other terms, the competitiveness of tourism enterprises depends solely on their ability to offer new products to meet the demands and requirements of potential customers and engage in innovative activities that can achieve higher-quality output at lower costs (Onan et al. 2020).

Flexible working hours, higher income, more free time, and the change in the value of holidays (seen as part of life) have created new lifestyles. Accordingly, customer requests and needs have also been altered. Punctuality, financial responsibility, convenience, speed, and fee have been perceived as essential service quality components. Therefore, tourism companies need to innovate to meet these changing customer types (Weiermair 2006). Innovation supports tourism companies in adopting new ideas, improving service processes, and boosting operational efficiency (Horng et al. 2016).

However, innovations for the tourism sector can be easily imitated by competitors. For this reason, the innovations must be sustainable and improved. This situation encourages tourism enterprises to compete and repeatedly innovate (Çamlı 2010).

According to Hjalager (2010), tourism is a sector with intense innovations. For example, Thomas Cook's first railway excursion on which he took a certain number of people to England, Disney movies and theme parks, Roy Kroc's acquisition of McDonald's, and making the company the world's number one in the fast-food sector are the examples of innovation in the tourism industry. Besides these, the creation of new tourism experiences can be seen as an innovation. For instance, consumer awareness toward the environment has led tourism companies to a process through which they can improve and renew their environmental performance. As a result, tourism types of eco-tourism and adventure tourism that can be considered innovations in the sector have emerged (Tuzlukaya 2009).

Furthermore, as a result of new technologies, there have been improvements in new skills, materials, services, and organization forms. For instance, due to the adaptation of e-commerce to the tourism sector, a new business domain called e-tourism has emerged. Therefore, new technologies can facilitate new technological innovations in the following phases in case of need (Coşkun 2013).

Schumpeter's innovation theory is regarded as a point of origin in the tourism literature (Alsos et al. 2014). According to Schumpeter, innovation involves the research, discovery, improvement, advancement, acceptance, and commercialization of new processes, new products, new organizational structures, and procedures. This definition is generally accepted in all sectors, including tourism (Nordin 2003). For example, influenced by Schumpeter's innovation theory, Hjalager (1997, 2002, 2010) categorized innovations in the tourism industry into five groups: Product/service innovation, process innovation, management innovation, institutional innovation, and marketing innovation.

1.2.1 Product/Service Innovation

Product/service innovation requires modern organizations to survive, grow, increase their market value, and maintain and improve their competitive position. Product innovation involves introducing a completely new or improved product and service that has been significantly improved in terms of its features or intended uses to the market (Eraslan et al. 2008). In other words, product/service innovations refer to changes observed directly by customers and accepted as new, either never seen at all or unique to specific enterprises or destinations. Nevertheless, such innovations are noticeable to customers and essential in purchasing decisions (Hjalager 2010).

Loyalty programs, environmentally sustainable lodging facilities, and organizations based on local traditions are examples of new tourism products developed in recent years (Hjalager 2002). Moreover, the concept of Formula 1 in the lodging industry is a generic innovation represented by the Accor Hotel chain. These hotels offer low-cost services without meeting the necessary and essential standards such as accessibility, hygiene, and comfortable bedding (Hjalager 2010).

1.2.2 Process Innovation

Process innovations often refer to behind-the-scenes initiatives aimed at enhancing efficiency, productivity, and workflow. Technology investments are supported by process innovation (Hjalager 2010). Process innovations improve the performance of existing processes through new or enhanced technologies or reorganization of the whole production line. Process innovation may be combined with or concluded in product innovation (Hjalager 2002). Restaurant kitchens pose important examples of process innovations. Foodservice technologies offer faster and best preparation methods, energy and labor savings, waste reduction, best sanitation, fast service, and high flexibility. On the other hand, with the invention of automatic check-in systems, both customers and employees save time (Hjalager 2010). Besides, using computer-aided management and monitoring systems in the tourism sector, robots, and self-service instruments in maintenance and cleaning businesses may be given as examples of process innovation (Hjalager 2002).

1.2.3 Managerial (Administrative) Innovation

It consists of management innovation, new business profiles, partnership structures, and authorization systems. A combination of new products, services, and production technologies exists. Staff empowerment is achieved through participation, training, and job enrichment. The unqualified ones are empowered with scientific management methods (Hjalager 2002).

Managerial innovation handles new means of organizing internal integration, staff empowerment and orientation, career building, and compensating work with paid benefits. One of the toughest challenges for many tourism companies involves keeping staff, maintaining flexibility, and controlling costs. Managerial innovation may also aim to improve workplace satisfaction, foster internal knowledge, and competition tools. Hjalager (2010) outlines that 'McDonald's early conceptual accomplishments in this particular field of innovation: well-planned training and socialisation, promotion from within, and enforcement of corporate values.' Various enterprises have adapted these methods and tried to improve them—for instance, the Disney Corporation.

On the other hand, reinforcing team spirit is also accepted as managerial innovation and is perceived as a requirement, especially in the knowledge-based segments of tourism. The first contribution to the comprehension of organizational innovation was made by Hochschild (1983). Hochschild asserted that successful airline management required the managed hearts of flight attendants and the products that contained human feelings. Again, attention has been drawn to human resources management, especially considering the lodging industry. Management innovation is a process that should occur not only for paid employees but also for the participation of voluntary staff (Hjalager 2010).

1.2.4 Institutional Innovation

The concept of institutional innovation is described as 'the implementation of a new organizational method in the commercial applications, workplace organizations, and external relations of the enterprises' (OECD/Eurostat 2005).

In other words, institutional innovation is the adoption of a new system, device, policy, process, program, product, and service, either developed or obtained from outside within the organization. In this context, a new product, service, production process, production technology, administrative system, or structure that concerns the institutional innovation organization and its members involve an innovation process that includes or interacts with a new plan or program (Uzkurt 2012b). Also, institutional innovations emerge as factors that contribute significantly to the exchange of information, learning ability, work efficiency, and quality with internal and external respondents with whom the organization is in contact. As a result, innovation would significantly improve organizations' performances (OECD/Eurostat 2005).

The importance of studies conducted on networks and partnerships, considered fundamental to support innovation in tourism research studies, has gradually increased. Nonetheless, new institutions may also affect enterprises and their customers by resulting in wide-range changes. For example, credit card–issuing banks represent an institutional innovation, along with their remote access applications. The intensive associations of the American Express with tourism actors indicate compulsory groupings/clusters (Hjalager 2010). Moreover, computerized reservation systems are institutional innovations that significantly impact access to products on a large scale, competition, and wages. When first introduced in the 1950s, licensing and franchising arrangements were also among the leading institutional innovations. Institutional innovations have significantly improved the spread and supply of product/service and process innovations to quite distant parts of the world (Hjalager 2010). Furthermore, financial incentive reforms that restructure social or health tourism; units that control access to sensitive domains, destination management systems; and changing conditions to obtain financial opportunities are other examples of institutional innovation in tourism (Eraslan et al. 2008, Hjalager 2002).

1.2.5 Marketing Innovations

Innovations regarding comprehension, practice, and processes that cover the entire marketing process or any phase of the marketing process are considered marketing innovations. Marketing innovation can emerge as a new technique in customer relations or a new marketing strategy to be implemented upon entering new markets. Considering that effective marketing strategies are crucial in enhancing the economic added value of innovations, it is essential to develop new marketing practices in marketing these innovations (Uzkurt 2012a). For example, the use of mobile communication technologies in the marketing of destinations can pose an example of marketing innovation in the tourism sector (Öztürk and Uşaklı 2013).

1.3 INNOVATION MODEL IN THE TOURISM SECTOR

In their study published in 1985, Abernathy and Clark developed a framework for determining the competitive impacts of innovation in the automotive industry. According to the application results of this framework based on the concept of transformation, innovations are divided into four classes: Architecture, orderly, niche, and revolutionary (Abernathy and Clark 1985). Later on, it has been tried to indicate that these innovations can be adapted to the tourism sector with the results of various studies (Bağıran 2015, Eraslan et al. 2008, Hjalager 2002). Hjalager (2002) adapted this model developed by Abernathy and Clark to the tourism sector. The horizontal axis of the model expresses whether specific innovations render existing corporate connections obsolete or whether they cause the reinforcement of existing relationships among businesses. The vertical axis refers to the information and competencies used for good or service production. Some models are more related to adaptation and further improvement of existing structures, while others are related to old and outdated ideas that need to be replaced (Hjalager 2002). In other words, some of the innovations are destructive in terms of competence and relationships, while others require protective and developer changes (Bağıran 2015). The model adapted to the tourism sector by Hjalager (2002) is illustrated in Figure 1.1.

The model posits four types of innovations regular, niche, revolutionary, and architectural. They have different implications in terms of collaborative structures and knowledge. The most comprehensive ones of these are architectural innovations. Architectural innovations imply changes within the industry and changes within the society in which they would be utilized. The least radical innovations are regular ones; however, their impacts after a certain period may be pretty remarkable. Finally, niche innovations tend to oppose collaborative structures, except for the strengths and knowledge.

Regarding innovations in the tourism sector, researchers and practitioners mainly concentrate on the opportunities offered by this category. Revolutionary innovations have radical impacts on competencies while keeping external structures fixed. For instance, the entire industry can be influenced by a collective change in the needed skills and competencies. Architectural innovations tend to shift all forms and set new rules that alter the tourism concept (Hjalager 2002).

Various examples of the tourism sector are given to the innovation in this model. Relevant examples are presented in Table 1.1.

1.4 DEVELOPMENT OF SUSTAINABLE TOURISM

Sustainable development was first coined in 1972 at the Stockholm Conference (the United Nations Conference on the Human Environment). At the conference, that economic development should be maintained in compliance with nature was brought forth. In the same year, the report entitled 'The Limits to Growth' was published. The report emphasized that collective action is required to prevent the uncontrolled

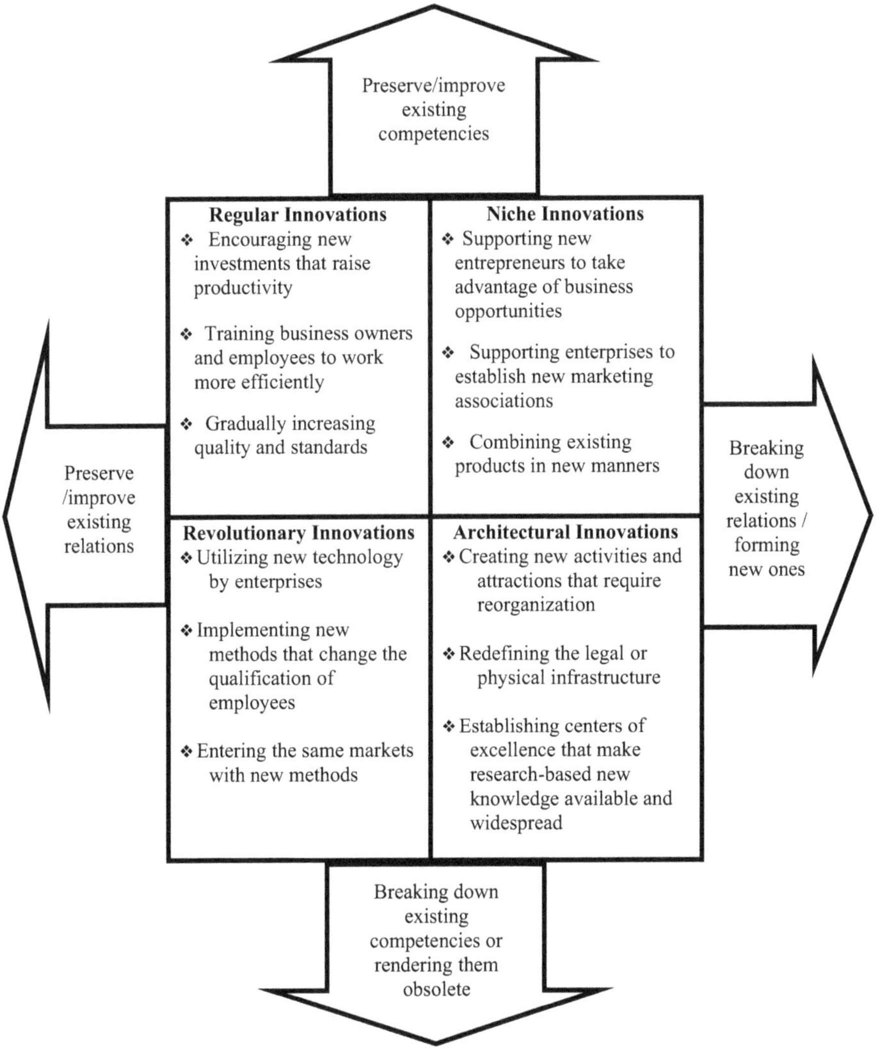

FIGURE 1.1 The Abernathy and Clark model (tourism perspective).

Source: Hjalager (2002).

growth of the economy (Göktepe 2011). Despite the preliminary studies, the primary research on the subject points out the 'Our Common Future' report (the Brundtland report), published by the United Nations World Commission on Environment and Development in 1987 (Serrano et al. 2019). This report emphasized that sustainable development was economic development, but justice should have been observed among people living today and living in the future. Later on, as of 1992, along with the Rio Declaration and Agenda 21, a global action plan for sustainable development was determined (Göktepe 2011). The essential detection was that economic

TABLE 1.1
Examples of Innovations for the Tourism Industry Based on the Abernathy and Clark Model

Regular Innovations	Niche Innovations
• Making new investments for larger structures. For example, larger hotels with a wide range of amenities. • Removing structural barriers by changing technology or time planning procedures. • Improving or increasing the service or offering additional advantages to the customer with internal staff training. • Raising quality standards in a well-defined system, for example, switching from two stars to three stars. • Approaching new markets with similar methods and products	• New business categories and product suppliers to complement existing businesses can be persuaded that the tourism industry would be a new marketplace for them. • Marketing associations can be established (for example, associations to be formed with specialized tour operators can be established to reach new customer groups). • New combinations of existing products may be generated.
Revolutionary Innovations	**Architectural Innovations**
• With the spread of new technology within the enterprise, staff will either stop what they have done so far or start doing it another way. An example of the most extreme case is the reduced need for culinary skills in restaurants, combined with the development of kitchen equipment and the supply of precooked foods. • While customers and suppliers are the same, electronic marketing and sales can be used instead of distributing brochures and flyers.	• It tends to change general structures and set new rules. Necessary changes are made in the understanding of tourism. Discovering new resources. For example, new designers, equipment, marketer, etc. to build ice hotels in Arctic tourism near the North Pole. • Redefining infrastructure (for example, as a result of environmental laws). The prohibition of new tourism opportunities along the coast requires the economic potential of other areas to be redefined.

Source: Coşkun (2013), Eraslan et al. (2008), Hjalager (2002).

development could not be achieved despite the environment, and the environment could not be protected by neglecting economic growth and development. Therefore, it has been decided to deal with environmental and economic development issues concurrently in a balanced and sustainable manner. It was pointed out that poverty, hunger, illness, illiteracy, and the deterioration of ecosystems were increasing. It was stated that the solution to these problems was not at the national level but at the global level. In the 'Johannesburg Declaration on Sustainable Development' of 2002, sustainable development's sociocultural, economic, and environmental dimensions were emphasized. Here, promises were made on poverty alleviation, changing consumption and production patterns, conserving and managing natural resources. Among the hardships encountered in achieving the goals, factors such as the deterioration of biodiversity, the deepening of the gap between the rich and the poor, the adverse impacts of globalization, and the decline in trust in democratic systems are indicated (Doğan 2014).

1.5 SUSTAINABLE TOURISM

In tourism, the idea of sustainability that emerged as a paradigm has generated sustainable tourism, a new approach toward tourism. Although it has been a long time since the Brundtland report was published, the meaning of sustainability in tourism and its current practical reflections are still disputable. Today, the sector's conceptual structure is being discussed by academics and professionals of the industry (Serrano et al. 2019).

The United Nations World Tourism Organization (UNWTO) defined sustainability in tourism as '*the principles that ensure the long-term balance established among environmental, economic and socio-cultural dynamics in the development of tourism*' (Günlü 2015).

The development of tourism by preserving the natural environment and historical-cultural and social environment constitutes sustainable tourism. The UNWTO defined sustainable tourism as 'fulfilling the needs of tourists and the host country without compromising the needs of future generations.' In this context, sustainable tourism development is to fulfill the needs of today's tourists and hosts based on the principle of preserving and improving social, environmental, and economic resources for the future. Furthermore, it aims to prevent poverty and maintain a world where future generations can perform tourism activities (Göktepe 2011).

Sustainable tourism is considered an alternative type of tourism that enhances the quality of life of the host society, offers high-quality experiences to visitors, and maintains the environmental quality upon which both visitors and the host society would depend. Therefore, it is one of the alternative development frameworks that mitigate the adverse impacts of mass tourism (Choi and Sirakaya 2005).

Sustainable tourism is defined as the actions and developments in the domain of tourism that fulfill the needs of today's tourists and the host society without hurting the environment, ecology, community, nature, and culture and without compromising the peace and welfare of future generations (Serrano et al. 2019).

The sustainability of tourism means knowing, protecting, developing, and attracting the local, regional, and national values that cause tourism (Sezgin and Karaman 2008).

Sustainable tourism development generates opportunities for creating a future while fulfilling the needs and expectations of contemporary tourists and host communities. In this case, while cultural integration, ecological environment, biodiversity, and vital systems are supported, the planning for managing all resources to fulfill economic, social, and aesthetic needs is realized. Therefore, the characteristics of sustainable tourism can be expressed as follows (Kahraman and Türkay 2014):

1. Natural, historical, and cultural resources are preserved for future use, and tourism's continuity benefits today's society.
2. Tourism development is managed and planned to not result in environmental and sociocultural problems in the touristic region.

3. Overall environmental quality is improved and maintained where it is needed.
4. High tourist satisfaction can be achieved by maintaining the marketability and popularity of the touristic destination.
5. The benefits obtained from tourism spread to a broader segment of society.

The long-term perspective, development and sustainability, and equality and fairness of outcome within and among generations comprise the basic principles of sustainable tourism. In summary, the core principles of sustainable tourism are as follows (Göktepe 2011):

- Minimizing environmental impacts.
- Achieving preservation results.
- Becoming different.
- Achieving originality.
- Reflecting social values.
- Comprehending and targeting the market.
- Improving the experience.
- Adding value.
- Acquiring good content.
- Enhancing the sense of space through design.
- Providing visitors and hosts with mutual benefits.
- Building local capacity.

Sustainable tourism tries to decrease the adverse impacts of tourism and travel activities. For this reason, it is included in the main subject of tourism. Sustainable tourism aims to enhance the economic benefit, improve the life quality of the local people, provide high-quality tourism experiences and social justice in both developing and developed countries, and preserve the environment. The broad scope of sustainable tourism has led to some controversy in the tourism literature. For instance, the concept has been used interchangeably with eco-tourism and sustainable development. Sustainable tourism is also responsible for increasing tourist satisfaction (Akbar and Zaim 2019). The benefits of sustainable tourism do not merely consist of environmental gains. There are also benefits to enterprises such as cost reductions, reputation enhancement, attracting wealthy customers, beneficial impression to investors, a pleasurable experience for visitors, job satisfaction for employees, and benefit to local communities (Hobson and Essex 2001).

1.6 SUSTAINABLE TOURISM DEVELOPMENT AND ITS DIMENSIONS

Economic, social, cultural, and technological changes experienced following the Industrial Revolution caused irreparable damages to the natural environment. Therefore, in the 1970s, organizations such as the United Nations and the World Bank put the concepts of *Sustainability and Sustainable Development* in the foreground by striving to prevent these problems. Based on these developments, a sustainable tourism map was created under the leadership of the UNWTO. As a result, the concept of sustainable tourism has been associated with sustainable development. Therefore, the idea of *sustainable tourism development* has loomed large as a crucial element of sustainable development (Çalışkan 2011).

According to the WTO, sustainable tourism development is defined as 'tourism that takes full account of its current and future economic, social and environmental impacts, addressing visitors' needs, the industry, the environment, and host communities' (UNEP/UNWTO 2005). Furthermore, sustainable tourism development is possible with a tourism comprehension that provides today's generation with assistance and support without compromising the needs and wishes of future generations (Sonuç 2014) and the preservation and development of natural, historical, cultural, environmental, and social values (Çalışkan 2011).

Translating the idea of sustainable development into tourism management has emerged due to the sector's dependence on the environment. If the resource quality deteriorates due to pollution and erosion, the demand for tourists will decline, and the economy and society may suffer. The environmental impact of tourism does not stem merely from tourist density. Besides, the activities of tourism-related organizations, pressure, and pollution caused by vehicles, water, energy consumption, waste generation, and purchasing strategies also account for the impact. Therefore, it is the responsibility of all tourism institutions and stakeholders to ensure the sustainable development of tourism (Hobson and Essex 2001).

Three (social, economic, and environmental) dimensions have emerged that form the basis of sustainable development. These three dimensions constitute the primary purpose of sustainable development (Byrd 2007).

1.6.1 Social and Cultural Sustainability

Social sustainability means reducing poverty, providing equal opportunities for all segments of society, and respecting human rights (Göktepe 2011). In addition, sustainability requires that all generations have equal access to resources. Social sustainability, one of the essential aspects of its sustainable development, concentrates on improving the living conditions of those who lack access to clean water and food. In this context, social sustainability is more about tackling poverty (Demircan 2016).

Cultural sustainability is the transfer of the cultural values of the current generation to the next generations by interacting with other generations and adding new ones to them (Demircan 2016). Tourism should not surpass the sociocultural capacity of the host society. In other words, it should not lead to the degeneration of cultural values. Sustainable tourism development considers the principle of preserving sociocultural values and transferring them to future generations (Çalışkan 2011).

1.6.2 Environmental Sustainability

Tourism develops mainly depending on the environment. In other words, the atmosphere is the most crucial attraction of a destination. For this reason, environmental preservation is of great importance for the future of tourism. Notwithstanding, the waste generated by the tourism sector and the environmental pollution caused by it is a significant problem to be taken into consideration. Tourism wastes cannot be controlled, especially in developing countries. In this context, environmental resources must be preserved and improved for tourism to grow in a sustainable environment (Çalışkan 2011).

Environmental sustainability means minimizing air, water, and land use and preserving biological diversity and natural resources (Göktepe 2011). In this context, aspects of sustainable tourism such as aiming at reducing CO_2 emissions, being compatible with the use of renewable energy resources, encouraging the efficient use of energy and water resources, preserving biodiversity, and promoting waste reduction are indicators of its contribution to environmental sustainability (Çelik 2016).

1.6.3 Economic Sustainability

The necessity to preserve the environment is clearly stated in the Common Future report. In addition, the report pointed out that environmental resources have been rapidly depleted, so the resources should have been used sustainably. In this context, reduction, reuse, and recycling have been adopted as basic environmental sustainability strategies. For example, reduce industrial waste and make less packaging, collect and reuse glass bottles, and use waste paper recycling and remaking paper (Demircan 2016).

In this context, sustainable tourism concentrates on protecting long-term economic welfare, creating employment, fair wages, new job opportunities, offering local products and services, and encouraging the determination of a sufficient fair wage level for these (Çelik 2016).

1.7 DEVELOPMENT OF INNOVATION AND SUSTAINABLE TOURISM

Innovation constitutes the basis of sustainable development, which is the most crucial issue of the tourism industry (Liu and Cheng 2018). Changes in social and environmental challenges indicate the necessity of sustainable innovation for the tourism industry. Sustainable innovation means intentionally changing the philosophy and values of the organization to generate social and ecological values besides economic gain. That is the transformation of an organization's supply of products and services (Bressan and Pedrini 2020).

Although it is stated that sustainable tourism development includes sustainability in tourism, these two concepts differ from each other. Tosun (2015) expressed this difference as follows:

> For example, sustaining mass tourism in its current state for a long time can be called sustainable tourism. On the other hand, for the current mass tourism to become a sustainable tourism development, it should contribute to the basic principles of sustainable development (the balance between economic, sociocultural and environmental development) or at least should not contradict these principles.
>
> *Tosun 2015*

In this context, it is necessary to examine tourism innovations in terms of the value they offer to both the sustainability of tourism enterprises and destinations and the principles of sustainable tourism development. On the other hand, these two concepts do not become entirely different from each other. On the contrary, its principles and features tend to overlap over time. Therefore, an innovation for tourism supports both sustainable tourism and sustainable tourism development.

1.8 SUSTAINABILITY OF TOURISM AND INNOVATION

Innovation developments in tourism products, services, activities, and processes enable tourism enterprises and destinations to continue in their current state or to continue their existence in the future by further improvement (Fayos-Solà and Cooper 2019, Kokkranikal and Morrison 2011). Innovations that support the sustainability of tourism are primarily technological (Horng et al. 2018). Therefore, tourism enterprises and destinations that adopt such innovations are preferred more since they differentiate themselves from their competitors. This contributes to the sustainability of tourism organizations as it increases customer satisfaction and loyalty (Çakıcı et al. 2016, Ribaric 2015). Similarly, the guests who are satisfied with the provided services tend to exhibit a commitment to the enterprise and recommend it. This situation offers a competitive advantage for tourism enterprises, increases the performance of the enterprises, and hence contributes to the survival of the enterprises (Booyens and Rogerson 2016).

For example, a growing number of hotel businesses in Taiwan are either adopting technology practices or using local culture to increase service quality and improve customer value. For instance, hotel Royal in Taiwan has switched to a check-in system utilizing iPads. In addition, it uses local cultural elements in decoration and building design (Horng et al. 2018). Besides, by courtesy of the widespread use of information technologies in tourism and innovations in transportation; faster and easier high-quality traveling facilities increase customer satisfaction (Özkök and Gümüş 2009). Furthermore, 100 innovations from passport to avatar expressed by Hjalager (2015) contribute tremendously to the sustainability of tourism enterprises and destinations.

Besides these, innovations such as smart cities and destinations, digital technologies, electronic word-of-mouth communication, and sharing economy, which result from the knowledge economy based on the possibilities emerging with technological change, are pretty crucial in terms of their contributions to the sustainability of tourism (Aydın and Boz 2018).

Innovative destination applications support the sustainability of tourism. By courtesy of information technologies, the needs of tourists can be determined more accurately. As a result, quick solutions to problems can be generated. Thus, the satisfaction level of tourists increases. Satisfied tourists repeatedly prefer and recommend the destination. For example, temporary interactive bus stops in Barcelona offer all kinds of information that tourists may need. These destinations, which support technological development and innovation, foster tourist experiences. Therefore, they are mostly preferred (Çoban and Eren 2018). So, for intelligent destinations, one can use the phrase 'sustainable destinations.' Digital technologies provide the managers of tourism enterprises and destinations important information in sounding out the tourists before, during, and after travel. For instance, tourists make their pretravel decision by conducting preliminary research on websites, virtual reality, social media tools, by sharing real time with mobile applications during travel, by reading comments about the place on social media, and by communicating with those who have visited the same destination before can share their experiences and opinions via websites and social media. Also, social media helps countries implement their tourism strategies. For example, the 'Tourism e-Kit' platform in Australia and the 'Discover Slovenia' platform in Slovenia both utilize social media tools such as Facebook, YouTube, Pinterest, Twitter, Foursquare to promote tourism destinations and attract tourists (Gençer and Mil 2018).

This information obtained from tourists would guide the relevant managers to ensure they revisit and experience the enterprise or destination in their current or a further improved state. Besides these, digital innovations such as NFC (Near-Field Communication), GPS (Global Positioning System), Virtual Reality-Augmented Reality, and Online Travel Agencies have an important place in tourism sustainability and the opportunities they provide to tourists, enterprises, and destinations. With GPS, tourists can determine their location, map their goal, and receive navigation services. Moreover, they can receive suggestions for restaurants, hotels, and cafes in the close vicinity of their sites. With NFC technology, tourists can shop and use their smartphones equipped with NFC technology on devices placed in touristic areas to acquire information about the location almost immediately. With online travel agencies, users can plan their travels concisely (Gençer and Mil 2018). Using virtual reality and augmented reality (AR) applications, tourists can visualize their destination, experience them virtually, and receive information about that place (Korkmaz Orhan 2019).

Again, one of the conveniences provided by digital innovations to the tourism industry is electronic word-of-mouth. However, compared to other product industries, tourism involves a high risk at the purchasing phase. Therefore, contemporary tourists decide by following comments and recommendations through sharing sites, blogs, personal sites, forums, and complaint sites. Thus, it minimizes the prepurchase risk. On the other hand, the managers of tourism enterprises and destinations monitor these platforms to acquire information about tourists and perform their marketing activities in compliance with this information. As a result, they may determine the expectations of the tourists more accurately (Boz and Demirel 2018).

Another important innovation that includes the tourism sector and emerged from internet technology is the sharing economy. In the tourism sector, many enterprises of the sharing economy offer services ranging from accommodation to travel. The most important of these can be shown as Airbnb, Tripping, HomeAway, HouseTrip, Uber, Lyft, and BlaBlacar. The sharing economy provides many economic, social, and environmental contributions to tourism enterprises and destinations. Therefore, it supports the sustainability of tourism. For example, the profits of enterprises included in the Airbnb network are higher than those of their competitors. Also, tourists are provided with low-cost accommodation options. Furthermore, the sharing economy is perceived as a consumption model that attracts environmentally and ecologically conscious consumers (Özkan and Duran 2018).

1.9 ECONOMIC, SOCIAL, AND ENVIRONMENTAL ASPECTS OF INNOVATION AND SUSTAINABLE TOURISM

In studies conducted on the relationship between innovation and sustainable tourism development, the concepts such as eco-innovation, environmental innovation, green innovation, social innovation, and sustainable innovation loom large. Environmental innovation concentrates on reducing environmental impacts, whereas eco-innovation focuses on both eco-designs and eco-labels. Green innovation is concerned with environmentally friendly processes and products. Subsequently, sustainable innovations concentrate on satisfying the dimensions of sustainable development (Triantafillidou and Tsiaras 2018). These innovations for the tourism sector are also associated with the dimensions of sustainable tourism development. They contribute to resolving economic, environmental, and social problems that the tourism sector has to deal with (Horng et al. 2016, Nunkoo et al. 2019). For this reason, innovation is an essential tool in achieving sustainable tourism goals, protecting cultural heritage and ecology, maintaining the continuity of social structure, employment, and human resources, and benefiting the local community (Hallenga-Brink and Han Brezet 2005).

Within this framework, in the following part, examining sustainable innovations within the scope of the values they offer to sustainable tourism development dimensions (economic, social, environmental) would provide a better comprehension of the subject.

1.9.1 Economic Development Dimension

In the tourism sector, process innovations are especially noteworthy in providing economic value to the industry. For example, along with the further development of existing technology or new technologies, the performance of tourism enterprises may increase, and the entire production line can be rearranged. Again, computerized management and control systems, robot technology in cleaning and maintenance, and self-service instruments may provide enterprises with economic savings. Also, new technologies open the path to higher incomes while creating new jobs. Again, as an example, with the help of Tourist Information Kiosks, transactions such as information search/scan, online purchases via credit cards, video, and commercial playbacks, ticket purchases, reservations, and direct phone access for more information are workable. All these improvements lead to a reduction in financial expenses (Özkök and Gümüş 2009).

Besides, important examples of innovation that offer economic value to the tourism industry include Thomas Cook, who escorted a certain number of people to England by train, Disney company's movies and theme parks, and Roy Kroc's acquisition of McDonald's and making the company number one in the fast-food sector in the World (Işık and Aydın 2016, Kokkranikal and Morrison 2011).

Another type of innovation that offers economic value to the tourism industry is social innovation. Social innovations in the tourism sector are essential in economic development, reduced poverty, aggravated social welfare, and sustainable tourism development (Zengin 2019). Also, within the context of soft tourism, eco-tourism comprehension, rural tourism, farm tourism, etc., as alternatives to the environmental damage of mass tourism, creating tourism types can be considered innovation. Thus, the positive economic impact of tourism can be sustained by developing a new product, and it can be ensured that resources are used without destruction through the elimination of the detrimental effects on the environment (Özkök and Gümüş 2009).

For tourists to visit the tourist attractions in a destination, these attractions need to be well introduced. Nevertheless, there may be some difficulties. The AR application provides significant convenience for both tourists and destinations. With AR technology, tourists can virtually access the information of historical and cultural values. This contributes to the development of both the local and national economies. It also contributes to the promotion and preservation of historical, cultural-artistic, religious, and traditional values. Therefore, AR should be perceived as an essential innovation in the sustainability goal in tourism (Jomsri 2019).

Also, green and ecological innovation practices in the tourism sector emphasize the economic dimension, although it is more related to the environmental size of sustainable development. Green management practices may strengthen the image and competitiveness of hotels. According to a study, 75 percent of customers prefer green hotels and do not hesitate to spend more on environmentally friendly hotels. It also contributes to customer satisfaction and loyalty, boosts profits, and finds new markets (Horng et al. 2018). Certain eco-innovations improve financial performance. For instance, they reduce resource utilization and operational costs while increasing labor productivity, market share, and sales (Wang et al. 2020). Eco-innovation aims at economic growth by enabling new professions and improving new products, services, and processes. Using alternative energy resources such as geothermal and solar energy in tourism enterprises is one of the leading eco-innovations and water storage and reuse. The importance of healthy food consumption in hotels and restaurants and eco-innovations, such as growing their vegetables in their gardens to serve them to their customers, provides tourism enterprises and destinations with sustainable advantages (Alonso-Almeida et al. 2016).

Green innovation offers hotel businesses the opportunity to enhance both environmental protection and financial performance. In addition, green innovation leads to differentiation as it provides hotel businesses with the opportunity to increase product design and quality. Therefore, hotel businesses may sell products at higher prices and profit margins. Besides, it provides resource efficiency by saving materials, reducing energy consumption, intensifying waste recycling, and ensuring less resource usage. Thus, it provides a competitive advantage.

Notwithstanding, investments in green innovation are essential for hotel businesses to realize sustainable development. Tourists mostly prefer hotel businesses with environmentally friendly practices. Moreover, the green invention provides businesses and destinations with advantages by fulfilling the demands of visitors regarding environmental protection in the places of visit. For this reason, hotel businesses implement ecological protection programs (recycling, water treatment) within the framework of green innovation. In addition, they install energy-saving systems and implement reuse programs for bedding sheets and towels and green building programs for constituting eco-friendly hotel environments. With these programs, hotel businesses attract new customers and aggravate resource efficiency (Gürlek and Tuna 2018). As a result, hotel businesses gain two main benefits from green practices. Firstly, they benefit from savings in consumption, and secondly, the increasing attention of customers on sustainable practices. Moreover, guests are willing to pay more to sustainable hotel businesses and are more likely to recommend them (Preziosi et al. 2019).

1.9.2 Social Development Dimension

Innovations pertinent to the tourism sector provide the sector with significant contributions in terms of economic as well as sociocultural aspects. Most of the time, they do this through social innovation. Social innovation enhances individual or social well-being by developing a participative culture. Thus, the qualities of both individual and social lives increase (Nunkoo et al. 2019). Social innovation is expressed as developing sustainable, effective, and innovative solutions to social problems (Aksoy et al. 2019).

The following applications are examples of social innovation in the tourism sector (Booyens and Rogerson 2016):

- Sports development programs.
- Skills and training-oriented development programs.
  - Community outreach programs for the public. For instance, vegetable gardens for the community.
- Using network structures to encourage tourism development in poor, rural regions.
- Providing education, medical care, and skill development through voluntary activities.
  - Visitor centers concentrate on social problems such as human rights, discrimination, genocide, and social justice.

Examples of social innovation include skills development and training programs supported by translation centers and museums (public benefit and nonprofit organizations); tourism operators (typically nonprofits organizations) make social and environmental innovations concentrated on nature preservation, health-care provision, education, and skills development in poor locations. Also, craft centers (tourism attractions) engage in social innovation through community outreach programs for skills development in crafts and arts as part of their duties and authority (Booyens and Rogerson 2016). For example, 'la Tablée des Chefs' in Canada is a program that teaches culinary workshops and teenagers in high schools and serves as platforms for hotels and restaurants to provide quality leftover food from chefs to food shelters (Aksoy et al. 2019).

In this context, one may consider social entrepreneurship, which aims to help people, as a social innovation (Peng and Lin 2016). Social entrepreneurship in tourism means supporting social and economic development. New products, services, processes, and procedures emerging due to social entrepreneurship activities fulfill the social needs and increase the well-being of both the individual and society (Booyens and Rogerson 2016). Social entrepreneurship, which is described as a process that explores opportunities to steer social change and deal with social needs, includes innovative use and combination of resources and contributes to the social goals of tourism destinations (Işık and Aydın 2017). In other terms, social entrepreneurship oriented with social purposes involves developing innovative ideas toward social change. Tourism attains an essential place in reducing poverty, especially in developing countries. In emerging destinations, social entrepreneurs tend to adopt a responsible approach that considers the social goals of sustainable tourism development (Altınay et al. 2015).

Another innovation approach that emphasizes the social dimension of sustainable tourism development is frugal innovation. Frugal innovation involves rethinking creation. It can do more with less by generating more employment opportunities and social values while reducing time, capital, and energy (Khan 2016). In other words, frugal innovation can be expressed as doing more things for a higher number of people using fewer resources. It can be characterized by the minor use of resources (production resources, raw materials, fuel, energy, waste, water financial resources) and is more affordable and better accessible than traditional innovation. This innovation approach concentrates on cost minimization, core functionality and performance maximization, fulfillment of the needs of the poor. It generates both business and entrepreneurship opportunities in underdeveloped regions and new jobs for both men and women. In addition, it implements innovative practices that enable low-cost transportation, energy, food, and beverages (Albert 2019).

1.9.3 Environmental Development Dimension

In the tourism sector, transportation from the airport to the hotel, excursions, meals, heating, cooling, cleaning, food, and product imports and travels to the place to be visited cause energy consumption. Due to such consumption, carbon dioxide emission and environmental degradation are on the rise. Therefore, climatic and environmental conditions must be preserved to maintain sustainable tourism improvements (Tandoğan and Genç 2019). Consequently, it is necessary to develop innovations to reduce the environment's detrimental effects or generate new products and processes that contribute to sustainable tourism development goals (Vatan and Poyraz 2016). Due to the increase in ecological consciousness toward the end of the 20th century, both travelers and industrial workers realized the necessity of preserving the environment. Toward the end of the 1970s, the WTO established an environment-oriented committee. In addition, sustainable tourism development was directly mentioned at the Rio de Janeiro Earth Summit held in 1992. Due to these developments and similar initiatives, tourism enterprises have made environmentally conscious or green innovations. For example, water conservation and towel reuse demands have become widespread in hotel businesses; nature-oriented recycling garbage bins and renewable energy systems have been seen in tourist locations. Therefore, besides environmental limitations and requirements, market forces have also encouraged tourism businesses to implement ecological innovations (Andereck 2009).

Along with the reduction of energy and wastes, companies can minimize damages to the environment. For instance, practices such as water softening, reducing the use of bleach, rainwater collection systems to mitigate the detrimental impacts of guests on the environment, composting of organic wastes based on recycling practices are conducted in small- and medium-sized tourism enterprises. Along with these practices, companies support environmental protection and reduce costs (Bressan and Pedrini 2020). Another method that would contribute to sustainable tourism development is organic and alternative food and beverage cultivation. For example, Mary, who is engaged in agricultural tourism in New South Wales (Australia), perceives the goal of 'working for a renewable and sustainable future' as 'a moral duty toward future generations' (Bressan and Pedrini 2020).

Besides, hotel businesses adopt environmentally sustainable innovations to be frugal in using water, energy, and perishable products, preventing waste and reducing greenhouse gas emissions. For instance, Hilton Hotels has saved approximately 9 million USD in 2 years by adopting sustainable innovations. At the same time, the demand for environmentally sustainable products, which ecologically friendly customers have appreciated, has increased. Also, sustainable enterprises engaged in environmental innovation can ensure customer loyalty and access to new markets (Smerecnik and Andersen 2011).

New tourism experiences may also be taken into account within the scope of environmental innovation. For instance, consumer consciousness toward the environment has led tourism businesses to a process through which they can improve and renew their ecological performances. Subsequently, tourism types such as eco-tourism and adventure tourism that can be considered as innovations have emerged in the sector (Tuzlukaya 2009). Furthermore, the ecological footprint can also be perceived as an environmental innovation. The implementation of environmental footprints ensures the attentiveness of consumers to the environment and ensures that environmental protection is guaranteed over time (Elmo et al. 2020).

Moreover, global warming, resource depletion, and environmental pollution problems experienced worldwide have led the tourism sector to implement sustainable innovations. Within the framework of this approach, studies on green innovation, ecological innovation, environmental or sustainable innovation have been explicated (Vatan and Poyraz 2016).

Green innovation involves reducing environmental damage and developing new products, ideas, attitudes, and processes to achieve sustainable development goals. Along with green innovation and environmental consciousness concepts, 'environmentally friendly hotel' has become increasingly crucial for the tourism sector. Environmentally friendly hotels are enterprises that save water and energy, manage solid and liquid wastes, care about the preservation of biodiversity, and mind such concepts as recycling and reuse (Işık and Barlak 2018). For example, the green hotel practice that offers environmentally friendly lodging contributes to environmental sustainability by helping energy-savings, carbon reduction, and the elimination of solid waste (Horng et al. 2018).

In this context, hotel businesses achieve blue flags, white stars, and green star certificates. These certificates are owned by enterprises that utilize a renewable energy system to inflict minor damage to the environment, separate harmful wastes through waste management, thus preventing them from entering nature, and recycle the dumped products. By courtesy of these certificates, tourism enterprises gain customer satisfaction and appreciation. For example, customers of the Crowne

Plaza Hotel in Copenhagen contribute to electricity generation by riding a bicycle connected to the generator for 15 minutes a day for free dinner and exercise. Thus, the damage caused by the hotel enterprise to nature is reduced (Yıldırım 2019). Also, one can include sustainability management, environmental communication, and resource conservation in environmentally sustainable innovation. *Green management* involves the extent to which hotel businesses implement sustainable practices. For example, hotel owners can establish environmental committees in compliance with the hotel's environmental policies or organize conferences to support sustainability consciousness. *Environmental communication* includes training of employees as well as customers and cooperation with stakeholders through dialogue among other stakeholders. *Resource preservation* includes saving resources, avoiding food waste, purchasing energy-saving materials and reusable products. Meanwhile, *energy conservation* concentrates on energy use in hotel businesses, for example, the adoption of renewable energy such as solar and wind energy by hotel businesses.

A similar type of innovation that adds value to the environmental dimension of sustainable tourism development is eco-innovation. Eco-innovation is the production, absorption, or utilization of product, service, process, and marketing innovations that are new to the organization and reduce environmental pollution and other adverse impacts (Wang et al. 2020). Besides its ecological effects, this innovation also offers value to customers, enterprises, and stakeholders. Eco-innovation in tourism can be defined as using and developing tourism resources to minimize environmental damage and provide value to enterprises, customers, and other stakeholders. It includes tourism enterprises with a competitive advantage, employee productivity, and ecological preservation (Tang et al. 2019). Eco-innovations attract tourists; eco-innovation is crucial for the tourism sector due to non-environmentally friendly products such as nonrecyclable packaging and non-disposable plastic containers in this sector (García-Pozo et al. 2016). Environmental protection and environmentally friendly approaches to resources are at the core of all eco-innovation definitions (Alonso-Almeida et al. 2018). For example, Club Med Finolhu Villas, built-in Maldives, and Stadthalle Boutique Hotel in Austria meet their energy needs via solar panels. Thus, they cause minor damage to the environment (Yıldırım 2019). Additionally, energy-saving, water-saving, water management, and the use of environmental or eco-tourism products may pose as other examples (Özkök and Gümüş 2009, 64, Wang et al. 2020). Moreover, biological agriculture, the application of environmentally oriented products and experiences, renewable energy technologies, eco-certification, and the incorporation of environmental precautions into the practices and management of an organization constitute the eco-innovation approaches that contribute to the environmental dimension of sustainable tourism development (Bell and Ruhanen 2016).

Eco-labels can be considered within the scope of eco-innovation in terms of sustainable tourism development. Eco-labels were developed in the 1990s and are environmental management and marketing tools to reduce detrimental impacts and provide competitive advantages (Arenado et al. 2017). For example, the blue flag fulfills legal requirements regarding hygiene, sanitation, and the environment. It is an assurance of safety for both residents and tourists. Its role as a management instrument is far more crucial, and it serves as a stencil for conducting environmentally conscious management and visitor satisfaction (Botero and Zielinski 2020). Customers exhibit an affirmative attitude toward green hotels certified with eco-labels. Customers show loyalty toward enterprises that implement such practices, and the customers' perception of hotel environmental communication is affected. By courtesy of green practices such as eco-labels, hotel businesses minimize their detrimental impacts on the environment, reduce environmental pollution, and prevent depletion of resources (Preziosi et al. 2019).

1.10 CONCLUSION

Economic, social, cultural, environmental, and technological development closely affected the tourism sector in today's world. These developments have increased the importance of sustainability and innovation to the tourism sector. Based on this importance, this issue has been addressed in many studies (Bramwell and Lane 2012, Bressan and Pedrini 2019, Fayos-Solà and Cooper 2019, Heslinga et al. 2019, Nunkoo et al. 2019, Smerecnik and Andersen 2011). However, the results are fragmented. For that reason, in this section, the relationship between innovation and sustainable tourism development has been revealed based on the results of related studies. The results are as follows: First, the studies on innovation and sustainability in tourism have increased over the last two decades.

Nonetheless, the extent to which innovation contributes to sustainable tourism development is still not clear. Although sustainable tourism and sustainable tourism development phenomena seem similar, specific differences account for this problem (Tosun 2001). Sustainable tourism involves a tourism business or destination that exists now in its current state and the future as being further improved. Therefore, technological innovations must be adapted to tourism. On the other hand, upon considering sustainable tourism development, this concept has stemmed from sustainable development. Thus, innovation should contribute to economic, sociocultural, and environmental improvements in tourism businesses and destinations. Therefore, it seems complicated to attribute innovations to sustainable tourism by ignoring the distinction between these two phenomena. Also, the conducted studies have interpreted sustainable tourism as an innovative concept and evaluated these two concepts as different, however, related ideas. Although these two concepts are related, the exact boundaries of their relationship are not clear (Bramwell and Lane 2012).

Second, tourism can have positive and negative impacts on the environment and the host communities. Innovations in the economic, social, and environmental domains are needed to eliminate these negativities and maintain the positive aspects. Therefore, innovation is perceived as the foundation of sustainable tourism development (Booyens and Rogerson 2016, Nunkoo et al. 2019). Besides, various articles, books, and consultant reports provide a great deal of information regarding the impacts of sustainable tourism on society and the tourism industry. Particular emphasis is placed upon the importance of innovation in causing beneficial outcomes of sustainable tourism in these studies. Innovation is perceived as the only response to social and environmental challenges. Moreover, innovation makes it easier to tackle the challenges required for achieving sustainable economic growth (Nunkoo et al. 2019).

Third, innovation activities contribute to the sustainability of tourism businesses by aggravating the satisfaction and productivity of tourism employees, tourists, and other stakeholders at the microlevel, providing institutionalization and branding. It has a crucial role in sustainable tourism development at the macro level through its contributions to the national economy, social welfare, employment, and environmental action (Kocabacak and Ertürk 2013).

Fourth, technological innovations for the tourism sector have made significant contributions to the sustainability of tourism. Along with the improvement of internet technology, such a contribution has increased exponentially. Innovations such as intelligent destinations, digital technologies (website, social media, virtual and AR, mobile technologies and applications, Network File System, GPS), sharing economy (Airbnb, Uber), and online travel agencies have provided the sustainability of tourism with significant benefits. These innovations form purchasing decisions of the tourists by giving them prepurchase confidence and reducing their purchase risks. It reduces the costs of tourism businesses and destinations by supporting their promotion and marketing activities. In addition, technological innovations provide both enterprises and destinations with economic, social, and environmental benefits through facilities such as energy-saving, waste reduction, and recycling. Thus, technological innovations directly support tourism's sustainability whereas indirectly support the principles of sustainable tourism development.

Fifth, besides technological innovations, innovation approaches such as energy, air, water-saving, frugal, social, and eco-innovation have supported sustainable tourism development as they offer value in sustainability's economic, social, and environmental dimensions. Furthermore, approaches such as eco-labels, frugal innovation, green, environmental, ecological, and sustainable innovation and innovative tourism approaches such as responsible tourism directly contribute to sustainable tourism development.

Finally, sustainable tourism development and innovation have been kept up to date from past to present, and tourism researchers have conducted various studies in these fields. Considering the COVID-19 pandemic, which negatively affected the whole world, sustainability and innovation issues would remain actual in the future. On the other hand, few studies aimed to explain the relationship between these two phenomena in the tourism industry. Therefore, studies to be conducted in this field would shed light on the future of the tourism industry. Therefore, this study is remarkable to provide sustainable tourism and innovation literature with related information.

REFERENCES

Abernathy, William J., and Kim B. Clark. 1985. "Innovation: Mapping the Winds of Creative Destruction." *Research Policy* 14, no. 1 (April): 3–22. https://doi.org/10.1016/0048-7333(85)90021-6.

Akbar, Iqbal, and Ilma Zaim. 2019. "Innovations in Service: Probing the Evidence in Sustainable Tourism." *The Asian Journal of Technology Management (AJTM)* 12, no. 2 (August): 132–48. https://doi.org/10.12695/ajtm.2019.12.2.5.

Aksoy, Lerzan, Linda Alkire, Sunmee Choi, Peter Beomcheol Kim, and Lu Zhang. 2019. "Social Innovation in Service: A Conceptual Framework and Research Agenda." *Journal of Service Management* 30, no. 3 (March): 429–48. https://doi.org/10.1108/JOSM-11-2018-0376.

Albert, Martin. 2019. "Sustainable Frugal Innovation—The Connection between Frugal Innovation and Sustainability." *Journal of Cleaner Production* 237, (July): 117749. https://doi.org/10.1016/j.jclepro.2019.117747.

Alonso-Almeida, Maria-Del-Mar, Alfredo Rocafort, and Fernando Borrajo. 2016. "Shedding Light on Eco-Innovation in Tourism: A Critical Analysis." *Sustainability* 8, (December): 1262. https://doi.org/10.3390/su8121262.

Alonso-Almeida, Maria-Del-Mar, Llorenç Bagur-Femenias, Josep Llach, and Jordi Perramon. 2018. "Sustainability in Small Tourist Businesses: The Link between Initiatives and Performance." *Current Issues in Tourism* 21, no. 1 (June): 1–20. https://doi.org/10.1080/13683500.2015.1066764.

Alsos, Gry A., Dorthe Eide, and Einar Lier Madsen. 2014. "Introduction: Innovation in Tourism Industries." In *Handbook of Research on Innovation in Tourism Industries*, edited by Gry Agnete Alsos, Dorthe Eide and Einar Lier Madsen, 1–24. Edward Elgar Publishing. https://doi.org/10.4337/9781782548416.00006.

Altınay, Levent, Roberto Daniele, and Victoria Waligo. 2015. "Social Entrepreneurship in Tourism." In *The 5th Advances in Hospitality & Tourism Marketing and Management (AHTMM) Conference*, edited by Doğan Gursoy, Medet Yolal, and Timothy Lee, 453–61. Beppu: Washington State University.

Andereck, Kathleen L. 2009. "Tourists' Perceptions of Environmentally Responsible Innovations at Tourism Businesses." *Journal of Sustainable Tourism* 17, no. 4 (July): 489–99. https://doi.org/10.1080/09669580802495790.

Arenado, Rocío, Rodríguez Ana, García López, and José L. Jiménez Caballero. 2017. "Has Implementing an Ecolabel Increased Sustainable Tourism in Barcelona?" *Cuadernos de Turismo* 40, (September): 1989–4635. https://doi.org/10.6018/turismo.40.309631.

Aydın, Şule, and Mustafa Boz. 2018. *Turizmde Güncel Konu ve Eğilimler II*. Ankara: Detay Yayıncılık.

Bağıran, Demet. 2015. "Destinasyon Yenilik Sürecinin Oluşturulmasında Ağ Yapısı ve Bilgi Yönetiminin Rolü." PhD diss., Dokuz Eylül University.

Bell, Chelsea, and Lisa Ruhanen. 2016. "The Diffusion and Adoption of Eco-Innovations amongst Tourism Businesses: The Role of the Social System." *Tourism Recreation Research* 41, no. 3 (June): 291–301. https://doi.org/10.1080/02508281.2016.1207881.

Booyens, Irma, and Christian M. Rogerson. 2016. "Tourism Innovation in the Global South: Evidence from the Western Cape, South Africa." *International Journal of Tourism Research* 18, no. 5 (December): 515–24. https://doi.org/10.1002/jtr.

Botero, Camilo M., and Seweryn Zielinski. 2020. "The Implementation of a World-Famous Tourism Ecolabel Triggers Political Support for Beach Management." *Tourism Management Perspectives* 35, (April): 100691. https://doi.org/10.1016/j.tmp.2020.100691.

Boz, Mustafa, and Nilgün Demirel. 2018. "Turizm Pazarlamasında Elektronik Ağızdan Ağıza Iletişim." In *Turizmde Güncel Konu ve Eğilimler II*, edited by Şule Aydın and Mustafa Boz, 47–60. Ankara: Detay Yayıncılık.

Bramwell, Bill, and Bernard Lane. 2012. "Towards Innovation in Sustainable Tourism Research?" *Journal of Sustainable Tourism* 20, no. 1 (January): 1–7. https://doi.org/10.1080/09669582.2011.641559.

Bressan, Alessandro, and Matteo Pedrini. 2020. "Exploring Sustainable-Oriented Innovation within Micro and Small Tourism Firms." *Tourism Planning and Development* 17, no. 5: 497–514. https://doi.org/10.1080/21568316.2019.1673810.

Byrd, Erick T. 2007. "Stakeholders in Sustainable Tourism Development and Their Roles: Applying Stakeholder Theory to Sustainable Tourism Development." *Tourism Review* 62, no. 2 (May): 6–13. https://doi.org/10.1108/16605370780000309.

Çakıcı, A. Celil, Harun Çalhan, and Kurtuluş Karamustafa. 2016. "Yi̇yecek ve Içecek İşletmeleri̇nde İnovasyon ve Sürdürülebi̇li̇r Rekabet Üstünlüğü İli̇şki̇si̇." *Kırıkkale Üniversitesi Sosyal Bilimler Dergisi* 6, no. 2 (July): 11–39.

Çalışkan, Caner. 2011. "Sürdürülebilir Turizm Gelişiminin Nesiller Arası Etki Boyutunun Algılanması: Alanya Örneği." M.S. thesis, Mustafa Kemal University.

Çamlı, Uğur. 2010. "Yeniliğin Müşteri Sadakati Üzerine Etkileri; Turizm Sektörüne Yönelik Bir Araştırma." M.S. thesis, Ankara University.

Çelik, Nur. 2016. "Sürdürülebilir Turizm Kavramı ve Gelişimi." In *Sürdürülebilir Turizm (Temel Kavramlar ve İlkeler)*, edited by Hüseyin Çeken, 67–83. Ankara: Detay Yayıncılık.

Ceylan, Yasemin. 2019. "Eco Labels in Tourism within the Scope of Sustainable Tourism." *Journal of Tourism Economics and Business Studies* 1, no. 1 (December): 65–80.

Choi, Hwan S.C., and Ercan Sirakaya. 2005. "Measuring Residents' Attitude toward Sustainable Tourism: Development of Sustainable Tourism Attitude Scale." *Journal of Travel Research* 43, no. 4 (May): 380–94. https://doi.org/10.1177/0047287505274651.

Çoban, Gamze, and Duygu Eren. 2018. "Bilgi Ekonomisi ve Akıllı Destinasyonlar." In *Turizmde Güncel Konu ve Eğilimler II*, edited by Şule Aydın and Mustafa Boz, 17–26. Ankara: Detay Yayıncılık.

Coşkun, Seval. 2013. "Stratejik Rekabet Üstünlüğü Sağlama Aracı Olarak Inovasyon Stratejileri: Kocaeli Otel Işletmeleri Üzerine Bir Araştırma." M.S. thesis, Düzce University.

Demircan, Şeyhmus. 2016. "Sürdürülebilirliğin Boyutları (Çevresel, Sosyal, Kültürel ve Ekonomik Boyutlar)." In *Sürdürülebilir Turizm (Temel Kavramlar ve İlkeler)*, edited by Hüseyin Çeken, 11–23. Ankara: Detay Yayıncılık.

Divisekera, Sarath, and Van K. Nguyen. 2018. "Determinants of Innovation in Tourism Evidence from Australia." *Tourism Management* 67, (January):157–67. https://doi.org/10.1016/j.tourman.2018.01.010.

Doğan, Mustafa. 2014. "Sürdürülebilir Destinasyon Yönetimi Bağlamında Adalar: Bozcaada Üzerine Bir Model Önerisi." PhD diss., Çanakkale Onsekiz Mart University.

Elmo, Grazia C., Gabriella Arcese, Marco Valeri, Stefano Poponi, and Francesco Pacchera. 2020. "Sustainability in Tourism as an Innovation Driver: An Analysis of Family Business Reality." *Sustainability (Switzerland)* 12, no. 15 (July): 1–14. https://doi.org/10.3390/su12156149.

Eraslan, Hakkı, Melih Bulu, and İsmail Bakan. 2008. "Kümelenmeler ve Inovasyona Etkisi: Türk Turizm Sektöründe Uygulamalar." *Seyahat ve Otel İşletmeciliği Dergisi* 5, no. 3 (September): 15–29.

Fayos-Solà, Eduardo, and Chris Cooper. 2019. *The Future of Tourism: Innovation and Sustainability*. Switzerland: Springer Nature. https://doi.org/10.1007/978-3-319-89941-1_3.

García-Pozo, Alejandro, Jose L. Sánchez-Ollero, and Míriam Ons-Cappa. 2016. "ECO-Innovation and Economic Crisis: A Comparative Analysis of Environmental Good Practices and Labour Productivity in the Spanish Hotel Industry." *Journal of Cleaner Production* 138, (January): 131–8. https://doi.org/10.1016/j.jclepro.2016.01.011.

Gençer, Kansu, and Burak Mil. 2018. "Turizmde Dijital Teknoloji." In *Turizmde Güncel Konu ve Eğilimler II*, edited by Şule Aydın and Mustafa Boz, 31–45. Ankara: Detay Yayıncılık.

Göktepe, Sevinç. 2011. "Sürdürülebilir Turizm Kapsamında İstanbul'daki 4 ve 5 Yıldızlı Otellerde Enerji Verimliliği." M.S. thesis, İstanbul University.

Günlü, Ebru. 2015. "Sosyal Girişimcilik Olgusun Un Kavramsal Analizi ve Turizmde Sosyal Girişimcilik." *Sosyal ve Beşeri Bilimler Araştırmaları Dergisi* 35, no. 16 (December): 23–42.

Gürlek, Mert, and Muharrem Tuna. 2018. "Reinforcing Competitive Advantage through Green Organizational Culture and Green Innovation." *The Service Industries Journal* 38, nos. 7–8 (November): 467–91. https://doi.org/10.1080/02642069.2017.1402889.

Hallenga-Brink, SuzanneC., and J.C. Han Brezet. 2005. "The Sustainable Innovation Design Diamond for Micro-Sized Enterprises in Tourism." *Journal of Cleaner Production* 13, no. 2 (December): 141–9. https://doi.org/10.1016/j.jclepro.2003.12.021.

Heslinga, Jasper H., Hans Hillebrand, and Tanja Emonts. 2019. "How to Improve Innovation in Sustainable Tourism? Five Lessons Learned from the Austrian Alps." *Journal of Tourism Futures* 5, no. 1 (March): 35–42. https://doi.org/10.1108/JTF-09-2018-0054.

Hjalager, Anne-Mette. 1997. "Innovation Patterns in Sustainable Tourism." *Tourism Management* 18, no. 1 (February): 35–41. https://doi.org/10.1016/S0261-5177(96)00096-9.

Hjalager, Anne-Mette. 2002. "Repairing Innovation Defectiveness in Tourism." *Tourism Management* 23, no. 5 (December): 465–74. https://doi.org/10.1016/S0261-5177(02)00013-4.

Hjalager, Anne-Mette. 2010. "A Review of Innovation Research in Tourism." *Tourism Management* 31, no. 1 (August): 1–12. https://doi.org/10.1016/j.tourman.2009.08.012. Hjalager, Anne-Mette. 2015. "100 Innovations That Transformed Tourism." *Journal of Travel Research* 54, no. 1 (December): 3–21. https://doi.org/10.1177/0047287513516390.Hobson, Kim, and Stephen Essex. 2001. "Sustainable Tourism: A View from Accommodation Businesses." *Service Industries Journal* 21, no. 4 (October): 133–46. https://doi.org/10.1080/714005050.

Hochschild, A. R. 1983. *The Managed Heart: Commercialization of the Human Feeling*. Berkeley: Berkeley University Press.

Horng, Jeou-Shyan, Chih-Hsing Sam Liu, Sheng-Fang Chou, Chang-Yen Tsai, and Da-Chian Hu. 2018. "Developing a Sustainable Service Innovation Framework for the Hospitality Industry Sustainable Service Innovation." *International Journal of Contemporary Hospitality Management* 30, no. 1 (August): 455–74. https://doi.org/10.1108/IJCHM-12-2015-0727.

Horng, Jeou-Shyan, Chung Jen Wang, Chih Hsing Liu, Sheng Fang Chou, and Chang Yen Tsai. 2016. "The Role of Sustainable Service Innovation in Crafting the Vision of the Hospitality Industry." *Sustainability (Switzerland)* 8, no. 3 (March): 17–20. https://doi.org/10.3390/su8030223.

Işık, Cem, and Ekrem Aydın. 2016. "Bilgi Paylaşımının Yenilikçi Iş Davranışına Etkisi: Ayder Yaylası Konaklama Işletmeleri Üzerine Bir Uygulama." *Girişimcilik ve İnovasyon Yönetimi Dergisi* 5, no. 2 (December): 75–103.

Işık, Cem, and Ekrem Aydın. 2017. "Kişisel Değerlerin Sosyal Girişimcilik Eğilimine Etkisi: Turizm Öğrencileri Üzerine Bir Araştırma." *Girişimcilik ve İnovasyon Yönetimi Dergisi* 6, no. 2 (December): 131–54.

Işık, Cem, and Sinem Barlak. 2018. "Otel Yöneticilerinin Yeşil İnovasyon Algıları: İstanbul İli Örneği." *Journal of Tourism Intelligence and Smartness* 1, no. 1 (July): 14–26.

Jomsri, Pijitra. 2019. "Creative Innovation of Augmented Reality for Promote Sustainable Tourism of Chiang Mai Moat." In *Paper presented at the Journal of Physics: Conference Series*, July 25–27, 1335. https://doi.org/10.1088/1742-6596/1335/1/012010.

Kahraman, Nüzhet, and Oğuz Türkay. 2014. *Turizm ve Çevre*. Ankara: Detay Yayıncılık, Ankara/Turkey.

Khan, Rakhshanda. 2016. "How Frugal Innovation Promotes Social Sustainability." *Sustainability* 8, no. 1034 (October): 1–29. https://doi.org/10.3390/su8101034.

Kocabacak, Ayşe, and Ebru Ertürk. 2013. "Otel Işletmelerinde Yeniliğin Önemi." In *Otel Işletmelerinde Yenilik Yönetimi*, edited by Muammer Mesci and Öznur Bozkurt, 1–22. İzmir: Sidas Medya Ltd.Şti.

Kokkranikal, Jithendran, and Alison Morrison. 2011. "Community Networks and Sustainable Livelihoods in Tourism: The Role of Entrepreneurial Innovation." *Tourism Planning and Development* 8, no. 2 (May): 137–56. https://doi.org/10.1080/21568316.2011.573914.

Korkmaz Orhan, Betül. 2019. "Turizmde Yeni Bir Akım: Sanal Gerçeklik." In *Turizm 4.0 Dijital Dönüşüm*, edited by Mete Sezgin, Seda Özdemir Akgül, and Ayşe Atar, 160–71. Ankara: Detay Yayıncılık.

Kuščer, Kir, Tanja Mihalič, and Harald Pechlaner. 2017. "Innovation, Sustainable Tourism and Environments in Mountain Destination Development: A Comparative Analysis of Austria, Slovenia and Switzerland." *Journal of Sustainable Tourism* 25, no. 4 (October): 489–504. https://doi.org/10.1080/09669582.2016.1223086.

Liu, Chia W., and Jen Son Cheng. 2018. "Exploring Driving Forces of Innovation in the MSEs: The Case of the Sustainable B & B Tourism Industry." *Sustainability (Switzerland)* 10, no. 11 (October): 1–19. https://doi.org/10.3390/su10113983.

Marakova, V., and M. Medved'ova. 2016. "Innovation in Tourism Destinations." *Forum Scientiae Oeconomia* 4, no. 1 (March): 33–43.

Nordin, Sara. 2003. *Tourism Clustering & Innovation: Paths to Economic Growth & Development*. Ostersund: European Tourism Research Institute, MID-Sweden University.

Nunkoo, Robin, Boopen Seetanah, and Shambhavi Agrawal. 2019. "Innovations in Sustainable Tourism Research." *Guest Editorial, Tourism Review* 74, no. 2 (April): 129–37. https://doi.org/10.1108/TR-04-2019-209.

OECD/Eurostat. 2005. *Oslo Manual, Guidelines for Collecting and Interpreting Innovation Data*. Vol. Third edit. Paris: OECD Publishing. https://doi.org/10.1787/9789264013100-en.

Onan, Gaye, Alper Duran, and Burçin Cevdet Çetinsiz. 2020. "Turizm Sektöründe Paydaşların Teknolojik Yeniliklere Karşı Algı ve Tutumlarının Belirlenmesine Yönelik Bir Araştırma." *Gaziantep University Journal of Social Sciences* 19, no. 4 (August): 1542–61.

Özkan, Çiğdem, and Erol Duran. 2018. "Turizm Endüstrisinde Paylaşım Ekonomisi ve Kısa Dönemli Kiralamalar." In *Turizmde Güncel Konu ve Eğilimler II*, edited by Şule Aydın and Mustafa Boz, 79–89. Ankara: Detay Yayıncılık.

Özkök, Ferah, and Fadime Gümüş. 2009. "Sürdürülebilir Turizmde Bilginin Önemi." *Yönetim Bilimleri Dergisi* 7, no. 1 (March): 51–71.

Öztürk, Yüksel, and Ahmet Uşaklı. 2013. "Global İnovasyon Endeksi: Akdeniz Çanağındaki Destinasyonlara Yönelik Karşılaştırmalı Bir Analiz." In *14. Ulusal Turizm Kongresi Bildiriler Kitabı*, edited by Kurtuluş Karamustafa, 1–19. Kayseri: Detay Yayıncılık.

Park, Eerang, and Sangkyun Kim. 2016. "The Potential of Cittaslow for Sustainable Tourism Development: Enhancing Local Community's Empowerment." *Tourism Planning and Development* 13, no.3 (December): 351–69. https://doi.org/10.1080/21568316.2015.1114015.

Peng, Kang-lin, and Pearl M.C. Lin. 2016. "Social Entrepreneurs: Innovating Rural Tourism through the Activism of Service Science." *International Journal of Contemporary Hospitality Management* 28, no. 6 (March): 1225–44. https://doi.org/10.1108/IJCHM-12-2014-0611.

Poudel, Surya, Gyan P. Nyaupane, and Megha Budruk. 2014. "Stakeholders' Perspectives of Sustainable Tourism Development: A New Approach to Measuring Outcomes." *Journal of Travel Research* 55, no. 4 (December): 465–80. https://doi.org/10.1177/0047287514563166.

Preziosi, Michele, Patrícia Tourais, Alessia Acampora, Nuno Videira, and Roberto Merli. 2019. "The Role of Environmental Practices and Communication on Guest Loyalty: Examining EU-Ecolabel in Portuguese Hotels." *Journal of Cleaner Production* 237, no. 117659 (July): 1–13. https://doi.org/10.1016/j.jclepro.2019.117659.

Prud'homme, Brigitte, and Louis Raymond. 2013. "Sustainable Development Practices in the Hospitality Industry: An Empirical Study of Their Impact on Customer Satisfaction and Intentions." *International Journal of Hospitality Management* 34, no.1 (September): 116–26. https://doi.org/10.1016/j.ijhm.2013.03.003.

Rasoolimanesh, S. Mostafa, and Mastura Jaafar. 2017. "Sustainable Tourism Development and Residents' Perceptions in World Heritage Site Destinations." *Asia Pacific Journal of Tourism Research* 22, no. 1 (April): 34–48. https://doi.org/10.1080/10941665.2016.1175491.

Ribaric, Robert. 2015. "Drivers of Innovation in Sustainable Tourism Development—The Concept and Case of Istria Destınation." In *3rd International Scientific Conference Tourism in Southern and Eastern Europe*, 3: 325–39.

Serrano, Laura, Antonio Sianes, and Antonio Ariza-Montes. 2019. "Using Bibliometric Methods to Shed Light on the Concept of Sustainable Tourism." *Sustainability* 11, no. 6964 (December): 2–25. https://doi.org/10.3390/su11246964.

Sezgin, Mete, and Abdullah Karaman. 2008. "Turistik Destinasyon Çerçevesinde Sürdürülebilir Turizm Yönetimi ve Pazarlaması." *Selçuk Üniversitesi Sosyal Bilimler Enstitüsü Dergisi*, 2008, no. 19 (February): 429–37.

Smerecnik, Karl R., and Peter A. Andersen. 2011. "The Diffusion of Environmental Sustainability Innovations in North American Hotels and Ski Resorts." *Journal of Sustainable Tourism* 19, no. 2 (March): 171–96. https://doi.org/10.1080/09669582.2010.517316.

Sonuç, Nil. 2014. "Sürdürülebilir Turizm: Tanımı ve İçeriği." In *Sürdürülebilir Turizm Kavramlar ve Uygulamalar*, edited by Metin Kozak, 13–29. Ankara: Detay Yayıncılık.

Tandoğan, Dilek, and Murat C. Genç. 2019. "Türkiye'de Turizm ve Karbondioksit Salımı Arasındaki İlişki: Rals-Engle ve Granger Eşbütünleşme Yaklaşımı." *Anatolia: Turizm Araştırmaları Dergisi* 30, no. 3 (November): 221–30.

Tang, Zi, Lin Liu, Xiaohong Li, Changbo Shi, Na Zhang, Zhengjie Zhu, and Jun Bi. 2019. "Evaluation on the Eco-Innovation Level of the Tourism Industry in Heilongjiang Province, China: From the Perspective of Dynamic Evolution and Spatial Difference." *International Journal of Sustainable Development and Planning* 14, no. 3 (September): 202–15. https://doi.org/10.2495/SDP-V14-N3-202-215.

Tosun, Cevat. 2001. "Challenges of Sustainable Tourism Development in the Developing World: The Case of Turkey." *Tourism Management* 22, no. 3 (June): 289–303. https://doi.org/10.1016/S0261-5177(00)00060-1.

Tosun, Cevat. 2015. "Sürdürülebilir Turizm-1." Uploaded on January 7, 2015. YouTube video, 34:50 min. www.youtube.com/watch?v=BXzLckt0Ui4&t=1276s.

Triantafillidou, Eleni, and Stefanos Tsiaras. 2018. "Exploring Entrepreneurship, Innovation and Tourism Development from a Sustainable Perspective: Evidence from Greece." *Journal for International Business and Entrepreneurship Development* 11, no. 1 (February): 53–64. https://doi.org/10.1504/JIBED.2018.090020.

Tuzlukaya, Şule. 2009. "Turizm Endüstirisi ve İnovasyon." *İz Atılım Üniversitesi Dergisi* 8, (June): 25–6. www.atilim.edu.tr/tr/press/page/3201/iz-dergisi.

UNEP/UNWTO. 2005. "Making Tourism More Sustainable: A Guide for Policy Makers." www.unep.frwww.world-tourism.org.

Uzkurt, Cevahir. 2012a. "Yenilik Çeşitleri ve Yeniliğin Yayılması." In *Yenilik Yönetimi*, edited by Cevahir Uzkurt and Ahmet E. Demirci. Eskişehir: Anadolu Üniversitesi.

Uzkurt, Cevahir. 2012b. "Yenilik Yönetimi ve Yenilikçi Örgüt Kültürü." In *Yenilik Yönetimi*, edited by Cevahir Uzkurt and Ahmet E. Demirci, 65–80. Eskişehir: Anadolu Üniversitesi.

Vatan, Ahmet, and Mine Poyraz. 2016. "Nasıl Sürdürülebilir Otel Olunur." *Çatalhöyük Uluslararası Turizm ve Sosyal Araştırmalar Dergisi* 1, no. 1: 15–30.

Wang, Yajun, Xavier Font, and Jingyan Liu. 2020. "Antecedents, Mediation Effects and Outcomes of Hotel Eco-Innovation Practice." *International Journal of Hospitality Management* 85, (July): 102345. https://doi.org/10.1016/j.ijhm.2019.102345.

Weiermair, Klaus. 2006. "Product Improvement or Innovation: What Is the Key to Success in Tourism?" In *Innovation and Growth in Tourism*. Paris: OECD Publishing. https://doi.org/10.1787/9789264025028-5-en.

Yıldırım, Özlem. 2019. "İstanbul'da Beş Yıldızlı Otellerde Yeşil Yıldız Uygulamasının Otellerin Iletmeciliğine Sağladığı Avantajların Analizi." PhD diss., İstanbul Ticaret University.

Zengin, Nilüfer. 2019. "Turizm Sektöründe Sosyal Inovasyon: Turizm ve Girişimcilik Eğitimi Alan Öğrenciler Üzerinde Bir Araştırma." M.S. thesis, Karabük University.

2 Alienation and Sustainability in Tourism Businesses

Eren Erkılıç

CONTENTS

2.1 INTRODUCTION

Individuals face multiple negations both in their social and business life because of the effect of rapid changes and developments in the world. The circumstances brought about by the mentioned progress and move can also trigger organizations to make modifications in many aspects such as structure, politics, and culture from the moment they are put into practice. [However, these shifts test the individual-organization relationship and induce displaying alienation behavior, known as the detrimental organizational behaviors. Alienation concept is one of the basic dilemmas of social psychology (Yüksel 2014). It is the situation in which individuals feel separated from the values of the society or the working environment in the workplace (Ankony and Kelley 1999).] Therefore, it cannot be qualified as an individual issue; alienation is a factor that hurts individuals' working lives. This harmful situation, voiced as organizational alienation, is one of the difficulties whose importance is arising day by day in business life (Nair and Vohra 2010). Organizational alienation is defined as a state where the employee cares less about his job, consumes less energy than usual, and focuses on external rewards (Agarwal 1993).

The tourism sector is one of the industries where most individuals are employed globally (Bamford 2012). However, qualified personnel do not want to work in the industry due to varied reasons and tend to move away (Türker 2016). Therefore, it can be uttered that organizational alienation behavior is also effectual on the tendency of employees to move away from the tourism sector even though the businesses operating in the tourism sector desire to maximize their service quality, the attitudes

DOI: 10.1201/9781003138051-3

and behaviors of the employees working in these businesses can invalidate these efforts. In such cases, business managers hold extensive duties, and it is required that business managers guide their employees in internalizing organizational values and goals. Hence, obstacles will arise in businesses unless managers pay attention to these issues, and the feeling of alienation in the employees may enhance and become a threat in the future (Babür 2009).

It is sighted among research carried out earlier on organizational alienation that the mutual relationship with alienation behavior such as demographic features (Yumuk 2011), human resource management practices (Erkılıç 2012), organizational dedication (Yıldırım 2009), organizational commitment, job satisfaction, tendency to quit (Uysaler 2010), total quality management (Er 2007), leadership (Sarros et al. 2002), social awareness (Holian 1972) have been explored. Although there is little research on organizational alienation, especially tourism businesses, it is possible to voice that there is little research on organizational alienation.

During the production and presentation of the product–service in tourism businesses, the businesses can carry off their goals with the communication that crops up between the employee and the consumer (Olalı and Korzay 2004), enabling these businesses to continue to serve sustainably. However, no matter what characteristics they have, tourism businesses cannot reach success without their employees. Therefore, determining the organizational alienation levels of employees in tourism businesses and revealing the factors that give rise to this behavior highlight the necessity of taking precautions by managers. It is unacceptable for the employees to exhibit alienation behavior toward their organizations in the tourism sector. Tourism businesses are in an industry where communication and relations are intense. In this context, it may be interpreted that the employees who have a sense of alienation and exhibit organizational alienation behavior are unlikely to succeed. Therefore, the tourism businesses where these employees work are unlikely to be successful and serve sustainably.

2.2 ALIENATION

Although the Latin origin of alienation is '*alienation*' (Schacht 1970), the root of the word is based on several words like '*alene*' in French, '*alienado*' in Spanish, and '*alienist*' in English, referring to a person who is separated or detached from himself (Fromm 1996). Being the subject of many studies in different disciplines, this concept has been defined in various ways. Hegel was the first to convey alienation (Salerno 2003). In contrast, alienation was firstly depicted by Karl Marx as losing the individual's individuality and is a situation that is not desired by the individual or society (Kanungo 1992). It is the testing of the individual's self-values and the emergence of inconsistency between these values and the values of the society that is tested (Shepard 1972); it is a disease that shows up depending on the conditions in the community and the personality of the individual (Seeman 1975), it is the feeling that an individual experiences given losing faith in the world and his character (Kohn 1976), it is the acceptance of oneself and the world as passive and behaving accordingly (Fromm 1992), it is the meaninglessness of the individual roles in the society where they belong to and the uncertainty in the community that arises with it (Levin 1994). Finally, it is a state where individuals must give up their other potential to realize their specific potential (Weiskopf 1996).

The concept of alienation has been examined associated with many different disciplines such as anthropology, criminology, political science, and sociology (Ray 1985). It is observed in research on the alienation concept that it has fundamental effects throughout the life span of individuals. When the historical evolution of the alienation concept is studied, it can be uttered that the works on alienation, which are still valid, have generally focused on the fields of religion and philosophy since the 18th century, on production and work relations, society, and individuals after the Industrial Revolution (Develioğlu and Tekin 2013).

Hegel examined the concept of alienation by focusing on the inside, not the social framework, and defined it as the soul's alienation and based the alienation on the 'id,' which is perceived as spiritual and explains the actual reality (Doğan 1998). In this context, it was emphasized that alienation is a process that must be overcome, and it is necessary for the Spirit (mind) to reach its structure and to form its essential character (Özbudun et al. 2008). However, Hegel adopted alienation as turbulence that is impossible to get rid of. In doing so, he stated that individuals should become conscious and direct their essence with the help of logic and mind (Silah 2005).

Marx stated that human beings are both natural and social beings and based the concept of alienation on the fact that human beings are in a construct that changes their environment while changing their environment (Tolan 1996). Unlike Hegel, Marx claimed that the essence of the individual is his essential being and maintained that he is alienated from this important being (Karakaya 2010). Marx argued that alienation is about division, labor, and specialization, and he associates alienation with capitalism (Doğan 2004). Marx characterized alienation as a concept related to the relationship between the minority that develops due to the competitive conditions of the capitalist system and concentrates on their needs and the majority who sell their labor. Marx examined alienation in four dimensions: '*alienation to labor, business process, self-environment, and society*' (Ferguson and Lavalette 2004).

Fromm discussed that people become alienated as they modernize, and social factors also lead to alienation. Fromm states that individuals are oppressed and feel bad due to the capitalist system. Thus, they cannot relate to the entities created by the system, cannot feel belonging to them, and that is why they become alienated from the structure. It turns out that the individual becomes a being striving to find a place for itself with alienation (Fromm 2004).

Seeman studied alienation by combining it with a historical and experimental perspective (Seeman 1959), indicating that alienation is a characteristic situation in modern society and reasoned that alienation should be considered as a social phenomenon, not an individual, and believed that it might cause many negative social consequences (Seeman 1967).

Mills denoted that alienation is individuals' spending their most productive ages for the wages they earn to survive and earn a living and stated that alienation arises because the individuals are directed to the division of labor and specialization. Thus, alienation is not only a bother of the working class but a common concern of all workers (Horowitz and Mills 1983).

Durkheim based the concept of alienation on anomie and related it to the division of labor. According to the concept of anomie, individuals are forced to be bound by the rules of society, succumb to the rules with reaction, and thus alienation prevails. Durkheim affirmed that the most significant factor in the emergence of this result is the division of labor. Durkheim communicated that alienation is the inability of individuals to accomplish satisfaction by limiting their duties in business life, resulting in alienation (Mercan 2006).

In line with the above explanations, it may be evidenced that the concept of alienation is generally that individuals are psychologically touched by the situation, event, behavior, or different reasons they face in their private and business lives. Moreover, alienation is the estrangement of individuals to their society, culture, workplace, social life, and colleagues and their failure to make sense of the community and culture they live in and their behavior in the form of indifference. To grasp this concept better, it is beneficial to touch on its dimensions, the causes, and consequences of the emergence of behavior and examine it from an organizational point of view.

2.3 DIMENSIONS OF ALIENATION

Individuals in modern societies must fight a lot to survive and are impacted by the community and culture they live in; they lose their characteristics, succumb to this struggle over time, and different dimensions of alienation are perceived in the individual subsequently (Yılmaz and Sarpkaya 2009). Although American sociologists studied alienation theoretically in the 1960s and later, they have determined its dimensions and examined it with many research methods (Eryılmaz 2010). Seeman designed alienation as '*powerlessness, meaninglessness, normlessness, isolation and self-alienation*' (Seeman 1959), while Dean sized it as '*Powerlessness, normlessness, social isolation*' (Dean 1961). Middleton put into the dimensions of '*Powerlessness, meaninglessness, normlessness, cultural alienation, social alienation, alienation from work*' (Middleton 1963), whereas Kohn categorized it as '*Powerlessness, self-alienation, irregularity, cultural alienation*' (Kohn 1976). Lastly, Mottaz dimensioned alienation as '*powerlessness, meaninglessness, self-alienation*' (Mottaz 1981).

The powerlessness dimension is a part emphasized by researchers from different scientific fields along with Seeman. In cases where individuals cannot reach their goals, individuals do not have control rights based on production; it is the feeling that individuals will be useless on their own and cannot impress their environment and that they are inadequate and unable to succeed (Soysal 1997; Tezcan 1983). According to Marx, this dimension is related to individuals' not being given decision-making authority about how they support production or during production. Likewise, individuals do not control production output (Marx 1970).

Similarly, Dean asserts that it is the loss of control over the product from the beginning to the end of production. Finally, alienation takes place with the effect of powerlessness. Thus, Dean supports Marx (Dean 1961). Likewise, Seeman affirms that individuals do not have any say in their product or any rights to control in the powerlessness dimension. This situation makes individuals feel worthless by dragging them into powerlessness (Seeman 1967).

Bacharach and Aiken put forward that it should be examined in two dimensions: individuals' ability to act freely and organizational decision-making effectiveness. The first dimension emphasized working hours and individuals' ability to perform freely about communication in the workplace. In contrast, they focused on the ability of individuals to be powerful in decisions regarding management and working conditions in the second dimension (Bacharach and Aiken 1979). Blauner positioned the powerlessness in four distinctive sizes (Blauner 1964):

- Employees do not have the right to own equipment and products.
- Employees do not have any efficiency regarding management.
- Employees do not have the right to choose their colleagues.
- Employees do not have the authority to control their jobs.

The reasons for the emergence of powerlessness can be listed as employees feel inadequate, employees are unable to solve the problems they find, employees do not experience the feeling of management and supervision during work, rule adjustments in the workplace, the effect of technological improvements, not being involved in management. Such reasons make employees feel excluded from the production or service process, thus pushing them to experience a feeling of powerlessness (Babür 2009).

The meaninglessness dimension is about individuals' inability to make sense of the situation or facts they meet. It can be articulated as the inability of individuals to make decisions by experiencing confusion when they need to make a decision. The individual in this position does not know what result he may get with his decision (Seeman 1959). For Bolton (1972), meaninglessness is that the individual does not know what to believe in the face of facts and that the truths shown to him are meaningless and not believing that the relevant truths may lead him to conclusions. Banai and Reisel (2007) proclaim that it is a confusion of concepts that individuals cannot foresee about the social events that the individuals may run into in the future.

The meaningless dimension covers the whole system of organizational objectives and sprouts with personal role conflicts in the business life of individuals and reveals a situation that prevents integration. With the division of labor, the employee only knows his duties and does not know about other jobs or how his duties contribute to the business or organization. Therefore, the employee becomes purposeless and supposes his duty makes little sense and has damaging feelings. Meaninglessness is when employees think that there is no link between the employees' jobs and the other jobs within the business or organization (Shepard 1973).

Meaningless dimension is a situation that relates to the perception of the events in which individuals are involved but cannot predict the consequences of their behavior toward beliefs (Seeman 1959). It can emerge on account of incompatibility between the duties of individuals and themselves in workplaces or within organizations. There should be no uncertainties in their responsibilities for individuals to make their duties meaningful, and individuals should feel that they think they are beneficial with their work (Durmaz 2015).

Normlessness dimension refers to the situation that turns into irregularity after meaningless and is derived from Durkheim's concept of anomie. Seeman stated that alienation reflects a sociopsychological status and suggested that this dimension is examined from individuals' point of view (Seeman 1975). Seeman (1959) described the normlessness dimension as a state in which the rules in the workplace become meaningless in the employees and the rules lose their effect, and the employees believe that they should act against the rules in reaching the targets. Put differently, it is the breakdown of the rules; the employees lose interest in the regulations and not adopting these rules; they become disinclined and alienated from the rules (Soysal 1997). Since the employees are in an environment against the value judgments, they cannot share their values. As a result, the existing rules seem meaningless to the employees, and thus a state of normlessness eventuates (Silah 2005). Marx first examined the social-isolation dimension as social alienation by the relationship between employee and employer. Social alienation is defined as the physical or mental distancing of the employee from other employees (Halbesleben and Clark 2010). Seeman verbalized social isolation as the individuals' inability to establish friendship and amity, communication, social relations, staying away from their social environment, and not establishing contact. In addition, Seeman explained that employees could not establish harmonious relationships at the organizational level (Seeman 1983). On the other side, Taviss altercated that the feeling of social isolation emerged in two ways. Firstly, the individuals do not belong to any group, and the feeling they experience after this leads them to experience a sense of isolation. Secondly, it is the feeling that others exclude the individual or personally reject the existing group (Tekin 2012). The situations that provoke the individuals to feel isolated can be listed as individuals' embarrassment of their job or the business or organization they are involved in, not being understood by others in the workplace, individuals' statements are perceived as wrong, they are excluded or not included in groups and individuals' inability to establish meaningful and healthy relationships with their colleagues (Bayat 1996). Indeed, individuals' feeling of isolation oppositely alters their physical and mental health and is discerned as an undesirable situation by society. Thus, this may cause alienation as a painful experience for the individual (Arokach 2006). *The self-isolation* dimension is the self-estrangement of individuals (Şimşek et al. 2006). The self-isolation dimension is that the employee does not feel the actions, behaviors, and attitudes belong to them. It is explained as controlling activities, behaviors, and attitudes (Soysal 1997).

Seeman defines this dimension as individuals' behavior that does not match their expectations or exhibit different behaviors than their expectations (Seeman 1959). According to Blauner, the alienated individual loses his sense of being himself, and the state of fear begins (Blauner 1964). Thus, the individual faced with this situation can be mentally injured by others (Gardner 2007). Fromm defines self-alienation as individuals' beholding that the talents do not belong to them (Fromm 1995a). Therefore, an individual who is estranged from themself loses connection with others as well. Besides, if the individual searches for status, he can market his abilities and himself similarly to the product for this purpose. This situation drives the individual away from himself (Boz 2014).

When the dimensions of alienation are examined from a general point of view, it is noticed that it can come about in situations such as individuals who do not enjoy their lives and have difficulty keeping up with the social structure of the society in which they live (Şimşek et al. 2006). Thus, it may be commented that individuals begin to be those who cannot contribute to the community and themselves with the alienation from their existence except for being satisfied with the conditions provided to them (Boz 2014).

2.4 ORGANIZATIONAL ALIENATION

The Industrial Revolution has reduced the influence of manpower in production and has promoted different resources in its place. However, it has also helped change the effects on individuals, accelerating alienation and becoming a topic studied by many researchers (Önal 2015). In other words, the differentiation of the relationship between the labor of the employee and the product is one of the variations it has brought about in business life due to industrialization. Mass production engendered a disconnection between the employee and the produced product and brought the beginning of organizational alienation (Kargı 2012). Among the reasons for alienation in business, life are the company's structure or organization, the nature of the job, and the work environment. For example, the expectations of the employees from the job and the meaningfulness of the job can arouse alienation. At the same time, the size of the business, bureaucracy, and management style can also compel alienation.

Additionally, many factors such as the existence of an unfair division of labor, monotony, working too long in the same job, incompatibility with the manager and the employee, not taking part in decisions, disagreements with colleagues, hardworking conditions are among the crucial factors of alienation within businesses and organizations (Şimşek et al. 2012). Organizational alienation springs up on employees' feeling incongruous because of the business conditions and corporate culture they face in the work environment. An employee's alienation from his organization means that their motivation has disappeared. However, it brings various opposing situations for the employee, forcing them to move away from themselves and enter a psychological process (Usta and Küçükaltan 2014). The employee who experiences alienation isolates himself from the society he is in and directs himself toward loneliness. In this way, it harms culture and nature itself. Likewise, employees who feel lonely, weak, and need to defend themselves are also alienated. This situation pushes the employees to be unhappy, and their performance decreases and prevents them from reaching the organization's goals (Bilir Güler et al. 2019). In addition to those, if the organizational culture and ethical rules are not compatible with the employees' values, it may cause organizational alienation (Sulu et al. 2010).

Regarding the alienation associated with the organization, Marx asserts a mismatch between the employees' job roles and their nature. This situation is that employees lose control over the business process and product. The nature of the job reveals the lack of specialization and control related to the job (Mottaz 1981). On the other hand, alienation from the job means employees' feeling of boredom with their businesses and the business environment, dissatisfaction with them, withdrawal from positions and less focus on their jobs, and low commitment to their jobs (Hirschfeld and Field 2000). Suppose employees cannot have a work environment as they hoped. In that case, if they experience the feeling of working like a robot or face harsh management, they may react with aggressive behavior by becoming alienated. Undesirable workplace behavior can be experienced with broken promises, arbitrary behavior, mutual hostility behaviors and feelings, lack of discipline, and work restlessness (Fettahlıoğlu 2006). The alienation concept has been studied and dimensioned by many researchers, and results have been obtained in many different fields of science. Therefore, researchers have suggested differing reasons for the emergence of alienation. For example, alienation may result from the society in which individuals live and the culture, family, or business environment, or spiritual reasons.

The reasons Marx lists for the alienation of individuals in the workplace or within the organization are as follows (Başaran 2000).

- In case of alienation, the tool, equipment, or product is not the employee's property.
- The specialization of an employee on a job forces the employee not to know what he produced and prevents the employee from developing creativity.
- An employee who works on a monotonous job and produces parts cannot make the product himself.
- Due to the technical compatibility, the employee cannot perform inspection, and the inspection task is given to the machine.
- The ability of the employee working with the machines to communicate with others is prohibited.
- Supervision is entirely under the organization's control, and the employee cannot control their future.
- The employee is estranged from his job because the employee refuses to control and manifest himself.
- Organization supervision directs the employee to move away from his job.

The reasons for alienation are listed in different studies by grouping them as characteristics of the age (industry, urbanization, environmental pollution, technology, etc.), living conditions of individuals (family, culture, health, etc.), characteristics of the workplace (management, structure, wage, etc.), the nature of the task (duration of work, control, supervision, etc.), and personal characteristics (mental health, social life, job satisfaction, etc.) (Hoşgörür 1997; Zorgül 2014). In another study, factors causing alienation were divided into organizational and environmental factors. Organizational factors are '*Management style, past events, and experiences, organization size, devolution of authority, expert personnel, information flow, group characteristics, modular relations, mode of production, division of labor, working conditions, beliefs, and attitudes*.' In contrast, the environmental factors are '*economic structure, technological structure, social and cultural structure, industrialization, urbanization and social disintegration, political and legal structure, union organizations, mass media*' (Demirel and Ünal 2011).

Due to the reasons for the emergence of alienation, alienating individuals display different attitudes and behaviors. These attitudes and behaviors are accepted because of alienation. They can cause many refusal behaviors such as

> Mental disturbances, low job satisfaction, feeling of stress, anxiety, and unwillingness, being bored with work, not performing the activity, self-estrangement, Being attached to other forces, deprivation, showing respective reactions in the society, showing suicidal tendencies, tendency to use drugs, avoiding marriage, turning to behaviors that do not obey the laws, not feeling happy, recognizing his job only as a vital movement, not knowing his position in business life, not being interested in matters outside of work, not having pride in the workplace, decreasing productivity, not taking responsibility, being interested in bureaucracy, being inclined to surrender and selfish.
>
> *Nettler 1957; Korman et al. 1981; Kanungo 1992; Fromm 1995a, 1995b; Mercan 2006; Zorgül 2014*

2.5 ORGANIZATIONAL ALIENATION IN TOURISM BUSINESSES

Tourism businesses can be exemplified as accommodation businesses, entertainment businesses, tour operators, travel agencies, and food and beverage businesses. It can be asserted that the most influential factor in the customers' evaluation of the service quality positively or unfavorably is the employees in these businesses in the tourism sector. These establishments serve labor intensively from the moment the guests start their holidays until their vacation ends. Factors such as the employees' trust in the businesses they work for, the quality of their working conditions, and management policies also have a prominent place in the tourism businesses to provide a quality service. Because contrary perception of such examples by employees can create negativities such as job dissatisfaction, loss of confidence, communication disconnections, and decreased motivation, and can directly reflect on customers. Thus, employees may become alienated from the businesses they work for.

If the employees within the business cannot work under the conditions they want, or if they start to regard themselves like robots during the production process, or if they come face to face with strict rules and bleak behaviors of the management, the employees exhibit aggressive behaviors or may experience alienation. This type of behavior stimulates arbitrary attitudes and behaviors and an atmosphere of uneasiness within the organization (Bingöl 1990). The attitudes and behavior of tourism employees toward customers necessitate those employees to keep their feelings under control. One of the requirements of working in the tourism sector is that they must be careful, cheerful, and calm (Yılmaz et al. 2010). This obligation causes the employees to feel under pressure and creates a ground for alienation. Due to factors such as working hours in the sector, heavy working conditions, wages not equivalent to the labor done, the employees' job satisfaction goes down. It, therefore, moves them to be exposed to stress during work. Hence, they drag employees toward burnout (Gürsoy 2014). The emergence of these conditions in tourism businesses is among the other reasons that constitute alienation.

Regardless of the business structure in the tourism sector, employees communicate directly with customers. For the quality of this communication, employees' performance must be high. Any sense of alienation that tourism sector employees will face may instigate businesses from experiencing negative consequences. For that reason, it is also a critical issue that business managers ensure employees' job satisfaction. The situations that incite the employees to be alienated should be determined, and necessary conditions should be provided to minimize this sense of alienation (Babür 2009). Unless these issues are stressed in tourism businesses, it is inevitable for the employees to go into deleterious feelings. The companies where employees with these feelings work may have challenges in achieving their goals and objectives, and their sustainability may be endangered. Ensuring sustainability in tourism businesses is closely related to the employees' positive and unneeded organizational behaviors to attain their goals and objectives. Therefore, examining the concept of alienation over different types of tourism businesses is also a significant issue that needs to be considered.

2.6 SUSTAINABILITY AND SUSTAINABILITY IN TOURISM BUSINESSES

Although sustainability started to be put into words in the early 1970s, it is among the issues that many countries, institutions, and organizations around the world have emphasized in recent years. Sustainability aims to employ all the society's resources (scientific, cultural, environmental, etc.) moderately by considering the future. Furthermore, it intends to create a social perspective acting following this view. It is a process that includes social justice, environmental science, politics, and law in many fields (Tıraş 2012). Sustainability is an issue that has been generally studied as sustainability on the environment in many sectors; it has become a topic that researchers and sector stakeholders are interested in economically, socially, culturally, and environmentally in the tourism sector under the concept of sustainable tourism. Sustainable tourism is defined as growth in which

> The environment by which human beings interact or do not interact is protected from deterioration or conversion, cultural integrity, ecological processes, biological diversity, and viable systems are maintained, all resources are managed in a way that they can meet the economic, social and aesthetic needs of the people and tourists visiting the region and meet the same needs of future generations
>
> *İlksen 1996 Dinçer 1996*

As can be understood from the definitions of the sustainability and sustainable tourism concepts, the main reasons for using these concepts together can be listed as follows (Gıran Taşçıoğlu 2016):

- Environmental and political changes.
- Considering the needs of communities and future generations.
- The demand for equal distribution of the shares between the lowest and the highest levels of the revenues obtained in the tourism sector.

- Ensuring the participation of all stakeholders in the tourism activity, the local people being.

It may be uttered that the realization of sustainable tourism practices in the tourism sector can be secured by incorporating sustainability into their practices. It also includes the management activities of the businesses and the employees controlled by these activities in the companies to perform their sustainable tourism activities. In many stages after establishing the companies, the management activities of the businesses are considered highly vital. Management activities on long-term success and sustainability require all stakeholders to gather and be involved in the same organizational goals. In this context, the businesses operating in the tourism sector must have employees who have the characteristics that can meet the conditions of the industry, the job, and the organization (Akbaba and Günlü 2011).

Table 2.1 displays 12 sustainable tourism goals stated by the United Nations Environment Programme and United Nations World Tourism Organisation (2005). These goals are examined in detail in many aspects regarding sustainable tourism. Tourism businesses should consciously take on their responsibilities for the purposes indicated above and contribute to sustainable tourism. As viewed in Table 2.1, the 5th of these 12 items emphasize visitor fulfillment. This chapter states that it is necessary to provide a safe and satisfying experience to all visitors without discrimination regarding race, gender, disability. For tourism businesses to ensure their sustainability, they need to evaluate themselves through management and employee policies. Tourism businesses can maintain their existence clearly if their employees fulfill their duties in a quality manner. In this scope, it can be stated that the behavior of employees is also an essential issue in revealing the quality of businesses and providing customer satisfaction.

Businesses or organizations claim that the most common setbacks encountered in sustainability are qualified employees and limited resources. It may be voiced that poor management becomes even more ineffective when faced with an emergency. Employees can't be compatible within the organization all the time. In this respect, reasons such as employees' inability to fully adopt the goals and lack of communication and coordination are potent on employees, and thus this can negatively affect sustainability (Chung et al. 2011). In general terms, employee behavior is undeniable in sustainable tourism and tourism businesses' sustainability. Therefore, it can be stated that positive and adverse employee behaviors are valid in the sustainability of tourism businesses.

2.7 ALIENATION AND SUSTAINABILITY IN TOURISM BUSINESSES

Success may be fulfilled in tourism businesses with the contributions of suitable employees for the job and who have adopted the organization's goals. However, this success has a significant impact on the sustainability of tourism businesses. This situation is related to the management style, the managers' attitudes and behaviors, and the power sources they employ. In this context, due to the management styles of the managers, employees can integrate with the organization and gain success or may

TABLE 2.1
12 Goals of Sustainable Tourism

1.	*Economic viability*	*'To ensure the viability and competitiveness of tourism destinations and enterprises, so that they can continue to prosper and deliver benefits in the long term'*
2.	*Local prosperity*	*'To maximize the contribution of tourism to the economic prosperity of the host destination, including the proportion of visitor spending that is kept locally'*
3.	*Employment quality*	*'To strengthen the number and quality of local jobs created and supported by tourism, including the level of pay, conditions of service and availability to all without discrimination by gender, race, disability or in other ways'*
4.	*Social equity*	*'To seek a widespread and fair distribution of economic and social benefits from tourism throughout the recipient community, including improving opportunities, income, and services available to the poor'*
5.	*Visitor fulfillment*	*'To provide a safe, satisfying and fulfilling experience for visitors, available to all without discrimination by gender, race, disability or in other ways'*
6.	*Local control*	*'To engage and empower local communities in planning and decision making about the management and future development of tourism in their area, in consultation with other stakeholders'*
7.	*Community wellbeing*	*'To maintain and strengthen the quality of life in local communities, including social structures and access to resources, amenities and life support systems, avoiding any form of social degradation or exploitation'*
8.	*Cultural richness*	*'To respect and enhance the historic heritage, authentic culture, traditions and distinctiveness of host communities'*
9.	*Physical integrity*	*'To maintain and enhance the quality of landscapes, both urban and rural, and avoid the physical and visual degradation of the environment'*
10.	*Biological diversity*	*'To support the conservation of natural areas, habitats, and wildlife, and minimize damage to them'*
11.	*Resource efficiency*	*'To minimize the use of scarce and non-renewable resources in the development and operation of tourism facilities and services'*
12.	*Environmental purity*	*'To minimize the pollution of air, water and land and the generation of waste by tourism enterprises and visitors'*

Source: United Nations Environment Programme and United Nations World Tourism Organisation (2005).

move away from the organization and exhibit alienation behavior, which is one of the undesirable organizational behaviors (Karaçor 2018).

The extension of technology in many industries has revealed mechanization and has been active in setting standards and expanding the control area. However, since the service is at the forefront only in tourism businesses, standardization could not be obtained sufficiently. Although mechanization and automation systems are included in the process, they remain limited. Although management thinking has transformed from a classical approach to a neoclassical approach, it has led to its centralization in management style, organizational structure, and employee management since this situation is not filled with mechanization and automation in tourism businesses. Employees have been tried to be managed like a machine, with a management approach similar to classical management, since these opportunities cannot be fully included in tourism businesses (Sert 2017). This management approach has laid the groundwork for employees to display alienation behavior in tourism businesses such as hotel businesses, tour operators, travel agencies, food, beverage, or entertainment businesses.

Even though tourism businesses supply physical conditions, they should ensure that their employees function effectively to compete with other companies in the sector and maintain their sustainability. This issue is even more prominent today for every business in the tourism sector (Kafalı 2017). Human resources have a consequential place in sustainability for tourism businesses. When the expectations and demands of the employees of the tourism businesses are met, the motivation of the employees boosts, and this positive effect contributes positively to the company's performance (Kutanis and Mesci 2010). Therefore, examining the alienation concept in terms of tourism businesses may be helpful in the context of revealing the effects of alienation on sustainability in more detail.

It is observed that sustainable resource management started in the 1980s in ***hospitality businesses***, but planned studies have been carried out since the 1990s. In this process, it has been determined that studies managed without a specific plan and policy did not produce sustainable results. In this case, the necessity of more systematic and professional approaches has come to the fore. Because the efficient use of resources should include commercial and social, economic, environmental, and human resources aspects involving the consumers, it should be assessed. The inclusion of humanitarian elements among the sustainability practices of hospitality businesses will make these practices more valuable (Demir 2014). The alienation behavior of the employees of the hospitality businesses is also among the humanitarian factors that should be considered in terms of sustainability.

In several research conducted on hospitality employees, it is grasped that the employees have gone through alienation. In these studies, it has been determined that if employees become alienated from society or workplaces, they will not be productive in their work and will experience alienation in terms of powerlessness, meaninglessness, and normlessness: Babür (2009) found out that there are significant differences between the demographic characteristics of the employees and alienation, and especially the front office employees experience higher separation than other department employees; Develioğlu and Tekin (2013) identified that employees who work emotionally in their work experience paradox and those who display alienation behavior experience this paradox more (Kaya and Serçeoğlu 2013). Furthermore, a study on male hotel employees in Israel concluded that alienation was higher among former Soviet-descent males and workers with heavy drinking–weed consumption (Islarowitz et al. 2012).

In food and beverage businesses, the output processes and tourism's environmental and social sustainability dimensions are more relevant (Özgen 2014). These service businesses need to be examined in terms of both human resources and sustainability. Food and beverage businesses offer catering services in line with the customers' preferences. In addition to the product that individuals consume in food and beverage businesses, they also attach importance to the service quality of these businesses. This mentioned quality is based on the fulfillment of the duties by the employees in the provision of food and beverages. Food and beverage businesses are places where individuals are concentrated, and circulation is high during their vacation periods. Especially at certain times of the day, this density may exceed the carrying capacity. Employees in these businesses can also be contrarily governed in terms of the management style, business conditions, or the opportunities offered by the business in this intense work tempo. In businesses where such excess conditions exist, these reasons may generate employees to exhibit alienation behavior. While food and beverage businesses are independent businesses, they are also included in hospitality businesses or serve as distinct departments. A similar situation can be experienced among the employees here.

Research on food and beverage business employees show that employees tend to be alienated in direct proportion to the support provided by the business, and there are significant differences between demographic characteristics such as marital status, age, education level, working hours in the sector, and alienation (Zaro 2018). Furthermore, an outstanding result has been achieved in a study carried on employees working in fast service restaurants in the United States, and it has been concluded that the alienation of the employees generally stems from the management style, not from the use of technology or machinery (DiPietro and Pizam 2008).

Entertainment businesses are one of the indispensable support parts of the tourism industry. Entertainment businesses can be classified in many ways. Entertainment products consumed quickly in the tourism sector (nightclub, disco, bar, amusement park, casino, etc.) are preferred by tourists. As in other businesses in the tourism sector, these businesses serve guests with people and reach their goals and targets through their employees. These businesses can provide services at different times of the day, and the working intensity of the employees can vary. Working conditions and workload in entertainment businesses can influence employees. Although they are expressed as entertainment businesses, entertainment words may not be the case for employees. These types of companies are companies with high customer density and circulation. Factors such as working conditions, working hours, type of business, and wages can negatively affect employees and get them to exhibit alienation behavior.

Individuals prefer transport businesses all over the world for transportation or other purposes. These can be large organizations or serve at the local level. Transportation businesses are among the first stages of reaching the goals in the tourism sector. They support individuals to reach their destination in an organized manner in a short time. The relationship of these businesses with sustainability often brings the environment to mind and is associated with the background mostly. However, it should not be forgotten that transportation companies are also a business. Challenging works are performed like providing active service on any day, and employees' working hours are arranged in shifts, long or short. Also, attention is on the front, and dangers cannot be disregarded in transportation companies. Transport businesses must also survive sustainably. This situation brings to the fore the need for qualified employees as in other tourism businesses. Transport business employees should also have specific technical and theoretical skills and experience because the working conditions and environment of the employees should be presented suitably while performing their duties. These businesses are those that may face significant risks. Being aware of this situation, employees want to be provided with the necessary opportunities regarding working conditions. The work conditions that employees encounter may have them exhibit surplus behaviors due to the risk effect in their jobs. Among these behaviors, alienation behavior can also find a place for itself. It was obtained in a study conducted on transport employees that intention to quit influenced loneliness and was entirely mediated by alienation from work (Gözükara et al. 2017).

Tour operators play a role as prominent actors in the realization of mass tourism movements worldwide. The tourism sector has reached another level with the mass tourism movements and has precipitated new investments in tourism every day. In consequence of these investments, the human resource needs of the other stakeholders of the tourism sector and the operators have expanded. Tour operators organize package tours to many parts of the world and provide individuals with other tourism opportunities. The quality of these operations is directly proportional to the fulfillment of their duties by the employees. As is generally the case with other tourism businesses, the drawbacks that employees may hit upon while performing their duties in tour operators can be listed as wages, working conditions, working hours, management style, relations with colleagues. Employees in question may be prompted by such practices and exhibit alienation behavior. In a study done on travel agency employees in Egypt, it was found that variables such as job-related income and experience have significant effects on employees' displaying alienation behaviors (Zaki and Al-Romeedy 2018). In addition, a study on tourism agency employees serving in Istanbul concluded that the demonstrated labor factor affected employee alienation (Kurt 2013).

With a general evaluation, employees' displaying alienation behavior in tourism businesses can be attributed to many reasons such as demographic characteristics (age, marital status, gender, educational status, experience, working time in the sector, etc.), work environment, working conditions, relations with other employees, managerial behavior, management style, business policies, and business culture. Alienation behavior is one of the offensive organizational behaviors that individuals exhibit in the face of any situation or phenomenon. Tourism businesses are labor-intensive and need human resources to survive in the future. Therefore, tourism businesses should also provide employees with opportunities in many aspects, significantly morale and motivation. Providing these opportunities is weighty for employees both in their internal relations with customers and in their ability to fulfill their duties in the business. Most notably, it is meaningful to ensure the existence of the company in the future.

2.8 CONCLUSION

Nowadays, individuals concentrate on their actions within the framework of the necessities of their living conditions rather than their wishes. Under these actions, individuals may exhibit a positive or unwelcome behavior toward their social life, culture, or the businesses they work in. The conditions of individuals naturally impact their lives, and this situation can also be reflected in their business life. The individuals who cannot pull off what they want in their living conditions, who cannot have a good business life, who are faced with the use of rules as a force, who have a disruption in communication, and who cannot get a reward for their work are more likely to exhibit alienation behavior, which is one of the unwanted organizational behaviors.

Since the income from tourism activities intensified, it has led countries worldwide to concentrate on tourism and wish to get a higher share of the economic benefits of tourism. With this rise, countries have significantly amplified their physical structures in tourism by providing opportunities to both public and private sectors. Moreover, it has led to the emergence of more alternative tourism types and transportation conditions. Along with the existence of the tourism movement, it laid the groundwork for progress toward food, beverage, and entertainment. In direct proportion to this course, the need for human resources in tourism businesses has augmented. The tourism industry is a sector where a lot of customer communication with employees takes place. An individual who carries out the tourism mobility communicates primarily with the employees in the industry during the vacation. Indeed, the behavior of the employees toward the demands and requests of the customers is a necessary condition in ensuring the continuity of the business. Providing the working and social needs of the employees in tourism businesses creates positive effects on the employees and contributes to the sustainability of companies. However, regarding the employees only as a mechanical part, the management policies and managerial behavior focusing on efficiency negatively influence the attitude of the employees toward their work and induce them to be alienated from their organizations. It can be stated that this unsatisfactory result may arise because the feelings and needs of employees may have been forgotten.

In addition to the physical characteristics in the tourism sector, a business's relationship with the customers in the tourism sector is a decisive issue. This sector obliges that employees fulfill their duties completely, comply with the customer–employee relationship within the framework of the rules, and behave smiling and kindly. Difficulties employees face in their lives, health, effects in their communication with family and colleagues, management policies can compel them to work without showing their feelings. When the individuals cannot get the reward for their efforts, such as wages, behavior, morale, or motivation, they move away from the organization and start worrying. The health of the employees who exhibit alienation behavior may deteriorate, and they may show many harmful behaviors such as stress, fear, anxiety, and deviant behavior. To prevent the employees in the tourism sector from exhibiting alienation behavior and to contribute to the sustainability of the businesses, the following suggestions can be presented to the companies:

- In addition to the working conditions, the areas that employees can use within the business should be prepared, and it should be ensured that they spend their rest periods in a quality way.
- As with the customer–employee communication sensitivity, the management–employee sensitivity of the service employees should be prioritized in the same way.
- Managers should make payments and pay rise on time by evaluating wage policies and country conditions. This situation may decrease the individual stress of the employees in their private lives and prompt them to pay more attention to their jobs.
- Psychological support programs and training should be included to address employees' troubles in their private and business lives.
- A homogeneous employee structure should be established, and duties and working hours should be distributed fairly.
- Business policies and rules should be clear, and employees should be informed about these.
- Regardless of which department or unit they work in, the wishes and complaints of the employees should be valued objectively, and the necessary solutions should be sought.
- Workload and pace of work should be adjusted according to the conditions, and human resources should be provided if necessary.
- Human resources should be selected and recruited according to the conditions and abilities required by the job.
- Employees should not be expected to be consistently successful, and the necessary sources of motivation should be prepared, and employees should not be left under stress.
- Promotion and reward opportunities should be made available within the businesses, and employees should be informed of these opportunities.
- Excessive grouping within the business should be prevented, and a good communication environment should be ensured between employees.
- A work environment should be created in which employees can make simple decisions about their jobs.
- Employees should be made aware that the tasks they perform have a meaning, and they should be disclosed that they have a share in the results achieved.
- Employees should be allowed to use their skills in the production or service process.
- Managers should know negative behaviors and should understand the causes and consequences of them well. In addition, managers should have the ability to investigate these behaviors, if necessary, or receive consultancy services.
- Attention should be paid to ensure that the diversity of duties assigned to employees is equal to other employees.
- Employees' opinions about organizational decisions should be taken, and when necessary, they should be included in managerial decisions.
- Employees should be approached relatively without any discrimination, and promotion and reward procedures should be carried out based on the duties and performances of the employees.

- A good communication network should be established between employees and management.
- Detailed explanations should also be made to the employees regarding the decisions taken by the management, and suspicious behavior should be avoided. It should not be forgotten transparent business management is a vital element that ensures order within the business.

On this account, there are plenty of types of businesses in the tourism sector. The employee is the most remarkable building block for these businesses to procure their goals and maintain sustainability. Hence, these enterprises offer their products and services through their employees and earn income. With the quality of the products and services provided, customer continuity may be ensured, and thus, quality workforce and service also gain importance. In this context, tourism businesses should know why alienation behaviors emerge and why their employees are likely to exhibit them. In this context, it is a dominant issue that tourism businesses should take measures and prevent disadvantageous situations that may arise and hinder the achievement of their goals and objectives. In this way, tourism businesses may succeed in terms of sustainability.

REFERENCES

Agarwal, Sanjeev. 1993. "Influence of Formalization on Role Stress, Organizational Commitment, and Work Alienation of Salespersons: A Cross-National Comparative Study". *Journal of International Business Studies* 24, no. 4 (December): 715–739. https://doi.org/10.1057/palgrave.jibs.8490252.

Akbaba, Atilla and Ebru Günlü. 2011. "Otel İşletmelerinde İşgören Bulma, Seçme ve Eğitim Sürecinin Stratejik İnsan Kaynakları Bakış Açısıyla Değerlendirilmesi: Beş Yıldızlı Otellerde Bir Araştırma". *The Journal of Social Economic Research* 11, no. 22 (December): 199–228.

Ankony, Robert C. and Thomas M. Kelley. 1999. "The Impact of Perceived Alienation on Police Officers' Sende of Mastery and Subsequent Motivation for Proactive Enforcement". *Policing: An International Journal of Police Strategies & Management* 22, no. 2 (June): 120–134. https://doi.org/10.1108/13639519910271193.

Arokach, Ami. 2006. "Alienation and Domestic Abuse: How Abused Women Cope with Loneliness". *Social Indicators Research* 78, no. 2 (September): 327–340. doi:10.1007/s11205-005-1603-x.

Babür, Serpil. 2009. "Organizational Alienation in Tourism Industry: A Study Concerning the Five Stars Hotels Enterprises in the District of Antalya". Master Thesis, Akdeniz University.

Bacharach, Samuel B. and Michael Aiken. 1979. "The Impact of Alienation, Meaninglessness, and Meritocracy on Supervisor and Subordinate Satisfaction". *Social Force* 57, no. 3 (March): 853–870. doi:10.2307/2577358.

Bamford, Kirsten L. 2012. "Undergraduate Student Perceptions of A Career in the Tourism and Hospitality Industry in New Zealand", Master Thesis, University of Otago.

Banai, Moshe and William D. Reisel. 2007. "The Influence of Supportive Leadership and Job Characteristics on Work Alienation: A Six-Country Investigation". *Journal of World Business* 42, no. 4, (December): 463–476. https://doi.org/10.1016/j.jwb.2007.06.007.

Başaran, İbrahim E. 2000. *Örgütsel Davranış*. Ankara: Feryal Matbaası.

Bayat, Bülent. 1996. “Comparative Investigation of Alienation Among Workers Working in Cement and Automotive Sectors”, PhD Diss., Gazi University.

Bingöl, Dursun. 1990. *İşyeri Disiplini ve Çalışma Barışı*. İstanbul: Özgün Matbaacılık.

Blauner, Robert. 1964. *Alienation and Freedom: The Factory Worker and His İndustry*. Chicago, IL: The University of Chicago Press.

Bolton, Charles D. 1972. “Alienation and Action: A Study of Peace-Group Members”. *The American Journal of Sociology* 78, no. 3 (November): 537–561. https://doi.org/10.2307/2776306.

Boz, Mehmet. 2014. “Alienation and Anger Relation in Educational Organizations (Şişli Technical and Industrial Vocational High School).” Master Thesis, Bahçeşehir University.

Chung, Huang F., Wang J. Jieh and Lin J. Tai. 2011 “Resource Sufficiency, Organizational Cohesion and Organizational Effectiveness of Emergency Response” *Nat Hazards*, 58, (December): 221–234. https://doi.org/10.1007/s11069-010-9662-y.

Dean, Dwight G. 1961. “Alienation: Its Meaning and Measurement.” *American Sociological Review* 26, no. 5 (October): 753–758. https://doi.org/10.2307/2090204.

Demir, Mahmut. 2014. “Sürdürülebilir Turizm ve Otel İşletmeleri” In *Sürdürülebilir Turizm* edited by Metin Kozak, 173–190. Ankara: Detay Yayıncılık.

Demirel, Göksu and Ünal Aydın. 2011. “Research to Analyze the Perception of Organisational Alienation within the Students Taking Tourism Education in the Vocational School.” 2nd International 6th National Vocational Schools Symposium, Aydın: Adnan Menderes University, May 25–27.

Develioğlu, Kazim and Ömer A. Tekin. 2013. “The Relationship Between Five Factor Personality Traits and Alienation: An Ampiric Study on Five Star Hotel Employees.” *Suleyman Demirel University: The Journal of Faculty of Economics* 18, no. 2 (June): 15–30. https://dergipark.org.tr/tr/pub/sduiibfd/issue/20818/222757.

DiPietro, Robin B. and Abraham Pizam. 2008. “Employee Alienation in the Quick Service Restaurant Industry.” *Journal of Hospitality & Tourism Research* 32, no. 1 (February): 22–39. https://doi.org/10.1177/1096348007309567.

Doğan, İsmail. 1998. *İletişim ve Yabancılaşma* (3rd. Ed.). İstanbul: Sistem Yayıncılık.

Doğan, İsmail. 2004. *Toplum ve Eğitim Sorunları Üzerinde Felsefi ve Sosyolojik Tahliller*. Ankara: Pegem Yayıncılık.

Durmaz, Merve. 2015. “Alienation Level of Health Workers: Isparta Sample.” Master Diss., Süleyman Demirel University.

Er, Kemal. 2007. “Total Quality Management Relation with Alienation from the Point of Employee: Example of Electronic Industry”, *International Journal of Human Sciences* 4, no. 1 (May): 1–40. www.j-humansciences.com/ojs/index.php/IJHS/article/view/42.

Erkılıç, Eren. 2012. “The Effect of Organizational Stress on Organizational Alienation: A Study on Five Star Hotels.” Master Diss., Afyon Kocatepe University.

Eryılmaz, Arzu. 2010. “Levels of Organizational Alienation for High School Teachers.” Master Diss., Hacettepe University.

Ferguson, Iain and Michael Lavalette. 2004. “Beyond Power Discourse: Alienation and Social Work.” *British Journal of Social Work* 34, no. 3 (April): 297–312. https://doi.org/10.1093/bjsw/bch039.

Fettahlıoğlu, Tamara. 2006. “Alienation Management in Organizations: The Comparative Survey in Private Enterprise and Public Sectors in Kahramanmaraş”, Master Diss., Kahramanmaraş Sütçü İmam University.

Fromm, Erich. 1992. *Marx'ın İnsan Anlayışı*. Translated by Kaan H. Ökten. İstanbul: Arıtan Yayınevi.

Fromm, Erich. 1995a. *Çağımızın Özgürlük Sorunu*. Translated by Bozkurt Güvenç. Ankara: Gündoğan Yayınevi.

Fromm, Erich. 1995b. *Umut Devrimi İnsancıllaşmış Bir Teknolojiye Doğru*, Translated by Şemsa Yeğin. İstanbul: Payel Yayınevi.

Fromm, Erich. 1996. *Özgürlükten Kaçış*, Translated by Şemsa Yeğin. İstanbul: Payel Yayınevi.

Fromm, Erich. 2004. *Çağdaş Toplumların Geleceği*, Translated by Gülnur Kaya and Kaan H. Ökten. İstanbul: Arıtan Yayınevi.

Gardner, Phyllis A. 2007. "Peoples Temple: An Analysis of Alienation in a Total Alienation", PhD Diss, Texas Woman's University.

Gözükara, İzlem, Çiğdem A. Mercanlı, Selçuk Capuk and Osman Yıldırım. 2017. "Impact of Turnover Intention on Loneliness and the Mediating Effect of Work Alienation." *Business Management and Strategy* 8, no. 1 (January): 18–38. https://doi.org/10.5296/bms.v8i1.10521.

Güler, Seyhan B., Tülay Demiralay and Vural M. Artin. 2019. "Impact of Organizational Culture on Organizational Alienation Behaviours", *Social Sciences Research Journal* 8, no. 1 (March): 209–222. https://dergipark.org.tr/tr/pub/ssrj/issue/43336/531993.

Gürsoy, Fadile. 2014. "The Level of Health Business Personnel's Alienation to the job Example of Van Province." Master Diss., Atılım University.

Halbesleben, Jonathon R. B. and Sara K. Clark. 2010. "The Experience of Alienation Among Temporary Workers in High-Skill Jobs: A Qualitative Analysis of Temporary Firefighters." *Journal of Managerial Issues* 22, no. 4 (Winter): 531–545. www.jstor.org/stable/25822529.

Hirschfeld, Robert. R. and Hubert S. Feild. 2000. "Work Centrality and Work Alienation: Distinct Aspects of a General Commitment to Work." *Journal of Organizational Behavior* 21, no. 7 (November): 789–800. https://doi.org/10.1002/1099-1379(200011)21:7<789::AID-JOB59>3.0.CO;2-W.

Holian, John. 1972. "Alienation and Social Awareness Among College Students." *The Sociological Quarterly* 13, no. 1 (January): 114–125. https://doi.org/10.1111/j.1533-8525.1972.tb02108.x.

Horowitz, Irving L. 1983. *C Wright Mills An American Utopian*. New York, NY: Free Press.

Hoşgörür, Vural. 1997. "Organizational Behaviours of The Teachers (Sample for the Central Schools for Secondary Education in the City of Samsun)" PhD Diss., Ankara University.

Dinçer, İlksen. 1996. "Sürdürülebilir Turizmin Hayata Geçirilmesi İçin Aktive Olması Gereken Dinamikler ve İşlevleri-Model Çalışması, Sürdürülebilir Turizm; Turizm Plânlamasına Ekolojik Yaklaşım", XIX. World Urban Day Colloquium, Mimar Sinan University, İstanbul, (342).

Islarowitz, Richard, Alexander Reznik and Yaniv Belhassen. 2012. "Work Alienation, Patterns of Substance Use and Country of Origin among Male Hospitality Workers in Israel", *International Journal of Mental Health and Addiction* 10, no. 6 (June): 923–926. https://doi.org/10.1007/s11469-012-9388-z.

Kafalı, Sedat. 2017. "The Effect of Internal and External Locus of Control on Organizational Alienation in Hotel Enterprises: A Case of Nevşehir." Master Diss., Nevşehir Hacı Bektaş Veli University.

Kanungo, Rabindra N. 1992. "Alienation and Empowerment: Some Ethical Imperatives in Business." *Journal of Business Ethics* 11, no. 5–6 (May): 413–422. https://doi.org/10.2307/25072290.

Karaçor, Musa. 2018. "A Research on the Effect of Power Sources Used by Managers to Organizational Identification and Organizational Alienation: A Case of Five Stars Hotel Business." Master Diss., Afyon Kocatepe University.

Karakaya, Fatih. 2010. "A Number of Modern Painting Proposal on Human and Alienation." Master Diss., İnönü University.

Kargı, Bilal. 2012. "Speculations About The (Re)Structuring of The Field of Economics in The Human Thought", *Gümüşhane University Journal of Social Sciences Institute* 3, no. 6 (June): 8–40. https://dergipark.org.tr/en/pub/gumus/issue/7515/99033.

Kaya, Ufuk and Neslihan Serçeoğlu. 2013. "Work Alienation Among Emotion Workers: A Research in Service Industry." *Çalışma ve Toplum Dergisi* 1: 311–345. www.calismatoplum.org/makale/duygu-iscilerinde-ise-yabancilasma-hizmet-sektorunde-bir-arastirma.

Kohn, Melvin L. 1976. "Occupational Structure and Alienation." *American Journal of Sociology* 82, no. 1: 111–130. https://doi.org/10.1086/226272.

Korman, Abraham K., Ursula Wittig-Berman and Dorothy Lang. 1981. "Career Success and Personal Failure: Alienation in Professionals and Managers". *Academy of Management Journal* 24, no. 2 (June): 342–360. https://doi.org/10.2307/255846.

Kurt, Zeylan. 2013. "Impact of Emotional Labour Factor on Alienation: A Research on Hotel Establishments and Travel Agents in Istanbul." Master Diss., Çanakkale Onsekiz Mart University.

Kutanis, Rana Ö. and Muammer Mesci. 2010. "Örgütsel Adaletin Çalışanların İş Tatminine Etkisi: Turizm Alanında Eğitim Veren Bir Yükseköğretim Kurumuna Yönelik Bir Örnek Olay Çalışması." *Sosyal Ekonomik Araştırmalar Dergisi* 10, no. 19 (June): 527–552. https://dergipark.org.tr/tr/pub/susead/issue/28416/302529.

Levin, William C. 1994. *Sociological Ideas: Concepts And Applications*, California: Wadsworth Publishing Company.

Marx, Karl. 1970. *Economic and Philosophic Manuscripts of 1844*. Translated by Martin Milligan, London: Lawrance and Wishard.

Mercan, Mustafa. 2006. "Organizational Commitment Organizational Alienation and Organizational Citizenship Behaviour of Teachers." Master Diss., Afyon Kocatepe University.

Middleton, Russell. 1963. "Alienation, Race, and Education." *American Sociological Review* 28, no. 6 (December): 973–977. https://doi.org/10.2307/2090316.

Mottaz, Clifford. J. 1981. "Some Determinants of Work Alienation." *The Sociological Quarterly* 22, no. 4 (September): 515–529. https://doi.org/10.1111/j.1533–8525.1981.tb00678.x.

Nair, Nisha and Neharika Vohra. 2010. "An Exploration of Factors Predicting Work Alienation of Knowledge Workers." *Management Decision* 48, no. 4 (May): 600–615. https://doi.org/10.1108/00251741011041373.

Nettler, Gwynn. 1957. "A Measure of Alienation." *American Sociological Review* 22, no. 6 (December): 670–677. https://doi.org/10.2307/2089196.

Olalı, Hasan and Meral Korzay. 2004. *Otel İşletmeciliği*. İstanbul: Beta Basım Yayımcılık.

Önal, Sibel. 2015. "Relation of Organizational Silence and Alienation: Research Upon Medium and Large Scaled Hotels in Çanakkale." Master Diss., Trakya University.

Özbudun, Sibel, George Markus and Temel Demirer. 2008. *Yabancılaşma ve...* Ankara: Ütopya.

Özgen, Işıl. 2014. "Sürdürülebilir Turizm ve Yiyecek-İçecek İşletmeleri", In *Sürdürülebilir Turizm*, edited by Metin Kozak, 191–206. Ankara: Detay Yayıncılık.

Ray, Nina M. 1985. "Channel Alienation: Sources and Consequences", PhD Diss., Texas Tech University.

Salerno, Roger A. 2003. *Landscapes of Abandonment Capitalism, Modernity and Estrangement*. New York, NY: State University of New York Press.

Sarros, James C., George A. Tanewski, Richard P. Winter, Joseph C. Santora and Iain L. Densten. 2002. "Work Alienation and Organizational Leadership." *British Journal of Management* 13, no. 4 (December): 285–304. https://doi.org/10.1111/1467-8551.00247.

Schacht, Richard. 1970. *Alienation*. New York, NY: Anchor Books.

Seeman, Melvin. 1959. "On the Meaning of Alienation." *American Sociological Review* 24, no. 6 (December): 783–791. https://doi.org/10.2307/2088565.

Seeman, Melvin. 1967. "On the Personal Consequences of Alienation in Work." *American Sociological Review* 32, no. 2 (April): 273–285. https://doi.org/10.2307/2091817.

Seeman, Melvin. 1975. "Alienation Studies." *Annual Review of Sociology* 1, no. 1: 91–123. https://doi.org/10.1146/annurev.so.01.080175.000515.

Seeman, Melvin. 1983. "Alienations Motifs in Contemporary Theorizing: The Hidden Continuity of the Classic Themes." *Social Psychology Quarterly* 46, no. 3 (September): 171–184. https://doi.org/10.2307/3033789.

Sert, Sertaç. 2017. "The Effect of Hotel Employees Perceptions About Job Characteristics and Organizational Structure on Alienation, PhD Diss., Gazi University.

Shepard, Jon M. 1972. "Alienation as a Process: Work as A Case in Point." *The Sociological Quarterly* 13, no. 2 (Spring): 161–173. https://doi.org/10.2307/4105773.

Shepard, Jon. M. 1973. "Technology, Division of Labor and Alienation," *The Pacific Sociological Review* 16, no. 1 (January): 61–88. https://doi.org/10.2307/1388654.

Silah, Mehmet. 2005. *Endüstride Çalışma Psikolojisi*, Ankara: Seçkin Yayıncılık.

Şimşek, Hüseyin, Refik Balay and Salih A. Şimşek. 2012. "Alienation from Work of Elementary School Teachers." *Journal of Educational Sciences Research* 2, no. 1, (June): 53–72. https://dergipark.org.tr/tr/pub/ebader/issue/44650/554618.

Şimşek, Mehmet Ş., Adnan Çelik, Tahir Akgemci, and Tamara Fettahlıoğlu. 2006. "Örgütlerde Yabancılaşmanın Yönetimi Araştırması", Selçuk Üniversitesi Sosyal Bilimler Enstitüsü Dergisi 15: 569–587. http://dergisosyalbil.selcuk.edu.tr/susbed/article/view/591.

Soysal, Abdullah. 1997. "A Theoric and Practices Study Regarding the fact of Alienation in Organizations." Master Diss., Selçuk University.

Sulu, Seyfettin, Adnan Ceylan and Ramazan Kaynak. 2010. "Work Alienation as a Mediator of the Relationship between Organizational Injustice and Organizational Commitment: Implications for Healthcare Professionals." *International Journal of Business and Management* 5, no. 8 (August): 27–38. https://doi.org/10.5539/ijbm.v5n8p27.

Taşcıoğlu, Sezen G. 2016. "The Development of Strategies for Sustainable Tourism: The sample of North Antalya and Tourism Conservation and Development Area." PhD Diss., Ankara University.

Tekin, Ömer A. 2012. "The Relationships between Five Factors Personality Traits and Alienation: An Examination on Five Star Hotel Employees in Kemer, Antalya." PhD Diss., Akdeniz University.

Tezcan, Mahmut. 1983. "Eğitimde Yabancılaşma." *Ankara University Journal of Faculty Educational Sciences* 16, no. 1 (1983):245–254. https://doi.org/10.1501/Egifak_000 0000927.

Tıraş, Hayrettin H. 2012. "Sustainable Development and Environment: An Examine in Theory." *Kahramanmaraş Sütçü İmam University Faculty of Economics and Administrative Sciences Journal* 2, no. 2 (June): 57–73. http://iibfdergisi.ksu.edu.tr/tr/pub/issue/10265/125901.

Tolan, Barlas. 1996. *Toplum Bilimlerine Giriş*. Ankara: Adım Yayıncılık.

Türker, Nuray, Mehmet Uçar and Muzaffer A. Ateş. 2016. "Perceptions of Tourism Students towards Tourism Industry: A study on Karabuk University Students, *Journal of Humanities and Tourism Research* 6, no. 2 (September): 311–333. https://dergipark.org.tr/tr/pub/joiss/issue/30780/323606.

United Nations Environment Programme and United Nations World Tourism Organisation. 2005. Making Tourism More Sustainable: A Guide for Policy Makers.

Usta, Işıl and Derman Küçükaltan. 2014. "Turizm İşletmelerinde Örgütsel Yabancılaşma" In Turizm İşletmelerinde Çalışan İlişkileri Yönetimi, edited by Şule Aydın Tükeltürk, Nilüfer Şahin Perçin, Berrin Güzel, 361–374. Ankara: Detay Yayıncılık.

Uysaler, Lütfi A. 2010. "The Relationship of Organizational Alienation with Organizational Commitment, Job Satisfaction and Turnover Intent and Organizational Alienation Management." Master Diss., Gebze Institute of Technology.

Weiskopf, Walter A. 1996. *Yabancılaşma ve İktisat*, Translated by Çağatay Koç, Yahya Madra, Değer Eryar, Kenan Erçel, Ceren Özselçuk, Alper Önder, Kemal Badur, Oya Köymen. İstanbul: Anahtar Kitapları.

Yıldırım, Tevfik. 2009. "The Influence of the Primary Education Administrators Personal and Organizational Worthy Accommodation on the Dedicating and Estrangement." Master Diss., Uşak University.

Yılmaz Gözde, Aşkın K. and Sayım Yorgun. 2010. "The Impact of Job Satisfaction on Life Satisfaction and Intention to Leave Among Unionized Lodging Sector Employees." *Paradoks, Journal of Economics, Sociology and Policy* 6, no. 1 (June): 87–107. https://dergipark.org.tr/en/pub/paradoks/issue/16358/171254.

Yılmaz, Sadi and Pınar Sarpkaya. 2009. "Alienation in Educational Organizations and Its' Management." *International Journal of Human Sciences* 6, no. 2, (September): 314–333. www.j-humansciences.com/ojs/index.php/IJHS/article/view/725.

Yüksel, Hasan. 2014. "Yabancılaşma Kavramı Paralelinde Emeğin Yabancılaşması ve Sonuçları" *Abant Izzet Baysal University Journal of Social Sciences* 14, no. 2: 159–188.

Yumuk, Yurdanur. 2011. The Effect of Work Alienation on Job Satisfaction in Hotel Operations: An Application in Nevşehir, Master Diss., Nevşehir University.

Zaki, Heba S. and Bassam S. Al-Romeedy. 2018. "Job Security as a Predictor of Work Alienation among Egyptian Travel Agencies' Employees." *Minia Journal of Tourism and Hospitality Research* 3, no. 1 (June): 47–64.

Zaro, Serkan. 2018. The Effect of Cuisine Employees' Organizational Support Perceptions' on Business Alienation Tendencies: An Investigation in Nevşehir Province, Master Diss., Nevşehir Hacı Bektaş Veli University.

Zorgül, Garip G. 2014. "Relationship Between Psychological Intimidations, to Which Elementary School Teachers Are Exposed, and Alienation to Job (Example Case in Avcilar Township of İstanbul Province)." Master Diss., Bahçeşehir University.

3 The Impact of Environmental Practices on Hotel Perceived Performance

Khaled Tamzini, Anissa Ben Hassine, Tahar Lazhar Ayed, and Mohamed Fadhel Djlassi

CONTENTS

3.1 INTRODUCTION

One of the main features of the last two decades is the increasing integration of the environmental dimension in company management. In this context, companies have gradually moved from a regulatory compliance strategy to a proactive environmental management strategy (Carmona-Moreno et al. 2004). While the 1960s and 1970s were marked by environmental crises and attempts to control the subsequent damage, in the 1980s, companies faced stringent regulations, leading to compliance difficulties and further cost. Since then, companies have adapted to these regulations by adopting environmental management systems and proactive strategies. Environmental management aims to predict the negative effect of the company's operations on the environment and take the necessary measures to alleviate it. In that

DOI: 10.1201/9781003138051-4

respect, ecological management is not just a statement of good intentions; it is beyond and above all managerial practices to be implemented to get a sustainable competitive advantage and superior performance compared to companies operating in the same sector (Hart 1995; Porter and Van der Linde 1995; Shrivastava 1995; Trung and Kumar 2005; Wu and Dunn 1995). Thus, several kinds of research raised the effect of environmental practices on competitive advantage and firm performance. Yet, these researches have not come up with conclusive and definitive answers (Margolis et al. 2007; Orlitzky 2011).

Although a plethora of research analyzing the link between environmental management and competitive edge (Chan 2013; Chen and Peng 2012; Lee et al. 2011; Leonidou et al. 2013; López-Gamero et al. 2009, 2010; Bonilla-Priego et al. 2011) may have led to results ascertaining that environmental management has a substantial impact on company performance, other research dealing with this relationship provided opposite results (Molina-Azorín et al. 2009). Adding to that, we noted that most of this research, with few exceptions (Molina-Azorín et al. 2009; Pereira-Moliner et al. 2015; Leonidou et al. 2013; López-Gamero et al. 2011), had been conducted in the industry sector (Llach et al. 2013; Carmona-Moreno et al. 2004). The service industry and the hotel and tourism sector have been little concerned by this type of research. However, they have the reputation of being 'silent destroyers of the environment' (Hutchinson 1996). In addition, almost all previous research in this managerial field appealed to the objective dimension of performance to measure it, neglecting its subjective size (see the summary of research related to the effect of the environmental size on business performance by Molina-Azorín et al. 2009: 518–519). The subjective measure of performance facilitates the measurement of complex performance dimensions, such as customer satisfaction, brand equity, etc.

In contrast, objective performance measures are challenging to obtain or not very reliable, sometimes because managers refuse to disclose this information and sometimes because of their lack of interest. Accordingly, the concept of 'perceived performance' emerged, allowing managers to measure their companies' performance against their main competitors (Molina-Azorín et al. 2009). This way, the dichotomy between objective and subjective performance measurement (see Gonzàlez-Benito and Gonzàlez-Benito 2005) is an important question that must be tackled with insistence since the researcher's choice between these two dimensions would have considerable consequences on the interpretation of its results.

Considering these findings, further research should address these critical questions and shed light on the link between environmental practices and business performance. Hence, this research aims to examine the impact of environmental management practices on the perceived performance of hotels. In the empirical section, our focus is led on a sample of Tunisian hotels.

This chapter is broken down into four parts. The first one is dedicated to the theoretical underpinning of environmental management practices and their relationships with perceived performance to come up with a set of hypotheses translated into a conceptual model. The second, third, and fourth parts are successively devoted to presenting the methodology, the results, and the underlying discussion, respectively. Finally, we set forth the contributions, limitations, and avenues for future perspectives by the conclusion.

3.2 LITERATURE REVIEW

Although it is often portrayed as an ancient phenomenon, corporate social responsibility (CSR) has become intensively debated among researchers and practitioners in recent years. It seems to be constantly renewed according to its application's events, circumstances, and territories. It also prompted debates on sustainability and controversies among academia and practitioners regarding the motivations explaining the responsible behavior of companies. While some companies use it to gain legitimacy, others consider it a tool to increase their competitiveness and maximize profit (Aguinis and Glavas 2013).

Drawing on the changing global environment, scholars have also gradually revisited CSR by focusing on managerial issues at the organizational level and expanding the scope of CSR to cover many practices dealing with the interests of different stakeholders. Thus, recent research tends to adopt the stakeholder perspective in CSR and to include the environmental practices (Wheeler and Sillanpaa's 1997; Turker 2009). CSR targeting the environment (ecological practices) includes investment in pollution control, the conception of strategies to reduce carbon emission, implementing environmental rules, and managing any waste (Nizamuddin 2018). The modern conceptualization of CSR has expanded to include controlling carbon emissions and the recycling of raw materials. Environmental protection represents a valuable public interest, where some authors argue that ecological performance is achieved through endeavors in three areas: Product technologies, the use of recycled raw materials and other programs that are likely to save resources; process technologies such as efficient production systems and end-of-pipe control; and management systems such as worker training programs and environmental audits (Mishra and Suar 2010). Henceforth, respect for the environment has become unprecedented over the past 15 years and has become a significant focus for companies. This issue already interests environmentalists, green groups, and stakeholders such as consumers, suppliers, certification associations, and shareholders.

To cope with the pressure of various stakeholders, companies have been compelled to take up the challenges related to ecological concerns and integrate them within their CSR strategies to alleviate the environmental effect generated by their operations (Chuang and Huang 2018). Thus, companies are constantly adopting new measures to live up to the needs of their relevant stakeholders regarding the natural environment and get a competitive advantage (Yadav et al. 2017).

Wiengarten and Pagell (2012) define environmental management as the interaction and influence of organizational activities concerned with the natural environment. It covers all activities that aim to alleviate the negative consequences of business operations on the natural environment (Cramer 1998). An initial categorization of environmental management activities makes the difference between 'pollution control' and 'pollution prevention' (Klassen and Whybark 1999; Hart 1995). Pollution control represents actions to limit pollution in the specifications (to abide by current legal standards). It is based on waste disposals and treatment techniques and usually involves using specific facilities that treat the waste generated by the company's activity (end-of-pipe approach). Pollution prevention is based on 'reduction at source,' i.e., avoiding waste before it is generated. Pollution prevention practices include techniques to reduce or eliminate the generation of pollutants through greater efficiency in using raw materials, energy, or water to protect natural resources through conservation (Hart 1995).

A second classification breaks down these activities into 'technical activities or practices' and 'organizational activities or practices' (Klassen and Whybark 1999; Cramer 1998). Carmona-Moreno et al. (2004) state that firms implement technical practices to reduce their costs, the risk of accidents, etc. (Klassen and Whybark 1999; Cramer 1998). These practices are qualified as 'tacit environmental management" (or minimum) . When it comes to organizational practices, referred to as 'explicit environmental management' or 'advanced environmental management,' they represent environmental protection activities carried out voluntarily, consciously, and explicitly by a company, reflecting its concern for environmental protection. Organizational activities are similar across industries, while technical activities depend on the sector (Alvarez Gil et al. 2001).

This research has adopted the second classification of environmental management activities. However, despite the vast body of studies dedicated to this field, the relationship between these two categories of ecological practices (or actions) and company performance is not conclusive. Accordingly, this relationship requires further investigation. The following development will be dedicated to the concept of performance and the hypotheses' formulation. According to Molina-Azorín et al. (2009), performance is generally measured by financial indicators such as return on assets 'ROA,' return on equity 'ROE,' return on sales, 'ROS,' etc. However, these indicators are applied mainly by companies operating in the industrial sector and may prove unsuitable for the hotel sector (Brown 1999 *in* Molina-Azorín et al. 2009). In this vein, Reichel and Haber (2005) *in* Molina-Azorín et al. (2009) point out that it would be more relevant to use indicators adapted to businesses that market intangible experiences. Hence, these indicators are commonly referred to as 'non-financial indicators of firm performance.' Furthermore, Fwaya (2006) and Fitzgerald et al. (1991) stressed that there had been a growing awareness in the hotel sector, whose service is essentially based on the quality of human resources, the importance and value of people, both employees, and customers, in the process of service delivery. This has prompted hoteliers to develop their information systems to evaluate their performance in employee morale and satisfaction.

Other dimensions of nonfinancial performance include competitiveness, service quality, customer satisfaction, organizational flexibility, resource use, and technology (Wadongo et al. 2010). For example, in the hotel industry, researchers have shown the importance of linking performance measures to strategic intent, competitive environment, revenue management, market orientation, and the service delivery process (Fitzgerald et al. 1991; Lynch and Cross 1995; Kaplan and Norton 1992; Haktanir and Harris 2005).

This research uses the performance conceptualization of Tarí et al. (2010), who consider its perceptual nature or perceived performance. This latter is perceptual, where it enables managers to measure their firm's performance concerning their main competitors (Molina-Azorín et al. 2009). Perceived performance is considered a subjective performance that is likely to facilitate the measurement of complex performance dimensions, such as customer satisfaction and brand equity (Molina-Azorín et al.

2009). It is also regarded as an objective performance in the sense of Gonzàlez-Benito (2005), and competitive performance in the mind of Molina-Azorín et al. (2009) since its indicators are obtained directly from the company and secondary sources.

Combining objective and subjective performance is of paramount importance in the accommodation industry (Reichel and Haber 2005 *in* Tarí et al. 2010). Notwithstanding, other researchers state that objective performance measures are challenging to obtain or not very reliable because of managers' unwillingness to disclose this information and sometimes lack interest (Gonzàlez-Benito and Gonzàlez-Benito 2005). In the grand schemes of things, this research adopts the approach of Molina-Azorín et al. (2009), who present perceived performance as made of 'competitive performance' and 'stakeholder satisfaction.' Adding to that, we adopt a subjective measure of the perceived performance. Likewise, the same authors distinguish between market share, average sales growth, income per room, wealth creation, etc., as indicators to measure competitive performance. Stakeholder satisfaction is also referred to as 'market success factors' (Llach et al. 2013). These success factors hinge around company image, customer satisfaction, and employee satisfaction.

3.3 HYPOTHESES

The hotel and tourism industry has received increasing pressure from different stakeholders and started participating in CSR-related activities to fulfill its environmental responsibility, such as energy, water, and waste management (Lin et al. 2021). Some researchers dealt with the consequences of ecological practices on competitive performance and stakeholders' satisfaction in this industry.

Garay and Font (2012) researched a sample of 400 small and medium enterprises operating in the hotel sector in the accommodation sector. Their findings show a positive effect on the financial performance of environmental practices (based on ecological cost savings). However, these ecological practices based on environmental cost savings are considered fundamental as they allow hotels to reduce expenditures and enhance revenues, generating higher performance levels. This is referred to as a direct effect on performance in the sense of Molina-Azorín et al. (2009).

Alvarez Gil et al. (2001) came to two main conclusions in their research conducted in the hotel sector in Spain. First, their results confirm that the age of the facilities, the size, affiliation or membership in a hotel chain, the environmental pressures of stakeholders, and the use of operational management techniques have a considerable effect on the implementation of environmental management practices by 3-, 4-, and 5-star hotels. Second, Alvarez Gil et al. (2001) showed a positive relationship between basic environmental rules and hotel financial performance. These results were later confirmed by Molina-Azorín et al. (2009), who researched the same Spanish hotel sector. Furthermore, a regression analysis on a sample of 301 hotels showed that their basic environmental practices significantly impact their competitive performance.

Along similar lines, Bagur-Femenias et al. (2013) investigated a sample of 448 travel agencies in Spain. They found a significant positive impact of basic environmental practices adopted by these agencies and their competitive performance. These researchers confirmed the results of Enz and Siguaw (1999), stating that integrating basic environmental practices is likely to influence competitiveness through the improvement of operational performance, which depends on a policy of saving on consumption, reducing operating costs, and improving general operating conditions (Bagur-Femenias et al. 2013). Llach et al. (2013) explained this impact because hotels' adoption of such practices directly and immediately influences their operational costs. Considering this development, the following hypothesis is posited:

Hypothesis 1a: Basic environmental practices are positively and significantly related to the competitive performance of hotels.

One of the reasons behind companies' engagement in environmental practices is to meet the concerns of major stakeholders (Angell and Klassen 1999). In addition, these authors point out that through implementing such sustainable procedures, companies look to improve customers' value. In this vein, Hui Fu et al. (2014) contend that environment-friendly practices are likely to impact a firm's image and reputation, which results in a high level of customer's trust and identification with the company, hence better customer satisfaction and loyalty.

Miles and Covin (2000) added that environmental management might lead to product differentiation along similar lines. More particularly, they stated that reducing pollution levels is likely to increase the demand from environmentally sensitive consumers. If the ecological features of products can become a new competitive argument appreciated by these 'green' customers, companies may get a higher environmental reputation.

Kassinis and Soteriou (2003) investigated the link between adopting environmental management practices (energy saving, recycling, and water-saving practices) and market performance in services, precisely the European hospitality industry via the mediation of customer satisfaction and loyalty. Their findings establish that the use of such practices (basic practices) is positively related to higher levels of customer satisfaction and, eventually, higher performance levels through enhanced customer loyalty, hence a positive relationship between environmental practices and customer satisfaction. Furthermore, Molina-Azorín et al. (2009) added that basic ecological techniques installing energy-efficient light bulbs and motion detectors represent easily identifiable and appreciable actions by both clients and employees. Thus, the results affirmed a significant and positive effect on stakeholder satisfaction.

Furthermore, it has been argued that customer satisfaction is commensurate with the perceived quality of services provided to customers. According to Kassinis and Soteriou (2003), this value created by satisfied and loyal employees is a function of costs to the customer and the results achieved for the customer. Some state that employee involvement in environmental practices, specifically the basic ones (as waste minimization), represents a critical capability related to the firm's ecological responsiveness (Hanna et al. 2000). More particularly, Enz and Siguaw (1999) stated that all operations named environmental best practice champions in a Cornell University study of best practices in the US lodging industry indicated that such practices were positively related to employee morale and satisfaction along with enhanced pride toward the hotel. Therefore, the following hypothesis is suggested:

Hypothesis 1b: Basic environmental practices are positively and significantly related to the hotels' stakeholder satisfaction.

The investigation conducted by Alvarez Gil et al. (2001) in the hotel sector in Spain and cited above confirmed a positive link between advanced environmental practices and the financial performance of hotels. Furthermore, Llach et al. (2013) researched the Spanish restaurant sector and confirmed the hypothesis that advanced environmental (or organizational) practices have a significant and positive effect on financial performance. The latter includes measurement indicators, including profit, market share, and occupancy rate. Furthermore, advanced environmental techniques were measured along with six dimensions: Ecological training, ecological initiatives, ecological marketing, ecological activities, long-term environmental strategic direction, and environmental savings and costs. In addition, the linkage between advanced environmental practices and competitive performance has been addressed by Molina-Azorín et al. (2009), who confirmed a positive and significant impact of the first variable (advanced environmental methods) on the second variable (competitive performance).

Kirk (1995) surveyed a sample of 53 hotels in the United Kingdom, specifically in Edinburgh, to decrypt the relationship between the environmental policies (and activities) of these hotels and their competitive performance (e.g., profitability). These environmental policies and activities form an ecological management program composed of practices and actions, such as savings on heating, recycling of bottles and cans, purchase of biodegradable detergents, modification of the towel supply policy, and installation of low-energy lighting. Thus, these practices could be considered advanced environmental practices. The development mentioned above leads to the following hypothesis:

Hypothesis 2a: Advanced environmental practices are positively and significantly related to the competitive performance of hotels.

The same research cited above and conducted by Llach et al. (2013) in the Madrid region (Spain), through personal interviews with managers of 374 establishments in the food and beverage services subsector, confirmed that there is a positive and significant association between advanced environmental practices (see list of these practices above) and stakeholder satisfaction as defined by these researchers in terms of 'key success factors (KSF).' Among these KSFs, they distinguish brand image, customer satisfaction, and employee satisfaction.

The research mentioned above conducted by Kirk (1995) on a sample of 53 hotels also led to a significant and positive effect of advanced environmental practices on stakeholder satisfaction: Customer satisfaction, employee satisfaction, improved relationship with the local community, improved public relations, acquisition and development of competitive marketing advantage. In addition, the results of the research cited above and conducted by Alvarez Gil (2001), Aragon-Correa et al. (2008), and Molina-Azorín et al. (2009) confirmed the impact of advanced environmental practices on stakeholder satisfaction. Thus, the following hypothesis is planned:

Hypothesis 2b: Advanced environmental practices are positively and significantly related to the hotels' stakeholder satisfaction.

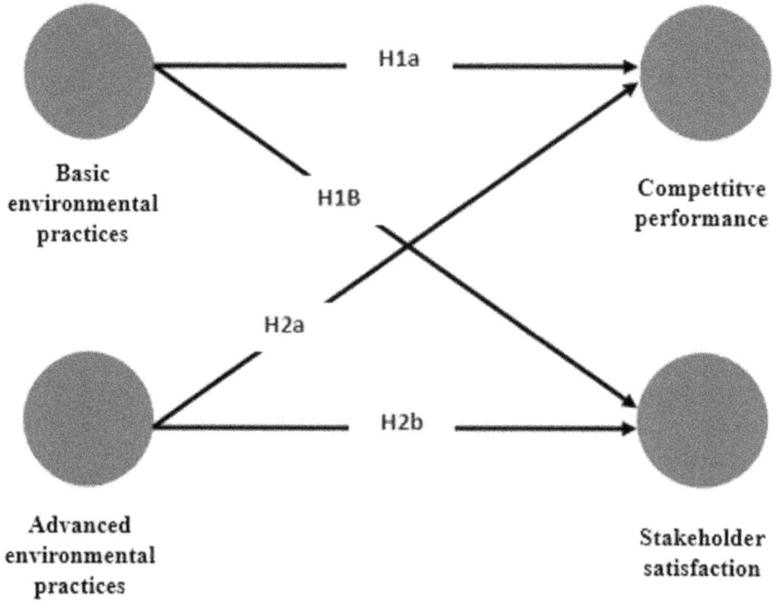

FIGURE 3.1 Conceptual model.

3.4 CONCEPTUAL MODEL

Based on the hypotheses presented above, we plot the conceptual model (see Figure 3.1). The latter draws the links between the two dimensions of environmental management: Basic environmental practices (or technical practices) and advanced environmental practices (organizational practices) and the two dimensions of hotels' performance, stakeholder satisfaction and competitive performance.

3.5 METHODOLOGY

3.5.1 Data Collection and Sample

Apart from the fact that most research in environmental management[1] has been conducted in the industrial sector (Llach et al. 2013; Carmona-Moreno et al. 2004) and that the service sector and the hotel and tourism sector have been sidelined despite their reputation as 'silent destroyers of the environment' (Hutchinson 1996), the choice of this sector was also motivated by contextual reasons. Firstly, a few academic research studies have been conducted in this sector in Tunisia, despite the recent crisis (a decline in the hotel and restaurant industry by 9.2%[2]). This crisis was triggered by the revolution of 2011 and aggravated by the wave of terrorist attacks between 2012 and 2015. Secondly, this sector is still relevant for the Tunisian economy since it contributes 7.5% of the national gross domestic product (GDP) and provides over 400,000 direct jobs (ONEQ 2013). Thirdly, introducing the ecological and environmental dimensions in the business model of superior category hotels (4- and 5-star hotels) allows them to be in line with the growing ecological awareness of their customers.

The target population of our study is composed of 4- and 5-star hotels. Among them are independent hotels and others affiliated to chains located in three prime Tunisian regions and tourist areas: Greater Tunis (North), Hammamet (Cap Bon), and Mahdia (Center). In line with the recommendations of Wadongo et al. (2010), the current study deals with this category of hotels. These authors consider that 5-star hotels are appropriate for this type of study because they are endowed with clear and coherent organizational structures. The results can also be generalized with a minor error, as the population is relatively homogeneous. In the same vein, Pereira-Moliner et al. (2015) consider that environmental management systems are more expanded international chains hotel. This could be explained by the fact that these establishments have more resources to build their environmental capacity. Therefore, in addition to the 5-star hotels, we included 4-star hotels in our sample. Two main reasons are behind this choice. Firstly, in Tunisia, the number of 5-star hotels is not very important compared to 4-star hotels. Secondly, apart from the respect of the classification of hotels, there is no significant difference between these two types of categories in terms of hotel management.

Given the above criteria, a sample of 45 hotels is selected using the judgmental non-probability method, which is one form of the nonprobability convenience method (Malhorta 2012). The study was conducted during the first quarter of 2017, and we opted for the traditional way of questionnaire administration, i.e., face-to-face distribution of printed questionnaires to guarantee the maximum number of responses, all the more so since we do not have the electronic (e-mail) addresses of our respondents. The questionnaire was therefore distributed directly to the top managers of the hotels. Senior managers were chosen as respondents because they are related directly to the strategic management of their hotels and are informed of the slightest changes in organizational improvement processes (Saeidi et al. 2015). Ideally, information should be collected from multiple respondents in each hotel to minimize the potential risk of bias from a single respondent. However, the strategic nature of the questions and the small size of some hotels limited the possibility of using multiple respondents per hotel. In addition, concerns about cost and sample size dictated the use of a single respondent.

Nevertheless, there are notable precedents in the environmental management literature for using a single, knowledgeable respondent. Examples include Henriques and Sadorsky's (1999) research work and Carmona-Moreno et al. (2004). Table 3.1 presents the profile of the selected hotels.

3.5.2 Measurement

Based on the literature review developed above and in light of the proposed research hypotheses, two variables are studied and measured: Environmental management practices and perceived performance.

3.5.2.1 Dependent Variable: Environmental Management Practices

The dependent variable is divided into technical and organizational practices (Klassen and Whybark 1999; Cramer 1998). These two dimensions were measured

TABLE 3.1
Hotels' Characteristics

Classification		Number	%
Hotel category			
	4 stars	15	33.3
	5 stars	30	66.7
Hotel capacity			
	Less than 200 rooms	21	46.7
	200–399 rooms	12	26.7
	400–700 rooms	9	20
	Over 700 rooms	3	6.7
Hotel affiliation			
	Independent hotel	27	60
	Chain-affiliated hotel	18	40
Specialization			
	Business and conference hotel	18	40
	Spa hotel	12	26.7
	Spa and conference hotel	15	33.3
Service level			
	High international level service	27	60
	Good-quality service	18	40

using a valid and reliable measurement scale (Cronbach's alpha for the first dimension: 0.83 and for the second dimension: 0.89) developed by Carmona-Moreno et al. (2004) and subsequently used by other researchers such as Molina-Azorin et al. (2009). Table 3.2 summarizes the type and nature of the scales used to measure the two dimensions of the 'environmental management practices' variable and the items of each scale.

3.5.2.2 Independent Variable: Perceived Performance

The literature review indicates that hotel performance is composed of competitive performance and stakeholder satisfaction (Molina-Azorín et al. 2009). These dimensions correspond to measurement indicators (see Table 3.3) frequently cited in the literature and commonly used and understood by hotel managers (Sainaghi et al. 2013 *in* Pereira-Moliner et al. 2015).

Both dimensions of company performance are considered perceptual and not objective variables in the sense of Pereira-Moliner et al. (2015). Thus, accurate and reliable measurement scales to measure them are adopted (Cronbach's alpha for the first dimension: 0.92 and for the second dimension: 0.71), developed by Molina-Azorín et al. (2009) by seeking the opinion of the various hotel managers in our sample concerning their known competitors (see nature of the scale: Table 3.3). Table 3.3

TABLE 3.2
Environmental Management Practices Measure

Variables	Scale	Nature	Items	
Technical (or basic) practices	Alvarez et al. (2001); Carmona-Moreno et al. (2004); Molina-Azorin et al. (2009)	7-point Likert scale ranging from (1) 'Strongly Disagree' to (7) 'Strongly Agree'	**6 items**	- The purchase of ecological products - Reducing the use of environmentally hazardous products - Facilitating environmental collaboration with the client - Practices to reduce energy and gas consumption - Practices to reduce the consumption of drinking water - Selective waste collection practices
Organizational (or advanced) practices		7-point Likert scale ranging from (1) 'Strongly Disagree' to (7) 'Strongly Agree'	6 items	- Employee training practices on environmental issues - Rewarding employees for ecological initiatives - Using environmental arguments in marketing campaigns - Care for the hotel's external environment - The long-term environmental approach of the hotel - Measuring the quantification of environmental savings and costs

summarizes the type and nature of the scales used to measure the two dimensions of the 'company's performance' variable and the items in each scale.

This study applies the partial least squares technique of the structural equation method. This technique entails two levels of analysis: The evaluation of the measurement model and the evaluation of the structural model. Concerning the assessment of the measurement model, it is carried out with the PLS-SEM software and aimed at verifying the reliability and validity of the selected scales. When evaluating the structural model, it seeks to check the hypothesized relationships in the research model while using the same software. The structural model test enables the validation of the hypotheses and leads to an empirically validated final research model.

TABLE 3.3
Perceived Performance Measure

Variables	Scale	Nature	Items	
Competitive performance	Das et al. (2000); Douglas and Judge (2001); Arawati (2005); Kassinis and Soteriou (2003); Molina-Azorín et al. (2009); Rodriguez-Anton et al. (2012); Rubio-Andrada et al. (2011)	7-point Likert scale ranging from (1) 'Much worse than competitors' to (7) 'Much better than competitors'	7 items	- Market share - Average sales growth over the last five years - Revenue per room - Total gross profit - Gross profit per room - Wealth creation (book value of the business versus market value) - Ability to generate a profit in times of crisis
Stakeholder satisfaction	Enz and Siquaw (1999); Russians and Soteriou (2003); Molina-Azorín et al. (2009)	7-point Likert scale ranging from (1) 'Much worse than competitors' to (7) 'Much better than competitors'	2 items	- Customers' satisfaction level - Employees' satisfaction level

3.6 RESULTS

3.6.1 The Measurement Model

Using PLS-SEM, we can address the limited number of respondents (our sample size is only 45 respondents) (Hair et al. 2016). The analysis evaluates the measurement model to avoid inappropriate results to ensure that all items contribute significantly to their constructs. For this purpose, the values of Outer loadings must be greater than 0.7 or even 0.8. Two items had to be eliminated in doing so: ENV2 and ENV10 (Henseler et al. 2009 2012; Hair et al. 2012), as stated in Table 3.4.

To evaluate the measure's reliability, the composite reliability is used and interpreted in the same way as Cronbach's alpha. Results are satisfactory when this reliability is more significant than 0.7 (Hair et al. 2012).

Concerning convergent validity, which guarantees the correlation of measures of the same construct (Carricano and Poujol 2008), Fornell and Laker (1981) propose to use the construct's average variance extracted (AVE), ensuring that it is well above 0.5 (Akrout 2010). Furthermore, outer loadings value greater than 0.7 also verifies convergent validity (Hair et al. 2012).

The discriminant validity assessment is done by applying the Fornell-Larcker criterion that compares the square root of the AVE with the correlations of the latent

TABLE 3.4
Outer Loadings Values

	Advanced environmental practices	Basic environmental practices	Competitive performance	Stakeholder satisfaction
ENV11	0.722			
ENV12	0.838			
ENV 1		0.893		
ENV 3		0.888		
ENV4		0.928		
ENV5		0.955		
ENV6		0.872		
ENV7	0.825			
ENV8	0.904			
ENV9	0.709			
PERF1			0.915	
PERF2			0.917	
PERF3			0.881	
PERF4			0.964	
PERF5			0.874	
PERF6			0.890	
PERF7			0.845	
PERF8				0.844
PERF9				0.833

variables, which must be higher than the highest correlation of each construct (Hair et al. 2012). All values are presented in detail in Table 3.5.

3.6.2 The Structural Model

The next step in the data analysis is to evaluate the structural model using a bootstrapping procedure (Hair et al. 2016). According to the results shown in Table 3.6, only basic environmental management practices are positively related to the two dimensions of perceived performance if its p-value is well above 0.05. To check the degree to which an exogenous construct helps explain an endogenous one, F squared (f^2) values are considered. It turns out that the competitive performance is illustrated with a significant effect because the f^2 value is greater than 0.35. As for stakeholder satisfaction, it was moderately impacted since the f^2 values are between 0.15 and 0.35 (Cohen 1988).

One way to measure the model's predictive accuracy is using the coefficient of determination (R^2) that represents the exogenous variable's combined effect on the endogenous variable(s). It is all about evaluating the variance of endogenous constructs explained by all the exogenous constructs related to them. The value of R^2 varies between 0 and 1. The results confirmed what we found previously, i.e., that the

TABLE 3.5
Reliability and Validity of the Scales

			Reliability	Validity	
			Internal consistency reliability	Convergent validity	Discriminant validity
Variables	Items	Outer loadings*	Composite reliability	Average Variance Extracted (AVE)	Fornell-Larcker Criterion
Basic environmental practices	ENV1	0.893	0.959	0.824	0.908
	ENV3	0.888			
	ENV4	0.928			
	ENV5	0.955			
	ENV6	0.872			
Advanced environmental practices	ENV11	0.722	0.900	0.645	0.803
	ENV12	0.838			
Competitive performance	PERF1	0.915	0.967	0.808	0.899
	PERF2	0.917			
	PERF3	0.881			
	PERF4	0.964			
	PERF5	0.874			
	PERF6	0.890			
	PERF7	0.845			
Stakeholder satisfaction	PERF8	0.844	0.825	0.702	0.838
	PERF9	0.833			

*Outer loadings > 0.7 or > 0.8.

two variables, competitive performance and stakeholder satisfaction, are powerfully explained by the independent variable as shown in Table 3.7.

Figure 3.2 schematically shows the results of the study. The thickness of the arrow indicates the size of the effect.

We summarize the tested hypotheses in Table 3.8, considering these results.

3.7 DISCUSSION

The findings led to two main conclusions: (1) Only basic environmental practices (as opposed to advanced environmental practices) are positively related to hotels' competitive performance and stakeholders' satisfaction. (2) This impact is significant. This result is consistent with the findings of the study conducted by Alvarez Gil et al. (2001), Molina-Azorín et al. (2009), and Bagur-Femenias et al. (2013). As mentioned earlier by Llach et al. (2013), this impact could be explained by the fact that the adoption by hotels of this type of practice directly and immediately

TABLE 3.6
Validation of Structural Paths

Structural paths	T statistics	p values	f^2
Advanced environmental practices -> Competitive performance	0.763	0.445	0.018
Advanced environmental practices -> Stakeholder satisfaction	1.005	0.315	0.024
Basic environmental practices -> Competitive performance	3.850	0.000***	0.366
Basic environmental practices -> Stakeholder satisfaction	3.134	0.002***	0.237

***Significant at 0.01.

TABLE 3.7
Coefficient of Determination (R^2)

Dependent variables	R^2	R^2 adjusted	p values
Competitive performance	0.553	0.532	0.000***
Stakeholder satisfaction	0.393	0.364	0.000***

***Significant at 0.01.

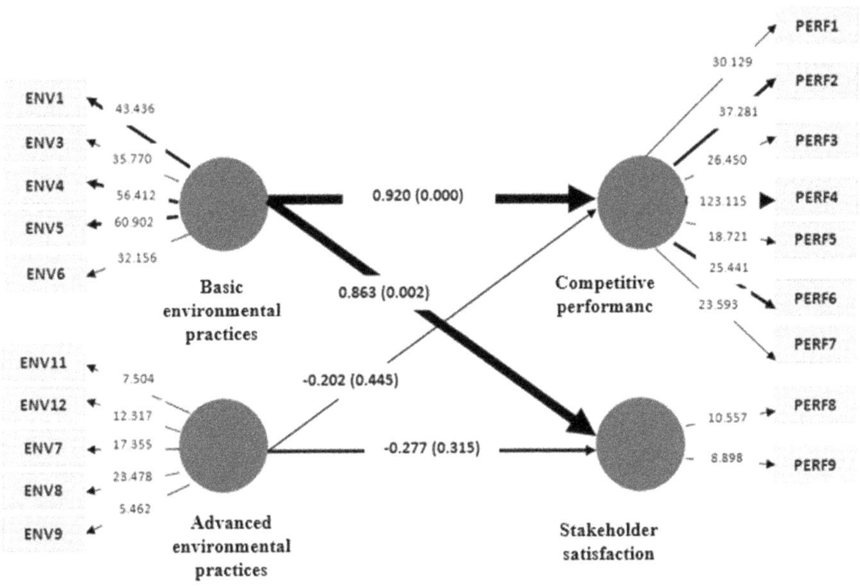

FIGURE 3.2 PLS-SEM results.

TABLE 3.8
Research Hypotheses Validation

Hypotheses	Hypothesis validation
Hypothesis 1a: Basic environmental practices are positively and significantly related to the competitive performance of hotels	Confirmed
Hypothesis 1b: Basic environmental practices are positively and significantly related to the hotel stakeholder satisfaction	Confirmed
Hypothesis 2a: Advanced environmental practices are positively and significantly related to the competitive performance of hotels	Rejected
Hypothesis 2b: Advanced environmental practices are positively and significantly related to the hotels' stakeholder satisfaction	Rejected

influences their operational costs. Likewise, these practices effectively reduce costs without altering the customer perceived value of the service offered and negatively impacting revenues (Bagur-Femenias et al. 2013). Furthermore, by allowing hotels to improve their economic performance, this type of reduction enables them to survive, particularly during a crisis. Thus, a reduction in fixed costs could make hotels more flexible and stable, as they could sell less and still master their costs (Llach et al. 2013). Finally, for Molina-Azorín et al. (2009), basic environmental practices represent easily identifiable actions by tourists and employees, hence their significant impact on their satisfaction (stakeholder satisfaction.

Unlike the effect of basic environmental practices on perceived performance, the current research showed that advanced environmental techniques have neither an effect on hotels' competitive performance nor their stakeholders' satisfaction. These results are partially shared by previous research. Thus, when it comes to the impact of advanced environmental practices on stakeholder satisfaction, our research is backed by the findings of Llach et al. (2013) and Pereira-Moliner et al. (2015) and does not lend support to those found by Alvarez Gil (2001), Aragon-Correa et al. (2008), and Molina-Azorín et al. (2009). Furthermore, regarding the effect of advanced environmental practices on competitive performance, our findings contradict those of Molina-Azorín et al. (2009).

The nonexistence of any relationship between advanced environmental practices and competitive performance could be explained by the fact that implementing these practices does not enhance the competitiveness of the hotel by promoting its image as a 'green' company and attracting a new category of clients, especially when most of these adopted endeavors are internal (e.g., the quantization of environmental savings and costs) and not external (e.g., the utilization of green arguments in marketing campaigns) and, therefore, customers are not aware of their service (Llach et al. 2013).

Given these findings and in light of results of previous research (Molina-Azorín et al. 2009; Pereira-Moliner et al. 2015; Llach et al. 2013) aiming to classify hotels in

Spain into different categories according to their 'proactivity' toward environmental management, we conclude that the Tunisian hotels in our sample are in the category called 'basic' or 'reactive.' However, other researchers point out that the hotels in this situation are in the 3-star category with an average size (in terms of the number of rooms) and are independent (i.e., they do not belong to hotel chains). Still, according to our results (Table 3.1), the hotels in our sample meet all of these criteria except the one related to category (number of stars), since all of our hotels are rated 4 and 5 stars.

3.8 CONCLUSION

This research aimed to examine the effect of environmental management on the perceived performance of Tunisian hotels. We first proposed a conceptual model grounded in the literature review and planned hypotheses showing the causal links between environmental management practices and perceived performance. In a second step, we surveyed a sample of Tunisian hotels (4 and 5 stars) to verify the hypotheses. The findings of this study confirm two of the four assumptions stating that environmental management through its so-called basic practices is positively and significantly related to the perceived performance of Tunisian hotels (competitive performance and stakeholder satisfaction). This conclusion could be considered a theoretical contribution per se supporting the results of previous research (see discussion of results). In addition, this research provides a significant contribution to environmental management. It leads to a better understanding of companies operating in the service and hotel sectors' ecological behavior. Ultimately, it provides new evidence of the importance of environmental practices in the services sector and their impact on business performance. This is likely to enrich the literature in the strategic management field.

Empirically, unlike most of those conducted, this research considered dimensions of hotel performance other than the financial one. Furthermore, this research provides managerial implications for managers looking to implement environmental practices since it sheds light on their nature and how they contribute to Tunisian hotels' performance. It should be noted that this study is not free of limitations. One limitation deals mainly with the lack of other research conducted in the hotel industry apart from Spain.

Future research could be directed at two levels. First, one avenue to be considered is the classification of Tunisian hotels (Through cluster analysis: The nonhierarchical statistical method of group classification) according to their degree of environmental 'proactivity.' This brings us back to the second stream that would address the degree of ecological 'proactivity' of the different hotels' performance classes. In this way, we could verify the fundamental hypothesis of the research of Molina-Azorín et al. (2009), which states that there is a significant link between the degree of environmental proactivity and company performance. To put it another way, the more the hotel's proactivity increases, the more its performance improves.

NOTES

1 With rare exceptions: Molina-Azorín et al. (2009); Pereira-Moliner et al. (2015); Leonidou et al. (2013); López-Gamero et al. (2011) (in Pereira-Moliner et al. 2015).

2 Source: Les effets de perturbations post révolution sur la croissance économique, 17 Octobre 2013. Publications centre tunisien de Veille et Intelligence Economique. www.economie.com.tn/?p=556.

REFERENCES

Aguinis, Herman and Ante Glavas. 2013. "Embedded versus peripheral corporate social responsibility: Psychological foundations," *Industrial and Organizational Psychology*, 6: 314–332.

Agus, Arawati. 2005. "The structural linkages between TQM, product quality performance, and business performance: Preliminary empirical study in electronics companies," *Singapore Management Review*, 27: 87–105.

Ajay Das, A., Robert B. Handfield, Roger J. Calantone and Soumen Ghosh. 2000. "A contingent view of quality management—The impact of international competition on quality," *Decision Sciences*, 31: 649–690.

Akrout, Fethi, 2010. *Les méthodes des équations structurelles* (Sfax), 1ère Edition URM, 273 Pages.

Alvarez Gil, Maria J., Jeronimo Burgoz Jimenez and Jose Cespesdes Lorente. 2001. "An analysis of environmental management, organizational context and performance of Spanish hotels," *Omega*, 29: 457–471.

Angell, Linda and Robert Klassen. 1999. "Integrating environmental issues into the mainstream: An agenda for research in operations management," *Journal of operations management*, 17: 575–598.

Aragon-Correa, Juan A., Nuria Hurtado-Torres, Sanjay Sharma and Victor J. Garcia-Morales. 2008. "Environmental strategy and performance in small firms: A resource-based perspective," *Journal of Environmental Management*, 86: 88–103.

Bagur-Femenias, Llorenç, Josep Llach and Del Mar Alonso-Almeida, Maria. 2013. "Is the adoption of environmental practices a strategical decision for small service companies? An empirical approach". *Management Decision*, 51: 41–62.

Bonilla-Priego, Maria J., Juan J. Nájera-Sánchez and Xavier Font. 2011. "Environmental management decision-making in certified hotels", *Journal of Sustainable Tourism*, 19: 361–382.

Carmona-Moreno, Eva, Jose Cespedes-Lorente and Jeronimo Burgoz-Jimenez. 2004. "Environmental strategies in Spanish hotels: Contextual factors and performance", *The Service Industries Journal*, 24: 101–130.

Carricano, Manu and Fanny Poujol. 2008. *Analyse de données avec SPSS [Data analysis with SPSS]*. (Pearson Education, Paris).

Chan, Siu W.E. 2013. "Gap analysis of green hotel marketing", *International Journal of Contemporary Hospitality Management*, 25: 1017–1048.

Chen, Annie and Norman Peng. 2012. "Green hotel knowledge and tourists' staying behavior", *Annals of Tourism Research*, 39: 2203–2219.

Chuang, Shun-Pin and Sun-Jen Huang. 2018. "The effect of environmental corporate social responsibility on environmental performance and business competitiveness: The mediation of green information technology capital," *Journal of Business Ethics, Springer*, 150: 991–1009.

Cohen, Jacob. 1988. *Statistical power analysis for the behavioral sciences* (Lawrence Erlbaum, Mahwah, NJ).

Cramer, Joseph. 1998. "Environmental management: from 'fit' to 'stretch'. Business," *Strategy and the Environment*, 7: 162–172.

Douglas, Thomas. J. and William Q. Judge Jr. 2001. "Total quality management and competitive advantage; The role of structural control and exploration," *Academy of Management Journal*, 44: 158–169.

Enz, Cathy A. and Siguaw, Judy A. 1999. "Best hotel environmental practices", *Cornell Hotel and Restaurant Administration Quarterly*, 40: 72–77.

Evo, Fwaya. 2006. *Human resource systems and competitive strategies in hospitality organizational performance in Kenya*, unpublished Msc thesis (Maseno University, Kisumu).

Fitzgerald, Lin., Johnston Robert, Brignall, T. J, Rhian Silverstro and C. Vos. 1991. *Performance Measurement in Service Businesses*, (CIMA, London).

Fornell, Claes and David F. Larcker. 1981. "Evaluating structural equation models with unobservable variables and measurement error", *Journal of Marketing Research*, 18: 39–50.

Garay, Luis and Xavier Font. 2012 "Doing good to do well? Corporate social responsibility reasons, practices and impacts in small and medium accommodation enterprises," *International Journal of Hospitality Management*, 31: 329–337.

González-Benito, Javier and Oscar González-Benito. 2005. "Environmental proactivity and business performance: An empirical analysis", *Omega*, 33: 1–15.

Hair, Joseph, Thomas Hult, Christian Ringle and Marko Sarstedt. 2016. *A primer on Partial Least Squares Structural Equation Modeling (PLS-SEM),* 2nd edition (Sage, Thousand Oaks, CA).

Haktanir, Mine and Peter Harris. 2005. "Performance measurement practice in an independent hotel context: a case study approach," *International Journal of Contemporary Hospitality Management*, 17: 39–50.

Hart, Stuart L. "A natural-resource-based view of the firm," *Academy of Management Review*. 20 (1995): 986–1014.

Henriques, Irene and Perry Sadorsky. 1999. "The Relationship between environmental commitment and managerial perceptions of stakeholder importance," *Academy of Management Journal*, 42: 87–99.

Henseler, Jörg, Christian Ringle and Marko Sarstedt. 2012. "Using partial least squares path modeling in international advertising research: Basic concept and recent issues," in *Handbook of Research in International Advertising*, ed. S. Okazaki. (Edward Elgar Publishing, Cheltenham) 252–276.

Hui Fu, Ye, Ben Hoabin Ye and Rob Law. 2014. "You do well and I do well? The behavioral consequences of corporate social responsibility," *International Journal of Hospitality Management*, 40: 62–70.

Hutchinson, Christopher. 1996. "Integrating environmental policy with business strategy," *Long Range Planning*, 29: 11–23.

James, Brown and Dev Chekitan. 1999. "Looking beyond RevPar". *Cornell Hotel and Restaurant Administration Quarterly*, 40: 23–33.

José Tarí, Juan, Enrique Claver-Cortés, Jorge Pereira-Moliner and José Molina-Azorín. 2010. "Levels of quality and environmental management in the hotel industry: The joint influence on firm performance," *International Journal of Hospitality Management*, 29: 500–510.

Joseph, Hair. M, Marko Sarstedt, Christian, Ringle and Jeannette Mena. 2012. "An assessment of the use of partial least squares structural equation modeling in marketing research," *Journal of Marketing Science*, 40: 414–433.

Kaplan, Robert and David Norton. 1992. "The balanced scorecard: measures that drive performance," *Harvard Business Review*, 70: 71–79.

Kassinis, George I., and Soteriou Andreas C. 2003 "Greening the service profit chain: The impact of environmental management practices." Production and operations Management, 12: 386-403.

Kirk, David. 1995. "Environmental management in hotels," *International Journal of Contemporary Hospitality Management*, 7: 3–8.

Klassen, Robert D. and Clay D. Whybark. 1999. "Environmental management in operations: The selection of environmental technologies," *Decision Sciences*. 30: 601–631.

Lee, Misung, Han H. Heesup and Greg Willson. 2011. "The role of expected outcomes in the formation of behavioral intentions in the green-hotel industry," *Journal of Travel & Tourism Marketing*, 28: 840–855.

Leonidou, Leonidas, Constantinos N. Leonidou, Thomas Fotiadis and Athina Zeriti. 2013. "Resources and capabilities as drivers of hotel environmental marketing strategy: Implications for competitive advantage and performance," *Tourism Management*, 35: 94–110.

Lin, Kuho, Mickael Y. Peng, Muhammad Khalid Anser and Arshian Sharif. 2021. "Bright harmony of environmental management initiatives for achieving corporate social responsibility authenticity and legitimacy: Glimpse of hotel and tourism industry," *Corporate Social Responsibility and Environmental Management*, 28: 640–647.

Llach, Josep, Jordi Perramon, Maria del Mar Alonso-Almeida and Llorenç Bagur-Femenias. 2013. "Joint impact of quality and environmental practices on firm performance in small service businesses: An empirical study of restaurants," *Journal of Cleaner Production*, 44: 96–104.

López-Gamero, Maria D., José F. Molina-Azorín and Enrique Claver-Cortés. 2009. "The whole relationship between environmental variables and firm performance: Competitive advantage and firm resources as mediator variables," *Journal of Environmental Management*, 90: 3110–3121.

López-Gamero, Maria D., José F. Molina-Azorín and Enrique Claver-Cortés. 2010. "The potential of environmental regulation to change managerial perception, environmental management, competitiveness and financial performance", *Journal of Cleaner Production*, 18: 963–974.

López-Gamero, Maria D., José F Molina-Azorín and Enrique Claver-Cortés. 2011. "The relationship between managers' environmental perceptions, environmental management and firm performance in Spanish hotels: A whole framework", *International Journal of Tourism Research*, 13: 141–163.

Lynch, Richard and Kelvin Cross. 1995. *Measure Up! Yardsticks for Continuous Improvement* (Blackwell, Oxford).

Malhotra, Naresh K. 2012. *Basic Marketing Research:* Integration of *Social Media*, 4th Edition. (Pearson, Boston).

Margolis, Elfenbein H.A. and J.P. Walsh. 2007. "Does it pay to be good? A meta-analysis and redirection of research on the relationship between corporate social and financial performance", *Ann Arbor*, 1001:1–68.

Mark. D.H., W.R. Newman and Pamela Johnson. 2000. "Linking operational and environmental improvement through employee involvement," *International Journal of Operations & Production Management*, 20: 148–165.

Miles, Morgan P. and Jeffrey. G Covin. 2000. "Environmental marketing: A source of reputational, competitive, and financial advantage," *Journal of Business Ethics*, 23: 299–311.

Mishra, Supriti and Damodar Suar. 2010. "Does corporate social responsibility influence firm performance of Indian companies?" *Journal of Business Ethics*, 95: 571–601.

Mohammed, Nizamuddin. 2018. Corporate social responsibility and corporate financial performance: An exploratory study of measurement-approach selection issues. *IUP Journal of Corporate Governance*, 17: 36–54.

Molina-Azorin, José F., Enrique Claver-Cortes, Jorge Pereira-Moliner and Juan José Tari. 2009. "Environmental practices and firm performance: an empirical analysis in the Spanish hotel industry," *Journal of Cleaner Production*, 17: 516–524.

ONEQ (Observatoire National de l'Emploi et des Qualifications). 2013. Rapport annuel sur le marché du travail en Tunisie. *Ministère de la Formation Professionnelle et de l'Emploi.*

Orlitzky, Marc. 2011. "Institutional logics in the study of organizations," *Business Ethics Quarterly*, 21: 409–444.

Paul, Shrivastava. 1995. "The role of corporations in achieving ecological sustainability," *Academy of Management Review*, 20: 936–960.

Pereira-Moliner, Jorge, José F. Molina-Azorin, Maria D. Lopez-Gamero, Juan J. Tari and Eva. M Pertusa-Ortega. 2015. "The Holy Grail: Environmental management, competitive advantage and business performance in the Spanish hotel industry," *International Journal of Contemporary Hospitality Management*, 27: 714–738.

Porter, Michael and Class Van der Linde. 1995. "Green and competitive: Ending the stalemate," *Harvard Business Review*, 73: 120–134.

Reichel, Arie and Sigal Haber. 2005. "A three-sector comparison of the business performance of small tourism enterprises: An exploratory study," *Tourism Management*, 26: 681–690.

Rodríguez-Antón, José Miguel, María del Mar Alonso-Almeida, María Soledad Celemín and Luis Rubio. 2012. "Use of different sustainability management systems in the hospitality industry. The case of Spanish hotels," *Journal of Cleaner Production*, 22: 76–84.

Rubio-Andrada, Luis, María Del Mar Alonso-Almeida and José Miguel Rodríguez-Antón. 2011. "Motivations and impacts in the firm and stakeholders of quality certification: Evidence from small- and medium-sized service enterprises", *Total Quality Management & Business Excellence*, 22: 833–852, doi: 10.1080/14783363.2011.593858.

Saeidi, Sayedeh, Sofian Parastoo, Saiedi Saudah, Saiedi Parvaneh, Pariza Sayyed and Seyyed A. Saiedi. 2015. "How does corporate social responsibility contribute to firm financial performance? The mediating role of competitive advantage, reputation, and customer satisfaction," *Journal of Business Research*, 68: 341–350.

Sainaghi, Ruggero, Paul Phillips and Valentina Corti. 2013."Measuring hotel performance: Using a balanced scorecard perspectives' approach", *International Journal of Hospitality Management*, 34: 150–159.

Trung, Do N. and S. Kumar. 2005. "Resource use and waste management in Vietnam hotel industry," *Journal of Cleaner Production*, 13: 109–116.

Turker, Duygu. 2009. "How corporate social responsibility influences organizational commitment," Journal of Business Ethics, 89: 189–204.

Wadongo, Billy, Edwin Odhuno, Oscar Kambona and Lucas Othuon. 2010. "Key performance indicators in the Kenyan hospitality industry: A managerial perspective," *Benchmarking: An International Journal*, 17: 858–875.

Wheeler, David and Mika Sillanpaa. 1997. *The Stakeholder Corporation: A Blueprint for Maximizing Stakeholder Value* (Pitman, London).

Wiengarten, Frank, and M. Mark Pagell. 2012. "The importance of quality management for the success of environmental management initiatives," *International Journal of Production Economics*, 40: 407–415.

Wu, Haw-Jan and Steven Dunn. 1995. "Environmentally responsible logistics systems," *International Journal of Physical Distribution and Logistics Management*, 25: 20–38.

Yadav, Nirmala, Shweta Sharma, Subhasini Sharma and Kanti P. Sharma. 2017. "Critical analysis of protective role of plants against gentamicin induced nephrotoxicity," *Indian Journal of Environmental Sciences*, 21: 1–34.

4 Economic Sustainability and Indicators of Most Visited Countries

Ahmet Vatan and Demet Tüzünkan

CONTENTS

4.1 INTRODUCTION

The word 'economy' means 'household management' means. Greek for 'home' and oikos, meaning 'tradition' or 'legal' meaning comes from the word nomos. The economy, the production of goods and services, is a social science that studies the factors that determine distribution and consumption. The ultimate aim of the economy is to improve the living conditions of people's daily lives (econation.co.nz 2021). In 2015, the adoption of the UN Sustainable Development Goals, the international community's economic, environmental, and social dimensions, represents a turning point in the decision-making in an integrated way to solve global problems by bringing together. The goal is to balance economic prosperity with environmental sustainability and social inclusion and cohesion, sustainable investment and innovation, good work, and encourage democratic participation and the rule of law (EESC 2021). The philosophical basis of a sustainable economy, producing not be perceived as humanity's common heritage of natural resources, fair share (intra-generational justice), and appropriate to future generations inherit pack release (as noted above) lies (Lorek and Spangenbeg 2014). A sustainable economy is an economy that does the most general welfare with minimum use of resources and environmental damage. From an economic perspective, to be truly sustainable, the total demand for natural resources (also known as ecological footprint foot) and the nature of supply from renewable sources (also known as biocapacity) should be less (econation.co.nz 2021).

Tourism is an economic activity that uses environment and culture as input. The focus on sustainable development in the world has made economic sustainability

DOI: 10.1201/9781003138051-5

more popular than other types of sustainability. Every tourist contributes economically to the destination. To benefit from tourism in the long term, the tourist flow must be sustainable. The sustainability of the tourist flow provides the basis for economic sustainability. For economic sustainability, seasonality in tourism should be resolved, economic leaks should be prevented, and plans and practices should be developed to support the competitiveness of businesses in the destination (Vatan 2019). This research aims to determine the economic sustainability of the most visited countries in the world in recent years. According to Mastercard's Global Destination Cities Index reports, the study sample consists of the top five most visited countries. To determine the economic sustainability of the most visited countries, indicators in the guide book titled indicators of sustainable development for tourism destinations posted by United Nations World Tourism Organization (UNWTO) will be used. The sustainable economy indicators of tourism destinations will be analyzed with the reports published by the countries.

4.2 THE ECONOMIC DIMENSION OF SUSTAINABILITY

Almost none of the economic development models in use today were created without taking environmental quality and natural resource deformation into account. These short-term models do not recognize borders in economic development and embrace development as decisive criteria in national economic competitiveness. The only long-term development model that considers environmental quality is sustainable development, which aspires for optimal development without wasting resources (Gürlük 2001). Until recently, developing countries assumed that achieving rapid and stable growth would meet the set requirement. Furthermore, the economics literature gave arguments that problems such as unemployment, income inequality, poverty, and ecocide would be solved as long as the economic growth target was achieved. However, the fact that economic growth, contrary to what is expected, has revealed alternative costs, such as increasing inequality in the distribution of income, impoverishment of the large masses, the destruction of the natural environment and natural resources to where long-term growth is no longer possible, and the deterioration of social peace, has prompted the emergence of a new growth and development approach. This understanding has revealed the notion of sustainable development, which places a high value on people and envisions the cautious consumption of natural and cultural resources considering the needs of future generations while also attempting to meet the economic and social needs of the current population (Sedefoğlu 2019).

According to neoclassical economic theory, sustainability can be explained by 'maximizing the welfare level.' Most economists have simplified the term as maximizing the benefit from consumption. This definition can be criticized for being very simplistic. However, this definition incorporates crucial aspects of human well-being such as clothing, food, home, health, and education. At the same time, the term has the advantage of reducing the problems to one dimension (Harris 2000).

On the other hand, this theory accepts unrestricted exploitation of the environment, or natural capital, to promote economic welfare and does not foresee any reason for environmental protection. While economic sustainability produces products and services that contribute to society, it also deals with the cost-benefit analysis of the business that aims to be profitable. This approach also strives to produce long-term value for stakeholders by assessing the opportunities and risks posed by economic, environmental, and social developments (Nemli 2004).

4.3 THE ECONOMIC DIMENSION OF SUSTAINABLE TOURISM

The notion of sustainability is founded on the principles of economic development, environmental resource protection, and ecological value transmission to future generations. When it comes to tourism, sustainability can be defined as managing tourism resources so that future generations can utilize them without being extinguished, polluted, or destroyed (Birkan 2001). Thus, sustainable tourism seeks to expand tourist capacity and improve the quality of tourist products while eliminating negative impacts on the natural and artificial environment, and human resources, which are critical inputs to the sector. However, with the development of tourism, several adverse outcomes have emerged, such as pollution and unusable resources, which have raised concerns. For this reason, to experience healthy growth and benefit future generations from touristic resources, a sustainable tourism understanding is required, which includes social responsibility, economic efficiency, and ecological sensitivity in every field (Beyhan and Ünügür 2005). Therefore, the importance of sustainable tourism is increasing even more. Sustainable tourism can be defined as the maintenance and development of regional and local attractions, which are the basis of tourism (Avcıkurt 2003). On the other hand, WTO (1998) defines sustainable tourism as

> development in which cultural integrity, ecological processes, biodiversity, and life-sustaining systems are maintained while preserving the environment in which humans interact or not, and at the same time, development in which all resources are managed in such a way as to satisfy the economic, social and aesthetic needs of people and tourists in the visited region, and in such a way that future generations can meet the same needs

and underlines that the resources that exist today must be met in a long-term and uninterrupted manner while preserving their value in the future. With Kuntay's (2004) definition, sustainable tourism is a tourism understanding that develops perspectives for the future, meets the current needs of tourists and the region that hosts them, and integrates the management of all resources with aesthetic, social, and economic conditions, taking into account the living systems, biological diversity, basic ecological processes, and cultural integrity.

The common elements in the definition of sustainable tourism are the optimum long-term use of natural and artificial resources, the preservation of the human settlement pattern, economic and social equality, devotion to the concept of quality, and social participation (Demir and Çevirgen 2006). Sustainable tourism requires both the sustainable increase of tourism's contribution to the economy and society and the sustainable use of resources and the environment based on tourism demand analysis. Effective tourism destination management causes applying a unique methodology based on the sustainability and performance of resources and capabilities

TABLE 4.1
Economic Dimension Indicators

Domains	Indicators
Seasonality	Bednights by month
	% of seasonal jobs
	Seasonality rate
	% of establishments open all year
Economic benefits	% Tourism on GDP
	Number of same-day visitors
	Number of tourists
	Daily spending per overnight tourist
	The average length of stay of tourists
	Establishments using local products
Employment	Employment/Total economy
	Employment by gender
	Employment by qualification

Source: UNWTO (2004, 2017). https://www.e-unwto.org/doi/book/10.18111/9789284407262

(Díaz and Rodríguez 2016). The competitiveness of a destination should focus on the ability to create added value by managing assets and processes. This can only be accomplished by stakeholder collaboration within a tourism planning model framework that considers the destination's natural, social, and economic resources for future generations (Enright and Newton 2004).

In many destinations where tourism is developed, sustainability-oriented plans, policies, strategies, and practices are carried out by various authorities at the local, regional, or national level. The UNWTO established tourism sustainability indicators in 2004 to facilitate sustainable, responsible, and environmentally sensitive tourism plans and practices. The UNWTO completed these indicators in 2017 after revising and expanding them in environmental, social, and cultural dimensions.

According to Table 4.1, there are three main headings in the economic dimension of sustainability. These are seasonality, economic benefits, and employment, and each is measured with different indicators.

4.3.1 Seasonality

Seasonality in tourism refers to the seasonal fluctuations and temporal imbalance of tourism over time. It is defined as the situation in which the number of tourists, overnight stays, and expenditures of tourists, and accordingly, the number of people employed in the tourism industry increases during certain times of the year and decreases during others (Kuşluvan and Kuşluvan 1998). Seasonality in the tourism industry is a factor that is considered creating a significant amount of social costs and large fluctuations in the revenues from the tourism industry for the country's economy. The most important basic social costs created by seasonality are low capacity utilization and seasonal unemployment. Seasonality can occur due to climatic conditions, industrial and institutional reasons, economic and social reasons, psychological reasons, and reasons related to special events (Günel 2009). Therefore, while seasonality, based not just on demand but also on supply, has positive effects, its adverse effects are relatively high. In destinations where the seasonality effect is visible, various economic, social, and environmental issues arise. As a result of this situation, researchers and practitioners regard seasonality, a structural aspect of the tourism industry, as a 'problem' that needs to be settled (Çoban et al. 2017: 348).

Within the scope of the UNWTO's economic sustainability indicators, seasonality is measured by night by month, the percentage of seasonal jobs, the seasonality rate, and the percentage of establishments open all year. In the light of the dashboards prepared by UNWTO, the seasonality chart of the most visited countries in the world in recent years is shown in Figure 4.1.

France, Spain, the United States, China, and Italy have ranked among the top five most visited countries in recent years. When we evaluate the tourist flow charts of these countries in the last five years (2020 was not included due to the epidemic), it is seen that four countries have seasonality problems. It is observed that the peak tourism seasons in the four most visited countries are comparable. We can conclude that China's seasonality graph fluctuates the least among these five most visited countries. The United States follows China. However, in the seasonality graph of the European countries, it was discovered that there are significant variances between months. In France, Spain, and Italy, the tourist flow, which begins to rise in April, peaks in the summer months compared to the northern hemisphere. Therefore, France appears to have the most seasonal problems of any European country.

4.3.2 Economic Benefits

According to E-UNWTO tourism statistics, international arrivals worldwide increased by 6% in 2019 compared to 2018. Approximately 1.5 billion people participated in tourism activities. The countries with the highest number of tourist arrivals were France, Spain, the United States of America, China, Italy, Turkey, Mexico, Thailand, Germany, and the United Kingdom. In contrast, the countries with the highest income from tourism were the United States of America, Spain, France, Thailand, the United Kingdom, Italy, Japan, Australia, Germany, and Macao, respectively (TUROB, 2020; E-UNWTO, 2021). The tourism industry, which, like many other industries, went through an extraordinary period as a result of the COVID pandemic, with a 74% drop in tourist arrivals and approximately 1.3 trillion dollars in tourism revenues in 2020, putting 100–120 million employees at the risk of losing their jobs (UNWTO, 2020). UNWTO has issued recommendations to all tourism stakeholders involved in this process to preserve the power of the positive effects of tourism on the economy. These recommendations include rendering tourism-related livelihoods in line with the sustainable development goals.

The direct economic contributions of tourism emerge in accommodation, food and beverage, retail, transportation, cultural sports, and entertainment sectors. On the other hand, the tourism industry makes indirect economic contributions in travel and

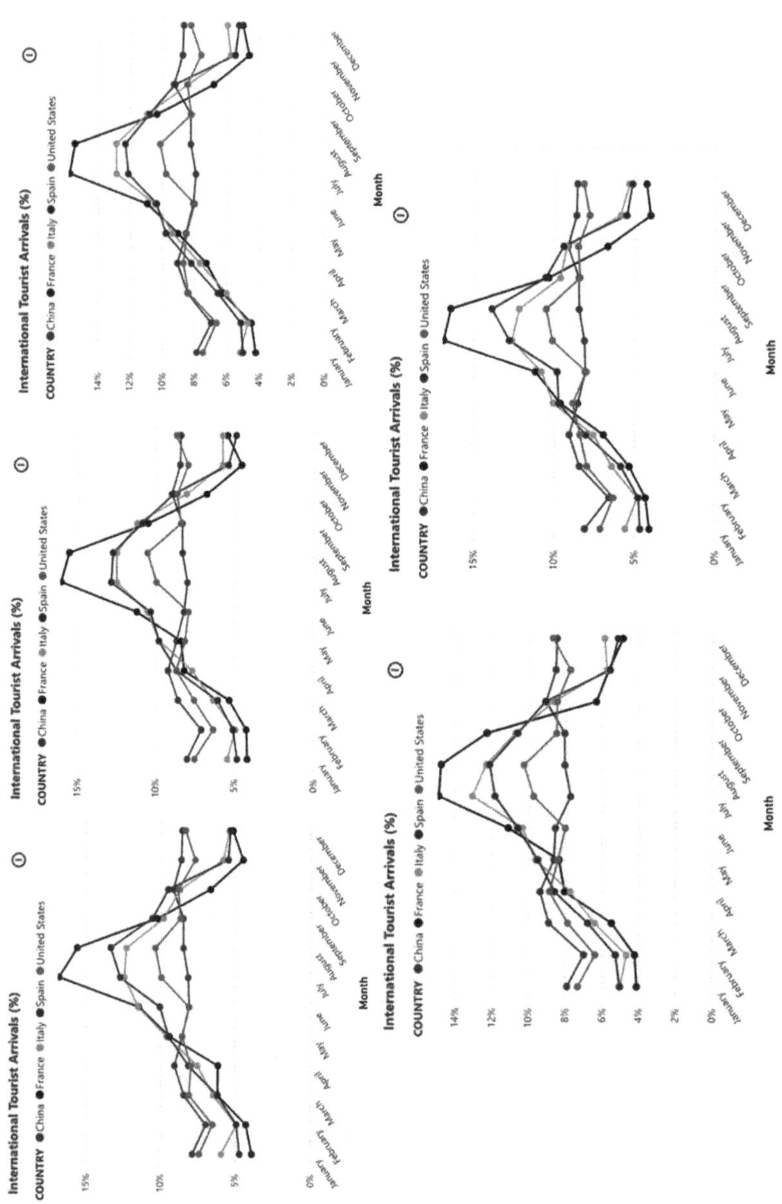

FIGURE 4.1 Seasonality of most visited countries by 2015–2019.

Source: UNWTO (2021).

tourism investments, government expenditures, and the effect of supplier purchases. The direct and indirect contributions of all these expenditures, in other words, the expenditures made by total employment, are also seen as derived economic contributions. Finally, its total economic contributions are Gross National Product and employment (Şit 2016: 109).

Tourism has positive economic effects. According to Kreag (2001), tourism:

- Increases income and living standards.
- Strengthens the local economy.
- Increases job opportunities.
- Increases investments, development, and infrastructure expenditures.
- Increases tax revenues.
- Improves public services infrastructure.
- Improves the transportation infrastructure.
- Increases shopping opportunities.
- Has direct, indirect, and induced effects on the economy.
- The income generated by tourism circulates within the economy, expanding its value.
- Develops new trade opportunities.
- Has a positive effect on foreign exchange earnings and balance of payments.

The UNWTO considers the percentage of tourism on GDP, number of same-day visitors, number of tourists, daily spending per overnight tourist, and the average length of stay of tourists as measurement indicators for the economic sustainability of tourism.

According to the UNWTO's Indicators of Sustainable Development for Tourism Destinations: A Guidebook, the number of tourists is crucial to evaluate the economic sustainability of a destination's economy within the scope of the economic benefits of tourism. Table 4.2 demonstrates that the number of tourists has increased continuously over the years when we look at France, Spain, the United States of America, China, and Italy, which have been the most visited globally in recent years. A particular focus should be placed on the United States of America and France for 2016 when both countries lost visitors due to political impotence and acts of terrorism.

TABLE 4.2
Tourist Numbers of Most Visited Countries (Million)

Country	2015	2016	2017	2018	2019
China	56.8	59.2	60.7	62.5	67.5
Spain	68.1	75.3	81.8	85.3	83.8
France	84.4	82.5	86.9	95.8	90.2
Italy	50.7	52.3	58.3	60.3	64.6
USA	77.4	75.6	76.9	78.3	78.7

Source: UNWTO (2021).

TABLE 4.3
Tourism Revenues of Most Visited Countries (USD)

Country	2015	2016	2017	2018	2019
China	44.969.000.000	44.426.000.000	38.799.000.000	39.468.000.000	34.458.000.000
Spain	56.309.000.000	60.351.000.000	66.682.000.000	69.023.000.000	71.200.000.000
France	66.441.000.000	63.557.000.000	67.717.000.000	73.044.000.000	71.011.000.000
Italy	41.415.000.000	42.423.000.000	46.719.000.000	51.602.000.000	51.910.000.000
USA	230.574.000.000	228.549.000.000	231.123.000.000	237.726.000.000	233.461.000.000

Source: UNWTO (2021).

One of the most important variables determining tourist flow is the region's security. In 2016, the tourist flow to these countries was disrupted by Trump's election in the United States and the bombings in France. Turkey, which ranks sixth among the world's most visited countries, also dropped in visitors in 2016 due to similar factors. Based on the three countries mentioned above, it can be concluded that regardless of the country's geography or development level, the keyword for tourists is always safety.

One of the issues to be considered in understanding the sustainability of a destination's economy is tourism income. When the countries that drew the most tourists in the world between 2015 and 2019 are studied in Table 4.3, it can be observed that Spain and Italy consistently grew their tourism revenues. The decline in tourist numbers experienced by the United States and France in 2016 appears to have had a comparable impact on tourism revenues. However, it is noteworthy that both countries experienced a decrease in tourism revenues in 2019 again, compared to the previous year. When it comes to China's tourism revenues, even though the number of tourists and the spread of tourism throughout the year are more stable than in other countries, there are still fluctuations in tourism revenues. It is seen that there has been a decrease in China's tourism revenues, particularly as of 2016.

Daily expenditure per tourist plays an essential role in the economic sustainability of a destination. Therefore, the average daily cost of tourists is one of the indicators that should be examined. Table 4.4 demonstrates that China's average daily tourist expenditures also dropped following a decrease in tourism revenues in 2016. Despite a drop in 2016, the average daily cost of tourists visiting Italy climbed in the following years. Spain is the most stable country regarding average daily expenditure by tourists, which has consistently increased over the years examined. The fall in the number of tourists in the United States and France in 2016, and the decline in tourism revenues, resulted in a directly proportional decrease in the average daily expenditure of tourists in 2016. However, the average daily expense of tourists increased in the following years in both countries. For 2019, no reliable data for China, Spain, or France could be obtained.

When looking at the average length of stay of tourists in the world's most visited countries in Table 4.5, the average length in four countries is continually changing

TABLE 4.4
Income per Tourist (USD)

Country	2015	2016	2017	2018	2019
China	336	313	252	255	*
Italy	511	500	519	553	554
Spain	569	580	624	653	*
France	327	313	327	345	*
USA	1.305	1.302	1.326	1.404	1.406

Source: worlddata.info (2021).
* (Not available)

TABLE 4.5
Average Length of Stay of Most Visited Countries

Country	2015	2016	2017	2018	2019
Italy	2.9	2.9	2.7	3.3	3.4
Spain	4.8	3.9	2.6	3.5	2.5
France	3.5	2.5	3.8	2.5	2.5
USA	9.9	10.3	9.9	9.8	9.8

Source: UNWTO (2021).

except for the United States of America. Italy is the only country among the countries studied that has increased the length of stay in recent years. In Spain and France, the average length of stay of tourists has decreased over the years. The average length of stay of tourists in the United States, which has a high percentage, is nearly identical between 2015 and 2019. It can be foreseen that the market change of countries may affect this. Therefore, a more accurate picture can be obtained by evaluating the combination of the length of stay with changes in the country's markets.

Tourism is one variable that contributes to a destination's 'sustainable economy,' as measured by its share in GDP. Spain is recognized as contributing the most to its GDP (see Table 4.6). Even though Spain's contribution to GDP from travel and tourism declined in 2019, there has been no surprising shift throughout the years. Until 2019, however, this rate has increased in Spain. Italy is the second country to contribute the most to the GDP in travel and tourism. While Italy experienced a decline in its contribution rate in 2016, travel and tourism to its GDP increased every following year. China is the third country that contributes the most to its GDP with its travel and tourism revenues. Although there was a decrease in 2019, it is observed that the contribution rate has increased continuously in previous years. Among the countries that attract the most tourists in the examined world, France is the fourth and the United States is the fifth in terms of travel and tourism revenues and their contribution

TABLE 4.6
Contribution of Travel and Tourism to GDP of Most Visited Countries (%)

Country	2015	2016	2017	2018	2019
China	10.49	10.98	11.04	11	10.95
Spain	14.04	14.17	14.53	14.57	13.31
France	9.51	9.32	9.35	9.54	9.56
Italy	12.75	12.71	12.99	13.18	13.31
USA	7.73	7.69	7.91	7.78	7.80

Source: Knoema, "Atlas". https://knoema.com/atlas (2021).

to GDP. Although tensions and progress have been experienced in both countries over the years, there are no surprising differences.

4.3.3 Employment

The tourism industry has become one of the most critical industries globally due to the significant foreign currency inputs it provides to the country's economy and the employment opportunities it creates through subsectors such as transportation, accommodation, food and beverage, recreation, and entertainment (Oral 2005: 13). Therefore, employment is a critical component of maintaining a long-term and stable tourism industry balance.

It is widely observed that female workers, part-time workers, those with a second job, and very young or older people are employed in the tourism industry. People who are not included in the unemployment statistics, such as stay-at-home parents, students, and retirees, are used intensely seasonally; therefore, the tourism industry's contribution to the solution of the unemployment problem is not as significant as it appears at first glance. On the other hand, some tourism enterprises demand seasonal labor by providing better working conditions or wages than the manufacturing industry, leading to a labor flow from these sectors to tourism. This feature of the tourism industry, particularly in developing countries, will play an essential role in developing this sector, increasing new job opportunities, and thus, employment (Şit 2016: 105).

The most critical element that decreases enterprise efficiency and impairs service quality is the inadequacy or absence of trained labor required in certain particular service areas in the industry. In the long run, inadequate services also cause a decrease in the demand for businesses, thus disrupting the market balance (Olalı and Timur 1988: 287). In this context, the employment dimension in economic sustainability indicators is measured by employment/total economy, employment by gender, and employment by qualification.

The economic sustainability of destinations is directly related to the employment rate of tourism in the region. Hence, one of the indicators of the economic sustainability of a goal is the direct contribution of tourism to employment. Table 4.7

TABLE 4.7
Direct Contribution of Tourism to Employment of Most Visited Countries

Country	2015	2016	2017	2018	2019
China	27.980.000	28.130.000	28.250.000	28.660.200	29.088.700
Spain	832.902	880.861	940.330	958.088	980.687
France	1.229.890	1.216.630	1.247.600	1.296.700	1.321.560
Italy	1.424.340	1.440.460	1.493.640	1.543.150	1.549.460
USA	5.494.920	5.763.240	5.743.740	5.793.430	5.905.230

Source: UNWTO (2021).

shows that China is the first country among the most visited countries where tourism contributes to work. It is observed that there has been a continuous increase in employment created by tourism over the years examined. The United States is the second country that makes the most employment through tourism. Despite a drop in jobs in the United States in 2017, the number of individuals employed in tourism climbed in the following years. In terms of tourism employment, Italy ranks top among European countries. In the years examined, the number of jobs in tourism has continually increased. France follows Italy. It is seen that France suffered a loss of employment in 2016. The decrease in the number of tourists and income that France experienced in 2016 impacted employment. Although Spain is one of the countries with the highest tourist flow, it has trailed behind other countries in tourism employment. However, in Spain, the employment graph in tourism has consistently increased over the years studied.

4.4 CONCLUSION

Economic sustainability, which focuses on the long-term availability of resources and low usage costs, is a subject many studies have carried out. Economic sustainability has become more popular than other types of sustainability since tourism is an economic activity, and, as a result, the global focus on sustainable development. To exemplify with a simple equation, every tourist who comes to the destination contributes economically. For the tourist, an economic resource, to provide economic input to the destination long term, the tourist flow must be continuous. When looking at the indications of a destination's economic sustainability, it is observed that more than half of them are linked to the tourist flow. Therefore, the sustainability of the tourist flow forms the basis for economic sustainability.

The number of tourists, tourism revenues, average daily expenditures of tourists, the average length of stay of tourists, the contribution of tourism to employment, and the country's GDP all provide information on whether a destination's economy is sustainable. When we examine the indicators of the five most visited countries globally, we can observe increasing tourist numbers. Only two countries (France and the United States of America) experienced a decrease in the number of tourists during the abovementioned period due to the security gap in the countries. There is a direct proportion between the variation in the number of tourists and tourism revenues. Only in China has the number of tourists increased over the years, while the country's income has decreased. The reason for this can be attributed to a shift in the country's tourism market. This direct ratio can be observed even in employment. When we look at the indicators for the countries studied, we can conclude that each of the five has a sustainable economy in terms of tourism. However, the most critical issue to be mentioned here is the seasonality problem, mainly seen in European countries.

The seasonality problem in tourism should be handled, leaks in the economy should be avoided, and policies and practices to promote the competitiveness of enterprises in the destination should be developed for economic sustainability. The concentration of tourist traffic at specific periods of the year and in particular locations directly negatively affects economic sustainability. Different studies have been carried out in the literature to eliminate seasonality, which is one of the adverse effects of tourism on the economic environment. Extending the tourism season and strengthening alternative tourism types are among the strategies to eliminate the seasonality problem. International tourist flow is usually the first thing that comes to mind when it comes to tourist flow. However, the development of domestic tourism also plays a vital role in ensuring the sustainability of the tourist flow.

For this reason, when the tourist flow is mentioned, the balances in the domestic market should be followed carefully. Maintaining low-price policies by airline companies, dividing school holidays into different dates throughout the year, lowering prices to sizes that domestic tourists can afford, and preparing travel programs by dividing domestic tourism into different sections are all the options that can be applied to help the development of domestic tourism. However, it is also worth noting that seasonality induces a concentration on time and space, which causes destination carrying capacity to be exceeded. In other words, the seasonality problem poses a threat to economic sustainability and environmental sustainability.

As a result, the economic sustainability of a destination depends on many factors. While many of these factors can be managed by goals, some cannot be governed by them. Sustainability of tourist flow, environmental sustainability, socio-cultural sustainability, economic sustainability, political sustainability, destination competitiveness, eliminating the seasonality problem, preventing leaks in the economy, supporting the competitiveness of businesses, creating an environment of trust in destinations, developing domestic tourism, and tourist satisfaction are among the elements that goals can manage. Economic sustainability can be attained if all of these prerequisites are accomplished.

REFERENCES

Cevdet Avcıkurt, *Turizm Sosyolojisi* (Ankara: Detay Yayıncılık, 2003).

Gülin Beyhan and Mete Ünügür, "Çağdaş gereksinmeler bağlamında sürdürülebilir turizm ve kimlik Modeli", *İtüdergisi/a mimarlık, planlama, tasarım*, 4(2) (2005): 79–87.

İbrahim Birkan, "Sürdürülebilirlik kavramı, turizm sektörü açısından sürdürülebilir gelişmenin önemi ve koşulları", in *I. Ulusal Turizm İşletmeciliği Kongresi Bildiriler Kitabı, Kızılcahamam, Ankara* (2001): 17–18.

Ömer Çoban, Mustafa Doğan and Ozan Kaya, "Etkinliklerin mevsimsellik sorununun çözümünde araç olarak kullanılması: Bozcaada örneği", *Journal of Tourism and Gastronomy Studies*, 5(4) (2017): 347–359.

Cengiz Demir and Aydın Çevirgen, *Ekoturizm Yönetimi* (Ankara: Nobel Yayın Dağıtım, 2006).

Econation, "Sustainable development". (2021). Online access: 12.03.2021, www.econation.co.nz/sustainable-development/.

Michael J. Enright and James Newton, "Tourism destination competitiveness: a quantitative approach", *Tourism Management*, 25 (2004): 777–788.

E-UNWTO, "International Tourism Highlights, 2020 Edition". (2021). Online access: 09.05.2021, www.e-unwto.org/doi/epdf/10.18111/9789284422456.

European Economic and Social Committee (EESC), "Sustainable development". (2015). Online access: 19.04.2021, www.eesc.europa.eu/en/policies/policy-areas/sustainable-development.

Özgür D. Günel, "Mevsimsellik, mevsimlik istihdam ve örgütsel bağlılık: konaklama işletmelerinde bir araştırma", *İşletme Fakültesi Dergisi*, 10(2) (2009): 199–219.

Serkan Gürlük, "Dünyada ve Türkiye'de kırsal kalkınma politikaları ve sürdürülebilir kalkınma", *Uludağ üniversitesi İktisat Fakültesi Dergisi*, 19(4) (2001): 1–6.

Jonathan M. Harris, "Basic principles of sustainable development", in Kamaljit S. Bawa & Reinmar Seidler (eds.). *Dimensions of sustainable development, volume I* (EOLSS Publishers/UNESCO, Paris, 2000).

Knoema, "Atlas". (2021). Online access: 03.03.2021, https://knoema.com/atlas.

Glenn Kreag, *The impacts of tourism* (Minnesota, MN: University of Minnesota Press, 2001).

Orhan Kuntay, *Sürdürülebilir turizm pazarlaması* (Ankara: Alp Yayınevi, 2004).

Salih Kuşluvan and Zeynep Kuşluvan, "Turizmde mevsimsellik: nedenleri, sonuçları ve yönetimi", *Pazarlama Dünyası*, 12(69) (1998): 18–29.

Sylvia Lorek and Joachim M. Spangenberg, "Sustainable consumption within a sustainable economy: beyond green growth and green economies", *Journal of Cleaner Production*, 63(1) (2014): 33–44.

Esra Nemli, *Sürdürülebilir kalkınma: şirketlerin çevresel ve sosyal yaklaşımları* (İstanbul: Filiz Kitabevi, 2004).

Hasan Olalı and Alp Timur, *Turizm ekonomisi* (İzmir: Ofis Ticaret Matbaacılık, 1998).

Saime Oral, *Otel İşletmeciliği ve Verimlilik Analizleri (5. baskı)* (Ankara: Detay Yayıncılık, 2005).

Díaz M. Rodriguez and Tomas F. Espino Rodríguez, "Determining the sustainability factors and performance of a tourism destination from the stakeholders' perspective", *Sustainability*, 8 (2016): 951.

Gülşah Sedefoğlu, "Sürdürülebilir kalkınma hedefleri çerçevesinde yoksulluk ve gelir eşitsizliği", in *Poedat Akademisi: 2. Buluşma*, 31 Temmuz-4 Ağustos (Muğla: Gümüşlük Akademisi, 2020).

Mustafa Şit, "Türkiye'de turizm sektörünün istihdama katkısı", *Akademik Yaklaşımlar Dergisi*, 7(1) (2016): 101–117.

TUROB, "İstatistikler". (2020). Online access: 09.05.2021, www.turob.com/tr/istatistikler/unwto--uluslararasi-turist-gelisleri-2019-yilinda-15-milyaroldu#:~:text=D%C3%BCnya%20%C3%A7ap%C4%B1ndaki%20uluslararas%C4%B1%20turist%20var%C4%B1%C5%9Flar%C4%B1,(1%2C461)%20milyar%20seviyesine%20ula%C5%9Ft%C4%B1.

UNWTO, The guidebook on indicators of sustainable development for tourism destinations (2004).

UNWTO, "Measuring sustainable tourism: a call for action—report of the 6th international conference on tourism statistics, Manila, Philippines, 21–23 June 2017". (2017). Online access: 09.05.2021, www.e-unwto.org/doi/pdf/10.18111/9789284418954.

UNWTO, "COVID 19 and tourism". (2020). Online access: 09.05.2021, www.unwto.org/covid-19-and-tourism-2020.

UNWTO, "Tourism dashboard". (2021). Online access: 03.03.2021, www.unwto.org/unwto-tourism-dashboard.

Ahmet Vatan, "Turist Akışının ve Rekabetçiliğinin Sürdürülebilirliği", in Oğuz Türkay & İsmail Çalık (eds.). *Sürdürülebilir Turizm: Gösterge Geliştirme ve Ölçme Yaklaşımı içinde* (Ankara: Detay Yayıncılık, 2019): 400–416.

worlddata.info, "Countries", 2021. Online access: 03.03.2021, www.worlddata.info/europe/index.php.

WTO, *Guide for local authorities on developing sustainable tourism* (1998). WTO, Madrid, Spain. Online access: 02.03.2021, https://www.eunwto.org/doi/book/10.18111/9789284402809

Part II

Tourism and Sustainability in the Digital Era

5 A New Age in Tourist Guiding

Digital Tourism and Sustainability

Hande Akyurt Kurnaz, Funda Ön, and Faruk Yüksel

CONTENTS

5.1 INTRODUCTION

The development of technology, which has progressed rapidly from the past to the present, has also enabled new products and services to be produced and marketed as quickly as its formation. The tourism sector has taken this form of production as an example, because society quickly adapted to technology. The tourism sector has had to follow and apply technology due to its human-based nature (Atar 2020). Along with technology, undoubtedly, the phenomenon of sustainable tourism has also been realized. With the increasing importance of this phenomenon, practices based on personality and environmental protection have been followed in the tourism sector. Care has been taken to establish tourism businesses under sustainability, such as recycling bins in lobbies, energy-efficient lighting and windows, in-room energy-saving devices, and green landscape works, which are taken care of in hotels (Millar and Baloglu 2011). Among the most important reasons for the rapid change of the tourism sector is its openness to technology and sustainability to protect the environment. As an industry that does not renew itself will not live very long, tourism is fed by environmental resources due to its characteristics. In this context, it needs to become a sector that prioritizes ecological factors. Continuing tourism is explained as sustainable and means the transferring of natural, cultural resources to future generations. If countries expect their tourism activities to continue, they should undoubtedly prepare the ground for the future in a sustainable manner and adapt the innovations in technology to themselves.

DOI: 10.1201/9781003138051-7

Tourism enterprises have paid attention to behave technological in all fields related to tourism to increase their preferability within sustainable tourism. Otherwise, businesses that cannot respond to the changing demands of society do not seem likely to survive (Atar 2020). The tourism sector consists not only of accommodation, transportation, and food and beverage departments. In tourism, tourist guides have a vital role in promoting, troubleshooting, organizing activities, and completing tours.

While intensive technological investments rise to the occasion in all subsectors of the tourism industry from travel to accommodation, the tourist guiding profession, an essential pillar of tourism, benefits from technological developments intensively today (Çakmak and Demirkol 2017). Tourist guides are tourism employees who embrace the destinations, ensure that the tours are completed in a quality way, and take part in the communication with tourists most intensely. When this is the case, tourist guides need to renew themselves in sustainable tourism and digital tourism. Thus, the attitude of the tourist guides to both technological developments and the phenomenon of sustainable tourism gains importance. In this direction, the chapter aims to reveal the perspective of tourist guides to sustainability in tourism and digital tourism and determine the place and significance of the tourist guiding profession in digital tourism.

5.2 DIGITAL TOURISM AND SUSTAINABILITY

One of the most significant developments in the tourism sector has been technological developments and changes (Middleton and Clarke 2001). As a result of digitalization, the era of digital tourism has begun. Digital tourism is related to the use of digital technologies in the tourism sector to enhance the experiences of current and potential tourists. It is defined as the support provided by digital technology tools for the tourist's experience before, during, or after tourism-related activities. This can be a recommendation system to help people find suitable accommodation while planning their vacation and a mobile guide application on their smartphone. The concept of digital tourism is not new. It encompasses many online activities that people today encounter with travel planning using Expedia and Tripadvisor, travel management with airline websites and Tripit, mobile tour guide applications on smartphones, and photo management, including Facebook, Flickr, iPhoto, or Picasa (Benyon et al. 2013).

With the advancement of technology, devices suitable for technology have been developed. With these devices, internet usage has become more widespread, and shares of information sharing over the internet have increased. Thus, by providing easy access to all kinds of information that people need, the transactions and processes they perform have become even more accessible (Demirezen 2019). Technologies designed and developed specifically for the tourism industry include managing various transport facilities, travel delivery systems, hospitality, and recreation and entertainment components (Hojeghan and Esfangareh 2011). Digital environments that allow individuals to share their experiences effectively affect the widespread technology and related developments in tourism. In the tourism sector, internet-based digital technology applications such as the internet, social media, cloud computing, and virtual reality play a role in changing individuals' expectations, demands, preferences, and experiences (Aksoy and Baş 2020).

Sustainability refers to an event or a process that can be continued at a certain level without specifying a period (Tokgöz and Önce 2009). Although sustainability is defined differently, it is perceived as the ability to continue the functions and processes of ecology and ecological systems and their productivity in the future (Chapin et al. 1996). There are three generally accepted dimensions of the concept of sustainability (Harris 2011):

- **Economic dimension:** An economically sustainable system should produce products and services based on certain principles, maintain the government's administration and external debt, and be protected from sectoral imbalances that harm agricultural and industrial production.
- **Environmental dimension:** An environmentally sustainable system should keep the resource base stable, avoid the misuse of renewable systems or environmental investment functions, and consume nonrenewable resources, only those that are adequately replaced by investments.
- **Social dimension:** A socially sustainable system should ensure adequate social services, including equality distribution, health, education, political responsibility, gender equality, and participation.

There have been essential revolutionary changes in the last century's technological, economic, and social fields. Undoubtedly, superior technological developments are at the roof of these changes (Acar and Tunca 2018). The digital transformation process provides businesses with the chance to continue their sustainability successfully. To ensure sustainability with digital transformation, it is essential to efficiently use the environmental effects of new activities and developments and protect and increase these values with economic development through tourism activities. With the increasing sensitivity to the environment and the importance of sustainability concepts, a tourism phenomenon that extends to surreal and virtual experiences has emerged, using technology excessively. With digitalization, tourism activities have added new situations to the value chain, the balance of current conditions has changed, and the number of work and transactions has decreased. With digitalization, intense competition, and increasing use of technology, businesses are trying to provide high value to customers while performing their activities and fulfill their wishes, desires, and feelings by revealing some situations hidden in customers by customer experience (Yavuz 2020).

Promotion stages in national and international platforms can be given as examples of the tourism sector and digitalization. Countries that want to be leaders by keeping the tourist attraction the highest level in the tourism market, increasing their share of income from the tourism sector, or continuing them sustainably, focusing on promotional activities. They do this by using the benefits of technology, digitally reaching a very dense tourist mass than expected. With the introduction of digital transformation, country promotional activities have become very effective in getting potential tourists. As the promotional activities of the country, today will be more effective and efficient, that they are carried out intensively through digital channels can be called a different innovation that it brought to tourism during the digital transformation promotion phase (Atar 2020). While sharing information about the tourism product, it also promotes hotels, tour and travel agencies, restaurants, and destination management organizations (DMO's) such as tourism industry networks and tourism operators (Turkalj et al. 2009).

Digitalization has undoubtedly had a significant impact on tourism for both providers and consumers (Turkalj et al. 2009). As people adapt, love, and wonder about technological developments, considerable changes have occurred in tourism and recreational activities. For example, many tourists have embraced the internet to search for travel information has forced countless tourism businesses and organizations to integrate themselves online into the virtual world. Based on this, adapting tourism businesses to developing technology provides customers with different experiences, saving time in running the business, increasing the quality of the service provided, and reducing operating costs (Aylan and Aylan 2020).

Ivanov and Webster (2017) state that with this wide area offered, hotels, restaurants, museums, airports, and train stations are among the places where the most contact with the customer are and that they are the most critical areas to test the robots and self-service technologies that have come into our lives with digital transformation. Robots and artificial intelligence applications, which many hotels chains have attached importance to and use in certain areas, contain a lot of information, can take on, and automatize more tasks than we can. In addition to these, speeding up the check-in process is one of the numerous contributions it provides to tourism (Yalçın-Kayıkçı and Kutluk-Bozkurt, 2018). Recently, it has been used in tourist guiding.

5.3 TOURIST GUIDING IN DIGITAL TOURISM

It is an essential issue that the personnel who will work in a service area where information technologies are used extensively, such as the tourism industry, have knowledge and experience in information technologies. Tourist guides are considered to be at the top of this qualified personnel, as they are in direct contact with the tourists who are the subjects of the tourism industry. Therefore, the people who carry out the tourist guiding profession must have many qualifications to fulfill the profession's requirements. The essential qualities are the sufficiency of knowledge levels and high communication skills (Okul and Şimşek 2020). Therefore, tourist guides have to keep up with changing technology.

At first glance, the effect of technology will be at the minimum level in the tourist guiding profession, where human relations are at the forefront. However, in addition to various applications that can be downloaded to mobile communication devices and used by people in the destinations they visit, starting from 1991, the increase in the number of robots that provide guidance services in closed areas such as museums and exhibitions in various countries around the world shows the exact opposite of this belief (Yıldız 2019). The study results, which deal with the effects of technological developments on the tourist guiding profession with SWOT (Strengths, Weaknesses, Opportunities, Threats) analysis, are given in Table 5.1 (Çakmak and Demirkol 2017).

It's striking that, as in all subsectors of the tourism industry, tourist guides also extensively use technology. Developments in the 'headset' system, GPS-navigation

TABLE 5.1
Effects of Technological Developments on Tourist Guiding Profession (SWOT Analysis)

Strengths	**Weaknesses**
• Tourist guides go on more tours due to the increase in the participation of people in the tour thanks to the developments in transportation technology • Traveling has become safer for both tourists and guides thanks to transportation technologies • Stronger relations between tourists and guides before and after the tour thanks to communication technologies • Thanks to navigation technology, problems in finding directions and alternative routes are minimized • The need for tourist guides to carry auxiliary resources with them has been eliminated	• Advanced information technologies bring about information pollution • Errors in using technology likely to cause serious problems • Possibility that guides or tourists may not master the technology fully • Rapid developments and innovations in technology create a necessary expense • The probability of the tour being interrupted as a result of not obtaining the expected benefit from every technological product
Opportunities	**Threats**
• Compared to the past, tourist guides can become culturally and geographically more informed in a shorter time • Thanks to advanced communication networks and social media, guides get an extra tour by contacting tourists directly • Technology acting as a driving force for guides to prepare themselves in a shorter time about geographies they have not been to before	• The risk that technology-based guidance applications will replace guides in the future • The possibility that guides who cannot adapt to developing technology will not compete

Source: Çakmak and Demirkol (2017: 233).

technologies, smartphones, and transportation systems that have been implemented in museums and archeological sites, on the other hand, affect the guides to perform their profession, is it considered that these developments affect the tourists participating in the tour significantly positively, increasing the participation or the efficiency taken (Çakmak and Demirkol 2017). The headset and audio guide systems used in Turkey facilitate the work of tourist guides (Yıldız 2019). To provide more comprehensive information in different languages to tourists visiting museums and archeological sites affiliated to the Republic of the Turkey Ministry of Culture and Tourism, the 'audio guide' application, an audio guide, is called an audio guide, has been used. In addition, a mobile microphone and headphone assembly are known as radiofrequency operating 'headset' is used for group tours. All of these exemplify the effects of technology on the tourist guiding profession in Turkey. Today, it is mandatory to use the headset system in İstanbul Kariye Museum, Konya Mevlana Museum, and İstanbul Hagia Sophia Museum. At the same time, it is compulsory to use an audio guide system in 22 museums and archeological sites (DOSİM 2021). In addition to these, with the new and modern technology, the number of interactive applications and examples that can be applied in all fields has been increasing. Recently, augmented reality, virtual reality, robots, and hologram subjects have attracted attention among the interactive applications in the academy and the tourism sector. These applications, which can be used in museums, archeological sites, and cultural heritage areas, also facilitate and support the narration of tourist guides (Akyurt Kurnaz and Ön Esen 2019).

Although the tools and applications that light with technology benefit tourist guides, it is a fact that they threaten the tourist guiding profession in the long term. Because advanced GPS-supported map applications and applications that provide detailed, written, and audio narratives about museums and sites can now offer tourists an alternative to travel without a guide, even at the destination they visit for the first time (İstanbullu Dinçer and Çakmak 2015). In addition, robot tourist guides used in various countries are used as a substitute for human tourist guides in museums and exhibition halls where they provide guidance services. In other words, there are robots and people in the tourist guiding profession in these countries. Unfortunately, this situation puts the human tourist guides at risk of losing their jobs (Yıldız 2019).

When the studies are examined, Mil and Dirican (2018) state that concepts such as tour guidance, museum guidance, and guidance license should be reevaluated, considering the development of hologram guidance (Mil and Dirican 2018). In their studies on cultural heritage and theme parks, reality applications positively increased the satisfaction level of the visitors. At the same time, they allowed tourists to access the information they wanted with no guide, and that they would be used more in the future (Fritz et al. 2005; Jung et al. 2015; Özgüneş and Bozok 2017). In this context, it is possible to say that the concept of new-generation guidance is defined as '*guides who can adapt digital innovations in digital tourism, apply them on their tours and present information about themselves to tourists through various social networks,*' has emerged (Akyurt Kurnaz and Ön Esen 2019, s.508). Thus, tourist guides have to keep up with technology in today's age.

5.4 RESEARCH METHOD

The study aims to reveal the perspective of tourist guides to the concept of sustainability in tourism and digital tourism, to determine the place and importance of the tourist guiding profession in digital tourism. A qualitative research method was used in this direction, and a semi-structured interview technique was used as a data collection tool. A semi-structured interview, which is frequently used in exploratory research, is the type of interview in which the main lines of the discussion are determined, the question order is not made, the order of the questions may change during the interview, and random questions can be asked (Robson 2015). For this reason, a semi-structured interview form was created by determining the questions following the purpose of the study. The relevant literature was examined while preparing the interview form, and the researchers made the questions. The interview questions designed to ensure the internal validity of the interview form were reviewed by two different researchers, and the interview form has been completed in line with the suggestions received. The interview form has included questions regarding sustainability, digital tourism, and tourist guiding in digital tourism. Following the demographic questions during the interviews, the following questions were asked for the study:

1. What are the five things that come to mind when it comes to sustainability?
2. What are the five things that come to mind when it comes to digital tourism?
3. Do tourist guides play a role in sustainable tourism? If so, how?
4. How do you evaluate the impact of tourist guides in digital tourism?
5. Does the tourist guiding profession matter within the scope of digital tourism? Please explain.
6. Are tourist guides essential in terms of sustainability in digital tourism? Please explain.
7. What do you think tourist guides should do to improve themselves within the scope of digital tourism?

The study has covered the tourist guides who work in the Muğla region. Tourist guides have been chosen as the sample within the scope of the study, as they are in constant contact with tourists and their profession is in danger due to changing technology. After the interview form was prepared, the people to be interviewed were contacted, and an appointment was made. The interviews were held between 01 April and 30 April 2021. Eight tourist guides who participated in the study voluntarily were included in the research sample. However, as the number of people interviewed increased, the data obtained decreased to repetition. Therefore, it was decided that the data had reached saturation, and the interview part of the study was ended. The interviews, which lasted 15–30 minutes, were recorded according to the participants' permission. The interviews were carried out via phone and the internet due to the pandemic period. During the transcription of the interviews, the participants were identified with codes (K1, K2, …).

In the research, the data were analyzed with the descriptive analysis technique. Descriptive analysis is a simple form of analysis in which data obtained from interviews are shown and explained as they are (Sönmez and Alacapınar 2014). In addition, direct quotations are frequently used to convey the opinions of the interviewed individuals correctly (Yıldırım and Şimşek 2013). Firstly, in the descriptive analysis, themes were created based on the prepared questions and the dimensions included in the interviews. Later, the pieces were arranged in a meaningful and logical way and supported by direct quotations.

5.5 VALIDITY AND RELIABILITY

To meet the validity and reliability criteria of the study, priority was given to the internal validity (persuasiveness), external validity (transmissibility), internal reliability (consistency), and external reliability (verifiability), which Merriam (1988) emphasized. A conceptual framework was formed while preparing the interview form to increase the study's internal validity due to the relevant literature review. The researcher did not act as a guide during the interview and stated that the data would be confidential. Thus, the data obtained in the discussion will reflect the truth. To ensure the external validity of the research, the research process, and what has been done within the scope of the study was expressed in detail, the study was compared with the investigations on the subject in the literature, and the volunteer participants were interviewed. To increase the internal reliability of the research, the findings were given directly. In addition, the data obtained were coded separately by the researchers, and as stated by Yüksel and Yüksel (2004), consistency percentages were harmonized. To increase the external reliability of the research, the method of data collection and analysis was explained in detail. The data obtained were kept, and an external expert confirmed all documents together with the themes created.

5.6 FINDINGS

The demographic information about the tourist guides participating in the study is included in Table 5.2. Participants were specified as K1, K2 during data analysis.

TABLE 5.2
Demographic Information of the Participants

Participant	Gender	Age	Education	Experience	Nationalities the Guide Works For	Languages That the Guide Works
K1	Female	43	Bachelor's degree	18 years	British, Scandinavian, Turkish	English, Turkish
K2	Female	41	Associate degree	19 years	British, Other European Countries, Turkish	English, Turkish
K3	Male	48	Bachelor's degree	21 years	British	English
K4	Male	32	Bachelor's degree	12 years	British	English
K5	Male	40	Associate degree	15 years	Middle Eastern/ European	Hebraic, English
K6	Female	34	Bachelor's degree	11 years	British, Polish	English
K7	Female	36	Associate degree	13 years	British, Turkish	English, Turkish
K8	Male	43	Bachelor's degree	20 years	British, Turkish	English, Turkish
K9	Male	33	Associate degree	9 years	British, Turkish	English, Turkish

The data obtained as a result of interviews with tourist guides were collected under two themes. These are ‘Sustainability’ and ‘Digital Tourism.’

- **Sustainability**

The study primarily aims to reveal the perceptions of the participants about ‘Sustainability.’ Therefore, participants’ perceptions of the concept of ‘Sustainability’ are given in Table 5.3.

When Table 5.3 is examined, it is seen that the words environment, nature, economy, preserving historical-cultural resources, and conservation and the future are in the foreground within the framework of the concept of ‘Sustainability’ in the memories of tourist guides. When the participants were asked questions about whether there is a role of tourist guides in sustainable tourism and to determine what they are,

TABLE 5.3
Words That Sustainability Concept Evocates

Participant	Word 1	Word 2	Word 3	Word 4	Word 5
K1	Environment	Economy	Tourism	Social circle	Service industry
K2	Energy	Agriculture	City	Natural habitat	Natural resources
K3	Agriculture	Trade	Tourism	Environmental protection	Marketing
K4	Environmental protection	Economic growth	Social progress	Health	Security
K5	Nature	Society	Culture	Nature	Economy
K6	Environment	Ecological process	Biological diversity	Cultural integrity	Maintaining and preserving the ordinary balance of life without deterioration
K7	The future of nature and ecological order	Importance of next generations	Use of existing resources	Responsibility	A good quality of life for all
K8	Protect the environment	Preserving local culture	Coordinated economic growth with locals	Conservation	Preserving historical and natural beauties
K9	Next generations	Production diversity	Production continuity	Our common future	Clean environment

all the tourist guides participating in the study stated that they have a role in sustainable tourism. Some of the participants' views are as follows:

> For sustainable tourism, it is important to protect the places such as environment and nature, archaeological sites, etc., and transfer them to future generations, guides who are active in the field can be more aware and effective in the protection of such places.
>
> *K3*

> As long as the tourist guides develop their knowledge and skills and reflect them on the field, they will continue to be an integral component and stakeholder for tourism.
>
> *K4*

> Tourist guides have a role in sustainable tourism. For example, they contribute positively to sustainable tourism by transferring their knowledge and experiences about natural or cultural heritage to incoming visitors.
>
> *K5*

> It is important for promoting sustainability projects. In the agency I worked for, I showed that electric boats were used within the scope of this project and were promoting it to incoming tourists.
>
> *K7*

> The guide, who dominates his region, also informs his surroundings. For example, professional support must be obtained for some stages of the Lycian Way. Raises awareness by informing local people about the historical and natural beauties of the geography they live in.
>
> *K8*

When asked the participants about the importance of tourist guides in terms of sustainability in digital tourism, they stated they are essential. They should learn the use of technology, which is very popular today, and develop themselves.

> Is important. Tourist guides are the most important face, no matter in which platform of this country.
>
> *K1*

> Considering that information cannot exist by itself in artificial intelligence and social media environments, and there is a lot of information pollution in the internet environment, tourist guides will work the same devotedly to their groups and provide the right information in the digital environment as well as the guidance they have done in the field. Since human beings are social creatures, they are always ready to travel, go on tours and discover new places. As these activities cannot take place in digital environments, tourist guidance will continue to exist.
>
> *K4*

> As members of a professional organization that constantly brushes up and renews itself in terms of knowledge, tourist guides are of great importance in terms of sustainability.
>
> *K5*

> Yes, there is. Trips, projects, and promotions made for the sake of sustainability can attract more tourists. The introduction of the work done on the digital platforms put one step ahead of other competitors. It becomes a reason for preference.
>
> *K7*

> No matter how much technological advances take place in alternative routes, it must have a human touch. The same way you find it objectionable to take a robot and guide you in nature. The guide should smell the flower, recognize the animal passing through its footprint, and create an alternative according to the instantaneous weather change. Yes, we know these. When we combine these talents in the digital environment, we will be more successful.
>
> *K8*

- **Digital tourism**

The study primarily aimed to reveal the participants' perceptions regarding the 'Digital Tourism' issue. The perceptions of the participants regarding the concept of 'Digital Tourism' are given in Table 5.4.

When Table 5.4 is examined, it is seen that the words social media, online vacation, virtual reality, and digitalization are in the foreground within the framework of the concept of 'digital tourism' in the memories of tourist guides.

When the participants were asked what the impact of tourist guides could be on digital tourism, they said that digital tourism benefits their profession. Some of the participants' views on the impact of tourist guides on digital tourism are given below.

> Informative and instructive videos prepared by guides are effective in digital tourism.
>
> *K1*

> During the pandemic period, there were friends who made online tours for a fee; many friends shared pictures of places to visit on social platform or gastronomy, trekking, etc., they have relevant accounts. It is becoming advertisement.
>
> *K2*

> Tourist guides can share the experiences that they have in the field over the years, and historical, cultural and artistic knowledge with tourist groups in digital media.
>
> *K4*

> By using social media, which is one of the main components of digital tourism, especially during the current period, tourist guides have made their voices heard by large masses.
>
> *K5*

TABLE 5.4
Words That Digital Tourism Concept Evocates

Participant	Word 1	Word 2	Word 3	Word 4	Word 5
K1	Online tourism				
K2	Travel planning	Accommodation	Transportation	Vehicle or equipment rental	New travel routes and tours
K3	Online marketing	Online holiday sales	Online vacation booking	Online procurement for vacationers' requirements that can be procured online	Obtaining, storing, and using all kinds of information
K4	Virtual reality	Artificial intelligence	Robotic	Blockchain	Social media
K5	Social media	360 Degree videos	Applications	Virtual reality	Digital marketing
K6	Tourism transforming from traditional to digital	Changing travel and decision-making habits	Increased content density related to destination or travel	Intensive sharing of experiences related to the destination or travel	Access to feedback in the fastest way possible, the use of digital data in tourism industry
K7	Easy access to information	Internet	The power of social media	Digital platforms where everyone is transmitting their bad or good experiences, such as Tripadvisor	Virtual travel programs
K8	Technological developments	Travel reservations on computers or smartphones	New software	Faster realization of tour or transfer needs	Access to information, fastest and truest websites
K9	All dynamics of social media–related to tourism	Digital-online reservation sales	E-mail feedback	Digital shopping	Online tour promotion

> At first glance, it creates a perception that it will take our jobs away from us. But I believe that the Professional guiding association can easily overcome the transition process in better understanding and using technology. We can crown guidance with digital developments.
>
> *K8*

Participants who perform the tourist guiding profession stated that digital tourism is vital for their job in terms of promotion. Some of the participants' views are as follows:

> It has. As in every subject, Professional suppliers who are vacation experts should be worked with. In the excursion part of tourism, if it has cooperated with the guides who are the experts of this business, more efficient results are obtained.
>
> *K3*

> Tourist guides have an important place in digital tourism, as they reach not only a limited area or audience but also a wide environment and masses by sharing their information flow through digital media.
>
> *K5*

> Guide's website, social media sites, YouTube channel, etc. are important to advertise his/her tours.
>
> *K7*

> No matter what technological advancements are, the service industry appeals to the emotion. It is necessary to give that feeling to the other side. We will continue to exist in this sector by blending our own experiences and emotions in the new tourism concept, accompanied by all kinds of developments.
>
> *K8*

One participant (K2) expressed by saying, '*Honestly, it has importance in promotions, but I am afraid that in time, many people will need us less with other services that they have already learned on the internet by traveling individually.*' that the digital tourism can affect their profession negatively as well as positively. Another participant emphasized that robot guides may come to the fore with digitalization, but they cannot replace human principles.

> It has. The tourist guide is skilled, knowledgeable, and hardworking. They can play an important role in the promotion of the sector. But is there a digital guide? The technology of the tourism industry is developing rapidly, but this is a service sector, yet people are not satisfied with the service of robots. Even in the production industry, which started to be digitalized a century ago, there are still artisans and engineers at the head of the machines. At the same time, a robot dog cannot be expected to walk tourists in an archaeological site. Because the tourist guide tells not only the history and pose a photo in front of the historical monument, they meet all the needs of the tourist during the tour by adhering to the timing, especially in unexpected situations (a situation requiring

first aid, unexpected service during the meal,…), they help with their experience, is solution-oriented. Tourists are not yet ready for robot guide service.

K9

In line with the information received from the participants, it is seen that tourist guides need to follow technology and improve themselves within the scope of digital tourism. Recommendations regarding what tourist guides should do in this respect are given in Table 5.5.

TABLE 5.5
Suggestions for Tourist Guides to Improve Themselves Within the Scope of Digital Tourism

Participants	Suggestions
K1	'To receive the necessary training to use digital platforms insufficient and quality way'
K2	'We, too, must make our websites, provide personalized services and specialize in some areas. New destinations can work on different routes'
K3	'Guides can be trained in using technology, and guides can work more intensively on the internet to promote the country, region, and company'
K4	'Tourist guides should continue to keep themselves up-to-date both professionally and socially, try new technologies, and not hesitate to adapt to them. They should share their knowledge with travelers and their experiences with other tourism stakeholders. Being professionally accessible is one of the requirements of our age'
K5	'Tourist guides should develop the knowledge that they have or resources also in digital environments that constantly improve themselves and share their new gains with the growing tourist guide candidates'
K6	'He/she should read more, have more knowledge for the internet and reflect his/her experiences continuously and in the best way'
K7	'They must keep up with developing technology'
K8	'It consists of education and training that you call life. One of the mottos in our life is that *you are never too old to learn.* We will keep pace with all developments in the digital field. The person who will participate in the tourism activity needs to have a general knowledge of the processes at all stages, from raising travel awareness to the end of the vacation. We should get Professional support on subjects such as how to make reservations, the meaning of codes, some terms, how to use technology, etc.'
K9	'First, they should learn to use computers and smartphones. They should then create a social media account for themselves. They should learn to manage the created social media account, especially even though YouTube and Instagram seem simple; certain device techniques are required for the sharing to be effective. They should make promotions and shares to promote and market their experiences and share them in the official languages. The posts made should be positively perceived and encouraging posts to attract tourists to their countries'

5.7 CONCLUSION AND RECOMMENDATIONS

According to Koo (2013), they provide appropriate destination information to tourists through information and communication technologies. Services such as food and beverage, transportation, guidance, and reservation can be seen as the convenience of digital tourism (Atar 2020). The tourist guiding profession, one of the sub-professions of tourism, a service sector, is among the jobs with their share of technological developments (Yıldız 2019). In this direction, it is aimed to reveal the perspective of tourist guides to the concept of sustainability in tourism and digital tourism, to determine the place and importance of the tourist guiding profession in digital tourism. As a result of the interviews with tourist guides, it has been determined that they have information about sustainability and digital tourism and that tourist guides are affected by digital tourism with today's technology age.

Sustainable tourism is an understanding of tourism that includes human activities. It affects the general experiences of visitors, causes significant economic, social, and environmental impacts on local communities, and aims to protect and maintain the world's natural resources due to economic development (Wan and Li 2013). Tourist guides fulfill their professions within the framework of this understanding. The tourist guides participating in the study confirm this. Acting as a cultural ambassador in the archeological sites, museums, or nature, the guide also protects historical, cultural, and natural areas, keeps traditions alive, and passes them on to future generations. Therefore, tourist guides are an indispensable stakeholder of the tourism sector as long as they fulfill their duties correctly, honestly, morally, and ethically.

Tourist guides are open to innovations as they need to keep their knowledge up-to-date, follow the plan, and refresh themselves as required by their profession. So for his reason, they have to keep up with the technology age we live in. In the study, it has been revealed that tourist guides were near to digital tourism. They were knowledgeable about this issue and used social media platforms and YouTube channels to introduce themselves. Tourist guides share innovative videos, pictures, take online tours, and write the information they have. In this context, tourism guides can reach more audiences thanks to digital platforms.

One of the noticeable results of the study is that digital tourism, which triggers continuous innovation and development and leads communities to digitalization with itself, can affect the profession of tourist guiding negatively and positively. Similarly, it also stated that robot tourist guides would increase in line with the developments in technology. Therefore, there will be the risk of replacing human tourist guides in the tourist guiding profession in the long term (Yıldız 2019). However, most tourist guides participating in the study do not see the developing technology as a risk. On the contrary, tourist guides say that developments in the digital world help them promote or perform their profession better. Furthermore, emotions are at the forefront in tourism, a labor-intensive service sector where warm smiles and hospitality occupy an essential place. Therefore, the mechanization that emerged with technology cannot replace human tourist guides.

On the other hand, Atar (2020) stated that as the rapid and continuous technological developments in the tourism sector reduce the need for people, tourism personnel may experience employment shortages over time. In addition, he states that the tourism sector is a human-based service sector, that personal touch is essential, so digital applications implemented can have positive effects on human capital for both and tourists (Atar 2020). It should also be noted that digital tourism can be about being creative and easily accessible, responding quickly to customers, and being in online media. Still, too much focus on technology should not affect the attention visitors deserve in their journey to the destination (Caraivan 2017).

Tourist guides need to follow technology to improve themselves in digital tourism. In this direction, the tourist guide should receive training if necessary, open social media accounts to introduce themself and try new digital media platforms. Similarly, Atar (2020) also stated that harmonizing tourism personnel with technology should be emphasized. The necessary training should be given; this may affect the motivation of the personnel, increase job performance, and enable the enterprise to achieve positive outputs (Atar 2020). In addition to this, he stated that the personnel who have been informed about the technologies used in the company could increase the preferability of the business by acquiring customer satisfaction by creating more robust communication with the tourist.

The most important constraint of the study is that the application is limited to tourist guides only. Different results may be obtained by using other research methods in future studies and conducting the sample on tourists and travel agencies. Despite the study's limitations, it will contribute to the literature because digital tourism has been addressed within sustainability—the lack of studies on how tourist guides known as cultural ambassadors are affected by digital tourism. In addition, it is also predicted that it will help tourist guides who are performing the profession draw attention to digital tourism and sustainability issues. The study maintains its importance in providing information about the profession by using the sustainable and digital concepts of tourist guiding, recently popular tourism.

REFERENCES

Acar, Ömer Faruk and Mustafa Zihni Tunca. 2018. "Sürdürülebilir Elektronik Ticaretin Ekonomik, Sosyal ve Çevresel Boyutları Üzerine Bir Araştırma." *Mehmet Akif Ersoy Üniversitesi Sosyal Bilimler Enstitüsü Dergisi* 10 (26): 549–565.

Aksoy, Güliz and Mehmet Baş. 2020. "Virtual Tour as a Tool Used in City Promotion Within the Scope of Digital Tourism." *Journal of Turkish Tourism Research* 4 (3): 2542–2564.

Akyurt Kurnaz, Hande and Funda Ön Esen. 2019. "Yeni Nesil Turist Rehberliği." In *Kavramdan Uygulamaya Turist Rehberliği Mesleği,* edited by Özlem Köroğlu and Özlem Güzel, 475–514. Ankara: Nobel Yayıncılık.

Atar, Ayşe. 2020. "Tourism Sector from Traditional to Digital." *Journal of Turkish Tourism Research* 4 (2): 1640–1654.

Aylan, Fatmanur Kübra and Serkan Aylan. 2020. "Reflection of Virtual Reality and Augmented Reality Applications to Recreational Activities: Digital Recreation." *Journal of Turkish Tourism Research* 4 (3): 2746–2760.

Benyon, David, Aaron Quigley, Brian O'Keefe and Giuseppe Riva. 2013. "Presence and Digital Tourism." *AI & Society* 29 (4): 521–529.

Çakmak, Tolga Fahri and Şehnaz Demirkol. 2017. "Teknolojik Gelişmelerin Turist Rehberliği Mesleğine Etkileri Üzerine Bir Swot Analizi." *Bingöl Üniversitesi Sosyal Bilimler Enstitüsü Dergisi* 7 (7): 221–235.

Caraivan, Luiza. 2017. "Digital Tourism: A Review of Trends in Promoting Tourism Activities." *Quaestus Multidisciplinary Research Journal* 11 (3): 159–162.

Chapin, Francis Stuart, Margaret Torn and Masaki Tateno. 1996. "Principles of Ecosystem Sustainability." *American Naturalist* 148 (6): 1016–1037.

Demirezen, Bilgehan. 2019. "Arttırılmış Gerçeklik ve Sanal Gerçeklik Teknolojisinin Turizm Sektöründe Kullanılabilirliği Üzerine Bir Literatür Taraması." *International Journal of Global Tourism Research* 3 (1): 1–26.

DOSİM (Döner Sermaye İşletmesi Merkez Müdürlüğü) "Sesli Rehberlik Listesi." May 03, 2021. www.dosim.gov.tr/sesli-rehberlik-listesi.

Fritz, Francisco., Ana Susperregui and María Teresa Linaza. 2005. "Enhancing Cultural Tourism Experiences with Augmented Reality Technologies" The 6th International Symposium on Virtual Reality, Archaeology and Cultural Heritage VAST.

Harris, Jonathan M. 2011. "Sürdürülebilir Kalkınmanın Temel Prensipleri." Çev. Emine Özmete, *Hacettepe Üniversitesi Sosyolojik Araştırmalar e- Dergisi*. May 03, 2021. www.sdergi.hacettepe.edu.tr/makaleler/EmineOzmet2eviri.pdf.

Hojeghan, Samira Borouji and Alireza Nazari Esfangareh. 2011. "Digital Economy and Tourism Impacts, Influences and Challenges." *Procedia Social and Behavioral Sciences* 19: 308–316.

İstanbullu Dinçer, Füsun and Tolga Fahri Çakmak. 2015. "Gözetim Toplumu Yönetiminin Turizm Açısından Değerlendirilmesi", I. Avrasya Uluslararası Turizm Kongresi, Selçuk Üniversitesi, Konya, Mayıs 28–30, 2015.

Ivanov, Hristov Stanislav. and Craig Webster. 2017. "Adoption of Robots, Artificial Intelligence and Service Automation by Travel, Tourism and Hospitality Companies, A Cost-Benefit Analysis", Prepared for the International Scientific Conference "Contemporary Tourism—Traditions and Innovations, Sofia University, October 19–21, 2017.

Jung, Timothy, Namho Chung and M. Claudia Leue. 2015. "The Determinants Of Recommendations To Use Augmented Reality Technologies: The Case of A Korean Theme Park." *Tourism Management* 49: 75–86.

Koo, Chulmo, Seunghun Shin, Keehun Kim, Chulwon Kim and Namho Chung. 2013. "Smart Tourism of the Korea: A Case Study", PACIS 2013 Proceedings.

Merriam, Sharan B. 1988. *Case Study Research in Education: A Qualitative Approach*. San Francisco, CA: The Jossey-Bass Education Series.

Middleton, Victor T. C. and Jackie Clarke. 2001. *Marketing in Travel and Tourism*. Oxford: Butterworth-Heinemann.

Mil, Burak and Cüneyt Dirican. 2018. "Industry 4.0 Technologies and Its Effects On Tourism Economics." *Journal of Multidisciplinary Academic Tourism* 1 (3): 1–9.

Millar, Michelle and Seyhmus Baloğlu. 2011. "Hotel guests' Preferences for Green Guest Room Attributes." *Cornell Hospitality Quarterly* 52 (3): 302–311.

Okul, Turan and Güntekin Şimşek. 2020. "Sanal Gerçeklik Uygulamalarının Turizm Rehberliği Bölüm Derslerinde Kullanımına Yönelik Bir Öneri." *Turist Rehberliği Nitel Araştırmalar Dergisi* 1 (1): 31–51.

Özgüneş, Reşad Emre and Düriye Bozok. 2017. "Turizm Sektörünün Sanal Rakibi (Mi?): Arttırılmış Gerçeklik." *International Journal of Turkic World Tourism Studies* 2 (2): 146–160.

Robson, Colin. 2015. *Bilimsel Araştırma Yöntemleri Gerçek Dünya Araştırması*. Çev. Ed. Şakir Çınkır ve Nihan Demirkasımoğlu. Ankara: Anı Publishing.

Sönmez, Veysel and Füsun G. Alacapınar. 2014. *Örneklendirilmiş Bilimsel Araştırma Yöntemleri*. Ankara: Anı Publishing.

Tokgöz, Nuray and Saime Önce. 2009. "Şirket Sürdürülebilirliği: Geleneksel Yönetim Anlayışına Alternatif." *Afyon Kocatepe Üniversitesi İktisadi ve İdari Bilimler Fakültesi Dergisi* 11 (1): 249–275.

Turkalj, Davorin, Antun Biloš and Renata Deželjin. 2019. "The Effects of Digital Promotion Investment in Croatia's Tourism Product." *ToSEE—Tourism in Southern and Eastern Europe* 5: 715–728.

Wan, Yim King Penny and Xiangping Li. 2013. "Sustainability of Tourism Development in Macao, China." *International Journal of Tourism Research* 15: 52–65.

Yalçın Kayıkçı, Meltem ve Ayşegül Kutluk Bozkurt. 2018. "Dijital Çağda Z ve Alpha Kuşağı, Yapay Zekâ Uygulamaları ve Turizme Yansımaları." *Sosyal Bilimler Metinleri* 1: 54–64.

Yavuz, Aslınur. 2020. "*Digital Transformation in Tourism: An Examination of Hotel Managers Perspectives*". Master's Diss., Düzce Üniversitesi.

Yıldırım, Ali and Hasan Şimşek. 2013. *Sosyal Bilimlerde Nitel Araştırma Yöntemleri*. Ankara: Seçkin Publishing.

Yıldız, Savaş. 2019. "Turist Rehberliği Mesleğinde Robot Rehberlerin Yükselişi." *Süleyman Demirel Üniversitesi Vizyoner Dergisi* 10 (23): 164–177.

Yüksel, Atila and Fisun Yüksel. 2004. *Turizmde Bilimsel Araştırma Yöntemleri*. Ankara: Turhan Kitapevi.

6 Socio-technological Sustainability in Tourism

Hasan Evrim Arici and
Nagihan Cakmakoglu Arici

CONTENTS

6.1 INTRODUCTION

The concept of sustainability covers all stakeholders, including governments, travelers, residents, tourism and hospitality organizations, and other tourism-associated companies. Sociocultural sustainability ensures an important development in local people's lives by enhancing tourism development's economic contribution to local destinations, preserving the natural environment, and providing high-quality travel experiences for tourists (Choi and Sirakaya 2006). With the advent of information technology and the internet, all stakeholders, including travelers, locals, and tourism service providers, must keep up with the new technology and apply current systems, triggering digital transformation and leading to transformative digital experiences in the tourism industry.

In the 21st century, with the fast development of the internet and mobile technology, digitalization has become an important actor and an efficient universal transformational impetus in travel and tourism, with consumer-generated content and social media having vital importance for the economic development of tourism destinations and companies (Gössling 2017). Furthermore, in tourism, the concept of

DOI: 10.1201/9781003138051-8

sustainability causes systematic training, development, observation, and cooperation, which could be succeeded by keeping up with new-generation technologies and digitalization (Benckendorff et al. 2014). Therefore, considering digitalization as a new dimension of sustainability could have positive outcomes for tourism development and transformative experiences of tourists.

In the sustainability literature, the theory of transformative learning developed by Mezirow (1991) has received growing attention and recognition. It is taken into substantial consideration for increasing and catalyzing socio-digital transformations toward sustainability. Recently, transformative learning theory has been adopted to explain traveler experiences in tourism (Pung et al. 2020). However, this theory, affected by several disciplines, including education, psychology, and sociology, is still in its infancy as a learning theory in tourism with particular features and discourses. Thus, the inquiry remains unanswered regarding how transformative learning theory has been adopted and put into practice in socio-technological sustainability and transformative digital learning research, and how research on sustainability and digital transformation in tourism could contribute to the future development of the comprehension of transformative experiences of tourism stakeholders.

To date, limited efforts have been made to examine the research mentioned above questions. Drawing on the hermeneutic approach, this study aims to expand the knowledge and understanding of sustainability's socio-technological transformation and its potential outcomes. The chapter proposes a new conceptual framework (see Figure 6.1), which first suggests that new technology and digitalization should be considered a new tourism actor. The sustainability concept embraces technology and digitalization as new dimensions and economic, sociocultural, and environmental dimensions. Second, this adoption could ease sustainable digital transformation in tourism as a catalyst. Third, this framework also suggests that such a digital transformation can provide unique and meaningful transformative experiences for all stakeholders, including tourists, hosts, and tourism companies. This chapter fills the theoretical gap in the tourism literature by discussing how the transformative learning theory is conducted in the sustainable digital transformation context.

In the wake of the purposes mentioned above, we first discuss the mainstream in transformative learning research and present sustainability literature. Second, we provide the methodology part. Afterward, the proposed framework of socio-technological sustainability is illustrated and critically discussed, followed by a conclusion and suggestions for further investigation and limitations.

6.2 LITERATURE REVIEW

6.2.1 Transformative Learning

Initially developed by Jack Mezirow (1991), the transformative learning theory identifies a change in an individual's perception, understanding, and beliefs, and consequently a group's future actions. According to this theory, individuals get a coherent body of experience—relationships, ideas, perception, values, senses, and conditioned responses—frames of reference, which describe their world (Mezirow 1997). Frames of reference refer to the forms of suppositions through which people perceive their world. They form and restrain our knowledge, understanding, sense, feelings, and expectations, and designate our actions. This theory suggests that we automatically change our activity. For example, we are more likely to refuse opinions, views, and plans, which cannot suit our perceptions (Mezirow 1991). Transformative learning theory includes obtaining a broader sense of the world, fostering novel abilities and capabilities (Mezirow 1991; Pearce and Foster 2007).

Transformational learning occurs when individuals begin to reflect critically on previous perspectives and recognize that these previously held predispositions have constrained their understanding of current contextual experiences through either a sudden or gradual process. Therefore, they begin to modify these presuppositions better to reflect the dynamics of these new contextual experiences.

Brookfield provides a complementary model that includes a series of steps that can be operationalized into transformative learning activities for individual or group settings, although not necessarily in an exact sequence. These steps are fluid and allow the exclusion of a stage without interruption of this transformative process (Brookfield 1987):

Step 1—Trigger. This is best described as a development that cannot be managed through the application of previous strategies.

Step 2—Appraisal. This occurs when the learner begins to grips with their incompetence in a new contextual experience.

Step 3—Exploration. This involves examining new and different ways of explaining or accommodating the experience that has led to discomfort for the learner.

Step 4—Alternatives. This allows for experimenting with a new role, new way of behaving, or new way of dealing with a problem.

Step 5—Integration. This takes place as these new ways become part of current behaviors and practices in daily life.

The works of Mezirow and Brookfield provide unique opportunities for practitioners to follow the guideline provided by the transformative learning theory to develop new and dynamic remedies that serve the transformational needs of the tourism industry in the digital era.

The theory of transformational learning suggests some insight into achieving change by developing key competencies to facilitate transformation. The critical traits listed in the transformational approach can easily change into competencies that can be set as strategical competencies and be of value in the development of resources: the ability to think critically and objectively to reflect on previous behaviors, the ability to collaborate with others and build consensus regarding the meaning of individual reflections, and the ability to create action plans for transforming resources.

Building on the earlier work of Mezirow on transformative learning, Wolf et al. (2017) developed a conceptual model that includes triggers of the transformative process and their outcomes. They suggest four dimensions of transformative tourism experiences: '(1) disorienting dilemma, (2) self-reflection, (3) resolution by exploring new actions, and (4) development of new skills, attitudes, and beliefs' (p. 1664). For example, tourism practitioners may face a disorienting dilemma in being confronted with a digital evolution encouraging people to transform existing norms and strategies or other social, cultural, natural, and politically intense situations for the first time (Walter 2016). Second, through self-reflection, they can resolve internal conflict by considering how their privilege has shaped their worldview and interacting with others (Wolf et al. 2017). Finally, the companies may reach an epiphany and resolve to act differently (Coghlan and Gooch 2011; Wolf et al. 2015). The third dimension of Wolf et al.'s model is resolution through exploring new actions. These actions may include searching for new ways to adapt digital transformation to the industry (Wolf et al. 2017). Robledo and Batle (2017) suggest that this dimension can be facilitated through sharing and solidarity. These feelings can enhance practitioners' desire to take action on their own to address and apply what they learned from the disorienting dilemma and self-reflection (Wolf et al. 2015).

The last dimension is the development of new skills, attitudes, and beliefs. Ultimately, the stakeholders could develop new skills in adapting to digitalization in the tourism industry. Reisinger (2013) and Noy (2004) refer to this outcome as long-term attribute-building. In sum, transformative development can include a broad gamut of physical and mental capabilities, such as managerial proficiency, cross-cultural understanding, endurance, and technology adaptation (Kirillova et al. 2017; Knollenberg et al. 2014).

6.2.2 Sustainability and Technology

The phenomenon of sustainable development is vague and thus frequently hard to employ in a socio-technological context. Sustainability refers to the ability to go further for an extended period. We may consider this concept as weak and strong sustainability. Weak sustainability is a prevalent concept. This concept includes the standard definition of Brundtland 'development that meets the needs of the present without compromising the ability of future generations to meet their own needs' (Brundtland 1987). Accomplishing sustainability is a matter of executing all resources that involve both natural and artificial resources.

On the other hand, the vital concept considers natural and artificial resources as distinct classes that must be protected uniquely. According to this concept, each species needs to be protected because anything else cannot be substituted. A compromise form concentrates on ecology and ecological issues, including the ozone layer, which has been supposed not to be substitutable by anything else.

More precisely, sustainability has been demonstrated by having three main components: sociocultural, environmental, and economic. Sociocultural sustainability is often described as involving various social and cultural shift components, as depicted by the World Tourism Organization (UNWTO)'s 'Respect the sociocultural authenticity of host communities, conserve their built and living cultural heritage and traditional values, and contribute to inter-cultural understanding and tolerance.' Sustainability principles refer to the environmental, economic, and sociocultural aspects of tourism development. To ensure long-lasting sustainability, an acceptable equilibrium must be conducted among these three components ('Sustainable Development | UNWTO' 2021).

Drawing on the definition mentioned above, 'development that meets the needs of the present without compromising the ability of future generations to meet their own needs,' this concept has been adjusted to tourism. Sustainable tourism has been comprehended as satisfying the needs and expectations of current travelers and locals by simultaneously preventing and increasing facilities for the future. However, there have been scarce implications that complete sustainable tourism has been accomplished or even sought (Byrd 2007). For example, Calvià, in the Balearic Islands, was an encouraging implication, yet for the moment, it is excluded from having been a sustainable tourism destination (Dodds and Kelman 2008). Therefore, there has been hopelessness concerning the probability of accomplishing a complete sustainable tourism development. Scholars like Armenta et al. or Weaver claim that sustainable development without technology is incomplete. A true technology-adjusted doctrine would be caused to warrant the future of sustainable development in tourism (Armenta et al. 2012; Weaver et al. 2017).

Thus, despite the development regarding sustainability (Butler 1991), sustainability in tourism has not reached the expected level despite various models and trials. Instead, the proper application of sustainability in tourism destinations needs more struggle to be successful. Especially the goals focusing more on mass touristic applications urgently need sustainability projects (Dwyer 2005; Hall 2019).

Developments in technology have recently developed into new phenomena like big data, the internet of things, machine learning, internet of services, social media, cybernetic-physical systems, and intelligent applications (Ali and Frew 2014; Weaver et al. 2017). These developments are primarily based on Industry 4.0, relating people, machines, devices, logistics systems, and products to communicate and collaborate (Kumar et al. 2020). These technologies help the theories to be implemented in real life. Relatedly, the potential of new technologies in creating real-life applications is of great importance. The relationship between new technologies and sustainability is elaborated mainly in two stages: tourism strategy and technologies that care for environmental sustainability. Within the last three decades, especially three notions have affected the tourism industry (Buhalis and O'Connor 2005; Cai et al. 2021; Law et al. 2019):

1. digitalization and technological developments
2. globalization of markets
3. need for sustainability

The sustainability model in tourism with high technology-focused markets triggers competition essentially. This integrates model technology as an added value for a more sustainable social, cultural, environmental, and economic development. Therefore, this digitalization has caused organizations to consider transforming sustainably a chance and a challenge (Gössling 2020).

The tourism industry worldwide has complex characteristics due to social, competitive, and economic factors (Huang et al. 2020; Radomskaya and Pearce 2021) and rapid integration with stakeholders. Thus, the circumstances require the tourism industry to adapt to the high technologies for more sustainable implementations.

Despite its importance, the relationship between sustainability and technology has been scarcely investigated by few scholars. For example, Liburd (2005) searched on the effects of mobile tourism applications on sustainability, focusing on equity, scale, and implementation elements. Another study concluded after they researched the sustainable tourism development of Manchester (UK) that IT was regarded to develop sustainability so that audio guiding and social media networks could inform tourists about sustainability standards (Touray and Jung 2010). Scott and Frew (2013) conducted a survey titled 'eTourism experts' focusing on IT implementations for more sustainability in tourism. They concluded that sustainability is essential in designing eTourism implementations like virtual reality, destination management systems, carbon calculations, intelligent transportation systems, social media platforms, etc. Most of them were appreciated for the customers' benefit, like reducing the prices of a hotel business in the low season. This study also suggested tourist management applications by controlling the numbers and flow and protecting vulnerable sites. For example, eco-labeling was recommended as a tool to support green tourism. Ali and Frew (2014) investigated sustainable tourism applications like energy and waste management. Moreover, research claim that more sustainable tourism causes constant training, control, and cooperation with the help of technology (Pierre J. Benckendorff et al. 2014). Furthermore, more recent research about technology and sustainability argued that technology has an influential role in sustainability in tourism (Gössling 2017).

The limited studies on the relationship of technology and sustainability mainly concentrated on information technology in tourism, which are related to the marketing, distribution, and profitability aspects of tourism but not with responsible tourism. Therefore, this chapter aimed to present a conceptual framework proposing socio-technological sustainability in tourism to achieve sustainable development better by keeping up with digital evolution.

6.3 METHODOLOGY

To understand the characteristics of socio-technological sustainability, this study conducted a hermeneutic approach and reviewed related literature on tourism sustainability and technology to make interpretations of these concepts. In developing a conceptual framework, the current study utilized tourism academic literature about technology and sustainability as a source to be analyzed and interpreted. The hermeneutic approach focuses on understanding rather than describing with the help of a spiraling method, moving from text to theory and back to the reader. Each movement includes dialectic dialogue of the author, critical questioning, practical wisdom, and ontological understanding of the relationship between technology and sustainability. Interpreting refers to unveiling the hidden part of sustainability in tourism, and dialectic questioning enhances these concepts' comprehension (Krausz 2002).

Therefore, our interpretation of socio-technological sustainability is based on the authors' readings of the most recent usage of the term in the tourism literature and subsequent questioning of the current and underlying theory. This resulted in outside and within the tourism, literature to further examine how sustainability develops due to digital transformation and to clarify the fundamental steps that could characterize this transformation.

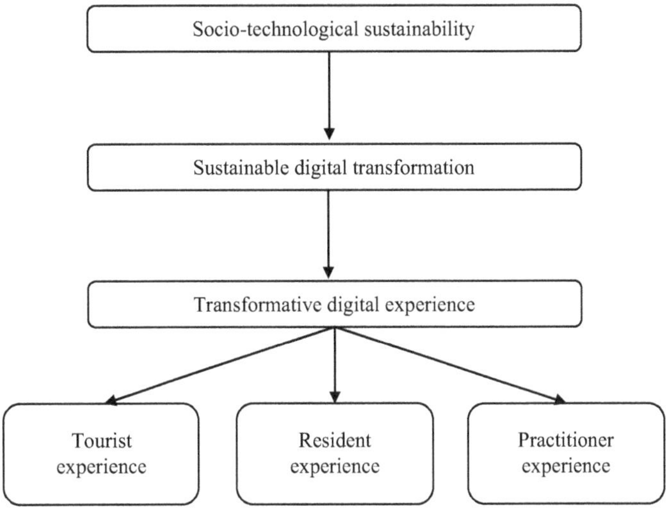

FIGURE 6.1 A proposed framework for a sustainable digital experience in tourism.

6.4 A TRANSFORMATIVE MODEL OF SUSTAINABLE DIGITAL TRANSFORMATION IN THE TOURISM INDUSTRY

6.4.1 Conceptual Framework

Figure 6.1 provides the conceptual model of the sustainable digital transformation in the tourism industry in the new world. Stakeholders in tourism first need to determine socio-technological sustainability. Then comes digital transformation that aids tourism stakeholders, including companies, locals, employees, and customers, to adapt new-generation technologies, revise existing resources and relationships, and clarify what new practices and resources they need for a sustainable digital transformation in tourism. Furthermore, this digital transformation leads to transformative experiences in the usage of new-generation technologies in tourism activities. This study delves into these transformative digital experiences for the three main stakeholders, namely, companies, locals, and tourists, separately. This framework informs tourism organizations how they should sustain technological transformation in the market or tourist destinations.

Moreover, this framework provides some avenues to show how tourism organizations offer technology-adapted services to their customers (i.e., artificial intelligence, service robotics, intelligent devices, etc.). Moreover, this framework provides a pathway illustrating how digital transformation could increase the quality of life of local people in a tourist destination. For example, smart cities, a recent trend, could be adopted to sustain digital transformation to contribute to tourism development and keep locals' life standards and sociocultural characteristics. Furthermore, this framework explains how digital transformation in tourism can lead to transformative learning for locals in a destination. Lastly, this study proposes that such digital transformation could enhance a traveler's excellent and sustainable, transformative experience in tourism. To achieve this, technological development or digitalization in tourism needs to ensure positive and authentic experiences for travelers. This framework also summarizes the ways of providing such transformative experiences as using service robots, intelligent applications, artificial intelligence, and their potential effects on travelers. Overall, this study claims that no matter which new technology or digitalization is preferred, tourism companies need to guarantee sustainable outcomes to protect the local culture and natural environment and look toward the future safely.

6.4.2 Socio-technological Sustainability

Drawing on the conceptual guidelines of transformative learning theory, this study proposes a framework explaining the process of socio-technological sustainability (Figure 6.1). We define socio-technological sustainability as ensuring sustainable digital transformation in tourism by protecting favorable transformative digital experiences of stakeholders, including tourists, residents, and practitioners. Our framework supposes that digitalization is inevitable in the industry. In particular, with the advent of the recent Covid-19 pandemic, the priorities of customers have changed from more personalized service to more distant service; many practitioners have realized the importance of adopting the new technology to be able to provide socially distance service to keep customers' safety and health; and many locals have learned to isolate themselves from the virus by obeying non-pharmaceutical precautions including wearing a mask, keeping social distance, and so on. This process leads to awareness of the importance of accomplishing technological adaptation in tourism.

The socio-technological sustainability proposed by this study requires achieving digital transformation in tourism and priorities to protect local culture, heritage, the social life of people, the natural environment of a regional destination, and the economic welfare of both destination and country. One of the most remarkable hesitations about fast-changing technological development is that novelties emerging from this technology accelerate consumption, with which the principle of sustainability is at odds. Even though the fact that technological innovations enable us to make numerous things more accessible and increase consumption seems like a positive development for tourism in the short run, these advances could have detrimental effects on social, cultural, and environmental aspects of real life in the long run. Therefore, we have to focus both on the technological transformation and at the same time on the sustainable results of this transformation. This can be achieved by concentrating on the social aspect of the change; technological transformation and digitalization should first preserve and contribute to the local culture and heritage. Thus, the point here for the tourism managers and marketers is to care about consumers' needs and preferences, namely, tourists, and consider the local people's expectations. For example, while planning intelligent cities for the travelers, besides designing cities satisfying the needs of the tourists, it is to be aimed to make the local people utilize these novelties at an optimal level. Only then a cumulative overall transformation or improvement starts to blossom. Therefore, the contribution of all tourism stakeholders to the development of the destination itself and the locals can be maximized, as suggested by social exchange theory. The theory has indicated that people positively react to the events that have benefited these individuals. Thus, there is a mutual relationship. In other words, reciprocal relations can direct people's responses to some circumstances. Similarly, collaboration theory suggests that local people need to be included in destination management and marketing processes since sustainable tourism development can only be accomplished by getting valuable contributions from all stakeholders.

Digital transformation in tourism should also mind protecting the local area. Technological change has facilitated many jobs and tasks to be conducted more efficiently and faster. Furthermore, it is possible to develop more green services and products thanks to technology. In other words, technology has to have a pretty important role in posing environmentally friendly applications and urging them to be utilized instead of being the reason for consumption and harming the environment. For example, many green practices in the hotel industry could be developed using new technologies effectively and efficiently. Such environmentally friendly implications as water savings, energy saving, and carbon emission could be sustained through benefitting new technologies and digitalization. Electric cars and sensor-based systems reducing energy usage are other reasonable examples that can be further utilized by tourism and hospitality firms.

The digital transformation is also expected to contribute to economic development. In other words, such change should ensure the sustainable economic development of a destination. Furthermore, it is clear that thanks to technological developments, many organizations may decrease their high costs and increase profitability by performing their tasks in a faster and cheaper way. That is, technology enables tourism companies to serve more with lower prices. Therefore, it could significantly increase tourism companies' financial performance and ensure sustained competitive advantage within the market.

Furthermore, the technological transformation can also support local people's economic welfare by generating new job opportunities for them directly and indirectly. With the advent of technology and the internet, many new jobs have been developed. For these available job positions, tourism companies need to hire new competent employees. Still, other firms from various sectors (mainly the IT sector) have employed many people to operate their businesses. This is an opportunity for locals because if local people could meet the standards of the job positions, they may have more chances to be recruited in these companies. Therefore, such a technological transformation can also contribute to the employment rate of the tourist destination and consequently the whole country.

Moreover, due to technological development, many promotion and marketing activities could be developed professionally to affect and attract target customers. For example, customer relationship management is a current system used by many tourism companies to recall previous customers, keep and retain existing customers, and catch future customers. Furthermore, several technological implications, like the Customer Relationship Management (CRM), could be effectively used to increase tourism companies' financial success, which leads to an increment in tourist destinations' economic development. Eventually, this socio-technological sustainability can result in an increment in a country's economic development.

Overall, socio-technological sustainability clarifies technological transformation in tourism by considering sustainable development's sociocultural, environmental, and economic dimensions. This concept suggests that technological change needs to improve the sociocultural characteristics of tourist destinations by ensuring local people's lives and protecting cultural heritage, increasing environmentally friendly implications, and contributing to the economic development of goals and countries. The following section explains how to achieve such a sustainable digital transformation by adopting conceptual guidelines of transformative learning theory in tourism.

6.4.3 Sustainable Digital Transformation

The concept of 'socio-technological sustainability' requires a transformation process that all stakeholders in the tourism industry can apply. A theoretical guideline, which is commonly accepted and implemented by previous studies, could direct us to achieve such digital transformation. Therefore, this study explains the process of sustainable digital transformation through adopting five phases of transformative learning theory. For each stage, this framework proposes practical implications for tourism stakeholders. This process starts with the need for a sustainable digital transformation. With the advent of technology, many professionals have begun to transform their existing situations into a new era. That is, technology has triggered the tourism industry to change. Today, tourism companies and other stakeholders are aware of the insufficiency of existing practices, approaches, and policies. This is the second phase of our transformation process, called 'appraisal.' In particular, the recent pandemic has forced us to reevaluate everything because we cannot operate our companies with the previous practices. Thus, there is a need for a sustainable technological transformation. The market encourages tourism professionals to explore new approaches, ways, and policies to achieve sustainable digitalization in the industry. Several alternatives will be evaluated, implemented, and revised (if necessary) to find the best solution for accomplishing such a sustainable digital transformation. Finally, the tourism industry could benefit from the social-technological sustainability of keeping our existing resources (including sociocultural characteristics, natural resources, and economic resources), developing new solutions and implementations for managing the industry more effectively and efficiently, and preparing the sector for the future generations. Each phase and specific examples have been briefly illustrated below.

Phase 1—Trigger. This is best described as a development that cannot be managed through the application of previous strategies. Digital evolution could be acknowledged as triggering all tourism stakeholders to revise and modify their existing processes.

Phase 2—Appraisal. This occurs when the learner begins to grips with their incompetence in a new contextual experience. The digital transformation has forced us to evaluate our existing situation and discuss how to integrate such a transformation into the tourism industry.

Phase 3—Exploration. This involves examining new and different ways of explaining or accommodating the experience that has led to discomfort for a person. Today, we are all aware of the incompetence of sustainability without adopting technology in tourism. Therefore, we may explore new and different avenues regarding digitalization in the world and tourism particularly.

Phase 4—Alternatives. This allows for experimenting with a new role, new way of behaving, or new way of dealing with a problem. We have several opportunities and methods for the adaptation of technology. This may also require additional roles and positions for all actors (including companies, locals, and travelers). As an alternative tourism actor, technology can be considered. Regarding sustainability, we may have to view technology as a new dimension of this concept and existing ones (i.e., environmental, sociocultural, and economic sustainability).

Phase 5—Integration. This takes place as these new ways become part of current behaviors and practices in daily life. Integration of technology into the sustainability concept is demonstrated in our framework. We discuss this phenomenon from the perspectives of tourism companies, residents, and customers. The new component of sustainability is named 'socio-technological sustainability.'

6.4.4 Transformative Digital Experience

In tourism, now, we know that digital transformation must be achieved to survive in the new era. Tourism and hospitality scholars, thus, need to set out to find possible ways and develop strategies for achieving such a digital transformation in the industry. As among the first attempts, this book chapter suggests that digital transformation must consider sustainability principles in tourism. First, the environmental component of sustainability requires protecting the natural environment from the potentially detrimental effects of rapid growth and development in tourism and related sub-sectors in tourist destinations. Second, technology can serve as a supporting constituent to protect the environment. For example, tourism companies could use green practices by controlling water usage, energy saving, and new technologies to reduce greenhouse gas emissions.

Digital transformation in tourism could develop the quality of life of local people. Many popular tourist destinations have tried to ensure the standards of a smart city (Monfaredzadeh and Krueger 2015; Cugurullo 2018; Girardi and Temporelli 2017) because it has a great potential to attract many visitors who are susceptible to technology. However, only equipping a town with innovative technologies is not adequate to ensure the sustainable competitiveness of the destination. Instead, new technology cannot present success for an extended period without embracing sustainability principles. Thus, digital transformation needs to protect the rights and benefits of local people. Still, it also contributes to their quality of life to better support tourism development in the tourist destination. The local people should be included in the destination marketing and management process. From the collaborative perspective, ignoring any stakeholder leads to failure to manage tourist destinations and achieve final goals. Hence, our framework suggests that socio-technological sustainability, considering all stakeholders' needs and expectations, could collaborate in managing and marketing tourist destinations.

On the other hand, our framework anticipates that digital transformation will inherently contribute to the economic development of tourism companies, destinations, and countries. Achieving adaptation of new technologies in a tourism company (e.g., hotel) will most probably increase the quality of service offered. Such technologies can also assist employees in customer service delivery design. The excellent service provided via integrating the new technologies would ensure higher levels of customer satisfaction in a hotel organization. The service profit chain model suggests that customers satisfied with the quality service will be loyal customers for hotel organizations (Heskett and Sasser 2010). The loyal customers will provide positive word of mouth and repurchase or revisit the hotel in the future. That is, these customers will be repeat guests. This process naturally leads to the financial success of hotel companies and eventually ensures sustained competitive advantage across rivals in the market. In sum, practical usage of the technology could improve the financial performance of tourism companies. The model is not limited to only tourism companies; rather, it can be applicable for all organizations in a tourist destination. The financial growth will contribute to the country's gross domestic product (GDP).

The framework proposes unique experiences for each stakeholder because everyone has different needs and expectations from the digital transformation. Drawing on this argument, we have provided specific transformative experiences for travelers, residents, and practitioners, respectively.

6.4.4.1 Tourist Experience

Customers give more positive responses for tourism organizations' sustainability activities once they are informed about its activities of responsible tourism by a neutral source like an independent business providing objective interpretations of business facilities instead of incorporation (Walker and Moscardo 2014).

The customers can be seen as solid stakeholders because they are a dependable source of sustainable communication (Tiago et al. 2021). Moreover, thanks to virtual technologies, customer word-of-mouth significantly impacts the prominence and dissemination of interaction ways (Liang et al. 2013). As a result, there has been a fundamental transformation in understanding distance and mobility through social media, with more accessible, cheaper, and more significant amounts of transportation, lower levels of greenhouse gas emissions, and environment-friendly applications.

Digitalization could change customer behaviors and expectations in the new era to pay more attention to more technology-adopted service designs. Thus, hospitality organizations need to develop a sustainable digitalization to satisfy customers' needs and expectations. In this sense, adopting new technology systems can offer excellent service to customers and transform hotel service experiences to reduce social interactions and improve cleanliness. Furthermore, recent research suggested that adaptation of new technology could change the conventional 'high-touch and low-tech' customer experience into 'low-touch and high-tech' customer experiences (Oktadiana and Pearce 2020; Cakmakoglu Arici and Güçer 2018; Cakmakoglu Arici 2018). This enables hospitality guests to possess mitigated interaction with service providers.

Furthermore, because physical, social distancing is a vital precaution to control the spread of the Covid-19 pandemic, new-generation technologies could decrease customers' risk of infection through constraining physical interactions with human employees in the hospitality setting. Moreover, recent implications of new-generation technologies in hospitality organizations confirm that the customers would welcome the offering of technological devices (Ivanov et al. 2018). Hence, hospitality firms must consider that their future survival and development rely on adopting sustainable digitalization in their service delivery design.

Moreover, digital transformation also encourages customers to adopt an 'intact lifestyle,' referring to consumer behavior that reduces face-to-face contact, as a self-preventive attitude to avoid risk and pursue safety, consisting of the usage of technology-based intact services and nondigitalized intact behaviors, including camping or hiking and special personalized services, such as room service or family unique dining rooms (Bae and Chang 2021). Furthermore, with the advent of the recent pandemic, tourists might be now looking for 'intact' services to minimize the risk that stimulates low-touch and high-tech service solutions in tourism companies. Hence, companies could consider the changing lifestyle of customers and adopt 'intact' service as an innovative type of service that is anticipated to minimize face-to-face interaction. In the short term, such services as contactless check-in and check-out, keyless room access, digital menu, and TV remote control could create a unique and trouble-free travel experience for the customers. In sum, the socio-technological sustainability suggests that an 'untact' lifestyle can spread among customers, significantly influencing travelers' pre- and post-buying behaviors and habits.

6.4.4.2 Resident Experience

Comprehending how local people perceive increases the applicability of destination management and sustainability models. Besides, rural development is closely connected with introducing particular local products or services.

A destination can be characterized as intelligent if human capital and conventional and novel technological infrastructure are supported with more investments in sustainability for a higher quality of life, with the help of proper strategies to protect natural sources and participatory management. Intellectual and human capitals are inevitable features of intelligent destinations, combining people, their relationships, training, and the business (Albino et al. 2015; Monfaredzadeh and Krueger 2015). A brilliant goal includes various opportunities to enable life-long learning, social heterogeneity, resilience, and participatory applications for all people. Thus, intelligent destinations involve innovative applications of intelligent people through the participation of urban and rural residents in public services. Additionally, a network of information, organizations of voluntary benefits, support for urban diversification, and research and development are other components of being an innovative destination.

Social and technological sustainability play essential roles in enriching the life quality of residents and aim at fostering more trained, sophisticated, and participatory residents. This can be achieved by enabling people's participation in the management procedure of the destination and by allowing them to become active citizens. For example, residents of a touristic destination aiming to be smart are to be involved in the processes of production and also governance to the degree they can be influential in the success of the goal (Monfaredzadeh and Krueger 2015). Therefore, digital transformation needs to provide positive outcomes for residents.

Moreover, digitalization in tourism can also lead to high technology-adopted services in tourism companies. This brings with it some dangers for local employees. For example, employees could be fired due to tourism and hospitality organizations' high-technology adapted service delivery design. Such a threat needs to be eliminated by considering local employees' rights and benefits. Therefore, socio-technological sustainability argues that companies also need to protect their employees' benefits when adapting new-generation technologies in service design. To achieve this, a mixed service delivery approach could be adopted based on human-technology collaboration in the service structure, combining the new-generation technologies and the human-based service delivery systems.

6.4.4.3 Practitioner Experience

Transformation of the tourism organization to take advantage of technological developments consists of changing business culture, new types of understanding, and evaluating and constructing new competencies for a more sustainable destination (Zhou et al. 2020; Cheer 2020).

The Internet has reconstructed interaction and communication in various settings. It has provided a virtual, joint, and global platform based on numerous contacts. Therefore, everybody can start and be involved in an interaction and cooperation organized for the future of a destination. The Internet has also accelerated organizational communication through word-of-mouth, mainly electronic word-of-mouth (Serra-Cantallops et al. 2020). Therefore, tourism organizations are urged to utilize social media and virtual platforms besides the conventional methods for better business communication (Chu et al. 2020; Nusair 2020).

Additionally, the close relationship between people and businesses is mainly characterized by the Internet in this digitalized world (Colleoni 2013). Web sites are tools of market interaction with responsible attitudes (Taylor and England 2006). People can quickly screen a tourism organization's responsibility facilities regarding social and environmental issues via World Wide Web. This corporate content is generally accessed directly through business websites or media reports available as links to other pages. The business facilities of sustainability presented on websites arouse the interest of tourism stakeholders, visitors, employees, and investors. Various stakeholders anticipate detailed information about the tourism organizations' sustainability reports' environmental, social, and governance facilities (Rodríguez and Cruz 2007; Uyar et al. 2020). Thus, the content quality of sustainability reports is based on competent web design and information presentation (Hsieh 2012).

Interaction in communicating is essential information conveying method for organizations because it has a significant role in social dynamics (Rodríguez et al. 2012; Zhang and Lin 2015). The collaboration based on web and data exchanges has improved the communication between tourism organizations and their related stakeholders (Kurgun et al. 2018; Novelli et al. 2006). The web-based cooperation allows them to interact with online users and gain popularity in marketing through word-of-mouth on virtual platforms.

Organizations are experiencing a significant transformation in the global network. Tourism organizations' guest relations and IT departments like hotels use social networking software (Garrido-Moreno et al. 2018; Kasavana et al. 2010). These technological developments could positively affect sustainable and responsible tourism because companies can access more stakeholders with the help of digital interaction (Ali and Frew 2014). Interactivity enabled by social networks has provided organizations to disseminate information more easily about their sustainable applications to their stakeholders (Chung and Koo 2015; Pierre J. Benckendorff et al. 2014). This novelty has strengthened the stakeholders since social media can disrupt business legitimacy (Xiang and Gretzel 2010).

Some global social software, such as blogs, Really Simple Syndication (RSS) feeds, forums, and social platforms, has attracted some consumer groups. Social media have a technological advantage to accelerate communication and interaction, contact and collaboration of businesses and other stakeholders. These interactions are called interactive 'viral' as ideas spread like epidemics through word-of-mouth, which is thought to be a dependable source (Leung et al. 2013; Munar and Jacobsen 2013; Sotiriadis and Van Zyl 2013; Litvin et al. 2008). Thus, tourism companies can adopt new technologies, including online tools, service robots, artificial intelligence, and intelligent devices, to market and promote their tourism products and services.

The technology can also be used to improve the quality of service offered. Technology integration into the service delivery design can be achieved by developing technology awareness of human labor (i.e., employees) in a tourism company. Tourism organizations could provide training for developing their employees' skills and knowledge about new-generation technologies. Such a service harmonizing employees and new-generation technologies can better satisfy customers' needs and expectations, resulting in higher customer loyalty and eventual financial success.

6.5 CONCLUSION

Drawing on the transformative learning theory, this study discusses and develops a framework proposing a new concept called 'socio-technological sustainability.' The present work has concentrated on developing a new idea of digital transformation by considering the main principles of sustainable development in the tourism industry. Studying sustainable digital transformation and the transformed tasks, functions, and responsibilities of the main three actors of the industry, namely, travelers, residents, and practitioners in the proposed framework based on the main dimensions of sustainability (i.e., sociocultural, environmental, and economic) are crucial to conceptualize the socio-technological sustainability concept in tourism since examination of sustainable digitalization in the tourism industry remains scarce. Only limited conceptual investigations consider the different characteristics of relevant automation and their international applications (Gössling 2017; Law et al. 2019). Through integrating sustainability and digital transformation in tourism, our study has proposed and demonstrated the conceptual framework including main phases and practical implications for the main actors of the tourism industry (i.e., tourists, residents, and practitioners), providing an essential contribution to our understanding on sustainable digitalization in the tourism industry.

Sustainability includes three main dimensions: sociocultural sustainability, environmental sustainability, and economic sustainability. However, digital evolution has entailed tourism industry practitioners and academicians to transform the overwhelming majority of existing models, concepts, and theories into the new millennium. Digitalization might be considered a milestone, which means that we could benefit from its advantages to improve local culture and residents' life quality, retain cultural heritage, protect the natural environment, and contribute to economic development in a tourist destination. We need to follow the newest technologies and consider our existing resources (i.e., financial, human, and physical resources) by doing a sustainable transformation. Underpinning the transformation process through transformative learning theory developed by Mezirow also expanded our understanding of tourism transformation. It sheds light on the importance of local or global events in changing human behaviors, attitudes, and beliefs (Kitchenham 2008; Mezirow 1997). The contribution of this chapter lies in suggesting a new concept of socio-technological sustainability for achieving long-term digital transformation in tourism and demonstrating the roles and functions of primary stakeholders in the proposed conceptual framework (Figure 6.1).

This book chapter suggests that digital transformation needs to consider the main dimensions of sustainable development and illustrate specific industry implications. For example, practitioners are companies and service providers who need to adapt new-generation technologies in the service delivery; tourists are customers looking for unique and more untact service experiences in the new era, particularly after the recent pandemic; and the residents are local people living in a tourist destination and have to be involved into destination management and marketing process actively. This framework could encourage further studies on the sustainable digital transformation of the tourism industry in the new era. This study also highlights how the digital transformation process would permanently impact the industry and its primary stakeholders.

The integration of sustainability and digitalization is more likely to change the industry's perceptions, behaviors, attitudes, and world beliefs. If the digital transformation could be sustained, sociocultural characteristics of local communities and the natural environment could be better protected. This process can also significantly support a tourist destination's economic welfare and development in the long term. The transformative process also changes people's perceptions of intelligent devices and robots, technology-oriented lifestyle, technological tools in interpersonal relations, and feeling drawn to technological development. The transformation of tourism and changes in attitudes and behaviors during travel have been studied by focusing on tourist experiences (Pung et al. 2020; Robledo and Batle 2017) and limitedly on tourism practitioners (Soulard et al. 2019). Yet, the transformative potential of sustainable digitalization in the tourism industry has not been examined to date. This study, thus, has a great potential to improve the knowledge and understanding of how digitalization could result in long-lasting, sustainable transformation in the tourism industry.

Furthermore, the current chapter presents to tourism and hospitality practitioners a new solution to consider digitalization as an opportunity to create a sustainable transformation in the services marketing process. The proposed framework recommends that hospitality practitioners first ensure the technological change in their companies when planning the strategy for providing their services. Tourism companies are stimulated to adopt new-generation technologies, increasing the awareness of the importance of the transformation, by conducting technical infrastructure and procuring the necessary equipment and intelligent devices, such as robotics and artificial intelligence; to minimize the interaction of frontline employees with customers due to recently spreading 'untact lifestyle,' particularly after the pandemic; and to enhance customers' experiences toward the technological innovations through offering virtual or innovative service implementations. In sum, a significant task for tourism practitioners is that management practices and marketing activities need to be transformed by following the latest technological development to deliver quality service, satisfying customers' needs and expectations. To trigger such a sustainable transformation in tourism and reinforce it, destination marketers and governments may have to provide political and financial support and incentives.

On the one hand, tourism practitioners should train their existing employees to improve their balance with technological innovation and enhance their skills and capabilities in utilizing these intelligent devices to play an active role during this transformation process. But, on the other hand, it is also vital for keeping the social life quality of locals.

The practitioners should also aid customers by intensifying their transformative learning about utilizing the new-generation technologies; inspire tourists to choose tourism and hospitality companies providing technology-centered service in their future travels. Furthermore, the permanent changes in tourist behaviors and attitudes due to the technological innovation in service delivery can also lead to positive word of mouth, triggering other customers to prefer such a tourism company. Through this process, the tourism industry would achieve a sustainable digital transformation.

Despite its importance, this chapter has some theoretical limitations. Although we gave full-time and energy to review the literature on relevant topics, it still can be lacking in interpreting the previous studies. Furthermore, our interpretations and conceptualizations of socio-technological sustainability lead to subjective outputs limiting the study's generalizability. However, besides utilizing empirical investigations, the current research ensures a deep discussion of interdisciplinary concepts and theories on digitalization, sustainability, and transformative learning to propose a sustainable digital transformation in the tourism industry. Future studies can expand our knowledge by focusing on specific implications of new-generation technologies in the tourism industry in general or its other subsectors (i.e., transportation and airline). The future investigation could also develop a specific framework on how to integrate frontline employees into the digitalization to minimize potential threats of transforming the service delivery, to generalize existing knowledge of the transformation procedure, and to make a contribution to the continuing conceptualization of socio-technological sustainability in the tourism and hospitality industry.

REFERENCES

Albino, Vito, Umberto Berardi, and Rosa M. Dangelico. 2015. "Smart Cities: Definitions, Dimensions, Performance, and Initiatives." *Journal of Urban Technology* 22 (1). Taylor & Francis: 3–21.

Ali, Alisha, and Andrew J. Frew. 2014. "Technology Innovation and Applications in Sustainable Destination Development." *Information Technology & Tourism* 14 (4). Springer: 265–290.

Armenta, Álvaro, Arturo Serrano, Mayer Cabrera, and Roberto Conte. 2012. "The New Digital Divide: The Confluence of Broadband Penetration, Sustainable Development, Technology Adoption and Community Participation." *Information Technology for Development* 18 (4). Taylor & Francis: 345–353.

Bae, So Y., and Po-Ju Chang. 2021. "The Effect of Coronavirus Disease-19 (COVID-19) Risk Perception on Behavioural Intention towards 'Untact' Tourism in South Korea during the First Wave of the Pandemic (March 2020)." *Current Issues in Tourism* 24 (7). Taylor & Francis: 1017–1035.

Benckendorff, Pierre J., Pauline J. Sheldon, and Daniel R. Fesenmaier. 2014a. "Sustainable Tourism and Information Technology." In *Tourism Information Technology*, edited by Benckendorff, P. J., Sheldon, P. J., Fesenmaier, D. R., 308–335. Wallingford: CABI.

Benckendorff, Pierre J., Pauline J. Sheldon, and Daniel R. Fesenmaier. 2014b. "Social Media and Tourism." In *Tourism Information Technology*, edited by Benckendorff, P. J., Sheldon, P. J., Fesenmaier, D. R., 120–147. Wallingford: CABI.

Brookfield, Stephen D. 1987. *Developing Critical Thinkers: Challenging Adults to Explore Alternative Ways of Thinking and Acting*. Jossey-Bass.

Brundtland, Gro H. 1987. "What Is Sustainable Development." *Our Common Future* 8 (9). Latrobe University: 1–40.

Buhalis, Dimitrios, and Peter O'Connor. 2005. "Information Communication Technology Revolutionizing Tourism." *Tourism Recreation Research* 30 (3). Taylor & Francis: 7–16.

Butler, Richard W. 1991. "Tourism, Environment, and Sustainable Development." *Environmental Conservation* 18 (3). JSTOR: 201–209.

Byrd, Erick T. 2007. "Stakeholders in Sustainable Tourism Development and Their Roles: Applying Stakeholder Theory to Sustainable Tourism Development." *Tourism Review*. Emerald Group Publishing Limited.

Cai, Wenjie, Brad McKenna, Philipp Wassler, and Nigel Williams. 2021. "Rethinking Knowledge Creation in Information Technology and Tourism." *Journal of Travel Research,* 60 (6). SAGE Publications Sage CA: Los Angeles, CA, 0047287520946100.

Cakmakoglu Arici, Nagihan. 2018. "The Antecedents of Revisit Intention in Medical Tourism: A Cross-Cultural Case." https://tezarsivi.com/the-antecedents-of-revisit-intention-in-medical-tourism-a-cross-cultural-case.

Cakmakoglu Arici, Nagihan, and Evren Güçer. 2018. "The Antecedents of Revisit Intention in Medical Businesses." *İşletme Araştırmaları Dergisi* 10 (2). İşletme Araştırmaları Dergisi: 740–757.

Cheer, Joseph M. 2020. "Human Flourishing, Tourism Transformation and COVID-19: A Conceptual Touchstone." *Tourism Geographies* 22 (3). Taylor & Francis: 514–524.

Choi, HwanSuk C., and Ercan Sirakaya. 2006. "Sustainability Indicators for Managing Community Tourism." *Tourism Management* 27 (6). Elsevier: 1274–1289.

Chu, Shu-Chuan, Tao Deng, and Hong Cheng. 2020. "The Role of Social Media Advertising in Hospitality, Tourism and Travel: A Literature Review and Research Agenda." *International Journal of Contemporary Hospitality Management* 32 (11). Emerald Publishing Limited: 3419–3438. doi:10.1108/IJCHM-05-2020-0480.

Chung, Namho, and Chulmo Koo. 2015. "The Use of Social Media in Travel Information Search." *Telematics and Informatics* 32 (2). Elsevier: 215–229.

Coghlan, Alexandra, and Margaret Gooch. 2011. "Applying a Transformative Learning Framework to Volunteer Tourism." *Journal of Sustainable Tourism* 19 (6). Taylor & Francis: 713–728.

Colleoni, Elanor. 2013. "CSR Communication Strategies for Organizational Legitimacy in Social Media." *Corporate Communications: An International Journal* 18 (2). Emerald Group Publishing Limited: 228–248.

Cugurullo, Federico. 2018. "Exposing Smart Cities and Eco-Cities: Frankenstein Urbanism and the Sustainability Challenges of the Experimental City." *Environment and Planning A: Economy and Space* 50 (1). SAGE Publications Sage UK: London, England: 73–92.

Dodds, Rachel, and Ilan Kelman. 2008. "How Climate Change Is Considered in Sustainable Tourism Policies: A Case of the Mediterranean Islands of Malta and Mallorca." *Tourism Review International* 12 (1). Cognizant Communication Corporation: 57–70.

Dwyer, Larry. 2005. "Relevance of Triple Bottom Line Reporting to Achievement of Sustainable Tourism: A Scoping Study." *Tourism Review International* 9 (1). Cognizant Communication Corporation: 79–938.

Garrido-Moreno, Aurora, Víctor J. García-Morales, Nigel Lockett, and Stephen King. 2018. "The Missing Link: Creating Value with Social Media Use in Hotels." *International Journal of Hospitality Management* 75. Elsevier: 94–104.

Girardi, Pierpaolo, and Andrea Temporelli. 2017. "Smartainability: A Methodology for Assessing the Sustainability of the Smart City." *Energy Procedia* 111. Elsevier: 810–816.

Gössling, Stefan. 2017. "Tourism, Information Technologies and Sustainability: An Exploratory Review." *Journal of Sustainable Tourism* 25 (7). Taylor & Francis: 1024–1041.

Gössling, Stefan. 2020. "Technology, ICT and Tourism: From Big Data to the Big Picture." *Journal of Sustainable Tourism* 29 (5). Taylor & Francis, 849–858.

Hall, C. Michael. 2019. "Constructing Sustainable Tourism Development: The 2030 Agenda and the Managerial Ecology of Sustainable Tourism." *Journal of Sustainable Tourism* 27 (7). Taylor & Francis: 1044–1060.

Heskett, James L., and W. Earl Sasser. 2010. "The Service Profit Chain." In *Handbook of Service Science*, edited by Paul P. Maglio, Cheryl A. Kieliszewski, and James C. Spohrer, 19–29. Service Science: Research and Innovations in the Service Economy. Boston, MA: Springer US. doi:10.1007/978-1-4419-1628-0_3.

Hsieh, Yu-Chin (Jerrie). 2012. "Hotel Companies' Environmental Policies and Practices: A Content Analysis of Their Web Pages." *International Journal of Contemporary Hospitality Management* 24 (1). Emerald Group Publishing Limited: 97–121. doi:10.1108/095961112.

Huang, Shanhui, Tao Xue, and Feiya Ma. 2020. "On the Conceptual Framework of Tourism Complex Research from the Perspective of the Theory of Complex Adaptive System." *Tourism Management and Technology Economy* 3 (1). Clausius Scientific Press: 1–15.

Ivanov, Stanislav, Craig Webster, and Peyman Seyyedi. 2018. "Consumers' Attitudes towards the Introduction of Robots in Accommodation Establishments." *Tourism: An International Interdisciplinary Journal* 66 (3). Institut za turizam: 302–317.

Kasavana, Michael L., Khaldoon Nusair, and Katherine Teodosic. 2010. "Online Social Networking: Redefining the Human Web." *Journal of Hospitality and Tourism Technology* 1 (1). Emerald Group Publishing Limited: 68–82. doi:10.1108/17579881011023025.

Kirillova, Ksenia, Xinran Lehto, and Liping Cai. 2017. "Tourism and Existential Transformation: An Empirical Investigation." *Journal of Travel Research* 56 (5). Sage Publications Sage CA: Los Angeles, CA: 638–650.

Kitchenham, Andrew. 2008. "The Evolution of John Mezirow's Transformative Learning Theory." *Journal of Transformative Education* 6 (2). SAGE Publications Sage CA: Los Angeles, CA: 104–123.

Knollenberg, Whitney, Nancy G. McGehee, B. Bynum. Boley, and David Clemmons. 2014. "Motivation-Based Transformative Learning and Potential Volunteer Tourists: Facilitating More Sustainable Outcomes." *Journal of Sustainable Tourism* 22 (6). Taylor & Francis: 922–941.

Krausz, Michael. 2002. *Is There a Single Right Interpretation?* Penn State Press.

Kumar, Ravinder, Rajesh Kr Singh, and Yogesh Kr Dwivedi. 2020. "Application of Industry 4.0 Technologies in SMEs for Ethical and Sustainable Operations: Analysis of Challenges." *Journal of Cleaner Production* 275. Elsevier: 124063.

Kurgun, Hülya, Osman A. Kurgun, and Erdem Aktaş. 2018. "What Does Web 4.0 Promise for Tourism Ecosystem? A Qualitative Research on Tourism Ecosystem Stakeholders' Awareness." *Journal of Tourism and Hospitality Management* 6 (1): 55–65.

Law, Rob, Daniel Leung, and Irene C. C. Chan. 2019. "Progression and Development of Information and Communication Technology Research in Hospitality and Tourism: A State-of-the-Art Review." *International Journal of Contemporary Hospitality Management* 32 (2). Emerald Publishing Limited: 511–534. doi:10.1108/IJCHM-07-2018-0586.

Leung, Daniel, Rob Law, Hubert Van Hoof, and Dimitrios Buhalis. 2013. "Social Media in Tourism and Hospitality: A Literature Review." *Journal of Travel & Tourism Marketing* 30 (1–2). Taylor & Francis: 3–22.

Liang, Silvia W.-J., Yuksel Ekinci, Nicoletta Occhiocupo, and Georgina Whyatt. 2013. "Antecedents of Travellers' Electronic Word-of-Mouth Communication." *Journal of Marketing Management* 29 (5–6). Taylor & Francis: 584–606.

Liburd, Janne J. 2005. "Sustainable Tourism and Innovation in Mobile Tourism Services." *Tourism Review International* 9 (1). Cognizant Communication Corporation: 107–118.

Litvin, Stephen W., Ronald E. Goldsmith, and Bing Pan. 2008. "Electronic Word-of-Mouth in Hospitality and Tourism Management." *Tourism Management* 29 (3): 458–468. doi:10.1016/j.tourman.2007.05.011.

Mezirow, Jack. 1991. "Transformation Theory and Cultural Context: A Reply to Clark and Wilson." *Adult Education Quarterly* 41 (3). Sage Publications Sage CA: Thousand Oaks, CA: 188–192.

Mezirow, Jack. 1997. "Transformative Learning: Theory to Practice." *New Directions for Adult and Continuing Education* 1997 (74). Wiley Subscription Services, Inc., A Wiley Company San Francisco: 5–12.

Monfaredzadeh, Tannaz, and Robert Krueger. 2015. "Investigating Social Factors of Sustainability in a Smart City." *Procedia Engineering* 118. Elsevier: 1112–1118.

Munar, Ana M., and Jens K. S. Jacobsen. 2013. "Trust and Involvement in Tourism Social Media and Web-Based Travel Information Sources." *Scandinavian Journal of Hospitality and Tourism* 13 (1). Taylor & Francis: 1–19.

Novelli, Marina, Birte Schmitz, and Trisha Spencer. 2006. "Networks, Clusters and Innovation in Tourism: A UK Experience." *Tourism Management* 27 (6). Elsevier: 1141–1152.

Noy, Chaim. 2004. "This Trip Really Changed Me: Backpackers' Narratives of Self-Change." *Annals of Tourism Research* 31 (1). Elsevier: 78–102.

Nusair, Khaldoon. 2020. "Developing a Comprehensive Life Cycle Framework for Social Media Research in Hospitality and Tourism: A Bibliometric Method 2002-2018." *International Journal of Contemporary Hospitality Management* 32 (3). Emerald Publishing Limited: 1041–1066. doi:10.1108/IJCHM-09-2019-0777.

Oktadiana, Hera, and Philip L. Pearce. 2020. "Losing Touch: Uncomfortable Encounters with Tourism Technology." *Journal of Hospitality and Tourism Management* 42. Elsevier: 266–276.

Pearce, Philip L., and Faith Foster. 2007. "A 'University of Travel': Backpacker Learning." *Tourism Management* 28 (5). Elsevier: 1285–1298.

Pung, Jessica M., Juergen Gnoth, and Giacomo Del Chiappa. 2020. "Tourist Transformation: Towards a Conceptual Model." *Annals of Tourism Research* 81. Elsevier: 102885.

Radomskaya, Valeriya, and Philip L. Pearce. 2021. "Adding Character: The Role of Destination Mascots in Tourism Development." *Tourism Management* 84. Elsevier: 104248.

Reisinger, Yvette. 2013. "Transformation and Transformational Learning Theory." *Transformational Tourism: Tourist Perspectives*. CABI Oxfordshire, 17–26.

Robledo, Marco A., and Julio Batle. 2017. "Transformational Tourism as a Hero's Journey." *Current Issues in Tourism* 20 (16). Taylor & Francis: 1736–1748.

Rodríguez, Beatriz, Julián Molina, Fátima Pérez, and Rafael Caballero. 2012. "Interactive Design of Personalised Tourism Routes." *Tourism Management* 33 (4). Elsevier: 926–940.

Rodríguez, Francisco J. G., and Yaiza d. M. A. Cruz. 2007. "Relation between Social-Environmental Responsibility and Performance in Hotel Firms." *International Journal of Hospitality Management* 26 (4). Elsevier: 824–839.

Scott, Mareba M., and Andrew J. Frew. 2013. "Exploring the Role of In-Trip Applications for Sustainable Tourism: Expert Perspectives." In *Information and Communication Technologies in Tourism 2013*, 36–46. Springer.

Serra-Cantallops, Antoni, Jose Ramón Cardona, and Fabiana Salvi. 2020. "Antecedents of Positive EWOM in Hotels. Exploring the Relative Role of Satisfaction, Quality and Positive Emotional Experiences." *International Journal of Contemporary Hospitality Management* 32 (11). Emerald Publishing Limited: 3457–3477. doi:10.1108/IJCHM-02-2020-0113.

Sotiriadis, Marios D., and Cinà Van Zyl. 2013. "Electronic Word-of-Mouth and Online Reviews in Tourism Services: The Use of Twitter by Tourists." *Electronic Commerce Research* 13 (1). Springer: 103–124.

Soulard, Joelle, Nancy G. McGehee, and Marc Stern. 2019. "Transformative Tourism Organizations and Glocalization." *Annals of Tourism Research* 76. Elsevier: 91–104.

"Sustainable Development | UNWTO." 2021. Accessed May 22. www.unwto.org/sustainable-development.

Taylor, Mark, and D. England. 2006. "Internet Marketing: Web Site Navigational Design Issues." *Marketing Intelligence & Planning,* 24 (1). Emerald Group Publishing Limited: 77-85. doi: 10.1108/02634500610641570.

Tiago, Flavio, Artur Gil, Sara Stemberger, and Teresa Borges-Tiago. 2021. "Digital Sustainability Communication in Tourism." *Journal of Innovation & Knowledge* 6 (1). Elsevier: 27–34.

Touray, Kabiru, and Timothy Jung. 2010. "Exploratory Study on Contributions of ICTs to Sustainable Tourism Development in Manchester." In *ENTER*, 493–505.

Uyar, Ali, Mehmet Ali Koseoglu, Merve Kılıç, and Fuad Mehraliyev. 2020. "Thematic Structure of Sustainability Reports of the Hospitality and Tourism Sector: A Periodical, Regional, and Format-Based Analysis." *Current Issues in Tourism,* 24 (18). Taylor & Francis, 2602–2627.

Walker, Kaye, and Gianna Moscardo. 2014. "Encouraging Sustainability beyond the Tourist Experience: Ecotourism, Interpretation and Values." *Journal of Sustainable Tourism* 22 (8). Taylor & Francis: 1175–1196.

Walter, Pierre G. 2016. "Catalysts for Transformative Learning in Community-Based Ecotourism." *Current Issues in Tourism* 19 (13). Taylor & Francis: 1356–1371.

Weaver, Paul, Leo Jansen, Geert Van Grootveld, Egbert Van Spiegel, and Philip Vergragt. 2017. Sustainable Technology Development. Routledge.

Wolf, Isabelle D., Gillian B. Ainsworth, and Jane Crowley. 2017. "Transformative Travel as a Sustainable Market Niche for Protected Areas: A New Development, Marketing and Conservation Model." *Journal of Sustainable Tourism* 25 (11). Taylor & Francis: 1650–1673.

Wolf, Isabelle D., Heidi K. Stricker, and Gerald Hagenloh. 2015. "Outcome-Focused National Park Experience Management: Transforming Participants, Promoting Social Well-Being, and Fostering Place Attachment." *Journal of Sustainable Tourism* 23 (3). Taylor & Francis: 358–381.

Xiang, Zheng, and Ulrike Gretzel. 2010. "Role of Social Media in Online Travel Information Search." *Tourism Management* 31 (2). Elsevier: 179–188.

Zhang, Chrystal B., and Yi Hsin Lin. 2015. "Exploring Interactive Communication Using Social Media." *The Service Industries Journal* 35 (11–12). Taylor & Francis: 670–693.

Zhou, Xiumei, Cheng Zhang, Zhuoqi Pan, and Peiling Wei. 2020. "Tourism Industry Is Leading the Digital Transformation of Cultural Heritage Management: Bibliometric Analysis Based on Web of Science Database." In *2020 Management Science Informatization and Economic Innovation Development Conference (MSIEID)*, 273–276. IEEE.

7 Information and Communication Technology Through a Decentralized Sharing Economy in the Tourism Industry

Senem Yazici

CONTENTS

7.1 INTRODUCTION

Information and communication technology (ICT) combines technologies that allow users to interact directly in the digital world (Rubtcova and Pavenkov 2019). ICTs and the Internet have transformed many business transactions in the digital world and online. After integrating ICTs with business, commercial operations then changed completely with creating a new form of business, known as e-business. It was the beginning of a digital transformation for many types of business. For example, the Internet has enabled customers to search for and buy products online using no intermediaries.

The online business world created new economic models like the sharing economy (P2P economy). The sharing economy became very popular after the Internet-enabled businesses reached many people worldwide and progressed the development of e-payment methods. PWC (2015) identified five dominant sharing economy sectors—travel, car sharing, finance, staffing, and music/video streaming—that will be worth $335 billion in 2025. The new generations like Gen Z and Alpha, who like to share, will continue to be the driving force in the sharing economy concept (Chang and

DOI: 10.1201/9781003138051-9

Wang 2018). Gen Z has preferences to share things quickly because they want to be more flexible and adaptable (Long and Wilhoit 2018). For example, Gen Z prefers to share taxis, travel, and hotel accommodation, but on their terms, not based on companies' rules and regulations (Tussyadiah and Pesonen 2018). Gen Z wants to enjoy a more accessible, flexible, comfortable, and easy-going lifestyle (Fodor and Jaeckel 2018). This generation was born in the sharing economy, and this is all they know. They will continue to push and develop what is possible regarding sharing economy models in the future.

After integrating ICT in the tourism industry, the industry's business operation changed utterly, and a new form of tourism was created, known as e-tourism. It was the beginning of a digital transformation for tourism. The Internet has enabled customers to search for and buy their travel products online using no intermediaries. However, the success of e-tourism depends upon effective e-payment systems. The online payment process was initially problematic and unsecured in currency change, bank commissions, transaction fees, and fraud. Blockchain technology with cryptocurrency could solve insecurity and instead offer transparency of online payment processes.

All sharing economy models are centralized and controlled by an organization. There are two well-known brands—Uber and Airbnb—offering shared economy services with a centralized settlement service. Centralized systems may not match future needs because of new generations' needs and wants. Blockchain is one of the latest technologies that will have a significant impact on most businesses. Even though blockchain technology is at the infancy stage in its development, tools such as cryptocurrencies, smart contracts, and decentralized applications have influenced online companies. Blockchain technology will change the sharing economy models because of decentralized data storage and communication usage (Pazaitis et al. 2017; Chang and Wang 2018). Trust is essential for upcoming generations, especially in the sharing economy (Hawlitschek et al. 2018).

This chapter focuses on the decentralized sharing economy in tourism. The systematic literature review examines tourism, ICT, and sharing economy literature. Web of Science and Scopus databases are used to search relevant articles. The inductive method is used to understand the two different disciplines. The main aim of this chapter is to explore new information about the decentralized sharing economy in tourism. Therefore, the first part of the chapter will focus on ICTs and online business developments. The second part will cover the digital economy within the tourism context in more detail. The third part of the chapter will examine the centralized and decentralized sharing economy model. The conclusion will deliver an overall evaluation of the integration of blockchain technology to enable a decentralized sharing economy in tourism.

7.2 EVOLUTION OF INFORMATION AND COMMUNICATION TECHNOLOGY (ICT) AND ONLINE BUSINESS

ICT has been widely studied in the literature (Law et al. 2019; Moreno and Tejada 2019; Purohit and Thakar 2019; Hamid et al. 2020). ICT goes back to the 1830s, with the invention of the telegraph by Samuel Morse (Ande et al. 2020), although

Kumar and Singh (2014) assumed that the term ICT started to be used around the late 1970s and early 1980s. From the 1990s, significant inventions like computers, personal computers, laptops, tablets, and smartphones emerged (Ande et al. 2020). Chandra et al. (2018) indicated that ICT development gets faster with intelligent mobile phones because information spreads quickly and easily. ICT became extremely popular at the beginning of the 21st century when computers and electronic devices usage became an essential part of people's business and personal lives (Söderström et al. 2012).

Technological inventions allowed faster ICT developments in many industries (Stratigea 2011). At the same time, scholars were suggesting new definitions of ICT to help the fast-developing concept. As a result, ICT started to be used in practical and academic life from the new wave of technological developments (Ande et al. 2020). However, the ICT term was difficult to define or explain for all uses in terms of its meaning. One of the early definitions was made by Blurton (1999), who defined ICT as 'a diverse set of technological tools and resources used to communicate and create, disseminate, store, and manage information.'

ICT is related to electronic technologies but cannot be explained just by the inventions of technologies. Michiels and Van Crowder (2001) have defined ICTs as 'a range of electronic technologies which when converged in new configurations are flexible, adaptable, enabling and capable of transforming organizations and redefining social relations.' Chapman and Slaymaker (2002) focused on using electronic device technology. They defined ICT as 'an expanding assembly of technologies that can be used to collect, store and share information between people using multiple devices and multiple media.' Chisenga (2006) indicated that ICTs embrace telecommunication technologies, digital technologies, and software applications simultaneously. ICTs include telephones, cable and satellite TV, radio, computer-mediated conferencing, video conferencing, computers, information networks, the Internet, intranets, and extranets.

ICT combines innovative technologies and many other aspects, as mentioned in the definitions. ICT is widely examined and used by many industries and academics (Ande et al. 2020; Law et al. 2019; Moreno and Tejada 2019). Therefore, the need arose to have a standard definition of the term ICT. In 2010, the International Organization for Standardization (ISO) published a worldwide ICT definition and standards for business and consumer applications. The International Organization for Standardization (ISO) (2010) proposed a standard definition as

> ICT includes the specification, design and development, integration and interoperability of systems, tools and applications dealing with the capture, representation, accessibility, processing, security, transfer, interchange, presentation, management, organization, storage and retrieval of information, and their related cultural, linguistic adaptability and societal aspects.

As Kimidi et al. (2018) stressed, ICT 'changed the scenario by breaking the access barriers and laid the path for the digital revolution where information storage, transfer, and retrieval are made very easy for information transfer.' ICT combines technologies that allow users to interact directly in the digital world (Rubtcova and Pavenkov 2019).

ICT developments started with the first invention of telecommunications and computer devices (Fourkas 2002). However, the real impact happened right after the Internet became widely available to the public (Packard 2020). Since the integration of ICTs with business applications, commercial operations have changed completely. The Internet has changed the way of doing business. The Internet created new business models, markets, and concepts, which reduced entrance barriers, start-up costs, and the cost of coordinating resources for new businesses (Chang et al., 2012; Allen 2015).

In the late 1990s, the World Wide Web (WWW), or the Internet, became a popular way of exchanging information through computer network connections. In 2000, Internet companies changed all traditional business models, and a new era started (Corr 2006). This beginning is also known as the 'Internet boom' because it has significantly impacted economies worldwide (Payne and O'Sullivan 2020). ICTs and the Internet have transformed many business transactions into digital or online platforms. ICT has changed the structure of a business and the way of delivering information (Hu and Yelland 2019); it has also had a significant role in changing the course of doing business. The Internet has also allowed a new form of business to be started up, known as e-business (Law et al. 2019), enabling customers to search for and buy products online using no intermediaries. It was the beginning of a digital transformation of traditional businesses (Novak and Schwabe 2009). ICT now plays the central role of exchanging information, buying, and selling products or services (Apulu and Latham 2011). Digital business has quickly adopted and altered communication and information exchange worldwide, expanding marketing and sales activities (Kokt and Koelane 2013).

ICT researchers have focused on teaching and learning (Naidoo 2020; Junaidi et al. 2020), entrepreneurship (Ismail and Idris 2006; Tang and Konde 2020), libraries (Mahanta 2020; Bello and Ezeri (2020), the economy (Amiri and Woodside 2017; Fosu 2019), tourism (Jaremen 2016; Dhaigude et al. 2016; Zaidan 2017; Spencer 2019; Adeola and Evans 2020), and online business (Gupta and Sharma 2012; Mundra and Rakesh 2014; Dharmawan and Hendrayati 2019; Szyjewski 2019; Kassem et al. 2019). Online business, the economy, and tourism were some of the most prominent early adopters of ICT.

The terms 'online business,' 'e-Business,' and 'e-Commerce' are used interchangeably in business literature (Gupta 2014; Correia 2019). However, all of them have separate concepts but very similar meanings. An online business can be described differently from the suppliers' and consumers' sides, respectively. Gupta and Sharma (2012) stated that online business enables millions of consumers to reach products or services anywhere in the world. Dharmawan and Hendrayati (2019) defined online business as 'the seller delivers the product they promise to the buyer.' Mundra and Rakesh (2014) described online business as 'the modern business methodology which uses direct marketing, selling, and services.' Gupta (2014) defined e-business or electronic business as 'the transformation of an organization's processes to deliver additional customer value through the application of technologies, philosophies and computing paradigms of the new economy.'

On the other hand, Correia (2019) defined e-commerce or electronic commerce as 'the purchase and sale of goods and services through an electronic network, especially the Internet.' E-commerce is more about the sale of all goods and services over the Internet. There are five different e-commerce types, namely: business-to-business (B2B), business-to-consumer (B2C), business-to-government (B2G), consumer-to-consumer (C2C), and mobile commerce (m-commerce) (Correia 2019). There is a specific difference between e-business and e-commerce. Gupta (2014) stressed that e-commerce uses ICT in B2B and B2C transactions, and e-business uses ICT to enhance business. Correia (2019) stated that the benefits of e-commerce are '24-hour availability, speed of access, wide availability of goods and services, easy accessibility and international reach.' The cost of starting a business has fallen because of the ability to start an online business through ICT (Kołodziej 2017). The economic benefits and ease of entry into the online business world have made the online business grow fast (Chou et al., 2014). Internet-based company numbers have increased markedly over the years with the growth of the online business. Table 7.1 shows the milestones of online business.

TABLE 7.1
Online Business Milestones

Date	Milestone
1969	CompuServe is founded
1979	Michael Aldrich invented the first online shopping system and coined the term 'e-commerce.' Aldrich connected a TV to a computer with a phone line. He created 'Teleshopping,' aka shopping from a distance
1980	The PC era begins (Desktop)
1981	Thomson Holidays UK started using Aldrich's 'Teleputer' as the first B2B shopping system
1982	The Boston Computer Exchange launched the first e-commerce platform
	Minitel was introduced nationwide in France by France Télécom and used for online ordering
1984	'Electronic Mall' was launched by CompuServe. Users could purchase items directly from 110 online merchants
	Gateshead SIS/Tesco became the first B2C shopping system
1985	Nissan UK sells cars and finance with credit checking to customers online from dealers' lots
1987	Swreg provides software and shareware for authors who sell their products online through an electronic Merchant account
1989	The e-commerce system Compumarket enables sellers to list items for sale and allows buyers to pay by credit card
	In May 1989, Sequoia Data Corp. introduced Compumarket, the first Internet-based system for e-commerce. Sellers and buyers could post items for sale, and buyers could search the database and make purchases with a credit card
1990	Tim Berners-Lee wrote the first web browser, the World Wide Web (WWW), using a next-generation computer
	The Web 1.0 era begins (WWW, basic HTML, e-mails)—information centered
	One hundred thirty websites are created (primarily read-only on the web)—14,161,570+ global users

(continued)

TABLE 7.1 (Continued)
Online Business Milestones

Date	Milestone
1991	The National Science Foundation allows the Internet to be used for commercial purposes
1991	The electronic AppWrapper, or the first app store, appears
1992	In Cleveland, Book Stacks Unlimited opens a commercial sales website (www.Books.Com) selling books online with credit card processing in the USA
	Terry Brownell launches the first fully graphical, iconic navigated bulletin board system for online shopping, using RoboBOARD/FX
1993	Paget Press releases Edition no. 3 of the first app store, the electronic Appwrapper
1994	The first official online transaction. One man sells a CD of Sting's *Ten Summoner's Tales* in what will become the world's first secure online purchase through the NetMarket retail and e-commerce platform
	Netscape released the Navigator browser in October under the code name Mozilla. Netscape 1.0 was introduced in late 1994 with SSL encryption that made transactions secure
	The Ipswitch Email server becomes the first software available online for sale and immediate download via a partnership between Ipswitch Inc. and Open-market
	Joe McCambley ran the first-ever online banner ad. It went live on HotWired.com and promoted seven art museums
	Pizza Hut offers online ordering on its web page
1995	Amazon.com launched as a bookstore
	Amazon sold its first item—a science textbook
	ebay.com launches as AuctionWeb, an auction site (the sharing economy starts); eBay sold its first item—a broken laser pointer
	The US National Science Foundation lifts its former strict prohibition of commercial enterprise on the Internet
	Thursday April 27, 1995, the purchase of a book by Paul Stanfield, the product manager for CompuServe UK, from WH Smith's shop within CompuServe's UK shopping center, is the UK's first national online shopping service secure transaction. At launch, the shopping service featured WH Smith, Tesco, Virgin/Our Price, Great Universal Stores/GUS, Interflora, Dixons Retail, Past Times, PC World (retailer), and Innovations
1996	The IndiaMART B2B marketplace was established in India
	The Ecplaza B2B Marketplace was established in Korea
	Excalibur BBS with replicated 'storefronts' was an early implementation of electronic commerce started by a group of cyber shops in Australia and copied to global partner sites
1997	Netflix.com (video on demand) was launched
	Dell was the first company to reach $1 million in online sales
1998	Paypal.com (online payment system) was launched
	Google was launched
	USPS launched stamps. Electronic postal stamps can be purchased and downloaded for printing from the web
1999	Zappo's, the first online-only shop, opens
	The Alibaba Group was established in China (alibaba.com)

TABLE 7.1 (Continued)
Online Business Milestones

Date	Milestone
	Business.Com was sold for US $7.5 Million to E-companies, purchased in 1997 for $149,000
	The peer-to-peer file-sharing software Napster launches
	ATG Stores launches, selling decorative items for the home online
2000	Global e-commerce transactions surpass $150 billion
	Complete Idiot's Guide To E-Commerce is released on Amazon
	The Web 2.0 era begins (social web, informative, interactive)—people-centric)
	17,087,182 websites now operate (the widely read-only web)—there are 413,425,190+ global users
2001	Amazon.com launched its first mobile commerce site
	Wikipedia launches
2002	Niche retail companies Wayfair And Net shops are founded, with the concept of selling products through several targeted domains, rather than a central portal
	eBay Acquires Paypal For $1.5 Billion
	LinkedIn launches
2003	The Bossgoo B2B Marketplace was established in China
	Skype launches
2004	Dhgate.Com, China's first online B2B transaction platform, is established, forcing other B2B sites to move away from the 'Yellow Pages' model
	Facebook was launched for college students
2005	Etsy launches as an online marketplace for handcrafted and vintage goods
	Yuval Tal founds Payoneer—a secure online payment distribution solution
2006	The Shopify API platform launches (Shopify enables the business to create an online shopfront with ease)
	Google acquires YouTube
	iTunes became the first digital musical retailer
	Twitter launches
2007	R.H. Donnelley acquires Business.Com for $345 Million
2008	The Magento e-commerce platform launches (launched as an online e-commerce storefront builder)
	Groupon is launched
2009	The Bigcommerce storefront platform launches
	Total e-commerce sales amounted to $143.4 billion
	Amazon.Com acquires Zappos.Com for $928 Million
	Retail Convergence, the operator of private sale website RueLaLa.com, was acquired by GSI Commerce for $180 million, plus up to $170 million in earn-out payments, based on performance through 2012
2010	Instagram is launched
	Pinterest (a photo-sharing website) launches
	Web 3.0 era begins (semantic web, personalized web)—machine centered
	1,775,801,725 websites now operate (the widely read-only web)—there are now 4.3 billion+ global users
2011	Quidsi.com, the parent company of Diapers.com, was acquired by Amazon.com for $500 million in cash plus $45 million in debt and other obligations

(continued)

TABLE 7.1 (Continued)
Online Business Milestones

Date	Milestone
	GSI Commerce, a company specializing in creating, developing, and running online shopping sites for brick and mortar businesses, was acquired by eBay for $2.4 billion
	Snapchat launches
	Internet users reached 2 billion in a year
2012	Instacart.com launches (food ordering and delivery)
	Zalora Group was founded and started operations in and around Asia
	Facebook acquires Instagram for $1 billion in cash and stock
2013	Vine, a widely popular video-sharing and social media service, launches shortly after being acquired by Twitter for $30 million
2014	Apple Pay (mobile app payment system) was launched
	US e-commerce and online retail sales reach $294 billion
	Overstock.com processes over $1 million in bitcoin sales
2015	Amazon's sales amount to more than half of all e-commerce growth
	Pinterest launches (buyable pins)
2017	Amazon acquires Wholefoods
	TikTok, a short video sharing and social media service, launches
	Cyber Monday sales exceed $6.5 billion, of which $2 billion represent mobile sales
2018	Walmart acquires Flipkart
	Global retail e-commerce sales reach $2.8 trillion
2020	Web 4.0 era begins (intelligent web, the WebOS, intelligent personal agents, distributed search, decentralized, private, and secure) agent-centered
2021	Retail e-commerce sales worldwide will probably surpass $4.8 trillion

Sources: Author adapted from Choudhury (2014), Maday (2020), Meerkerk (2020).

After technological developments enabled personal computers and the Internet to be available to the broader public, personal Computers (PCs) and the Internet became part of people's daily and business lives (Fourkas 2002). After the Internet provided a new market arena for business, many Internet-based companies were established between 1990 and 2000. The first Internet-based businesses were books.com (1992), Amazon (1994), eBay (1995), Netflix (1997), Paypal (1998), Alibaba (1999), and Google (1998) (Sandulli et al. 2014).

One of the first Internet companies, 'Amazon,' is the world's most valuable company, worth $220B (Visualcapitalist 2020). E-commerce has changed traditional business and transactions when buying and selling products. eBay and Amazon are pioneers of e-commerce worldwide (Correia 2019). E-commerce has enabled international transactions to be made more easily than before. This is reflected in the customer numbers as well as the revenue of firms. There are 4.57 billion worldwide Internet users; the most extensive number of Internet users is in China, with 854 million in 2019 (Statista 2020). The Emarketer global e-commerce 2019 report prepared by Lipsman (2019) estimated the critical numbers of e-commerce by saying

> Global e-commerce will rise by 20.7% in 2019, to $3.535 trillion. Despite its strong growth rate, 2019 will experience a decline from the previous two years, when e-commerce grew 28.0% in 2017 and 22.9% in 2018. By 2021, we expect that global e-commerce will approach $5 trillion, though growth rates will fall below the 20% threshold beginning in 2020.

The top countries for e-commerce sales in 2019 were China, the US, the UK, Japan, South Korea, Germany, France, Canada, India, and Russia (Lipsman 2019).

At the beginning of 2020, the COVID-19 pandemic hit the world's business and personal life badly, affecting the global economy (Gössling et al. 2020). Web 4.0 and Industry 4.0 strived to solve many problems, like fighting COVID-19 (Javaid et al. 2020) and facilitating distance learning (Nadeak 2020). People could not travel during the pandemic restrictions. Wen et al. (2020) stated that many people now work from home, engage in distance learning, do transactions with online banking, and order goods and services online. In March 2020, e-commerce sales increased by 97% in home products and furnishings, 136% in DIY products, 163% in garden essentials, 26.6% in electronics, while decreases were reported of –60% in ticketing sales, –44% in travel bookings, and –8.9% in online dating (Helpnetsecurity 2020). During the pandemic lockdown, people wanted to connect and talk to each other. The Zoom video communication e-commerce company increased its revenue by 78% in quarterly sales growth (Tilley 2020).

This can be called a big jump in digital activity because of the lockdown in many countries, with many travel restrictions. As a result, people indulge in online grocery shopping plus buying other goods and services online (Kim 2020). In addition, they spend more time on social media, video games, and e-sport sites, which delivers an incredible opportunity for digital advertisers (Kemp, 2020). The Hotsuits (2020) report indicates that online and digital activities have increased by 57% in terms of watching shows and films on streaming services; 47% spend longer using social media; 46% spend time on communication services such as Messenger; 39% listen more to music streaming services; 36% spend more time on mobile apps; 35% spend more time playing computer or video games; 15% create and upload videos, and 14% listen to more podcasts. In the month that the pandemic began, Internet user numbers reached 4.57 billion, which is 59% of the total global population (Hotsuits 2020).

The most used social platforms are Facebook, YouTube, WhatsApp, FB Messenger, Instagram, TikTok, Snapchat, Twitter, and Pinterest (Hotsuits 2020). Global e-commerce activity increased by 81% regarding searching and 74% in buying (Hotsuits 2020). Unfortunately, the pandemic period has negatively affected some areas, like sharing economy activities. Gerwe (2020) pinpoints that 'the coronavirus pandemic turned each sharing economy strengths into a weakness.' The sharing economy started in 1995 when eBay launched the world's first auction website (Tura and Vaskelainen 2018). The global sharing economy reached $520 billion in 2018 (Media OutReach 2019). The following section will feature the sharing economy and the digital sharing economy and tourism transformation.

7.3 THE DIGITAL SHARING ECONOMY AND TOURISM

The sharing economy, a new economic model, which is called the sharing economy, has changed the way to share goods and services (Martin et al. 2015; Cheng 2016; Graham and Anwar 2018; Mallinson et al. 2020; Gerwe 2020). Some products are easy to share, and some of them are not so easy to share. For example, holiday (vacation) homes, lawnmowers, canoes, cars, and medical equipment are among the easiest things to share (Keohane and Shubber 2016).

The most difficult to share category includes food processors, headphones, and iPads (Keohane and Shubber 2016). Wang and Nicolau (2017), Davlembayeva et al. (2019), Sdino and Magoni (2017), and many other scholars have agreed that the sharing economy is 'a socioeconomic system.' This socioeconomic system includes 'peer-to-peer-based activity' (Hamari et al. 2016), 'using technology to reach suppliers without a middleman' (Heylighen 2017; Davlembayeva et al. 2019), 'the pooling of human and physical resources' (Sdino and Magoni 2017), 'buying and selling' (Ganapati and Reddick 2018) and 'online platforms' (Balogh 2018; Turi et al. 2017; Davlembayeva et al. 2019; Andreoni 2020). One of the unique sides of the sharing economy is enabling selling and buying activity among strangers, nationally or internationally (Schor and Fitzmaurice 2015). Allen (2015) explains that the sharing economy is 'a suite of emerging software platforms acting as an intermediary between private buyers and private sellers, allowing them to share their existing resources and a market catalyzed by disruptive technologies.' Similarly, Hamari et al. (2016) define the sharing economy as 'the peer-to-peer-based activity of obtaining, giving, or sharing the access to goods and services through community-based online services.'

Ecosystems often differ significantly between countries due to differences in market competition. In the ecosystem of the sharing economy business model, companies are not separate entities. Instead, business dynamics require various supply chains influenced by cross-industry impacts, typically linked to technological advances and innovation. Sharing economy platforms interact with suppliers, asset providers, regulators, competitors, and the final consumer. Shared economy businesses have been able to bring users and suppliers together in an open and accessible marketplace, boosting innovation by providing a compelling option to customers or even replacing established players.

It is essential to mention that ICT is the source of enabling sharing through online platforms (Pouri and Hilty 2018). All definitions of the sharing economy have in common that sharing through online media with strangers, either nationally or internationally, is possible without an intermediary. Pouri and Hilty (2018) suggested that technology (ICT) enables connectivity, and connectivity enables formalized sharing practices. There are three key actors in the sharing economy: owners, seekers, and platforms (Ritter and Schanz 2019). Owners and seekers access products or services via the platform. The venue is a market that provides a link between owners and seekers, with a renting fee. The market segments in the sharing economy include four ideal-type market segments of the sharing economy (singular transaction models, subscription-based models, commission-based platforms, and unlimited platforms) (Ritter and Schanz 2019).

The sharing economy and tourism have a long history in the literature (Law et al. 2014; Hossain 2020). All tourism facilities go under the commission-based platform

(Ritter and Schanz 2019). The digital revolution has changed tourism and opened more room for sharing economy platforms to expand (Zsarnoczky 2018; Pencarelli 2020). In tourism, different stages of the sharing economy impact and create a new way of delivering services to tourists. These are pre-trip (booking), journey, destination, and post-trip (Rashideh 2020). Pre-trip includes accommodation, traditional house swaps between two individuals, house sitting, work in exchange for accommodation, hotel booking resale platforms between individuals, review platforms, and exchange of information between users.

One of the famous and pioneer pre-trip (booking) sharing platforms is AirBnB, which is now more significant than the world-renowned giant hotel chains (Sainaghi et al., 2020; Kilhoffer, 2020; Dogru et al. 2020). Uber is an excellent example of a journey stage of a sharing economy (Geissinger et al. 2020). 'GearCommons.com' is an example of peer-to-peer outdoor gear rental at the destination (Chasin et al., 2018). Airbnb does not own any properties or rooms, but the digital sharing platform has been valued at $31 billion because of its business model of selling other people's properties or rooms (Blal et al., 2018). Airbnb offers flexible, easy access, different choices, and unstandardized accommodation (Forgacs and Dimanche 2016). Priporas et al. (2017) found that 'Airbnb guests have meager expectations of the amenities and services available at the lodgings.' Airbnb sells other people's rooms for a fee, while couchsurfing.org offers rooms for free (Decrop et al. 2018; O'Regan and Choe 2019; Juric et al. 2021).

Many tourism-centered sharing Internet-based companies start up every year at the journey, destination, and post-trip stages. The accommodation, transportation, dining, and travel sectors share Internet-based companies that offer various services to tourists internationally (Tussyadiah and Sigala 2018). Airbnb, Couchsurfing, Bookabach, and Homeaway are good examples of sharing accommodation platforms (OECD 2016). Blablacar, Uber, Drivy, and Lyft are good examples of the transport sector (OECD 2016). Eatwith, VizEat, and Feastly are good examples of the dining sector (OECD 2016). VoomaGo, Vayable, Withlocals, and tours by locals.com are good examples of travel services sites (OECD 2016). Buhalis et al. (2020) found, however, that the sharing economy has grown fast and uncontrollably, which creates a dark side to the sharing economy, delivering disruption to community lives and displacements. They also mentioned that dishonesty makes problems among users and locals, a phenomenon that has been published on online review platforms. This is happening in the last two stages of the sharing economy of the tourism customer journey, namely, destination and post-trip media. Dedeoglu et al. (2020) suggested that practitioners encourage old customers to share experiences at the post-trip stage to increase brand awareness, reliability, and trust. Therefore, another issue has acquired importance in creating healthy sharing systems for customers and locals.

7.4 DECENTRALIZED SHARING ECONOMY WITH BLOCKCHAIN TECHNOLOGY

Tourism has continued to evolve with new technologies, and these changes have continued rapidly. Blockchain technology, one of these new technologies, has found usage areas in tourism and has started to produce solutions to many problems that have not been solved for years. While providing the Internet connection, the blockchain has enabled secure transactions. The tourism and travel industry will derive many benefits by using blockchain technology. It will improve decentralization, transparency, process times, data security, low distribution cost, and lower transaction fees for tourism sharing platforms. Kundu (2019) believed that blockchain technology represents trust and that it is the best solution for implementing a smart city as fully digital. Rahman et al. (2019) also suggested that blockchain technology can support security and privacy with smart contracts to use the sharing economy in smart cities.

In some products and services, technology facilitates trust (Hawlitschek et al. 2016; Harrison and Hair 2017), but unique services like tourism require a bit more care to earn tourists' trust. E-commerce and online payment systems create a trustful environment with a central control mechanism like a bank (Liu et al., 2011). Trust is more accessible to lose in tourism than any other business, especially after adverse events or bad reviews (Eitzinger and Wiedemann 2008; Schuckert et al. 2015; Erceg et al. 2020). Will blockchain technology with decentralized systems and smart contracts change the sharing economy models in tourism and other sectors? The following section will cover the discussion of blockchain technology with smart contracts' impact on the sharing economy.

Tourism sharing platforms offer goods and services exchanges with a stranger, especially within international destinations. Schor and Fitzmaurice (2015) argued that this increases the issue of trust and reputation. Tourists trusted tour operators and travel agencies as the middlemen for their holiday components at the origin-destination (Novak and Schwabe 2009). Still, e-commerce via the Internet has changed the buying behavior, with trust between tourists and suppliers now seen in a good way (Albayrak et al. 2020; Tran and Strutton 2020). Tourists can reach the tourism supplier directly at a lower price. There are more alternatives available on online platforms (Cesarani and Nechita 2017). However, trust/distrust is an issue in using tourism-related sharing platforms or buying travel-related services over the Internet (Cheng et al. 2019; Sthapit and Björk 2019; Erceg et al. 2020).

The sharing economy will enter a new era as blockchain and decentralized markets arise. One of the essential characteristics of decentralization is the elimination of intermediaries such as centralized controlled platforms. Service fees can be considerably lowered in a decentralized sharing network. For example, Uber and Airbnb are sharing economy platforms but not decentralized. This type of platform avoids actual peer-to-peer connections by restricting communications, removing intermediaries provides a real peer-to-peer link. A peer-to-peer blockchain link would allow users to connect and decide the value and terms of the share transaction between themselves. No service fees would be incurred if intelligent contracts were used to carry out the agreement's provisions automatically.

There are flaws in the centralized sharing economy model. It charges high fees for using the network, putting individual users at a disadvantage while benefiting the company—the differences between the traditional centralized sharing economy model and decentralized sharing economy model. Thellmann (2018) proposed a new model based on blockchain technology with Ethereum, DApp, and IPFs systems. The centralized design of the sites means that consumers are not involved in any stage of the transaction process. Moreover, platforms may gain access to private data without the knowledge of their customers. These are the downside of the centralized sharing economy platform business. The decentralized sharing economy model will provide a real peer-to-peer experience. The decentralized model makes it convenient and straightforward for businesses to create and manage asset and service listings. The decentralized platform allows buyers and sellers to interact, search listings, and start businesses.

Trust used to be provided by middlemen and third parties. A new demand is to share things peer to peer without a mediator. In this way, many benefits come from cutting service costs, commission, extra costs, and hassle to reach the final product. Blockchain is helping to build trust between peers (Erceg et al. 2020). Blockchain also creates a new digital-based business world controlled by people with transparency and protection of their sharing experience with a profit or without profit.

7.5 CONCLUSION

Blockchain technology is new and developing quickly. On the other hand, the sharing economy is growing day by day. The sharing economy has reached the stage of implementing smart contracts without a third party. However, there is little research on combining these two fields to explain how a decentralized sharing economy organization will work in tourism. More research needs to cover this area in the future. This study has combined two subject disciplines into one and has examined future solutions. First, blockchain with smart contracts will change the sharing economy structure, especially in tourism. Blockchain technology and smart contracts will be future solutions for digital sharing economy problems for many reasons. First, smart contracts enable automated processes in a decentralized organization. Second, the future of sharing economy organizations must consider the security of users' data, trust-free sharing services, authorization, and confidentiality. Yuan and Wang (2018) suggested that the 'decentralized sharing economy blockchain can serve as a key enabling technology for the next generation of the sharing economy.' Blockchain technology is known as a trust-free technology. Therefore, the sharing economy 2.0 and 3.0 will depend on blockchain technology and developments (Hawlitschek et al. 2018). Third, the e-tourism system has made the already very complex traditional system even more difficult. While the number of intermediary businesses was a problem, tourism and travel companies that have opened on the Internet have increased the number of intermediaries with online travel agencies (OTAs). The tourist must now filter more information and determine the holiday they want, and they also must feel safe. At this point, blockchain technology will have an important place in solving the problems of this complex and multi-mediated system of tourism (Pilkington 2017). One of the main problems experienced by the tourism industry is that the product cannot be transferred to another account, so there is an insufficient/faulty baggage tracking system (Rashideh 2020). In addition, he stated that there are problems in identity checking processes and security gaps in payments and double bookings.

On the other hand, blockchain technology has many benefits in tourism, like visibility of information, reducing service costs, and improving trade quality (Erceg et al. 2020). Blockchain tourism is a new way of storing databases for travel companies and tourists. Many new blockchain-based tourism projects like Winding Tree, ShoCard and SITA, Trippki, Cool Cousin, Webjet, Sandblock, Accenture, and Travel Chain have started establishing blockchain's position in offering solutions for the tourism and travel industry (Coita and Ban 2020). The world's largest tourism and travel company, TUI, is the world's first tourism company to integrate blockchain technology into the travel industry (Onder and Treiblmaier 2018). TUI is currently implementing its in-house blockchain technology, called Bed Swap (Vinod 2020). The tourism and travel industry will see more blockchain-based applications in the future. Today, there are certain areas that blockchain technology has adopted in tourism.

However, technology will increase day by day. Blockchain technology can be used to secure payment, protect customer identification, manage baggage, have a customer rewards system, control overbooking, have faster payment systems, and lower transaction fees. Trust is the main issue between tourists, sharing economy platforms, and suppliers. Blockchain technology may solve some problems in the travel and tourism industry. However, experts in blockchain technology must work closely with tourism experts to create the best solutions needed by the industry. Smart contracts may be the most powerful part of using blockchain that may influence customer and supplier relations. However, tourism professionals must trust blockchain technology before adopting anything. As a supplier, they must put their faith in this technology and be open to opportunities like enhancing security and transparency for their customers. Therefore, they need to work closely with blockchain experts. Tourism has had difficulty adopting emerging technologies, so it may take more time to adopt blockchain because it is disruptive.

Blockchain technology is a disruptive technology in travel and tourism. It may influence loyalty schemes, contracting, protecting identity, secure payment, and revenue management. There are many advantages to using blockchain technology in travel and tourism. However, the industry is at the early stage of using and adopting blockchain technology in all areas. Blockchain will change travel and tourism because of the trust, transparency, security, and a new way of storing data for future travelers.

REFERENCES

Adeola, Ogechi, and Olaniyi Evans. 2020. "ICT, infrastructure, and tourism development in Africa." *Tourism Economics* 26, no. 1: 97–114.

Albayrak, Tahir, Sezer Karasakal, Özge Kocabulut, and Aslıhan Dursun. 2020. "Customer loyalty towards travel agency websites: The role of trust and hedonic value." *Journal of Quality Assurance in Hospitality & Tourism* 21, no. 1: 50–77.

Allen, Darcy. 2015. "The sharing economy." Institute of public affairs review: A quarterly review of politics and public affairs, *The Sharing Economy* 67, no. 3: 24–27.

Amiri, Shahram, and Joseph M. Woodside. 2017. "Emerging markets: The impact of ICT on the economy and society." *Digital Policy, Regulation and Governance* 19, no. 5: 383–396.

Ande, Ruth, Bamidele Adebisi, Mohammad Hammoudeh, and Jibran Saleem. 2020. "Internet of Things: Evolution and technologies from a security perspective." *Sustainable Cities and Society* 54: 101728.

Andreoni, Valeria. 2020. "The trap of success: A paradox of scale for sharing economy and degrowth." *Sustainability* 12, no. 8: 3153.

Apulu, Idisemi, and Ann Latham. 2011. "Drivers for information and communication technology adoption: A case study of Nigerian small and medium sized enterprises." *International Journal of Business and Management* 6, no. 5: 51.

Balogh, Ádám. 2018. "Sharing economy as a new business model or just a phenomenon?." *Köz-gazdaság-Review of Economic Theory and Policy* 13, no. 3: 111–123.

Bello, Samuel Akande and Chioma Nnalu Ezeri. 2020. "Globalisation of library and information services: An assessment of the level of ICT deployment in academic libraries in Oyo State, Nigeria." *Library Philosophy and Practice* 3881: 1–19.

Blal, Inès, Manisha Singal, and Jonathan Templin. 2018. "Airbnb's effect on hotel sales growth." *International Journal of Hospitality Management* 73: 85–92.

Blurton, Craig. 1999. "New directions of ICT-Use in education". www.unesco.org/education/educprog/lwf/dl/edict.pdf.

Buhalis, Dimitrios, Luisa Andreu, and Juergen Gnoth. 2020. "The dark side of the sharing economy: Balancing value co-creation and value co-destruction." *Psychology & Marketing* 37, no. 5: 689–704.

Cesarani, Maurizio, and Florin Nechita. 2017. "Tourism and the sharing economy. An evidence from Airbnb usage in Italy and Romania." *Symphonya. Emerging Issues in Management* 3: 32–47.

Chandra, Natalia, Raymond S. Chin, Eric Cardova, and Meidica D. Pratiwi. 2018. "Implementation of gyroscope sensor to presentation application on Android smartphone." In 2018 Indonesian Association for Pattern Recognition International Conference (INAPR), pp. 197–201. IEEE.

Chang, Hsin H., Chin-Ho Lee, and Chi-Yuan Lai. 2012. "E-Service quality and relationship quality on dealer satisfaction: Channel power as a moderator." *Total Quality Management & Business Excellence* 23, no. 7–8: 855–873.

Chang, Wei-Lun, and Jia-Yin Wang. 2018. "Mine is yours? Using sentiment analysis to explore the degree of risk in the sharing economy." *Electronic Commerce Research and Applications* 28: 141–158.

Chapman, Robert, and Tom Slaymaker. 2002. "ICTs and rural development: Review of the literature, current interventions and opportunities for action." (Working Paper 192). www.odi.org/sites/odi.org.uk/files/odi-assets/publications-opinion-files/2670.pdf.

Chasin, Friedrich, Moritz von Hoffen, Marcus Cramer, and Martin Matzner. 2018. "Peer-to-peer sharing and collaborative consumption platforms: A taxonomy and a reproducible analysis." *Information Systems and e-Business Management* 16, no. 2: 293–325.

Cheng, Mingming. 2016. "Sharing economy: A review and agenda for future research." *International Journal of Hospitality Management* 57: 60–70.

Cheng, Xusen, Shixuan Fu, Jianshan Sun, Anil Bilgihan, and Fevzi Okumus. 2019. "An investigation on online reviews in sharing economy driven hospitality platforms: A viewpoint of trust." *Tourism Management* 71: 366–377.

Chisenga, Justin. 2006. "Information and communication technologies: Opportunities and challenges for national and university libraries in Eastern, Central and Southern Africa., 2006." In Standing Conference of African National and University Libraries of Eastern, Central and Southern Africa, Dar es Salaam (Tanzania), 9–10 July 2006.

Chou, Chien-Hsiang, Yu-Yin Wang, Yi-Shun Wang, and Tzung-I. Tang. 2014. "Exploring the determinants of repurchase behavior in C2B e-commerce." *International Journal of e-Education, e-Business, e-Management and e-Learning* 4, no. 4: 271.

Choudhury, Nupur. 2014. "World wide web and its journey from web 1.0 to web 4.0." *International Journal of Computer Science and Information Technologies* 5, no. 6: 8096–8100.

Coita, Dorin C., and Olimpia Ban. 2020. "Revolutionizing marketing in tourism industry through blockchain technology." In Strategic Innovative Marketing and Tourism, pp. 789–797. Springer, Cham.

Corr, Thomas A. 2006. "Boom, bust, boom: Internet company valuations-from Netscape to Google." *Financier* 13, no. 14: 66–84.

Correia, Arnaldo A. 2019. "Challenges and strategies for entry into the sports nutrition market in Portugal: A case study." PhD Diss. https://repositorio.iscte-iul.pt/bitstream/10071/19974/1/Master_Arnaldo_Ribeiro_Correia.pdf.

Davlembayeva, Dinara, Savvas Papagiannidis, and Eleftherios Alamanos. 2019. "Mapping the economics, social and technological attributes of the sharing economy." *Information Technology & People* 33, no. 3: 841–872.

Decrop, Alain, Giacomo D. Chiappa, Jérôme Mallargé, and Pietro Zidda. 2018. "Couchsurfing has made me a better person and the world a better place": The transformative power of collaborative tourism experiences." *Journal of Travel & Tourism Marketing* 35, no. 1: 57–72.

Dedeoglu, Bekir B., Babak Taheri, Fevzi Okumus, and Martin Gannon. 2020 "Understanding the importance that consumers attach to social media sharing (ISMS): Scale development and validation." *Tourism Management* 76: 103954.

Dhaigude, Amol S., Rohit Kapoor, and Sudhir Ambekar. 2016. "A conceptual model for adoption of information communication technology in the travel and tourism industry." *Tourism Recreation Research* 41, no. 1: 49–59.

Dharmawan, Fahmi, and Heni Hendrayati. 2019. "Customer-based brand equity in digital age: A conceptual approach." *KnE Social Sciences* 3, no. 13: 986–1007.

Dogru, Tarik, Makarand Mody, Nathan Line, Courtney Suess, Lydia Hanks, and Mark Bonn. 2020. "Investigating the whole picture: Comparing the effects of Airbnb supply and hotel supply on hotel performance across the United States." *Tourism Management* 79: 104094.

Eitzinger, Claudia, and Peter M. Wiedemann. 2008. "Trust in the safety of tourist destinations: Hard to gain, easy to lose? New insights on the asymmetry principle." *Risk Analysis: An International Journal* 28, no. 4: 843–853.

Erceg, Aleksandar, Jovanka Damoska Sekuloska, and Ivan Kelić. 2020. "Blockchain in the tourism industry—A review of the situation in Croatia and Macedonia." *Informatics*, 7, no. 1: 1–16.

Fodor, Mónika, and Katalin Jaeckel. 2018. "What does it take to have a successful career through the eyes of generation Z-based on the results of a primary qualitative research." *International Journal on Lifelong Education and Leadership* 4, no. 1: 1–7.

Forgacs, Gabor, and Frederic Dimanche. 2016. "Revenue challenges for hotels in the sharing economy: Facing the Airbnb menace." *Journal of Revenue and Pricing Management* 15, no. 6: 509–515.

Fosu, Agyei. 2019. "The use of ICT by SMMEs in a digital economy: A case study in Buffalo City Metropolitan in South Africa." In InSITE 2019: Informing Science+ IT Education Conferences: Jerusalem, pp. 521–522.

Fourkas, Vassilys. 2002. "Cyber-space: Toward an integrated approach." *Revista Teknokultura* 2, no. 15: 3–11.

Ganapati, Sukumar, and Christopher G. Reddick. 2018. "Prospects and challenges of sharing economy for the public sector." *Government Information Quarterly* 35, no. 1: 77–87.

Geissinger, Andrea, Christofer Laurell, and Christian Sandström. 2020. "Digital Disruption beyond Uber and Airbnb—Tracking the long tail of the sharing economy." *Technological Forecasting and Social Change* 155: 119323.

Gerwe, Oksana. 2020. "Is the sharing economy over?." *EIX.org* https://eiexchange.com/content/is-the-sharing-economy-over.

Gössling, Stefan, Daniel Scott, and Colin Michael Hall.2020. "Pandemics, tourism and global change: a rapid assessment of COVID-19." *Journal of Sustainable Tourism* 29, no. 1: 1–20.

Graham, Mark, and Mohammad A. Anwar. 2018. "Two models for a fairer sharing economy." Davidson, N. Finck, M. and Infranca, J.(eds), The Cambridge Handbook of the Law of the Sharing Economy, Cambridge University Press, Cambridge: 328–340.

Gupta, Anjali. 2014. "E-Commerce: Role of E-Commerce in today's business." *International Journal of Computing and Corporate Research* 4, no. 1: 1–8.

Gupta, Pooja, and Manisha Sharma. 2012. "Ecommerce applications and flavors: Customers and business companion." *Asian Journal of Research in Business Economics and Management* 2, no. 3: 81–101.

Hamari, Juho, Mimmi Sjöklint, and Antti Ukkonen. 2016. "The sharing economy: Why people participate in collaborative consumption." *Journal of the Association for Information Science and Technology* 67, no. 9: 2047–2059.

Hamid, Zuliah A., Shazali Johari, and Puvaneswaran Kunasekaran. 2020. "Exploring Social media's influence on sustainable indigenous tourism." *International Journal of Psychosocial Rehabilitation* 24, no. 2: 1084–1091.

Harrison, Dana E., and Joseph F. Hair. 2017. "The use of technology in direct-selling marketing channels: Digital avenues for dynamic growth." *Journal of Marketing Channels* 24, no. 1–2: 39–50.

Hawlitschek, Florian, Benedikt Notheisen, and Timm Teubner. 2018. "The limits of trust-free systems: A literature review on blockchain technology and trust in the sharing economy." *Electronic Commerce Research and Applications* 29: 50–63.

Hawlitschek, Florian, Timm Teubner, and Christof Weinhardt. 2016. "Trust in the sharing economy." *Die Unternehmung* 70, no. 1: 26–44.

Helpnetsecurity. 2020. Pandemic driving global e-commerce growth, but fraud is on the increase too, www.helpnetsecurity.com/2020/04/09/e-commerce-increased-fraud/

Heylighen, Francis. 2017. "Towards an intelligent network for matching offer and demand: From the sharing economy to the global brain." *Technological Forecasting and Social Change* 114: 74–85.

Hossain, Mokter. 2020. "Sharing economy: A comprehensive literature review." *International Journal of Hospitality Management* 87, no. 102470: 1–11.

Hotsuits. 2020. Digital in 2020 report. https://wearesocial.com/digital-2020.

Hu, Xinyun, and Nicola Yelland. 2019. "Changing learning ecologies in early childhood teacher education: From technology to stem learning." *Beijing International Review of Education* 1, no. 2–3: 488–506.

International Organization for Standardization. 2010. ISO/IEC JTC 1 long term business plan. ISO/IEC JTC 1 N 10013, www.iso.org/files/live/sites/isoorg/files/archive/pdf/en/jtc_1_long_term_business_plan.pdf.

Ismail, Rahmah, and Idris N. A. Haji. 2006. "The impact of information and communication technology utilisation on firm performance: A case study of women entrepreneurs." *Malaysian Management Journal* 10, 1, no. 2: 19–32.

Jaremen, Daria E. 2016. "Advantages from ICT usage in hotel industry." *Czech Journal of Social Sciences Business and Economics* 5, no. 3: 6–18.

Javaid, Mohd, Abid Haleem, Raju Vaishya, Shashi Bahl, Rajiv Suman, and Abhishek Vaish. 2020. "Industry 4.0 technologies and their applications in fighting COVID-19 pandemic." *Diabetes & Metabolic Syndrome: Clinical Research & Reviews* 14, no. 4: 419–422.

Junaidi Junaidi, Budianto Hamuddin, Wendy Simangunsong, Fathu Rahman, Tatum Derin. 2020. "ICT usage in teaching English in Pekanbaru: Exploring junior high school teachers' problems." *International Journal of Advanced Science and Technology* 29, no. 3: 5052–5063.

Juric, Jana, Jörg Lindenmeier, and Christian Arnold. 2021. "Do emotional solidarity factors mediate the effect of personality traits on the inclination to use nonmonetary peer-to-peer accommodation networks?" *Journal of Travel Research* 60, no. 1: 47–64.

Kassem, Rassel, Mian Ajmal, Angappa Gunasekaran, and Petri Helo. 2019. "Assessing the impact of organizational culture on achieving business excellence with a moderating role of ICT: An SEM approach." *Benchmarking: An International Journal* 26, no. 1: 117–146.

Kemp, Simon. 2020. Digital 2020: April Global Statshot, https://datareportal.com/reports/digital-2020-april-global-statshot.

Keohane, David and Shubber, Keohane. 2016. We thought the sharing economy was dead. https://ftalphaville.ft.com/2016/06/09/2165717/we-thought-the-sharing-economy-was-dead/.

Kilhoffer, Zachary. 2020. "Platform work and participation: Disentangling the rhetoric." In *Using New Media for Citizen Engagement and Participation*, edited by Adria Marco, 1–15. Hershey, PA, USA: IGI Global.

Kim, Rae Y. 2020. "The impact of COVID-19 on consumers: Preparing for digital sales." *IEEE Engineering Management Review* 48, no. 3: 212–218.

Kimidi, Siva Shankar, Ch Mallikarjuna, and Saket Asthana. 2018. "Research archive of Indian Institute of Technology, Hyderabad (RAIITH)." *Informatics Studies* 5, no. 1: 52–60.

Kokt, Deseré, and Thakane Koelane. 2013. "Reflecting on Information and Communication Technology (ICT) in marketing from a marketers and student perspective." *African Journal of Business Management* 7, no. 31: 3098–3108.

Kołodziej, Monika. 2017. "Virtual reality as the indicator of the modern banking." *Nauki o Finansach* 2, no. 31: 44–51.

Kumar, Arun, and Priyadarshani Singh. 2014. "Transfiguration of multiple careers: ICT as mutant." *Academic Research International*, 5, no. 4: 213–218.

Kundu, Debasish. 2019. "Blockchain and trust in a smart city." *Environment and Urbanization ASIA* 10, no. 1: 31–43.

Law, Rob, Dimitrios Buhalis, and Cihan Cobanoglu. 2014. "Progress on information and communication technologies in hospitality and tourism." *International Journal of Contemporary Hospitality Management* 26, no. 5: 727–750.

Law, Rob, Daniel Leung, and Irene Cheng Chu Chan. 2019. "Progression and development of information and communication technology research in hospitality and tourism: A state-of-the-art review." *International Journal of Contemporary Hospitality Management* 32, no. 2: 511–534.

Lipsman, Andrew. 2019. Emarketer: Global ecommerce 2019 report www.emarketer.com/content/global-ecommerce-2019.

Liu, Xumin, Athman Bouguettaya, Jemma Wu, and Li Zhou. 2011. "Ev-lcs: A system for the evolution of long-term composed services." *IEEE Transactions on Services Computing* 6, no. 1: 102–115.

Long, Ziyu, and Elizabeth D. Wilhoit. 2018. "Disciplined freedom, branded authenticity, and dependable independence: How tensions enact flexibility in lifestyle blogging careers." *Journal of Applied Communication Research* 46, no. 3: 368–387.

Maday, Josh. 2020. The history of e-commerce: A long and winding road, www.the-future-of-commerce.com/2020/01/30/history-of-e-commerce/.

Mahanta, Prafulla Kumar. 2020. "Usage of information and communication technology in the degree college libraries of Assam: A study." *Library Philosophy and Practice (ejournal)* 3829: 1–13.

Mallinson, Daniel J., Göktuğ Morçöl, Eunsil Yoo, Shahinshah Faisal Azim, Eli Levine, and Saahir Shafi. 2020. "Sharing economy: A systematic thematic analysis of the literature." *Information Polity* 25, no. 2: 143–158.

Martin, Chris J., Paul Upham, and Leslie Budd. 2015. "Commercial orientation in grassroots social innovation: Insights from the sharing economy." *Ecological Economics* 118: 240–251.

Media OutReach. 2019. CXC public chain third party application—Consensus planet culture education interactive entertainment platform comes right away. www.businessinsider.sg/cxc-public-chain-third-party-application-consensus-planet-culture-education-interactive-entertainment-platform-comes-right-away.

Meerkerk. 2020. What is ecommerce? http://blog.meerkerkonline.com/what-is-ecommerce/.

Michiels, Sabine I., and Loy Van Crowder. 2001. "Discovering the Magic Box: Local appropriation of information and communication technologies (ICTs)." SDRE, FAO, Rome.

Moreno, Pilar, and Pilar Tejada. 2019. "Reviewing the progress of information and communication technology in the restaurant industry." *Journal of Hospitality and Tourism Technology* 10, no. 4: 673–688.

Mundra, Ankit, and Nitin Rakesh. 2014. "Online hybrid model for online fraud prevention and detection." In Intelligent Computing, Networking, and Informatics, pp. 805–815. Springer, New Delhi.

Nadeak, Bernadetha. 2020. "The effectiveness of distance learning using social media during the pandemic period of COVID-19: A case in Universities Kristen Indonesia." *International Journal of Advanced Science and Technology* 29, no. 7: 1764–1772.

Naidoo, Gedala Mulliah. 2020. "Digital communication: Information communication technology (ICT) usage for teaching and learning." In Handbook of Research on Digital Learning, pp. 1–19. IGI Global, Hershey.

Novak, Jasminko, and Gerhard Schwabe. 2019. "Designing for reintermediation in the brick-and-mortar world: Towards the travel agency of the future." *Electronic Markets* 19, no. 1: 15–29.

OECD. 2016. Re-thinking policies for the tourism sharing economy, www.oecd.org/cfe/tourism/re-thinkingpoliciesforthetourismsharingeconomy.htm.

Onder, Irem, and Horst Treiblmaier. 2018. "Blockchain and tourism: Three research propositions." *Annals of Tourism Research* 72, no. C: 180–182.

O'Regan, Michael, and Jaeyeon Choe. 2019. "Managing a non-profit hospitality platform conversion: The case of Couchsurfing.com." *Tourism Management Perspectives* 30: 138–146.

Packard, Noel. 2020. "The ARPANET into the internet: A tale of two networks." *Studies in Media and Communication* 8, no. 1: 37–49.

Payne, Will B., and David O'Sullivan. 2020. "Exploding the phone book: Spatial data arbitrage in the 1990s internet boom." *Annals of the American Association of Geographers* 110, no. 2: 391–398.

Pazaitis, Alex, Primavera De Filippi, and Vasilis Kostakis. 2017. "Blockchain and value systems in the sharing economy: The illustrative case of Backfeed." *Technological Forecasting and Social Change* 125: 105–115.

Pencarelli, Tonino. 2020. "The digital revolution in the travel and tourism industry." *Information Technology & Tourism* 22, no. 3: 455–476.

Pilkington, Marc. 2017. "Can blockchain technology help promote new tourism destinations? The example of medical tourism in Moldova? SSRN, June 11: 1–12. Available at SSRN: https://ssrn.com/abstract=2984479 or http://dx.doi.org/10.2139/ssrn.2984479.

Pouri, Maria J., and Lorenz M. Hilty. 2018. "Conceptualizing the digital sharing economy in the context of sustainability." *Sustainability* 10, no. 12: 4453.

Priporas, Constantinos-Vasilios, Nikolaos Stylos, Roya Rahimi, and Lakshmi Narasimhan Vedanthachari. 2017. "Unraveling the diverse nature of service quality in a sharing economy: A social exchange theory perspective of Airbnb accommodation." *International Journal of Contemporary Hospitality Management* 29, no. 9: 2279–2301.

Purohit, Atul, and Urjita Thakar. 2019. "Role of information and communication technology in improving loyalty program effectiveness: A comprehensive approach and future research agenda." *Information Technology & Tourism* 21: 259–280.

PWC. 2015. The sharing economy—Sizing the revenue opportunity, www.pwc.com/gx/en/about/global-annual-review-2015/colliding-megatrends/thesharing-economy.html.

Rahman, Md Abdur, Md Mamunur Rashid, M. Shamim Hossain, Elham Hassanain, Mohammed F. Alhamid, and Mohsen Guizani. 2019. "Blockchain and IoT-based cognitive edge framework for sharing economy services in a smart city." *IEEE Access* 7: 18611–18621.

Rashideh, Waleed. 2020. "Blockchain technology framework: Current and future perspectives for the tourism industry." *Tourism Management* 80: 104125.

Ritter, Martin, and Heiner Schanz. 2019. "The sharing economy: A comprehensive business model framework." *Journal of cleaner production* 213: 320–331.

Rubtcova, Mariia, and Oleg Pavenkov. 2019. "The involvement of parents in the educational process through information and communication technologies." In RW-544th International Conference on Internet Technologies and Society (ICITS). Chennai, Tamil Nadu, India, vol. 23.

Sainaghi, Ruggero, Mehmet Ali Köseoglu, Francesca d'Angella, and Fuad Mehraliyev. 2020. "Sharing economy: A co-citation analysis." *Current Issues in Tourism* 23, no. 8: 929–937.

Sandulli, Francesco D., Antonio Rodríguez-Duarte, and Daría C. Sánchez-Fernández. 2014. "Value creation and value capture through internet business models." In Handbook of Strategic e-Business Management, pp. 83–108. Springer, Berlin, Heidelberg.

Schor, Juliet B., and Connor J. Fitzmaurice. 2015. "Collaborating and connecting: The emergence of the sharing economy." In Handbook of Research on Sustainable Consumption. Edward Elgar Publishing, Cheltenham.

Schuckert, Markus, Xianwei Liu, and Rob Law. 2015. "Hospitality and tourism online reviews: Recent trends and future directions." *Journal of Travel & Tourism Marketing* 32, no. 5: 608–621.

Sdino, Leopoldo, and Sara Magoni. 2017. "The sharing economy and real estate market: The phenomenon of shared houses." In International Conference on Smart and Sustainable Planning for Cities and Regions, pp. 241–251. Springer, Cham.

Söderström, Tor, Jörgen From, Jeanette Lövqvist, and Anette Törnquist. 2012. "From distance to online education: Educational management in the 21st century." *European Journal of Open, Distance and E-learning* 15, no. 2: 85–95.

Spencer, Andrew. 2019. "ICT and Caribbean tourism." In Travel and Tourism in the Caribbean, pp. 95–114. Palgrave Macmillan, Cham.

Statista. 2020. Internet usage worldwide—Statistics & facts, www.statista.com/topics/1145/internet-usage-worldwide/#dossierSummary__chapter1.

Sthapit, Erose, and Peter Björk. 2019. "Sources of distrust: Airbnb guests' perspectives." *Tourism Management Perspectives* 31: 245–253.

Stratigea, Anastasia. 2011. "ICTs for rural development: Potential applications and barriers involved." *Netcom. Réseaux, Communication et Territoires* 25, no. 3/4: 179–204.

Szyjewski, Grzegorz. 2019. "Expanding an open source e-commerce with a separate ICT system." *Procedia Computer Science* 159: 2091–2101.

Tang, Yee Kwan, and Konde, Victor. 2020. "Differences in ICT use by entrepreneurial micro-firms: Evidence from Zambia." *Information Technology for Development* 26, no. 2: 268–291.

Thellmann, Pascal. 2018. Blockchain is the infrastructure for a new decentralized sharing economy, https://hackernoon.com/blockchain-is-the-infrastructure-for-a-new-decentralized-sharing-economy-f715da32bece.

Tilley, Aaron. 2020. Zoom video posts fourth-quarter net profit on 78% revenue growth, *The Wall Street Journal*, www.wsj.com/articles/zoom-video-posts-fourth-quarter-net-profit-on-78-revenue-growth-11583363098.

Tran, Gina A. and Strutton. 2020. "Comparing email and SNS users: Investigating e-servicescape, customer reviews, trust, loyalty and E-WOM." *Journal of Retailing and Consumer Services* 53: 101782.

Tura, Nina, and Taneli Vaskelainen. 2018. "Exploring problems associated with the sharing economy." *Electronic Journal of Business Ethics and Organization Studies* 23, no. 1: 37–45.

Turi, Abeba Nigussie, Josep Domingo-Ferrer, David Sanchez, and Dritan Osmani. 2017. "A co-utility approach to the mesh economy: The crowd-based business model." *Review of Managerial Science* 11, no. 2: 411–442.

Tussyadiah, Iis P., and Juho Pesonen. 2018. "Drivers and barriers of peer-to-peer accommodation stay–an exploratory study with American and Finnish travellers." *Current Issues in Tourism* 21, no. 6, 703–720.

Tussyadiah, Iis P., and Marianna Sigala. 2018. "Shareable tourism: Tourism marketing in the sharing economy." *Journal of Travel & Tourism Marketing* 35, no. 1, 1–4

Vinod, B. 2020. "Blockchain in travel." *Journal of Revenue and Pricing Management* 19, no. 1: 2–6.

Visiualcapitalist. 2020. The top 10 most valuable brands, www.visualcapitalist.com/ranked-the-most-valuable-brands-in-the-world/.

Wang, Dan, and Juan L. Nicolau. 2017. "Price determinants of sharing economy based accommodation rental: A study of listings from 33 cities on Airbnb. com." *International Journal of Hospitality Management* 62: 120–131.

Wen, Jun, Metin Kozak, Shaohua Yang, and Fang Liu. 2020. "COVID-19: Potential effects on Chinese citizens' lifestyle and travel." *Tourism Review* 78, no. 1: 74–87.

Yuan, Yong, and Fei-Yue Wang. 2018. "Blockchain and cryptocurrencies: Model, techniques, and applications." *IEEE Transactions on Systems, Man, and Cybernetics: Systems* 48, no. 9: 1421–1428.

Zaidan, Esmat. 2017. "Analysis of ICT usage patterns, benefits and barriers in tourism SMEs in the Middle Eastern countries: The case of Dubai in UAE." *Journal of Vacation Marketing* 23, no. 3: 248–263.

Zsarnoczky, Martin. 2018. "The digital future of the tourism & hospitality industry." *Boston Hospitality Review* 6: 1–9.

8 Innovative Digital Ideas in Presenting Cultural Heritage in the Tourism Industry

Özge Çalhan

CONTENTS

8.1 INTRODUCTION

The sustainability of tourist products is getting shorter day by day due to increasing and changing tourist demands. Therefore, introducing new and more effective products is becoming a necessity every day. To meet this need and to remain competitive in the global tourism market, innovation is needed. While there is no precise concept of innovation in tourism, it is generally understood to include something defined as novel and distinct from business as usual or previous practice (Johannessen et al. 2001; Hjalager 2010). Besides four essential issues in the determination of innovativeness, the extent to which a product or service is based on new knowledge and other resources, the area to which the product or service is new to the market, the extent to which the production process relies on new technologies, and the area to which the product requires the establishment of new networks and collaborative links (Hjalager 2014). The ability to maintain and grow market share, reach new markets, and boost the ability to produce new products faster and at lower costs are the most significant effects of innovation on results (Clausen and Madsen 2014). Innovative digital ideas should be included in the components in the tourism industry such as tour

DOI: 10.1201/9781003138051-10

operators, travel agencies, destination decision makers, transportation, restaurants, accommodation, and so on. There have already been several examples; Thomas Cook provides a unique trip and other experiences for a completely new segment of consumers, Disney Corporation provides movie and media-synergized theme parks, and Ryanair provides incredibly low fares using remote airports, allowing new customers to fly (Alsos et al. 2014). Airlines delivered more service than many customers would demand. New market innovations discovered and exploited this in new business models (Hjalager 2014). For the abandoned rural destinations, trekking and wilderness experiences for specific categories of tourists can be attractive; food festivals or local celebrities, events, and guided tours also can be a different alternative for tourists in the local destinations (Hall and Boyd 2005). All innovative movements are done for the customer, users, or tourism aspects for the tourists. So, determinants of innovativeness are the customers, users, or tourists.

8.2 INNOVATIVE DIGITAL IDEAS FOR CULTURAL HERITAGE

For the promotion and communication of cultural tourism, it is critical to comprehend how cultural heritage assets can become vital elements of destination tourist goods (Ho and McKercher 2004). Consumers may be classified as buyers, users, or payers. Customers now have access to tour operators' potential offers (videos, content, and so on). Customers may also design their package tours and become more involved in the visiting process due to the various aspects associated with the principle mentioned above of creativity. The three roles (buyer, consumer, and seller) are not mutually exclusive; they coexist. From the innovative cultural offer of well-known sites, it emerges a clear understanding of the need to bring creative forms to a sector, such as archeology, that needs 'rejuvenation,' both through the use of information and communication technology techniques and the enrichment of the archeological heritage. These projects are essential tools for educating the local community about the value of its heritage, especially the tourist-drawing sites. According to people holding a managerial position offering creativity in tourist use and technical solutions promotes good/services use and communicates a different interpretation of archeological sites and besides providing creativity in tourist use and technical applications promotes good/service use and further understanding of archeological culture (Corte et al. 2009). Cultural heritage items are created as a result of the presence of cultural visitors, regardless of their diverse needs and desired experiences. Therefore, it is necessary to develop a proper cultural heritage product. To fully realize the potential of a heritage asset, it must be transformed and created into a tourist-friendly product (Ho and McKercher 2004). Audiovisual presentations, computer programs, and hands-on exhibitions are under pressure to upgrade at cultural heritage attractions. Since, as time passes, visitor preferences develop and become more challenging (Fyall and Garrod 1998). As the cultural tourist changes, digital access to destinations or cultural sites should integrate with innovative movements to get the best tourist experiences about the locations. The cultural and literary tourist wants to access a range of academic experiences that reveal the complexities of the city's history via the built environment (Carson et al. 2017).

Technical information and communication techniques should be used to introduce creative ways to cultural heritage areas. Innovation has the potential to alter the value creation of cultural heritage dramatically.

The innovation for the usage of cultural assets allows the relationship between the visitors and destination with the acculturative. For instance, the audiovisual presentations provide more depth for the tour. Visitors will discover exciting and different experiences if the package tour involves scenic tableaux, directional sound, special effects, sculpted figures, three multimedia displays that use large-format screens, technical and architectural details of the buildings (Prentice et al. 1998). There are many possible ideas to increase influential heritage for society, such as employment and economic gains. First, it needs to make renovation works in the heritage area. Then the conservation is another important work, and it takes a long time (OECD 2005). Without being part of an integrated development plan, cultural heritage cannot benefit society and be sustainable for long periods. The city has cultural heritage assets that offer effective vehicles to reach cultural sites and some supportive services for tours. Cultural heritage interpretation for the tourist's experiences should be enhanced while they follow the routes provided in the tour. There should be some innovation to increase the tourist experiences (Mitsche et al. 2013). Users can interact directly with their artistic backgrounds thanks to innovative fictional works and graphic design technologies. Using programs like Google Maps, building an interactive map has become a relatively simple task with options for customization to meet the needs of specific groups of users. However, even though the technologies on offer are interactive and provide the 'modern tourist' with a variety of personal entry points to different sites or experiences, combining government policy initiatives with cultural heritage, literary history, and new technologies that could open up a room for visitor interaction while reflecting layers of scholarly output poses a challenge (Carson et al. 2017). The tourists should have easy access to cultural heritage information, individual attractions, programs, and tickets. The cultural distribution system, channels, and national and regional tourist offices should promote cultural heritage destinations.

Hua, Chen, Fang, and Wang attempted to obtain Hakka culture components and skills and combine realistic 3D (three-dimensional) digital interpretations of Hakka culture for Internet-based immersive virtual experiences and cultural tourism information services. The researchers use technological databases to define cultural assets (Hua et al. 2018). The opportunities to innovate information and communication technology are essential to cultural heritage, thus owing to the high demand for knowledge and information, during the process of production of cultural information with the systems, which are developed for specific functions for the tourist, which are global positioning system (GPS), devices such as 3G mobile phones and portals which used to provide updated information on tourism services (transportation, overnight stays, opening hours of archeological and museum sites, and any some other helpful information that need for organizing a tourist itinerary). ArtBase, an Amsterdam-based international cultural listings company, has a database of over 200,000 cultural events at 25,000 cultural venues worldwide. Consumers can purchase tickets for several of these events online.

In addition, ArtBase is currently collaborating with NBBS, a Dutch tour operator, to develop versatile cultural tourism products that enable consumers to book vacations (Richards et al. 2001). Visitors visit many museums through Google Arts and Culture and Clark, which provide virtual tours for visitors to different destinations. Especially cultural heritage artifacts can be seen. There are 2000 museums and cultural institutions on this platform. This platform has supplied records, archived digitally, and shared the world's most significant cultural values since 2003 (https://cyark.org/ourMission/).

San Matteo Museum in Pisa is a virtual museum that serves as a model for all other museums in the province of Pisa and around the world. It allows visitors to see a city's medieval art in a digitally restored medieval environment (Barone et al. 2012).

Virtual museums supply innovative digital ideas for visitors. For instance, the Rijksmuseum in Amsterdam gives opportunities to the visitors to save the works they like in their studio, sharing their created galleries with others, using the artifacts as poster paper. Typically, artworks need to be moved to a display to the public from one place to another for the organized exhibition. Thanks to the concept of virtual museums, the artifacts or the data can be visualized in different ways, such as stereo projection systems, Web3D content management, and 3D model software. The tourists can visit these digital museums and other cultural heritage values that serve digitally by themselves or with the help of a screen.

Innovation in cultural offers can occur in three ways: technological, experiential, and systemic, as seen in Figure 8.1. Technological innovations can be used more in museums (projected presentation, virtual reality (VR), 3D technology, and so on) or

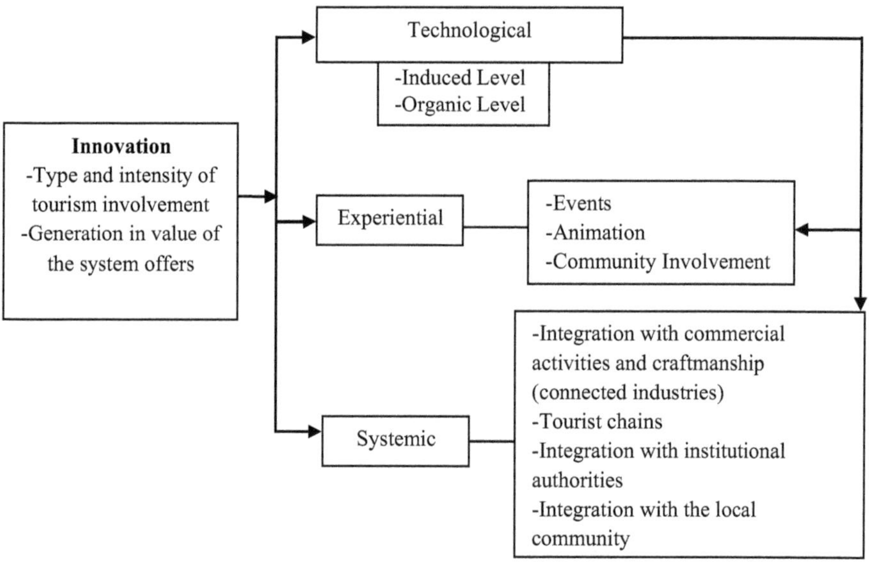

FIGURE 8.1 Different types of cultural offers innovation.

Source: Corte et al. (2009, p. 229).

historical sites (headsets that can be borrowed in the entrance of the archeological areas or museums, maps with QR codes, and so on). Cause these places are more suitable for technological innovation. Some alternative tourism types for the destination can be classified as experiential innovation. New events or festivals for the goal can be innovative. Other recent tours can be organized besides existing ones that can be innovative for the destination. The destination may have the potential for new alternative terms. Even if the goal has no potential for unique alternative tours, the destination can be attracted with differentiation and innovative ideas. Collaboration with other cultural sites for cultural circuits is better for promoting integrated offers. Interconnectedness among the different aspects of innovation is a part of systemic innovation forms.

To implement the digital ideas in cultural heritage values, both visitors and practitioners should consider these ideas in moderation and understand their importance. It is seen that there are studies in the literature that examine the attitudes of both tourists (Michael et al., 2010; tom Dieck and Jung, 2018)., who are consumers of

TABLE 8.1
Examples for Digital Ideas Used in Cultural Heritage Aspects

Cultural Heritage Values	Digital Ideas
Heritage monuments and statues	The Buddha statue which was exploded in the Bamyan Valley reflected in a Holographic 3D Model, Sutra inscriptions in China visualized by high-resolution 3D data, The Regolini Galassi Tomb has been reconstructed in 3D, 3D scanning and modeling the Bismarck Monument in Hamburg
Heritage buildings	A light show of La Sagrada Familia, 3D representation of the Umayyad City Walls, virtual reality of Notre Dame, 3D in the Famosa Fortress in Melaka in Malaysia
Museums	Virtual reality in Freud Museum (London), augmented reality and 3D scanning at Acropolis Museum, touch screen computers, virtual tour in Louvre Museum, multimedia contents and audio information delivered via headphones, audio story platform in the museum of technology in Helsinki, three different augmented reality applications in Leventis Municipal Museum in Nicosia
Heritage sites	Augmented reality in Olympia Archeological Site, 3D reconstruction of Pompei ancient city, virtual reality of Aspendos ancient city, 3D reconstruction of Roman Cologne, ground spectroradiometric measurements in Kouklia Palaepaphos archaeological site in Cyprus, GIS and 3D models used in archaeological excavation in Nelson Island
Heritage assets (clothes, foods, beliefs, traditions, customs, myths)	Realistic 3D digital representations of Hakka culture, 3D digitization of Idalion Tablet found in Cyprus, the inscription of Gortyna in Greece via 3D documentation, 3D reconstruction of Peranakan culture

cultural heritage, and decision makers, who are practitioners toward these practices. Due to high prices for implementing digital ideas, heritage organizations hesitate to implement such innovations. They may think that they will suffer financial loss if visitors do not accept them. For this reason, the acceptance of digital ideas becomes essential for their wider use. Studies on this subject in literature are essential in researching and revealing the reservations about using technological innovations in cultural heritage.

8.2.1 Innovative Digital Ideas for Conservation of Cultural Heritage

Digital applications can transfer cultural resources to the next generations in a way. In today's world, when we consider the damages that humanity has given to these values, it is the goal to archive and stores each cultural inventory through digital technologies. To share cultural heritage and establish interculture communication, Internet-based experiences and technological uses of databases are needed. Many cultural heritage assets are damaged due to natural (flood, earthquake, volcanic explosion, climate change, fire) and human-caused (war, terrorism, remissness, dilapidation) threats. Measures can be taken against these damages within the scope of innovative digital ideas, such as archiving these cultural values in an electronic environment, keeping their 3D images, keeping their drawings and photographs in a cloud environment, and storing memories that do not have a long life span. Cultural heritage asset protection is a critical problem for future generations and the entire world. These heritage artifacts reflect our history for the public's long-term understanding. Digital 3D documentation is a method of restoration and security that combines surveying and building computing to bridge the gap between reality and the virtual world. A growing number of cultural organizations recognize the importance of capturing 3D datasets of these heritage values (Cheng et al. 2010).

For a cultural archive to be helpful, four items are needed. The first one is the dataset that should be completed. The second one is that the dataset should be recorded with an automated system. The third one is the human resources that need to have the necessary skills to access the data. The last one is that the database should be constructed. Using tools such as a Geographic Information System (GIS) program to access cultural tourism records aids in good information access. The accuracy of the information provided is critical to providing a high-quality visitor experience. This knowledge could be real tangible artifacts in a museum or exhibition. It could be found in tangible ways like a historical monument or archeological site or records of intangible culture like dance, music, or gastronomy. Image databases, interactive visitor information, and displays are required from tourists. Visitors can learn about the time, place, genre, style, and culture by looking at these elements. These use simple technologies that include standardized data recording, storage, and manipulation, though the data can be used in other formats later on, such as the development of a catalog or multimedia. Before being updated, cultural material should be safeguarded, archived, and registered (Shackley 1997).

High-resolution 3D measuring tools and techniques that are innovative for documentation, analysis, and protection were used to capture stone inscriptions in the province of Sichuan in China's southwest. Thanks to this innovative technology, the copies of the original note can be visualized (Schmidth et al. 2010). Geoinformatics creates new perspectives in conserving cartographic heritage by digitizing, georeferencing, visualizing, and comparing data (Kyriazi et al. 2010). Society needs to realize its cultural heritage values, and while these cultural values turn to heritage tourism, it is essential to conserve their value (Rakitocav and Urasevic 2017). In an academic study about the human and environmental threats to the island of Crete, the threats were examined using a GIS that is one of the modern technologies such as remote sensing (RS) and GPSs. They are a vital technique for preserving cultural heritage (Alexakis and Sarris 2010).

8.2.2 Innovative Digital Ideas for Management of Cultural Heritage

Cultural tourism and the preservation and management of cultural heritage have always had a close relationship. For successful tourism movements, it is required to manage cultural heritage. The better the cultural heritage is controlled, the more successful tourism promotion can be achieved. With the successful management of cultural heritage, its sustainability is ensured by preserving cultural heritage, and in this case, it positively affects tourism movements. Some platforms are about heritage management programs. Arches are one of them, and the Arches platform helps the project and data management, data discovery, and visualization (www.archesproject.org/). New developments in cultural heritage data management and visualization are helpful tools for analysis and data exchange. Cause the information management of the cultural values is essential for cultural travel routes maps, the general information about the cultural destinations for tourists to plan their travel and stay. For that reason, innovative digital ideas have an enormous impact on both cultural heritage destinations and information management. With the successful management of cultural resources information by the creative digital ideas, which are setting the stage for virtual tourism, the tourists stimulate their interest and increase their travel motivation to the destination. The innovative digital ideas give a chance to cultural heritage assets to easier management; operations cataloging and survey, archeological, documentary, and historical data. Thanks to managing cultural heritage values by innovative digital ideas, the tourists, visitors, or consumers can interact with the cultural heritage product and benefit from new heritage information services (Borowiecki and Navarrete 2017).

8.2.3 Innovative Digital Ideas for Interpretation of Cultural Heritage

After cultural heritage assets are revealed, documented, and protected, they are presented to the tourists. Bringing these assets together for visitors is very important in terms of awareness of history. Today, cultural values are provided to meet with tourists with innovative digital ideas. Digital ideas can enhance the visitor experience by presenting the information more effectively. Creative digital ideas can interpret cultural heritage contents, primarily published online on websites, social media platforms, and various portals (Borowiecki and Navarrete 2017). There are some examples of the interpretation of cultural heritage assets. For instance, Russian museums have incorporated information technologies. Nowadays, all museums have their websites. All these types of equipment (multimedia, TicketNet, QR codes, projectors, plasma displays, web cameras, touch-sensitive screens) help to show the intangible nonmaterial cultural heritages (Madirov and Absalyamova 2015). In addition, on-site VR, two-dimensional augmentations (photos and text), and 3D augmentations, which include static 3D models of ancient sites and interactive animated 3D models, help users find not only information about tourism artifacts but also imagine the cultural properties (Cirulis et al. 2015).

Tourists can watch and listen to stories about cultural heritage and hear about the historical meaning of the artifacts chosen by visitors for virtual games. The apps are generally available online or as a smartphone download, but they can also be set up in museums. Thanks to these applications, interactive 3D models of cultural heritage artifacts, the visitor has different interpretation experiences. For instance, White Bastion is a fortress that overlooks Sarajevo and has served as a castle for various civilizations. Visitors can display ten digital stories on demand and engage with six immersive virtual versions of the castle. More information on incidents and characters related to the castle during the medieval, Ottoman, and Austrian-Hungarian periods can be found in medieval, Ottoman, and Austrian-Hungarian stories. Legends or other characters may be used to enhance the interpretation of this castle (Rizvic et al. 2019). Visitors to the Technology Museum in Helsinki, Finland, can record their stories, connect them to objects, and share them with other visitors using the website. That is another example of the interactive interpretation (www.myhelsinki.fi/en/see-and-do/sights/museum-of-technology). These innovative digital ideas enhance the visitor experiences by telling hidden stories and guiding users in their virtual tours. Digital pictures support the interpretation of exhibits in museums and other cultural heritage areas. When interpreting cultural heritage, the narrative method is essential to raise the attractiveness for the tourists. For the practical, interactive interpretation of digital ideas, it is necessary to present cultural heritage assets to attract the attention of tourists. Cause these digital ideas help the functional performance of cultural heritage. Cultural artifacts that only a tiny part of them have survived until today can be visualized and understood by visitors by using digital ideas. They provide the visitor with a full detailed view of these cultural heritage assets. Based on historical and archeological sources interpretation, the Etruscanning 3D model of the Etruscan Regolini-Galassi tomb depicts the tomb as it might have been during the Etruscan era, with the objects contextualized inside. This example shows the importance of interpreting the cultural heritage assets (Hupperetz et al. 2012). The digital map library has been created for the heritage assets as a new interpretation tool for the touristic destination Mytilene. It allows online access for educational, recreational, and touristic activities. It provides powerful tools for data interpretation for visitors (Kyriazi et al. 2010).

The different digital ideas used in cultural heritage assets allow the cultural heritage to interpret and have other presentation methods. Mr. Tien-seng Poo's sculptures were presented in the study using three different digital ideas: augmented reality, VR, and rapid prototyping. Visitors who used VR in this study changed their viewing angles to watch sculptures from multiple perspectives. The details of the sculptures can be seen as the distance between tourists and photos varies. As a result, unlike exhibition settings, visitors may communicate closely with the statues. Visitors who used augmented reality and wore polarized 3D glasses connected to a wireless remote control device could freely walk around the virtual exhibition room, giving them the sensation of being submerged in the virtual space with the 3D sculptures. Furthermore, rapid prototyping allows for the replication of complete or reduced-size digitalized sculptures to achieve promotion results (Huang 2010). Aegaron (Ancient Egyptian Architecture Online) application presents drawings of Egypt's archeological and cultural values to the visitors of the website (http://drupaldev.aegaron.ucla.edu/search/plans).

8.3 IMPORTANCE OF DIGITAL IDEAS FOR CULTURAL HERITAGE

Technology is becoming indispensable for all areas of life all day by day. The inclusion of technology in human life at this level causes people to need to use technology. While it is possible to do their work faster and more effectively thanks to technology, doing without technology is no longer almost selectable for people. This shows the importance of technology to make the best use of time. Travelling has also become more accessible with technology. Technology can be used before the beginning of travel (making reservations, renting a car, buying museum tickets, learning the opening and closing hours of historical sites, check-in, and so on).

In addition, technology, which is used in different parts every day, has already been used in matters such as revealing, preserving, archiving, and presenting cultural heritage. Thanks to these innovative digital ideas used within the scope of cultural heritage, these assets can be transferred to future generations more effectively and offered to today's tourists. For example, visitors can access an interactive archive of photographs and text at the Micro Gallery in the Sainsbury Wing of the National Gallery in London, containing 2,200 paintings and 1,000 illustrations. Aside from the Holocaust Memorial Museum in Washington, DC, there are video clips of scenes from WWII. Touch screens are available to visitors (Markwell et al. 1997).

According to Qi and Li (2012), cultural tour's significant development cannot be achieved without the support of technology. The traveler's needs change rapidly. Constructions of the technological systems in the cultural heritage places help transform the cultural heritage resources. In this way, satisfaction can be supplied from the visitors. Considerable success was achieved in these exhibitions with the help of using a sound explanation system (large high-tech projector, high-quality commentator) (Qi and Li 2012). In May 2007, the Masada National Park and an ambitious museological experience were added to the Masada offering. This involves a theatrical setting and a radio play and audio descriptions to go along with it. The critical supply source is technologically advanced tools, especially audio guides, and a preshow movie presentation museum. The combination of archeological artifacts, theatrical productions, music, and video creates an unforgettable experience that invites visitors to take on the role of the first player in Masada history. This is a groundbreaking approach that will mark a turning point in museum presentations in Israel and abroad. Masada National Park offers a creative supply in an archeological site where tourists can participate in daytime musical and cultural activities. Furthermore, the organization would strengthen cultural and religious programs to increase the cultural offering (Corte et al. 2009). In the study conducted by Dieck and Jung in 2017, augmented reality in cultural heritage has cultural, historical, educational, economic, experiential, epistemic values, and contributes to tourists' positive learning experiences. Furthermore, augmented reality in cultural heritage contributes to conserving history, increasing tourists' satisfaction, and positive word of mouth (tom Dieck and Jung 2017).

8.4 POSITIVE IMPACTS OF DIGITAL IDEAS USED IN CULTURAL HERITAGE IN THE TOURISM INDUSTRY

Digital technologies supply new opportunities for the cultural assets to sustain the traditional functions of the cultural assets by providing and preserving them. They also offer different information techniques for tourists (Tariffi et al. 2004). Integration with technology is essential in all sectors. In tourism, for cultural heritage, technology is also critical. In cultural heritage attractiveness, it is possible to use technological devices. In this way, the heritage places can be more attractive. Thanks to technology, tourists can reach cultural information more quickly. Thanks to information technology, tour operators can participate in the mass customization of items, such as cultural attractions and activities. Following the 1990s, mass-market tour operators started to focus on the cultural heritage market. The tour program of mass-market operators began with a city break program, which offered nothing more than the opportunity to visit cultural attractions at a low cost. City break programs have added particular cultural features such as trips to art galleries, the theatre, musicals, and opera.

Some big distributors, such as TUI in Germany, have begun to produce unique brochures related to cultural activities. By creating new ones, mass-market operators may retain their management skills. New cultural items lose their unique appeal as soon as they are experienced by mass tourists (Richards et al. 2001).To provide more information about cultural assets, it needs to use digital information technology. A growing number of cultural organizations recognize the value of digital tools and services that add value to their offerings. Due to digitization programs, increased access to cultural heritage material can be considered a valuable public service to artistic institutions (Manaf and Ismail 2010).

8.4.1 Positive Impacts for Cultural Travel Experiences of Tourists

Travel experiences of tourists are often very fragile and affected by the events experienced during the tours. Planned or unexpected positive changes experienced during the time reflect positively on the travel experiences of the visitors. To increase the trip's experiences, travel agencies, tour guides, or people responsible for that travel make an effort to prevent anything negative from happening. Positive developments in the travel experience that will delight tourists are supported for this purpose. One of the things that can positively change tourists' travel experience is innovative digital ideas. Especially in cultural travel experiences, tourists can perceive and learn the tangible and intangible cultural heritage inventories they encounter more efficiently with digital innovations. This experience positively affects their travel experiences.

Considering some studies on innovative digital ideas used in cultural heritage values and the tourists' satisfaction from the travel experiences, it is observed that the tourists are satisfied with these digital innovations ideas. Tourists were pleased to take advantage of the valuable educational tool that enhanced their trip. They were delighted with the AR, 3D, film, and audio displays in ancient city Olympia in Greece. Younger visitors, who can be described as those with the highest degree of computer skills, were the most passionate of all. Some digital ideas help the tourists better understand the sites' history and use an example developed for this ancient site (Vlahakis et al. 2001). Tourists want to see the types of applications such as mobile augmented reality applications with cultural heritage tools because they explained that they both enjoyed the experiences and these applications helped them achieve some learning goals. The increase in the information and the system quality of these innovative digital ideas and the ease of use also enable visitors to use these ideas (Haugstvedt and Krogstie 2012; tom Dieck and Jung 2018). The tourists explained their augmented reality experience in a former synagogue building in the United Kingdom; a small Jewish museum displays a historical collection of Jewish items and artifacts as a way of preserving Jewish heritage. This was a precious learning experience for the visitors. Moreover, integrating innovative digital ideas into cultural heritage assets promotes the future revisit intention of the visitors (Moorhouse and Jung 2017).

In many museums of the World, the visitors can have a chance to use the applications containing native languages and download via Wi-Fi access or use QR codes with the help of their smartphone. The number of young people visiting museums that use this device has risen dramatically. Innovative digital ideas allow the visitors/tourists to live the old times by explaining historical heritage assets. Augmented, virtual, and mixed reality are examples of digital concepts. When they are used in museums, the visitors can have a chance to see the artifacts in very different dimensions. When they are used in historical sites, the tourists can have an opportunity to see old buildings in their full versions. Thanks to digital technologies, both time and cost can be saved. Large exhibitions or museums are visited digitally, although it may not be like seeing them with their own eyes, this visit may satisfy the tourists. Cultural heritage assets can be remotely accessible thanks to digital ideas. The person who visits the museum with a virtual tour may want to wonder about it and visit it at a more suitable time in detail thanks to this virtual tour. These virtual visits can be evocative for the person who wants to see the reality as well. Virtually seeing the entire work may increase the motivation of visit to these cultural assets. Another contribution of VR to museums is tourist satisfaction. Visitors can see the digital applications in closed-to-heritage destinations damaged by terrorism or war thanks to virtual interpretation. In this way, tourists can have the opportunity to see these cultural assets that they will never see—their satisfaction level of travel experiences increases. Cultural heritage values can become more functional as a social benefit when developed interactively with digital ideas to feed their creativity and be inspired by these works. The innovative digital ideas for cultural heritage allow visitors to think even more significantly and capture their imagination and attention. In this way, the visitors are encouraged for a deeper exploration of cultural heritage (Garau and Ilardi 2014).

8.4.2 Positive Impacts for Cultural Heritage Products

Cultural heritage products enhance the destination's competitiveness by offering varied experiences to tourists. When digital ideas are used in cultural heritage products, these cultural products can be a different new product for the tourism industry. Developing a new tourism product in the destination provides synergies between the primary touristic products and the new touristic products. Tourists who visit one attraction may visit others (Benur and Bramwell 2015). The growing divide between dynamic and less dynamic cultural heritage products is focused on the liveliness and livability of intangible heritage elements such as customs, language, faith, music, folklore, and gastronomy, rather than the actual existence of buildings, galleries, or historical environments, language, religion, music, folklore, and gastronomy. Destinations, especially in cases where physical heritage assets are scarce or nonexistent, have a chance to compete in the cultural tourism market. The challenges lie even more in innovation and creativity (Picard and Robinson 2006). One example of creative interactive ideas in 3D investment in 3D technology represents cultural product creativity and may serve as a 'fresh deal' foundation. The deployment of visitor-facing ICT at heritage sites may be motivated by a variety of factors. These can include (Kaminski et al. 2010):

- 'Improve the user's experiences,
- Increase visitor numbers,
- Improve educational effects,
- Some combination of the above.'

The heritage buildings are examples of cultural heritage products that are needed for an advanced online web page. The primary characteristics that these web pages should have had given as follows (Andaroodi and Kitamoto 2010):

- 'Provide multiple schemas to cover different attributes such as history, physical features, environment, management, and preservation,
- Provide multiple bibliographic referencing,
- Use metadata standards to describe building attributes or annotate the dataset,
- Link every textual entity with visual data, such as images, movies, or architectural drawings, to validate the textual descriptions.'

With the different digital ideas applications, cultural heritage products can be preserved, archived at different levels, and have effective visual presentations.

8.4.3 Positive Impacts for Destination Tourism Movements

Considering the current rate of widespread use of technology, innovative investments can be a chance to raise the number of tourists. A study revealed that new technologies used to increase the museum visit experiences of visitors could make an economic contribution by increasing the number of visitors. As the visitors express their satisfaction, the interest in seeing the cultural heritage values where digital ideas are applied will increase, and the number of visitors will increase (vom Lehn and Heath 2005). The primary driver for the usage of innovative digital ideas in cultural heritage in tourism is economic. Governments, both public and private, finance these ideas when cultural heritage assets are combined with creative digital ideas can be used by both destination and regional tourism movements for artistic and commercial purposes (Borowiecki and Navarrete 2017).

Innovative digital ideas served a role for the destination that the participation in heritage and preserve the local heritage for the goal strengthened the connections between people and environment in the destination (Tait et al. 2016). The usage of virtual tour applications in ancient cities can attract more tourists. Tourists need to visualize these old settlements as close as possible. They prefer to visit these ancient sites more than the other attractiveness. The cultural tourists have different travel experiences as they can connect with the past and the culture. If innovative digital ideas make it easy for tourists, tourists may prefer that destination more. Innovative technologies are integrated into cultural heritage sites offer valuable visitor experiences (Pallud and Monod 2010). Besides, these experiences can create competitiveness between the destinations (Moorhouse and Jung 2017).

The widening access for all users to cultural heritage assets through innovative digital ideas is emerging as a significant opportunity for urban destinations, heritage organizations, and tourism providers. To generate more benefit for the goal, it is necessary to increase access to heritage by digitizing more cultural material and making it more widely accessible to the public (Paskaleva-Shapira et al. 2008).

REFERENCES

Alexakis, D., and Sarris, A. 2010. Environmental and human risk assessment of the prehistoric and historic archaeological sites of Western Crete (Greece) with the use of GIS, remote sensing, fuzzy logic and neural networks. In *Euro-Mediterranean Conference* (pp. 332–342). Springer, Berlin, Heidelberg.

Alsos, G. A., Eide, D., and Madsen, E. L. 2014. "Introduction: Innovation in tourism Industries" in *Handbook of Research on Innovation in Tourism Industries*, Eds: Gry Agnete Alsos, Dorthe Eide and Einar Liner Madsen. Edward Elgar Publishing, USA.

Andaroodi, E. and Kitamoto, A. 2010. Architectural heritage online: ontology-driven website generation for world heritage sites in danger. In *Euro-Mediterranean Conference* (pp. 277–290). Springer, Berlin, Heidelberg.

Barone, V., Licari, D., and Nardini, F. M. 2012. RICH: research and innovation for cultural heritage. *Conservation Science in Cultural Heritage*, *12*, 109–133.

Benur, A. M. and Bramwell, B. 2015. Tourism product development and product diversification in destinations, *Tourism Management*, *50*, 213–224.

Borowiecki, K. J. and Navarrete, T. 2017. Digitization of heritage collections as indicator of innovation. *Economics of Innovation and New Technology*, *26*(3), 227–246.

Carson, S., Hawkes, L., Gislason, K., and Cantrell, K. 2017. Literature, tourism and the city: writing and cultural change, *Journal of Tourism and Cultural Change,* 15 (4), 380–392.

Cheng, H. M., Yen, Y. N., Chen, M. B., and Yang, W. B. 2010. A processing for digitizing historical architecture. In *Euro-Mediterranean Conference* (pp. 1–12). Springer, Berlin, Heidelberg.

Cirulis, A., Paolis, L. T., and Tutberidze, B. 2015. Virtualization of digitalized cultural heritage and use case scenario modeling for sustainability promotion of national identity, *Computer Science,* 77, 199–206.

Clausen, T. H. and Madsen, E. L. 2014. "Innovations, their knowledge sources and their effects in experience-based tourism", in *Handbook of Research on Innovation in Tourism Industries*, Eds: Gry Agnete Alsos, Dorthe Eide and Einar Liner Madsen, Edward Elgar Publishing, UK, 113–131.

Corte, V. D., Savastano, I., and Storlazzi, A. 2009. Service innovation in cultural heritages management and valorization, *International Journal of Quality and Service Sciences,* 1 (3), 225–240.

Fyall, A. and Garrod, B. 1998. Heritage tourism: at what price?, *Managing Leisure*, 3 (4), 213–228.

Garau, C. and Ilardi, Emiliano. 2014. The "Non-Places" Meet the "Places:" Virtual tours on smartphones for the enhancement of cultural heritage, *Journal of Urban Technology*, 21 (1), 79–91.

Hall, M., and Boyd, S. 2005. Nature-based Tourism in Peripheral Areas: Introduction, in *Nature-based Tourism in Peripheral Areas: Development or Disaster?,* Michael Hall and Stephan Boyd (Eds.), 3-20, Channel View Publications/Multilingual Matters, Clevedon.

Haugstvedt, A. C., and Krogstie, J. 2012. Mobile augmented reality for cultural heritage: A technology acceptance study. In *2012 IEEE International Symposium on Mixed and Augmented Reality (ISMAR)* (pp. 247–255). IEEE.

Hjalager, A. M. 2010. A review of innovation research in tourism, *Tourism Management*, 31 (1), 1–12.

Hjalager, A. M. 2014. Disruptive and sustaining innovations: the case of rural tourism, in *Handbook of Research on Innovation in Tourism Industries,* Eds: Gry Agnete Alsos, Dorthe Eide and Einar Liner Madsen (Eds.), Edward Elgar Publishing, USA, 56–83.

Ho, P. S. and McKercher, B. 2004. Managing heritage resources as tourism products, *Asia Pacific Journal of Tourism Research*, 9 (3), 255–266. https://cyark.org/ourMission/.

Hua, L., Chen, C., Fang, H., and Wang, X. 2018. 3D documentation on Chinese Hakka Tulou and internet-based virtual experience for cultural tourism: a case study of Yongding Country, Fujian. *Journal of Cultural Heritage,* 29, 173–179.

Huang, Y. H. 2010. The digital archive of sculptures of Tien-Shen Poo in early Taiwan history. In *Euro-Mediterranean Conference* (pp. 343-355). Springer, Berlin, Heidelberg.

Hupperetz, W., Carlani, R., Pletinckx, D., and Pietroni, E. 2012. Etruscanning 3D project. The 3D reconstruction of the Regolini Galassi Tomb as a research tool and a new approach in storytelling. *Virtual Archaeology Review*, 3 (7), 92–96.

Johannessen, J., Olsen, B., and Lumpkin, G. 2001, Innovation as newness: what is new, how new, and new to whom?, *European Journal of Innovation Management*, 4 (1), 20–31.

Kaminski, J., McLoughlin, J., and Sodagar, B. 2010. Assessing the socio-economic impact of 3D visualisation in cultural heritage. In *Euro-Mediterranean Conference* (pp. 240–249). Springer, Berlin, Heidelberg.

Kyriazi, E., Soulakellis, N., Tataris, G., and Lappas, S. 2010. Use of geoinformatics for the digitization and visualization of cartographic heritage: the case of an early 1920s Mytilene town map. In *Euro-Mediterranean Conference* (pp. 193–205). Springer, Berlin, Heidelberg.

Madirov, E. and Absalyamova, S. 2015. The influence of information technologies on the availability of cultural heritage, *Social and Behavioral Sciences,* 188, 255-258.

Manaf, Z. A. and Ismail, A. 2010. Malaysian cultural heritage at risk?: A case study of digitisation projects, *Library Review,* 59 (2), 107–116.

Markwell, S., Bennett, M., and Ravenscroft, N. 1997. The changing market for heritage tourism: a case study of visits to historic houses in England, *International Journal of Heritage Studies*, 3 (2), 95–108.

Michael, D., Pelekanos, N., Chrysanthou, I., Zaharias, P., Hadjigavriel, L. L., and Chrysanthou, Y. 2010. Comparative study of interactive systems in a museum. In *Euro-Mediterranean Conference* (pp. 250-261). Springer, Berlin, Heidelberg.

Mitsche, N., Vogt, F., Knox, D., Cooper, I., Lombardi, P., and Ciaffi, D. 2013. Intangibles: enhancing access to cities' cultural heritage through interpretation, *International Journal of Culture, Tourism and Hospitality Research*, 7 (1), 68–77.

Moorhouse, N., and Jung, T. 2017. Augmented reality to enhance the learning experience in cultural heritage tourism: an experiential learning cycle perspective. *eReview of Tourism Research*, 8, 1–5.

OECD. 2005. Culture and local development. www.myhelsinki.fi/en/see-and-do/sights/museum-of-technology. http://drupaldev.aegaron.ucla.edu/search/plans. www.arches project.org/.

Pallud, J. and Monod, E. 2010. User experience of museum technologies: the phenomenological scales. *European Journal of Information Systems* 19: 562–580.

Paskaleva-Shapira, K., Azorin, J., and Chiabai, A. 2008. Enhancing digital access to local cultural heritage through E-governance: innovations in theory and practice from Genoa, Italy. *Innovation: The European Journal of Social Science Research*, 21 (4), 389–405.

Picard, D, and M. Robinson (Eds.). 2006. *Festivals, Tourism and Social Change, Remaking Worlds*, Channel View Publications, Clevedon.

Prentice, R. C., Witt, S. F., and Hamer, C. 1998. Tourism as experience the case of heritage parks, *Annals of Tourism Research*, 25 (1), 1–24.

Qi, Z. and Li, Q. İ. 2012. A humble on the development strategies for Bohai Rim cultural tour industry, *Physics Procedia*, 24, 2245–2249.

Rakitovac, K. A. and Urosevic, N. 2017. Models of valorisation of cultural heritage in sustainable tourism, *Management*, 12 (3), 199–215.

Richards, G., Goedhart, S., and Herrijgers, C. 2001. "The cultural attraction distribution system", in *Cultural Attractions and European Tourism*, Greg Richards (Ed.), 71–90, CABI Publishing, New York, .

Rizvic, S., Boskovic, D., Okanovic, V., Sljivo, S., and Zukic, M. 2019. Interactive digital storytelling: bringing cultural heritage in a classroom. *Journal of Computers in Education*, 6 (1), 143–166.

Schmidt, N., Boochs, F., and Schütze, R. 2010. Capture and processing of high resolution 3D-data of sutra inscriptions in China. In *Euro-Mediterranean Conference* (pp. 125–139). Springer, Berlin, Heidelberg.

Shackley, M. 1997. Saving cultural information: the potential role of digital databases in developing cultural tourism, *Journal of Sustainable Tourism*, 5 (3), 244–249.

Tait, E., Laing, R., Grinnall, A., Burnett, S., and Isaacs, J. 2016. (Re) presenting heritage: laser scanning and 3D visualisations for cultural resilience and community engagement. *Journal of Information Science*, 42 (3), 420–433.

Tariffi, F., Morganti, B. and Segbert, M. 2004. Digital cultural heritage projects in Europe: an overview of TRIS and the take-up trial projects. *Program*, 1, 5–28.

tom Dieck, M. C., and Jung, T. H. 2017. Value of augmented reality at cultural heritage sites: a stakeholder approach. *Journal of Destination Marketing and Management*, 6 (2), 110–117.

tom Dieck, M. C. and Jung, T. 2018. A theoretical model of mobile augmented reality acceptance in urban heritage tourism. *Current Issues in Tourism*, 21 (2), 154–174.

Vlahakis, V., Karigiannis, J., Tsotros, M., Gounaris, M., Almeida, L., Stricker, D., and Ioannidis, N. 2001. Archeoguide: first results of an augmented reality, mobile computing system in cultural heritage sites. *Virtual Reality, Archeology, and Cultural Heritage*, 9 (10.1145), 584993–585015.

Vom Lehn, D., and Heath, C. 2005. Accounting for new technology in museum exhibitions. *International Journal of Arts Management*, 7 (3), 11-21.

9 An Evaluation of Big Data Use for Fraud Detection in Hotel Enterprises

İlknur Eskin and Emel Adamış

CONTENTS

9.1 INTRODUCTION: BACKGROUND AND DRIVING FORCES

Big data covers various resources to obtain data such as social networks, videos, digital visuals, sensors, and sales transaction registries. Analyzing all these data aims to access valuable and quality information about the users generating the data. Absorbing the core meaning/reality behind the data paves the way for a timely response to incidents and almost certain inferences depending on the cases. For instance, in the case of Swine influenza virus (SIV), through regional statistics of around 40 terms related to swine influenza made concerning search engines, the US health-care providers correctly forecasted where and to what extent the virus spread and in which regions it had potential progression despite very few patient application yet. Therefore, health-care service coverage was shifted to those regions beforehand, and the spread of the virus could be prevented (Aktan 2018; Onay 2020). Big data can provide beneficial results for fraud risks and detection as well. Though fraud dates to old times, the scandals influencing the markets like Enron and WorldCom have revealed that effective measures should be taken against fraud and corruption (Doğan and Kayakıran 2017). On the other hand, the difficulty in uncovering the fraud compels the researchers to develop new methods. Particularly proactive approaches produced for combating against fraud have gained prominence to notice the presence of fraud from the very beginning and obstruct its harm before it is large scaled (Ertikin 2017). Accordingly, the opinion that big data and big data analytic techniques will provide remarkable benefits in fraud detecting is prevailing today. While the study discusses

DOI: 10.1201/9781003138051-11

and elaborates the use of big data in determining the risk of fraud in different sectors and hotel enterprises, the rest of the chapter can be summarized as follows. Section 9.2 deals with the frauds encountered in enterprises. Section 9.3 explains big data as well as its strategic effects. Section 9.4 discusses the impacts of big data on fraud detection and auditing. Finally, Section 9.5 evaluates the use of big data in detecting fraud specific to hotel enterprises, and Section 9.6 presents the general evaluation drawn from the previous areas.

9.2 FRAUD

As a global problem and multidisciplinary concept, fraud is one of the significant threats to the sustainability of organizations in any industry. However, since it is mainly concealed, hardly ever reported, and therefore undetected, it remains a big challenge to explore the actual losses. Moreover, the victims of fraud can range from individuals or public sectors to businesses (Mojtahed 2019). Fraud encompasses deceptive actions such as manipulating or illegally capitalizing on business assets or resources by employees or/and third parties. Thus, it differs from other activities like theft. In addition, it is often performed by well-educated people who know the business or organization well, which causes another challenge for detection and prevention. The world's largest anti-fraud organization based in the USA, ACFE, (Association of Certified Fraud Examiners 2020) classifies frauds encountered in organizations into three categories as asset abuse, corruption, and fraudulent financial statements, which is also known as 'Fraud Tree.' *Asset abuse* (misappropriation) includes stealing or misusing the employing organization's resources. *Corruption* includes bribery, defalcation, extortion, economic blackmail, and using organization assets for personal benefits.

Financial statement frauds such as false disclosures, omissions in financial statements, and fictitious income are usually actions committed at the managerial level (Sunarti et al. 2020). They are also named corporate fraud or fraudulent financial reporting. Fraudulent financial statements are the most difficult to detect and, therefore, have the lowest share of profession-related frauds. However, they are reported as the ones causing the highest average lows (Ertikin 2017). In the ACFE's recently released 'Report to the Nations: 2020 Global Study on Occupational Fraud and Abuse,' the damages and losses caused by fraud are explained sectoral. Occupational fraud losses were most excellent in the mining ($475,000) and energy ($275,000) sectors.

On the other hand, the loss reported for the foodservice and hospitality industry was $114,000, with a high rate of corruption (39%). Apart from the economic losses, fraud and similar offenses were reported to diminish corporate social responsibility (CSR) and sustainability of an organization over time (Jurkiewicz and Giacalone 2016), and service technology was found to represent an antecedent of procedural corruption in the North American hotel industry (Gillard et al. 2018). This may also endanger the competitiveness of hotels in the hospitality industry, which seems paramount and requires awareness of fraudulent actions, devising measures to prevent and detect. Undoubtedly, no organization is expected to be immune to fraud. However, since fraud is not an industry-specific financial crime, the hotel industry is also susceptible to high risks of fraudulent actions. It gets its share due to its service and labor-driven characteristics and other reasons such as a load of monetary transactions, diversity of income units, sales of products with high unit values, and a variety of stocks. The risks are usually induced by unawareness of mistakes or ignoring or feeling no need for correction.

Furthermore, hotels have various cash-intensive outlets like rooms, spas, bars, cafes, restaurants, etc. Therefore, fraudulent behaviors are commonly observed in room revenues, food and beverage revenues, bar revenues, cash funds, credit slips, purchasing, receipt and inventory procedures, and operations administered by senior/top management. For detecting these frauds, computerized accounting information systems may not be adequate because the perpetrators may not be from low-level employees but also the managerial level.

9.3 BIG DATA

This section deals with the characteristics of big data and its effects on businesses in detail.

9.3.1 Characteristics of Big Data

The concept of big data is mainly defined as 'a new generation of technologies and architectures, designed to economically, the separate value from huge volumes of a wide variety of data, by enabling high-velocity capture, discovery, and analysis.' This definition associates big data with 3Vs, which are volume, velocity, and variety. Subsequent studies revealed that 3Vs do not explain today's big data. Two other representing qualities, 'veracity' and 'value,' were added (Jain et al. 2016). Therefore, five vs. of big data can be explained as follows:

Variety: The fundamental and most challenging nature of big data analysis includes various qualities and types. Variety of data, one of the basic distinctions between traditional and big data analysis, refers to data coexisting in different formats such as structured, semi-structured, or unstructured numbers, text, images, audio (Durmuş and Kar 2019).

Volume: Insanely increase of high-speed data production thanks to big data causes a massive rise in global data volume. Mobile appliances and wireless data processes in every sphere of daily life have constantly been producing data and providing millions of data over internet-based applications. However, storage of high amounts of data should also be considered. New technologies entail growth in generated data and data processing, storage, aggregation, and archiving challenges. Today, widespread cloud technology allows easy data storage and availability on demand (Yılmaz et al. 2017).

Velocity: It refers to how fast the data is generated and processed, which means real-time occurrence and a constant repeat of the data obtained from traditional and digital sources. In that way, increasing speed in data can be processed, stored, and analyzed by databases. For example, with its over 20,000 stores in 28 countries, the largest retailer Walmart has formed the most significant cloud in the world to process 2.5 petabytes of data per hour. In addition, people upload videos on YouTube for hours every day and every minute and send over 200 million emails (Ishwarappa and Anuradha 2015). When these facts are considered, the critical role of big data seems more understandable.

Value: Traditional data used in organizations are not sources providing essential information for the future as they are in static and archived condition. Analysis of future trends, getting ready in case of possible alterations, and taking necessary decisions will be possible through the value of big data. In this sense, big data provides remarkable contributions to organizations and businesses regarding the generation and processing of data by adding value. Real-time inputs for decision-making are essential in making sound and accurate judgments (Yılmaz et al. 2017).

Veracity: The truthfulness or reliability of big data can be evaluated under two aspects: high reliability of data source and appropriateness of data for the target audience. The data captured for big data are primarily from various sources, so they are not usually available to be checked for accuracy by the organizations reaching them. Accordingly, in today's world, where such a variety of data is encountered, assurance of accurateness depends on source data accurateness (Durmuş and Kar 2019).

As a company providing big data solutions, IBM originated 'veracity' to represent the unreliability inherent in some data sources. For instance, customer emotions in social media are obscure due to containing specific judgments. However, it should be kept in mind that these emotions may also include valuable information. Because of this, the need for the assessment of obscure data has led to the development and employment of different tools to manage obscure data (Gandomi and Haider 2015).

9.3.2 Strategic Impacts of Big Data

Our interaction on the internet has also increased with the rise of internet use in our daily life. This enables enterprises to gather more and more information about what we do, what we like, and where our location is. Enterprises need to go beyond conventional calculation methods to make those complex and varying data produced at any moment (Gillon et al. 2014). For that reason, computer clusters and distributed file systems such as HDFS—Hadoop Distributed File System, RDD—Resilient Distributed Datasets, and platforms have open-source software frameworks like Hadoop, Spark, MapReduce, Pig, and Hive are becoming widespread. Hadoop, the most well-known software, is an open-source software solution designed to work on big data. Hadoop is currently used for big data analytics in many leading IT companies, such as Yahoo, Amazon, Facebook, LinkedIn, Twitter, IBM, and Adobe. These technologies that are started to be used in data storage and processing have triggered the development of methods like data mining, text and web mining, artificial intelligence, machine learning, deep learning, and all utilized to analyze data (Atalay and Çelik 2017; Aktan 2018). Enterprises using big data aim to gain benefits in various fields such as e-commerce, e-government, science, health, and security. Benefits perceived as 'values' by enterprises depend on their strategic objectives regarding the use of big data (Günther et al. 2017). Big data is new products, new services, and new business opportunities. Big data provides a competitive advantage and effectively creates sustainable value by improving the data-based decision-making processes of enterprises

TABLE 9.1
Benefits of Big Data

Benefit Dimension	Subdimensions
IT infrastructure benefits	- Creating business flexibility for current and future changes - Lowering IT costs - Increasing IT infrastructure capacity
Operational benefits	- Decreasing costs - Developing production - Enhancing quality - Improving customer services
Management benefits	- Better management of resources - Development of decision-making and planning processes - Performance improvement
Strategic benefits	- Realizing growth targets - Providing cooperation - Developing innovation processes - Creating cost leadership - Ensuring product differentiation - Connecting with stakeholders
Organizational benefits	- Improving working models - Facilitating organizational learning - Creating a shared vision

Source: Wang et al. (2018, p. 5).

and increasing innovation opportunities. In addition, big data provides support in many areas, such as better understanding of customers, optimizing supply chain and human resources, and improving financial indicators (Wamba et al. 2015). According to Wang et al. (2018), big data benefits IT infrastructure, operational, organizational, management, and strategic fields. These benefits are summarized in Table 9.1.

Big data causes significant changes also in the business models. These changes are summarized in two company-based cases (www.bernardmarr.com): Firstly, Rolls-Royce uses big data in design, manufacturing, and after-sales support services. A large quantity of data is created in simulations used at the designing phase of the product, and they are processed, visualized, and determined which part of the design to improve. Quality is increased in the manufacturing system through the Internet of Things (IoT) and advanced measurement systems. Data from the sensors installed on the products and manufacturing equipment are stored in cloud technology and subsequently analyzed. In this way, big data facilitates improving the design process, reducing the time for product development, and increasing the quality and performance of the products while also lowering the costs.

Secondly, movements, heart and breathing rates, daily step numbers of and calories burned by the users are transferred to the cloud with the help of sensors on the PoloTech shirt developed by Ralph Lauren apparel company, and these data are analyzed. Users can watch these data and have access to exercise programs designed specifically for them. Moreover, big data offers essential data for researchers. For example, social media data are used to research customers' lifestyles instead of traditional data collection methods such as questionnaires and phone interviews. One of the most popular location-based social networks globally, foursquare keeps 5 billion check-in records of approximately 55 million users. These data provide a rich data resource for various research studies such as customers' lifestyles (Mannan et al. 2019).

9.4 BIG DATA AND AUDITING

Big data use has also developed accounting and auditing practices. It contributes to accounting practices through video, audio recordings, and software alternatives. Instead of determining inventory costs via traditional methods, it enables data obtained from the Radio-Frequency Identification (RFID) system, one of the big data resources. Besides, the information provided by big data helps accounting transactions to be performed with accounting information systems in the electronic medium in real time (Avunduk and Kızgın 2020). Warren et al. (2015) state that big data increases accounting information quality. The authors also stress that it will decrease the difference between GAAP and IFRS in the USA since it allows global data sharing. Accordingly, it will help fair value accounting develop into a worldwide accounting model. By examining the accounting system of the HUAWEI technology enterprise, which uses big data, Yang (2020) draws our attention to the trust-establishing role of big data in terms of currency and accuracy of the information generated during the accounting process. The author also concludes that constant communication between accounting and other departments is achieved, and enterprise resources are scientifically and efficiently managed. As is known, big data comprises a multi-type data combination of traditionally structured financial and nonfinancial data, logistics data, sensor data, emails, phone calls, social media data, blogs, and a mix of other internal/external data. This extensive database has caused changes in auditing methodology (Onay 2020). It enables auditors to reach financial (accounting records) and nonfinancial (board decisions, customer agreements/contracts, etc.) information faster. In addition, it provides auditors applying analytical auditing procedures with an opportunity to compare previous years' data of enterprise being audited with sectoral data efficiently, which leads to more apparent risk determination for the concerned enterprise (Tang and Karim 2019). The current literature on big data and auditing relationships has highlighted several points. According to Yoon et al. (2015), big data assists the trustfulness assessment of audit evidence.

In contrast to traditional auditing, which examines commercial transactions manually to obtain evidence, today's use of GPS enables data confirmation more reliably. In addition, various analysis techniques for gaining evidence analyze data. Cao et al. (2015) and Zhang et al. (2015) claim that big data enhances the efficiency of financial statement auditing.

Similarly, Christea (2020) asserts that big data eases accounting procedures for financial statement auditing, decreases risk, and improves organizational performance. As a result, big data brings new opportunities to auditing practices in China.

Furthermore, since it has improved auditing processes, it reduces subjective judgments and helps for objective results. Zhu and Huang (2019) support this view, who conclude that bid data enables more accessible data analysis and comparison by providing standardization and increases auditing quality due to subjectivity reduction.

9.4.1 Big Data and Fraud

The purpose of fraud auditing is to reveal and investigate suspected fraud transactions. Mainly suspicious transactions are investigated in fraud auditing. There is usually either an estimate or a denouncement when choosing an account. The fraud auditor analyzes all operations covered by eliminating sampling errors. Process in the traditional method includes document review, investigation of external data, and interviews (Ertikin 2017). Unfortunately, the risk of fraud is a highly complex and subjective judgment that the auditor must make in the audit. The auditor's traditional audit procedures in determining the risk of fraud do not always yield effective results. Technological tools should ensure that standard fraud risk checklists and standard planning programs give results in fraud detection. In this process, big data analysis methods such as data mining and data analytics (e.g., predictive modeling) effectively determine fraud risks. For example, the correlation between financial and nonfinancial data in measuring the performance of an enterprise might be an indicator of the manipulation of financial information (Brown-Liburd et al. 2015). Recently, considerable literature has grown up around the theme of fraud and big data analytics. It will be helpful to mention some examples to understand better big data use methods in fraud detection. For instance, Jain (2017) investigated data mining practices in detecting frauds in the telecommunications industry, and Mishra and Kumari (2020) in detecting credit card fraud. Srinivasan and Arunasalan (2013) announced new applications using big data to detect fraud, abuse, waste, and fault in private health insurance claims. Furthermore, it has been stated that these practices determine the source of the high costs of private health insurance and detect malicious patterns. Çalış et al. (2014) analyzed a private hospital's health supplies purchasing data according to the digital analysis method and identified fraudulent transactions in the purchasing department. The study emphasized that traditional fraud control methods are insufficient in detecting fraud. Fraud can be detected in advance by analyzing the information in the database thanks to information technologies. Laha (2016) stated that big data analytics play an essential role in detecting credit card fraud. Thanks to this system, the customer's past transactions provide crucial information about the accuracy of the current transaction, and a possible fraudulent situation can be determined. Suppose the credit card company detects a suspicion in the customer's transaction. In that case, the transaction is declined or sends the message to the mobile phone asking the customer for the validity of the transaction and the correctness of the credentials. If the information requested from the customer is provided, the transaction is allowed. Otherwise, the customer's credit card is canceled, and a new credit card is issued. Another study by Jianhao (2019) examined the 'credit risk control anti-fraud project' process by using the big data applications of banks. This process consists of four modules (retail credit application, cabinet gateway, query pre-management platform, and offline data processing platform) to prevent fraud by detecting risks before, when, and after the credit is given. Differently, in the health-care sector, Georgakopoulos et al. (2020) detected fraudulent transactions using big data tools to detect financial and medical frauds. Using big data, financial institutions can see the details of money movements, anticipate and prevent theft, and better understand consumer behavior. International banks benefit from big data in many areas such as customer behavior analysis, cross-product sales, legal compliance management, reputation risk management, and dealing with financial crimes (Srivastava and Gopalkrishnan 2015). For example, Chen et al. (2015) examined the fraud risk management of Alibaba Company, one of the most famous e-commerce companies in the world. Big data-based fraud risk management system predicts misuse and incorrect transactions. In addition, the Ant-Buckler system based on big data ensures the prevention of fraudulent actions for merchants and banks in the online environment. In summary, data mining and machine learning techniques are extensively investigated in detecting credit card frauds in the literature (Carneiro et al. 2017; Dornadula and Geetha 2019; Itoo et al. 2020). With the intense use of electronic payment systems, credit card fraud has increased, and this situation has caused severe financial losses to the related parties. This has forced service providers to continually improve their systems to detect fraud (Jurgovsky et al. 2018). On the other hand, cybercriminals' development of fraud models has required service providers to apply advanced and dynamic techniques. Among these techniques, data mining and machine learning techniques have been the most discussed topics.

9.5 THE USE OF BIG DATA FOR DETERMINING FRAUD IN HOTEL ENTERPRISES

Characteristics of hotel enterprises make them more vulnerable than other businesses. They are often small scaled but with a large scale of cash transactions due to many revenue centers and high-value stocks such as seafood and wine, and these stocks might be easily consumed by employees (Geller 1991). However, grouping the business processes of hotel enterprises in two main titles as administrative and technical services (human resources, marketing, maintenance, security, etc.) and accommodation, food and beverage, and guest entertainment activities (spa, health center, etc.) make their management difficult (Radojevic and Radovic 2014). Considering these differences, a system that will detect fraud in advance should be established. Otherwise, unauthorized commercial transactions, errors in financial transactions, fictitious sales, cash frauds, deficiencies such as contracts approved without notification, and consequently, the institution will face financial loss. This can also have various consequences, such as business bankruptcy (Aktürk 2015). Therefore, it is essential that businesses operating in the hospitality industry ensure the confidentiality, monitoring, and safety of the data they handle and process. In a study by Okutmuş and Uyar (2014), fraudulent transactions were detected in a hotel business's food and beverage department. The hotel's document and book examination revealed the difference between the amount used in the food department and the amount usually used. It has been determined that this difference stems from the relationship of interest between the kitchen manager and the supplier company and has caused financial losses due to the employee's use of business assets for his benefit. It is also stated that cybercrime has become more critical for this industry since most of the cyberattacks have been carried out in hotels and resorts since 2016 (Chen and Fiskus 2018). It is easy for cybercriminals to steal all the information at once, primarily since chain hotels use integrated systems to manage their assets and customers. There have also been incidents of credit card fraud (CARD Payment card fraud) in cyberattacks, and users' information is stolen. Nwachukwu et al. (2021) stated that data mining, one of the big data analysis methods, is used intensively in detecting fraud. Big data plays a vital role in managing the risk of fraud in the hospitality industry and other industries. In addition to structured data obtained from corporate systems such as food and beverage services, information systems, customer information and order management systems, accounting and stock management systems, access control systems, hotel management and reservation systems in the hotel business; semi-structured–unstructured data (Esen and Türkay 2017) obtained from blogs, websites, social media, mobile phone applications, location information can be analyzed for fraud risk management. For example, in their study concerning this issue, Gray and Debreceny (2014) pointed out that fraud can be detected by performing data mining techniques on many data sets like internal (such as daily customer check-ins) and external (such as social media) sources.

Hajek and Henriques (2017) examined big data analysis techniques in predicting financial statement fraud. They analyzed the financial information and managerial comments obtained from the corporate annual reports of 311 public companies using text mining and machine learning techniques. In addition, they examined the extent to which these techniques helped to predict financial statement fraud. The study findings revealed that revenues and earnings estimates play a critical role in financial statement fraud, and negative, uncertain, and controversial language variables are significantly associated with the fraud. Therefore, big data provides essential risk management and fraud detection (Corckcroft and Russell 2018). In their study, Vasarhelyi et al. (2015) concluded that the uses of big data could be on a larger scale, such as security videos receipts and exits, news videos marketing activities, management of social networks customer relations, RFID inventory confirmation, web hits revenue prediction, mobile calls staff cost estimation and observation. Thus, an auditor can evaluate much more evidence during fraud examinations. Furthermore, Tang and Khondkar (2019) proposed a six-stage model for fraud detection: initial data collection, data integration, fraud indicator identification, group meetings and discussions, drawing conclusions, and documentation. Since big data and data analytics are used in this model, it is reported that accurate audit evidence is obtained in detecting fraud and that the analytical audit procedure results are reliable. To support this, it is stated that big data and big data analytics increase audit quality and effectively detect fraud (Ballios 2021).

9.6 CONCLUSION

When current literature is examined in line with the purpose of the study, it is seen that big data is used significantly in accounting auditing and in managing the risk of fraud. The studies emphasize that it is possible to detect fraudulent transactions and form audit opinions based on more robust justifications using big data analysis techniques. The literature reveals that fraud is domain specific with no one-solution-fits-all method among fraud detection techniques (Mojtahed 2019), and the use of big data in fraud detection varies according to companies and sectors. For example, while big data analysis techniques are mainly used to detect credit card frauds in the financial industry, they are used to detect financial and medical fakes in the service industry like the health-care sector. In the hospitality industry, especially in terms of hotels, the room sales are the primary revenue items. In addition, having income from operational departments (food and beverage, sports center, spa, etc.), having high unit value stocks, being intense in monetary transactions and in labor force lead to high risk of fraud.. Advanced techniques are needed to manage these risks to make the various internal or external data types more significant and valuable for effective benefiting. Big data analysis techniques play a crucial role in analyzing these data and managing the risk of fraud resulting from the analysis. Undoubtedly, big data analytics is an efficient and intelligent tool helping to identify and avoid the risk of security and fraudulent behavior. Big data also provides new insights for fraud detection and prevention strategies, including real-time detection (Madhuri et al. 2021). However, despite the importance of big data use and its remarkable potential in fraud detection, there remains a lack of studies with a concentration of the hospitality industry, which deserves full attention. The major limitation of this study is the evaluation of big data use in detecting fraud in hospitality (hotels) within the literature framework. The issue of fraud detection via big data in the hospitality industry is intriguing and could be deeply explored in further research. Further case studies and more significant efforts are required to fully understand its practical implications and how big data analysis techniques are used in fraud risk management of hotel enterprises.

REFERENCES

Aktan, Ertuğrul. 2018. "Büyük Veri: Uygulama Alanları, Analitiği ve Güvenlik Boyutu". *Bilgi Yönetimi Dergisi*, 1(2): 2–12.

Aktürk, Ahmet. 2015. "Konaklama İşletmelerinde Etkin Bir İç Kontrol Sisteminin Tesisi Bağlamında Muhasebe Sistem Organizasyonu: Bir Vaka Analizi". *Journal of Accounting, Finance and Auditing Studies*, 1(4): 108–127.

Association of Certified Fraud Examiners. 2020. Report to the Nation 2020 Global Study on Occupational Fraud and Abuse. https://acfepublic.s3-us-west-2.amazonaws.com/2020-Report-to-the-Nations.pdf

Atalay, Muhammet and Enes Çelik. 2017. "Büyük Veri Analizinde Yapay Zeka ve Makine Öğrenmesi Uygulamaları". *Mehmet Akif Ersoy Üniversitesi Sosyal Bilimler Dergisi*, 9(22): 164.

Avunduk, Hüseyin and Merve Kızgın. 2020. "Büyük Veri ve Sürekli Denetimde Veri Analizi". *Journal of Business in the Digital Age*, 3(1): 78.

Ballios, Dimitris. 2021. "The Impact of Big Data on Accounting and Auditing". *International Journal of Corporate Finance and Accounting*, 8(1): 1–14.

Brown-Liburd, Helen, Hussein Issa and Daielle Lombardi. 2015. "Behavioral Implications of Big Data's Impact on Audit Judgment and Decision Making and Future Research Directions". *Accounting Horizons*, 29(2): 451–468.

Çalış, Yıldırım, Emrah Keleş and Ahmet Engin. 2014. "Hilenin Ortaya Çıkartılmasında Bilgi Teknolojilerinin Önemi ve Bir Uygulama". *Muhasebe ve Finansman Dergisi*, 63: 93–108.

Cao, Min, Roman Chyhyla and Trevor Stewart. 2015. "Big Data Analytics in Financial Statement Audits". *Accounting Horizons*, 29(2): 423–429.

Carneiro, Nuna, Gonçalo Figueira and Migel Costa. 2017. "A Data Mining Based System for Credit-Card Fraud Detection in e-Tail". *Decision Support Systems*, 95: 91–101.

Cecconi, Federico and Marco Campennì (Eds.). (2019). *Information and Communication Technologies (ICT) in Economic Modeling. Computational Social Sciences.* Chapter 11 by Mojtahed V., *Big Data for Fraud Detection.* doi:10.1007/978-3-030-22605-3.

Chen, Hsinchun and Joseph Fiscus. 2018. "The Inhospitable Vulnerability: A Need for Cybersecurity Risk Assessment in the Hospitality Industry". *Journal of Hospitality and Tourism Technology*, 9 (2): 1–13.

Chen, Jidong, Ye Tao, Haoran Wang and Tao Chen. 2015. "Big Data Based Fraud Risk Management at Alibaba". *The Journal of Finance and Data Science*, 1: 1–10.

Christea, Lavinia Mihaela. 2020. "Innovations in Financial Audit Based on Emerging Technologies". *Audit Financiar*, 18(3): 513–531.

Cockcroft, Sophie and Mark Russell. 2018. "Big Data Opportunities for Accounting and Finance Practice and Research". *Australian Accounting Review*, 28(2): 1–11.Doğan, Saime and Dilek Kayakıran. 2017. "İşletmelerde Hile Denetiminin Önemi". *Maliye Finans Yazıları*, 108: 168.

Dornadula, Vaishnavi Nath and Sa Geetha. 2019. "Credit Card Fraud Detection Using Machine Learning Algorithms". *Procedia Computer Science*, 165: 631–641.

Durmuş, Cem and Tuğba Kar. 2019. "Muhasebe Bilgi Sistemleri Doğrultusunda Büyük Veri Kullanımı: Büyük Veri'yi Etkin Olarak Kullanan İşletmeler Üzerine Bir Araştırma". *Mali Çözüm Dergisi*, 29(156): 169–193.

Ertikin, Kıvanç. 2017. "Hile Denetimi: Kırmızı Bayrakların Tespiti için Kullanılan Proaktif Yaklaşımlar". *Muhasebe ve Finansman Dergisi*, 75: 89–91.

Esen, Fevzi and Bahar Türkay. 2017. "Turizm Endüstrilerinde Büyük Veri Kullanımı". *Journal of Tourism and Gastronomy Studies*, 5(4): 92–115.

Gandomi, Amir and Murtaza Haider. 2015. "Beyond the Hype: Big Data Concepts, Methods, and Analytics". *International Journal of Information Management*, 35(2): 137–144.

Geller, A. Neal. 1991. "Rule out Fraud and Theft: Controlling Your Food-Service Operation". *The Cornell Hotel and Restaurant Administration Quarterly*, 32(4): 55–65.

Georgakopoulos, Spiros, Parisis Gallos and Vassilis P. Plagianakos. 2020. "Using Big Data Analytics to Detect Fraud in Healthcare Provision". doi: 10.1109/MECBME 47393.2020.9265118.

Gillard, Evelina, Ming-Hsiang Chen and Wan Qing Lv. 2018. "Procedural Corruption in the North American Hotel Industry". *International Journal of Hospitality Management*, 72: 154–167.

Gillon, Kirstin, Sinan Aral, Ching-Yung Lin, Sunil Mithas and Mark Zozulia. 2014. "Business Analytics: Radical Shift or Incremental Change?", *Communications of the Association for Information Systems*, 34: 139.

Gray, Glen and Debreceny Roger. 2014. "A Taxonomy to Guide Research on the Application of Data Mining to Fraud Detection in Financial Statement Audits". *International Journal of Accounting Information Systems*, 15: 357–380.

Günther, Wendy, Mohammad Mehrizi, Marleen Huysman and Frans Feldberg. 2017. "Debating Big Data: A Literature Review on Realizing Value from Big Data". *Journal of Strategic Information Systems*, 26: 191.

Hajek, Petr and Roberto Henriques. 2017. "Mining Corporate Annual Reports for Intelligent Detection of Financial Statement Fraud—A Comparative Study of Machine Learning Methods". *Knowledge-Based Systems*, 128(15): 139–152.

Ishwarappa Kalbandi and J. Anuradha. 2015. "A Brief Introduction on Big Data 5 Vs Characteristics and Hadoop Technology". *Procedia Computer Science*, 48: 320.

Itoo, Fayaz, Meenakshi Mittal and Satwinder Singh. 2020. "Comparison and Analysis of Logistic Regression, Naïve Bayes and KNN Machine Learning Algorithms for Credit Card Fraud Detection". doi:10.1007/s41870-020-00430-y

Jain, Priyank, Manasi Gyanchandani and Nilay Khare. 2016. "Big Data Privacy: A Technological Perspective and Review". *Journal of Big Data*, 3: 1.

Jain, Vanita. 2017. "Perspective Analysis of Telecommunication Fraud Detection Using Data Stream Analytics and Neural Network Classification Based Data Mining". *International Journal of Information Technology*, 9: 303–310.

Jianhao, Yu. 2019. "Design and Implementation of Bank Wind Control Anti-Fraud Project Based on Big Data Technology". doi:10.1088/1742-6596/1345/2/022064.

Jurgovsky, Johannes, Michael Granitzer and Konstantin Ziegler. 2018. "Credit-Card Fraud Detection". *Expert Systems with Applications*, 100(15): 234–245.

Jurkiewicz, Carole and Rebert A. Giacalone. 2016. "Organizational Determinants of Ethical Dysfunctionality". *Journal of Business Ethics*, 136: 1–12.

Laha, Arnab. 2016. Statistical Challenges with Big Data in Management Science. In: Pyne S., Rao B., Rao S. (eds.) *Big Data Analytics*. New Delhi: Springer India.

Madhuri, Talapuru, Sirisha, E. Ramesh Babu, B. Uma and B. Muni Lakshmi. 2021. "Big-Data Driven Approaches in Materials Science for Real-Time Detection and Prevention of Fraud". *Materials Today: Proceedings*, 15 May, 1–8.

Mannan, Muhammad, Saboohi Mehmood, Muhammad Shafiq and Aqeel-ur Rehman. 2019. Data Management and Visualization Using Big Data Analytics. In: García M.F., Lev B. (eds.) *Data Science and Digital Business*. Switzerland: Springer.

Mishra, Smita Prava and Priyanka Kumari. 2020. Analysis of Techniques for Credit Card Fraud Detection: A Data Mining Perspective. In: Patnaik S., Ip A., Tavana M., Jain V. (eds.) *New Paradigm in Decision Science and Management. Advances in Intelligent Systems and Computing*. Springer.

Nwachukwu, Chijioke, Timothy Usman, Sadiq Akhor and Agboola Oladipupo. 2021. "Auditing in the New Age of Industry 4.0: The Need for more Research". *International Journal of Business Strategy and Automation*, 2(1): 17–28.

Okutmuş, Ercüment and Süleyman Uyar. 2014. "Konaklama İşletmelerinde Yiyecek-İçecek Departmanında Yapılan Hilenin Tespiti: Vaka Analizi". *Mali Çözüm Dergisi*, 24(12): 35–54.

Onay, Ahmet. 2020. "Büyük Veri Çağında İç Denetimin Dönüşümü". *Muhasebe Bilim Dünyası Dergisi*, 22(1): 136–141.

Radojevic, Tijana and Nikica Radovic. 2014. Application of Information Systems and Internal control in Hotel Business. doi:10.15308/sinteza-2014-777-781.

Srinivasan, Uma and Bavani Arunasalam. 2013. "Leveraging Big Data Analytics to Reduce Healthcare Costs". *IT Professional Magazine*, 15(6): 21.

Srivastava, Utkarsh and Santosh Gopalkrishnan. 2015. "Impact of Big Data Analytics on Banking Sector: Learning for Indian Banks". *Procedia Computer Science*, 50: 643–652.

Sunarti, Nyoman, Putu Kurniawan, Edy Sujana and I. Nyoman P. Yasa. 2020. "Fraud Risk Management: An Anti-Fraud Model for Tourist Accommodation in Bali". *Asia Pacific Fraud Journal*, 5(1): 137–146.

Tang, Jiali and Khondkar Karim. 2019. "Financial Fraud Detection and Big Data Analytics—Implications on Auditors' Use of Fraud Brainstorming Session". *Managerial Auditing Journal*, 34(3): 324–337.

Vasarhelyi, Miklos A., Alexander Kogan and Brad M. Tuttle. 2015. "Big Data Accounting: An Overview". *Accounting Horizons*, 29(2): 392.

Wamba, Samuel, Shahriar Akter, Andrew Edward, Geoffreay Chopin and Denis Gnanzou. 2015. "How "Big Data" Can Make Big Impact: Findings from a Systematic Review and a Longitudinal Case Study". *International Journal of Production Economics*, 165: 234–246.

Wang, Yichuan, Lee Ann Kung and Terry A. Byrd. 2018. "Big Data Analytics: Understanding Its Capabilities and Potential Benefits for Healthcare Organizations". *Technological Forecasting & Social Change*, 126: 3–13.

Warren, J. Donald, Kevin C. Moffitt and Paul Byrnes. 2015. "How Big Data Will Change Accounting". *Accounting Horizons*, 29(2): 397–407.

Yang, Wang. 2020. "Analysis on the Influence of Big Data Era on Enterprise Financial Accounting—A Case Study of HUA WEI Technologies Co., Ltd". doi:10.1051/e3sconf/202021401004

Yılmaz, Bülent, Samet Bülbül and Murat Atik. 2017. "Büyük Verinin (Big Data) Muhasebe Üzerindeki Etkisi ve Muhasebeye Sağladığı Katkıların İncelenmesi". *Kara Harp Okulu Bilim Dergisi*, 27(1): 79–112.

Yoon, Kyunghee, Lucas Hoogduin and Li Zhang. 2015. "Big Data as Complementary Audit Evidence". *Accounting Horizons*, 29(2): 431–438.

Zhang, Juan, Xiongsheng Yang and Deniz Appelbaum. 2015. "Toward Effective Big Data Analysis in Continuous Auditing". *Accounting Horizons*, 29(2): 469–476.

Zhu, Yangpeng and Bingbing Huang. 2019. "Summary of Research on the Application of Big Data in Auditing". 674–676. doi:10.1109/CISCE.2019.00156

https://publicaffairs-sme.com/PatriotFamily/_from_cloud_at_Walmart_23_Jan_2017.pdf (11.02.2021)

www.ber nardmarr.com/default.asp?contentID=684 (01.03.2021)

10 Digital Change for Sustainable Restaurant Systems

Bükre Aslan Savaşan

CONTENTS

DOI: 10.1201/9781003138051-12

10.1 INTRODUCTION

Considering worldwide, it is possible to say that half of the world's population works in the food sector if we talk about the population that lives in the countryside and works in food production and processing in the cities. However, it can be understood through the worldwide increasing diseases originating from nutrition that the concept of food, the most fundamental necessity, is not given enough importance. Most of the techniques employed in this field are unfortunately of unsustainable quality. Food products that are tasteless, standardized, unecological, and harmful in terms of community health are produced most of the time. A system of production aims for easily merchantable, commercialized instead of the best product has been created. The organic structures of the food have been spoiled, and biological variety has been reduced. A severe natural disaster has been caused by contaminating the land and the air, applying to polluting fuels. Instead of putting an end to world hunger, a global system that disrespects the effort of billions of people has been created. The concept of sustainability that aims to leave a better world than it was, not taking anything more than needed, not harming the environment or the world, and correcting the mistake should there is any, is the only way to sort these courses of events out. If we can provide sustainability for the food system, we can produce and consume the best possible food. Even though this condition is a natural and right wish to be made, it is not considered severe and necessarily enough. The sustainable food system can be explained as a process related to all social, psychological, cultural, and political factors that include farming and food production, selling, and consumption. The purpose of the studies of sustainable food systems is to implement traditional principles of sustainable development. When the sustainable food system includes the responsibility of eco-nutrition against economic, socio-cultural, and environmental sustainability and sticks to the most convenient health standards of the community members, it can prove the community can develop socially and economically. The sustainable food system can contribute to creating sustainable factors related to a destination directly or indirectly. It supports agriculture and food production, prevents unauthentic production, increases appealingness, empowers the local community and pride, and provides a trademark and identity based on food experience. The sustainable food system in a destination also contributes a lot to sustainable tourism by expanding and developing the area of the sources of the local tourism, providing added value to the authenticity of the destination, empowering the local economy in terms of tourism and agriculture sectors, and ensuring an eco-friendly infrastructure. Sustainable food systems cause sustainable restaurants. Restaurants can monitor energy, food, and waste streams, help human health and the environment, and share and educate customers. They can lay the groundwork for local food economies by working together. Restaurants connect with their customers through their food and decide where the food comes from and how it will be prepared. As a critical component of the food and beverage industry, the restaurant industry can significantly impact the food inventory network in terms of sustainability. Restaurants can move toward sustainability in a variety of ways. Given that restaurants are involved in the purchasing, planning, and sale of food to consumers, they can play a role in empowering consumers to spend less unexpectedly by moving to sustainability. There is a variety of practices ranging from local sourcing to reusing or energy efficiency to accomplish. Supplying ethical food while supporting nearby obtainment, practical cultivating, and angling can contribute to the local food economy. They can assess energy use in carbon emissions and the supply chain and implement measures to make energy more productive. They can bolster environments through water use, waste transfer, and sympathy toward biodiversity. Restaurants that resolve these concerns will be more sustainable, and sustainable restaurants will contribute to a more sustainable tourism industry (Gore 2008). It is wise to use technology to implement sustainable systems in restaurants. Digital concepts brought by technology such as blockchain and big data have become inevitable for restaurant operators. For this reason, it is imperative to include these digital concepts in restaurant applications. Various ways of using these new concepts for sustainability are discussed in this section. However, the use of these technologies, which will become widespread in the future, in restaurants is currently limited.

10.2 THE CONCEPT OF SUSTAINABILITY

Many associations and organizations have given the concept of sustainability definitions since it became a current issue. Scientist Hans Carl von Carlowitz first used 'Sustainability' by definition in his *Sylvicultura Oeconomica* book. The concept of sustainability was put forward three centuries ago to manage forest and wildlife, then began to be used as related to fishing in the first half of the 20th century. In addition, there had been discussions about soil failure and the methods of sustainable soil cultivation in agriculture to prevent this failure, especially in the 1930s (Vehkamaki 2005; Brander 2007).

Dyllick and Hockerts (2002) have indicated that sustainability has been one of the most repeated words of the 21st century and emphasized that sustainability is the promise for the protection of the natural environment and cultural experiences for future generations and the excellent evolution of the community toward a more equal and healthier world. Sustainability has been defined as the ability of any system such as a community or an ecosystem to execute its works without an interruption, breakdown, and excessive consumption or the power of a plan to continue without excessively depending on the primary sources of which it vitally relies on. This can be explained in this way: Leaving the world in a better condition than it was found as not taking more than what is needed, trying not to damage the world or the environment, and correcting the mistake made (Hawken 1993). The concept of sustainability is related to the appearance of the concern about things being 'unsustainable.' When the adopted production types (energy, agriculture, industrial manufacturing, etc.) are considered unsustainable, changing these types into a new alternative has been suggested (Şahin 2004).

10.2.1 Sustainable Development

When mentioning sustainability, it is necessary mainly to consider economic concepts as well. For this reason, sustainability and sustainable development has been used most of the time simultaneously. In the World Commission on Environment and

Development description, the concept of sustainable development is mentioned as 'meeting the needs and abilities of today's people and future generations with no sacrifice.' According to this World Commission on Environment and Development description, sustainability is ensured through all human activities and involves many different topics (WCED 1987).

The concept of sustainable development is a profound concept consisting of three dimensions. These dimensions were first schematized as economic, social, and ecological dimensions by the economist René Passet in 1979 (Passet 1979; Kongoli 2016).

The 'The Future We Want' report was published at the World Sustainable Development Summit (Rio + 20) held in Rio in 2012. According to this report, to achieve sustainable development goals, it is necessary to integrate the economic, social, and environmental dimensions and understand their intersections well (Boas et al. 2016; Turhan et al. 2017).

10.2.1.1 Environmental Sustainability

Environmental sustainability is the ability to increase the value and characteristics of nature by protecting ecological resources and ecological heritage, allowing them to be renewed (Hürol 2014). Minimizing air, soil, and water pollution and protecting biological diversity are among the main objectives. In addition, managing nonrenewable resources is an essential concept to handle (Duran 2018). A sustainable system as environmentally should stabilize its primary resource and avoid the exploitation of the primary resources or its environmental investment functions and use up the inedible resources only which are replaced with investment. This process should also involve the biological variety, atmospheric balance, and the protection of the functions of other ecosystems, which are not classified as economic resources (Holmberg and Sandbrook 1992).

10.2.1.2 Social Sustainability

Social sustainability is the ability of every individual in society to access essential services such as welfare, health, education, and security rights equally, without social class and gender discrimination (Hürol 2014). Equality of generations and transferring social sustainability to future generations is also an important issue in social sustainability. The practices of today's age should not put future generations in a disadvantageous position (McKenzie 2004). A socially sustainable system should adequately realize even distribution, health and education, gender equality, and social services involving political responsibility. Social sustainability is defined as internalizing the excess input locally or nationally by society and maintaining this character with no social incompatibility in the short or long run (McKenzie 2004).

10.2.1.3 Economic Sustainability

Economic sustainability is creating income and employment to protect the population (Hürol 2014). While conducting economic activities, the ecological balance should not be ignored, and care should be taken in using nonrenewable resources (Duran 2018). Economic sustainability is related to other dimensions of sustainability. Ecological and social problems will also affect economic sustainability in the long run (Özdemir 2018). An economically sustainable system should be productive based on the lasting fundamentals of goods and services, provide the management of the governmental and external debts steadily and avoid sectoral instabilities that damage the agricultural and industrial production (Holmberg and Sandbrook 1992).

10.2.2 The Significance of Sustainable Development in Terms of Countries and Regions

Today, sustainability is defined with a multidimensional integrative perspective such as the superiority of law, information society, international competitive power, sustainable development, human development, and economic development. Some significant defining factors of the developing process are the progress in the technological field. The level of the developed countries is related to their capacity to produce technology and innovations provided in the technical area during both the developing process and the new developing process in which information comes into prominence. The quality and evolution of sustainable development can be tracked through activities carried out on international platforms. The adventure that began in 1972 in Stockholm has made it 40 years with the meeting of 2012 Rio (Rio + 20). In this process, sustainable development has gained international qualification due to a series of conferences and decisions.

The studies of sustainable development that aim to involve all world countries have shown activities in the last 15 years. It has been mainly carried out among international institutions and developed countries. Especially, the United Nations (UN) and side organizations, UN Development Programme (UNDP), UN Environment Programme (UNEP), UN Industrial Development Organization (UNIDD), and UN Food and Agriculture Organization (UNFAO), have been carrying out studies intensively in terms of sustainable development (Yılmaz 2014). Just as it aims to meet the fundamental human needs and expectations, sustainable development is considered a solution for rapid population growth, hunger, and unemployment caused by international struggles and the reduction of natural resources that directly concern human life. For this reason, sustainable development possesses an essential element regarding countries and regions.

10.2.3 Corporate Sustainability

The efforts of all stakeholders, including governments, nongovernmental organizations, individuals, and businesses, are essential for sustainable development to take place. Corporate sustainability is the implementation of the concept of sustainable development by companies. It is defined as adopting business strategies that meet the needs of the business and business stakeholders while protecting human and natural resources (WCED 1987; Mukumbi 2013). Financial performance and profit today no longer guarantee the long-term survival of a company. Therefore, a company should also integrate nonfinancial performances such as social responsibility projects and environmental protection practices into its strategic planning. Recent research has shown a positive relationship between corporate solid sustainability policies and the profitability of companies.

Furthermore, companies with corporate concrete sustainability policies have more responsible attitudes toward their employees; they use the concept of 'long-term planning' required by corporate sustainability (Lin 2010; Sprinkle and Maines 2010). Especially, in developed countries, businesses are more expected to care about sustainability by the public. As a result, companies are obligated to explain their economic, social, and environmental sustainability practices and report their sustainability manifestos. There are also restaurants that we can give examples of these companies. The studies revealed that consumers showed positive approaches to the restaurants that do sustainable practices. It was stated that announcing these practices of restaurants to the public would provide them with a competitive advantage (Hu et al. 2010; Freeman 2011). For example, the 3 Michelin star restaurant Azurmendi, located in Bilboa, has prepared a report that shows; all the 17 Sustainable Development Goals in the Sustainable Development 2030 Agenda of the UN (United Nations 2015) have been practiced by the Restaurant Azurmendi. In addition, the report shows the sustainable practices it has carried out by the restaurant (Restaurant Azurmendi 2018). There are also more examples of sustainability reports prepared by different restaurants in the world. For instance, Restaurant Relae (2016) in Denmark published its sustainability report in 2016, emphasizing the company's environmental and social sustainability practices, and the restaurant group Café de Coral (Café de Coral Group 2018), which published its sustainability report in 2018. Thus, it is possible to observe many companies from different industries publishing corporate sustainability reports such as these restaurants.

10.3 SUSTAINABLE RESTAURANT SYSTEM

Restaurants administer energy, food, and waste streams, support the environment, and share and educate customers. They can have a positive impact on local food economies through collaborative efforts. Restaurants bond with their customers and decide where the food comes from, how it will be prepared and discarded, and who will be involved in that preparation. As a critical component of the food and beverage industry, the restaurant industry can significantly impact the food inventory network in terms of sustainability.

Sustainable restaurants are defined as food and beverage establishments where environmental practices such as waste recycling, water-saving, and energy-saving are carried out (Chen et al. 2011). These restaurants provide a more environmentally friendly service for consumers, distributors, and producers (Kurnaz and Özdoğan 2017). Sustainable restaurant buildings are designed as energy-efficient and environmentally friendly. These structures may be newly built or renovated facilities (Namkung and Jang 2017). Sustainable restaurants focus on increasing their revenues by reducing their costs and concentrate on efficiency and energy-saving by acting on the principle of reducing, recycling, and reusing (Cousins et al. 2011). All elements of the sustainable restaurant movement are implemented at businesses, groups, and individuals. While this movement handles consumers, it is green marketing and corporate social responsibility activity. Corporate social responsibility refers to the concept that enterprises integrate the needs and interests of shareholders, suppliers, employees, customers, and the whole world into corporate strategy (Legrand et al. 2010). Many restaurant owners are hesitant about sustainable practices. Because they think that these applications are costly and can reduce the quality of service. However, implementing environmentally friendly applications is not just a social responsibility project; it is a development that will gain a competitive advantage by providing image reputation and cost savings in the long term to the company. In addition to the competitive advantages, consumers' demand for environmentally friendly products and services is increasing. This increasing demand encourages restaurant owners to do sustainable practices (Jeong 2015). The concept of sustainability and a sustainable restaurant system has been examined until this part of the chapter. Now, how restaurants can benefit from technological innovations to be socially and environmentally sustainable will be presented.

10.4 ENVIRONMENTAL IMPACT OF RESTAURANTS

Restaurants are great consumption machines, where food is produced by using energy, fuel, water, and natural resources, and a large amount of waste is generated in the meantime. Restaurant enterprises, which constitute a large part of small and medium-sized enterprises, are the enterprises that pollute the environment the most and affect climate change the most among SMEs (Salzberg 2006). Some researchers have seen restaurants as the least sustainable economic sector globally compared to their economic benefits and the greenhouse gas effect they create (Wang et al. 2013).

Davies and Konisky presented the conceptual framework by collecting the environmental impacts of restaurants on three channels. These three channels are direct ecological impact, ecological impact toward the producer, and environmental impact toward the consumer. While direct environmental impact refers to the effect directly created by the restaurants themselves, the producer's environmental impact occurs within the scope of the restaurant's suppliers. The last category, the consumer-oriented environmental impact, is the impact of restaurants on consumers (Davies and Konisky 2000).

Environmental impact of restaurants (Davies and Konisky 2000; Chen 2014):

- Environmental impacts for the producer
    - Agriculture
    - Fishing
    - Farming
- Direct environmental impacts
    - Energy consumption
    - Water consumption
    - Solid waste generation
    - Air pollution
    - Environmental impacts for the consumers

10.4.1 Direct Environmental Impacts

Direct environmental impacts are categorized into four: Energy consumption, solid waste generation, water consumption, and air pollution (Davies and Konisky 2000).

10.4.1.1 Energy Consumption

Restaurants are businesses with very high energy consumption (Szuchnicki 2009). According to Pacific Gas and Electric Food Service Technology Center, restaurants use almost five times more energy per square meter than other industrial buildings (Wang et al. 2013). Energy costs make up 30 percent of a typical commercial building's annual budget, which increases by an average of 6–8 percent annually. Therefore, growing restaurants' energy and water efficiency can reduce greenhouse gas emissions by providing restaurant owners with an estimated savings of 10–20 percent on bills (Freeman 2011).

10.4.1.2 Water Consumption

The concept of water management has become more critical today. Water management defines the use, planning, and distribution of water resources considering future generations' needs. Within the scope of water management, sectors with high water use must prevent water losses by using water-saving practices, evaluate wastewater, develop basin waters by not forgetting that groundwater is an exhaustible resource, and use water efficiently (Turhan et al. 2010). It is essential for our future that restaurants, which are among the sectors that use water intensively, pay attention to water management. Water is vital for restaurant business operations. Restaurants use water for production, cleaning, and service of food. An average of 60 liters of water is used for each meal served in restaurants (Vanschenkhof 2011). In addition, oil, heavy metals, pathogens, preservatives, and chemicals in restaurants' water drainage can cause water pollution if the correct drainage systems are not used (Chen 2014).

10.4.1.3 Solid Waste Generation

Food waste and packaging waste are the primary sources of solid waste generated in restaurants (Chen 2014). These wastes from restaurants negatively affect the economy, the environment, and the welfare of future generations. It is essential that restaurants, the raw materials of which are mainly food, be careful about food waste. The three main types of restaurant food wastes are ready meals (food leftovers) that arise as a result of overproduction in restaurants, wastes (production wastes) that are produced as production losses during the preparation of meals, and food discarded by consumers (plate wastes) (Chen 2014). In addition, foods that have expired due to not tracking products and become unusable due to not complying with the correct storage conditions create food waste in restaurants and increase costs. Solid wastes created by restaurants are not just food waste. Packaging waste is also a part of the solid waste generated. Restaurants buy some products in packages. As a result, there is a solid-developed solid waste mass after used products that reach the restaurant as packaged by the glass, plastic, paper, and tin. Restaurants also create solid waste while processing and preserving food. Aluminum foil, wax paper, plastic piping bags, and stretch films are generally used once and disposed of. Since these products are a constant need for restaurants, they contribute to both cost increase and solid waste generation. There are also packaging wastes generated by restaurants during service. Plastic beverage cans, plastic forks, knives, plastic water bottles, packaging papers, aluminum, Styrofoam, and polystyrene boxes used in packaging, mainly used in fast service restaurants, can be given examples.

10.4.1.4 Air Pollution

The pollutant concentration that causes air pollution varies according to cooking, cooking oil, and energy source. Regardless of the type of energy source and the material used in the meal, it was determined that the cooking method that has the most effect on air pollution is frying with oil. The impact of cooking oil type on air pollution varies depending on the smoking temperature of the oil (Paras 2018). The most striking factor in the studies about air pollution impact of restaurants was the type of energy source used in cooking. The three most common energy sources used in cooking are gas, electricity, and solid fuels. While gas and electricity are used mainly in developed countries, solid fuels are used more frequently in undeveloped countries. Among these three energy sources, the source that pollutes the air the most is solid fuels. Solid fuels are coal and biomass (wood, crop residues, fertilizer, etc.). Solid fuels, which can be used in traditional and modern cooking methods, are the most polluting cooking energy sources (Paras 2018). Charcoal grills used in restaurants are one of the sources that use solid fuels that cause air pollution.

10.4.1.5 Technological Solutions to Reduce Direct Environmental Impacts of the Restaurant Businesses

For restaurants to make energy-saving and more effective, methods such as using solar energy to construct the building, building sheathing, using double glazing should be preferred. Today, with the development of technology, the use of intelligent building systems has increased. As a result, restaurants installed in smart buildings can save energy. Technology is developing in the production of kitchen equipment. Ovens, deep fryers, small equipment, and refrigerators consume much less energy than their previous versions are available today. Selecting A++ equipment by following up-to-date technologies saves energy. Using technological systems such as sensor faucets, waterless urinals, applying slow flow systems to toilet faucet ends, and using pressure flushing systems that use less water in toilets should be preferred. Methods should be approved, such as providing water recovery with rainwater collection tanks, intelligent building systems, applying gray water recycling systems to reuse in toilets, garden irrigation, and rough cleaning by collecting less polluted wastewater. To minimize food waste, software such as MICROS that monitors and uses food products supplied and stored by the restaurant should be used. This software records the foods that are provided and stored, and as they are used, the inventory is automatically reduced. Innovative options that do not harm the environment, such as bamboo straws, which are developed as an alternative to environmentally harmful products such as plastic straws and cutlery, should be preferred. In addition, to decrease solid waste generation, Quick Response (QR) code menu applications prevent unnecessary waste of paper for menu cards. If the restaurant offers take-away service, it should do so with less environmentally damaging electric vehicles. In addition, electric vehicle charging stations in the restaurant car park will be an attractive element for customers who care about the environment.

10.4.2 Environmental Impacts for the Consumers

Restaurants affect public health with the food they offer. Today, consumers go to restaurants to fill their stomachs and have different experiences, socialize, and have fun. Moreover, since they prefer to eat in restaurants, they can travel long distances and make specific preferences (Akbaba 2016). In this context, restaurants can directly affect consumers' health with the products they prefer to use in their meals and the cooking techniques. Therefore, even if restaurants are organizations with commercial concerns and aim to profit, they should seek ways to offer more beneficial and healthy foods to society and explain these healthy options in their menus (Jeong 2015).

10.4.2.1 Technological Solutions to Reduce Environmental Impacts of the Restaurant Businesses for the Customers

Shortly, the authenticity and reliability of online restaurant reviews will be revealed through blockchain technology. This will eliminate fake reviews and information. Restaurants must provide their guests with reliable and accurate information. Thanks to the blockchain, the traceability of foodborne diseases will also increase.

10.4.3 Environmental Impacts for the Producer

The sustainable food system is defined as the system that provides healthy food that will have the most negligible negative impact on the environment for generations and protects the ecosystem in this process (Shimokawa 2016). The global food system allows restaurants to access a wide range of products from almost anywhere in the world, in all seasons of the year. Although most restaurants follow a food-purchasing process based on specific preferences and cost, how food is produced and how far it travels to reach the restaurant are essential issues that affect the environment. Restaurants impact the sustainability of the food system with their food-purchasing preferences.

10.4.3.1 Sustainable Agriculture

Agriculture is the starting point as the primary production of the food chain. Sustainable agriculture includes the system and practices that will develop the preserving of farmed land, farmers, environment, and natural farm resources and the production of good food ingredients of high quality at reasonable costs. Sustainable agriculture is a way of farming that corresponds to today's requirements for the next generations without endangering the resources. Sustainable agriculture assembles three main goals: Environmental health, economic profits, and social and economic equality. The convenience of the environment is making sustainable agriculture possible in all farming lands by utilizing land, air, and water consciously and protecting nature.

Sustainability in terms of the economy should be considered providing the income necessary to producers for farmers today and in the future. The acceptability in terms of social is the convenience of the necessities of producers for the new technologies and regional ethical values. The supportability in terms of politics, however, includes topics such as the selling of seeds, manures, credits at the cost of the product.

10.4.3.2 Sustainable Fishing

Restaurants that include seafood in their menus must support sustainable fishing and supply fish from producers with a sustainable fishing certificate. Restaurant Septime, located in France, which operates a sustainable restaurant system, announced its fish supply motto in its manifesto. It states that it only supplies products from anglers who use sustainable methods and whose boats don't exceed 12 meters. Furthermore, the restaurant emphasizes that it prefers less fashionable fish than the species with high consumption and the fish on the menu vary according to the type of fish caught that day. It also states that it pays 20 percent more than the market to support the producer from whom it purchases sustainable fish (Aslan and ve Akbaba 2018).

The world's leading ecology experts predict that we can no longer consume seafood in the next 40 years. Considering that the world's population of one billion people depends on fish for protein and that future generations cannot consume seafood, the importance of fish producers preferred by restaurants is revealed (Cordey and Pitcher 2009).

10.4.3.3 Sustainable Farming

Scientific data show that the livestock sector has an important place in the world economy and politics. When we look at global figures, we see a sector worth 1.4 trillion dollars and employs at least 1.3 billion people (Thornton 2010). While the demand for animal products and the human population in the world is increasing rapidly, it is estimated that the global meat production, which was 229 million tons in 1999, will increase to 465 million tons in 2050, and the milk from 580 to 1043 million tons. In 1980 and 2002, total meat production tripled, rising from 45 million tons to 134 million tons. Today, the surface area allocated to animal husbandry in the world corresponds to 30 percent of the ice-free terrestrial surface area of the planet (Steinfeld et al. 2006; Thornton 2010). The feed and food growing area required to feed the animals is also included when calculating this surface. Therefore, the livestock sector is considered whole with the global effects of feed cultivation and industry. In addition, the livestock sector has many impacts on the environment. It affects global warming, decreases biodiversity, and consumes an enormous amount of water.

The livestock sector handles some of the gases that cause the warming of the atmosphere. The livestock sector is a significant player responsible for 18 percent of greenhouse gas emissions. The livestock sector handles 91 percent of the extinction of amazon forests (Sergio 2003). The most important reason for the destruction of rainforests has taken place in the literature as livestock and feed production (Veiga et al. 2003; Yale School 2019). With the disappearance of these forests, 137 plants, animals, and insect species are disappearing every day. The livestock sector causes a decrease in biodiversity (Andersen 2014). The livestock sector is a sector that consumes a large amount of water. The amount of water required to produce 1 kilogram of beef is 43,000 liters (Pimentel et al. 2004). With the environmental impact of livestock farming in the limelight, restaurants purchase large quantities of meat.

10.4.3.4 Technological Solutions to Reduce Environmental Impacts of the Restaurant Businesses for the Producer

Sustainable restaurants prefer products that are produced with the least harm to the environment. Blockchain technology, which we have heard frequently today, has gained importance. Thanks to this technology, it has become possible for sustainable restaurants to access reliable information about the source of the products they supply. By using blockchain, the clarity and accuracy of specific product labels can be solved. A company called ‘Where Foods Come From’ in Castle rock, Colorado, will provide label verification and validation services to rule the accuracy of food labels. This label verification service uses QR codes and can provide the required information almost immediately. This has brought considerable benefits to society, but by adopting blockchain technology, the services provided by the company can be raised to a whole new level of honesty and trust. With the help of blockchain, all records and reports can and will be available and traceable within a few seconds to ensure that the advertisements on the product label are accurate, credible, and reliable. Blockchain enables restaurant and retail owners to be held accountable for their product proclamations and statements (Willie 2019). Previous research has demonstrated that blockchain technology has numerous advantages, one of which is identity management. In the supply chain, blockchain can be used to store and share data with others (such as suppliers and customers) or correlate received data with other data from nodes. Blockchain provides suppliers with increased visibility, allowing them to see who is doing what, when, and where. Blockchain technology can also circumvent third parties and auditors, thereby lowering costs and increasing efficiency. Furthermore, blockchain technology provides transparency and aids in creating distributed and immutable records, allowing for input traceability. Blockchain technology’s traceability mechanism also aids in the prevention of fraud throughout the supply chain (Bumblauskas et al. 2020).

REFERENCES

Andersen, K., Kuhn, K. (Producers), Kip, A., Kuhn, K. (Directors). 2014. Cowspiracy: The Sustainability Secret [Documentary—Movie]. Los Angeles: A.U.M. Films NS First Spark Media..

Akbaba, A. 2016. Yiyecek İçecek İşletmelerinde Sosyal Sorumluluk Uygulamaları. O. N. Özdoğan (Editör), Yiyecek İçecek Endüstrisinde Trendler, Kavramlar, Yaklaşımlar, Başarı Hikâyeleri. (1. Baskı). Ankara: Detay Yayıncılık, 31–50.

Aslan, B., Akbaba, A. 2018. Ödüllü Sürdürülebilir Restoranların Uygulamalarının İncelenmesi. VIII. Ulusal IV. Uluslararası Doğu Akdeniz Turizm Sempozyumu E-Kitabı, Hatay, 777–787.

Boas, I., Biermann, F., Kanie, N. 2016. Cross-Sectoral Strategies in Global Sustainability Governance: Towards a Nexus Approach. International Environmental Agreements: Politics, Law and Economics, 16(3), 449–464.

Brander, J.A. 2007. Sustainability: Malthus Revisited. The Canadian Journal of Economics, 40(1), 1–38.

Bumblauskas, D., Mann, A., Dugan, B., Rittmer, J. 2020. A Blockchain Use Case in Food Distribution: Do You Know Where Your Food Has Been?. International Journal of Information Management, 52, 102008.

Café de Coral Group. 2018. Sustainability Report 2017/18. www.cafedecoral.com/tch/corp_social_respon/csr_reports/images/SR2018/CDCSRE17-18/index.html (Erişim Tarihi: 20.03.2021).

Chen, C.J., Gregoire, M.B., Arendt, S., ve Shelley, M.C. 2011. College and University Dining Services Administrators' Intention to Adopt Sustainable Practices: Results from US Institutions. International Journal of Sustainability in Higher Education, 12(2), 145–162.

Chen, T.B. 2014. Consumers' Perspectives of Environmental Values and Attitudes Influence on Green Purchase Behaviour and Green Restaurant Intention in Malaysian Service Sector. Doctoral Dissertation, Multimedia University, Malaysia.

Cordey, H., Pitcher F. (Producers). 2009. South Pacific [Documentary Video File]: BBC and Discovery UK (Production Companies).Cousins, J., Foskett, D., Pennington, A. 2011. Food and Beverage Management for the Hospitality, Tourism and Event Industries. Oxford: Goodfellow Publishers Ltd.

Davies, T., Konisky, D.M. 2000. Environmental Implications of the Foodservice and Food Retail Industries. Washington, DC: Resources for the Future.

Duran, B. 2018. Sürdürülebilirlik Kavramının Önemi, Karşılaşılan Sorunlar ve Şirketlerin Sürdürülebilirlik Raporlarının İncelenmesi. Ankara: Yüksek Lisans Tezi, Ankara Başkent Üniversitesi Sosyal Bilimler Enstitüsü.

Dyllick, T., and Hockerts, K. (2002). Beyond the Business Case for Corporate Sustainability. Business Strategy and the Environment, 11(2), 130-141.

Freeman, E.M. 2011. Restaurant Industry Sustainability: Barriers and Solutions to Sustainable Practice Indicators. Master's Thesis, Arizona State University, ABD.

Gore, A. 2008. Worldchanging: A User's Guide for the 21st Century. New York, NY: Harry N Abrams Incorporated.

Hawken, P., Shah, K. 1993. The Ecology of Commerce: A Declaration of Sustainability (Vol. 5). New York, NY: Harper Business.

Holmberg, J., Sandbrook, R. 1992. Sustainable Development: What Is to Be Done? Making Development Sustainable: Redefining Institutions, Policy, and Economics (Ed. J. Holmberg). International Institute for Environment and Development, 19–38. Washington, DC: Island Press.

Hu, H.H., Parsa, H.G., Self, J. 2010. The Dynamics of Green Restaurant Patronage. Cornell Hospitality Quarterly, 51(3), 344–362.

Hürol, H.Y. 2014. A Study on Social Sustainability: The Case of Doğanbey Urban Renewal Project in Bursa. Ankara: Yüksek Lisans Tezi, Orta Doğu Teknik Üniversitesi Fen Bilimleri Enstitüsü.

Jeong, E. 2015. Restaurant Customers' Healthy Menu Consumption Intention: An Investigation on Motives, Barriers, and Restaurant Environmental Factors. Doctoral Dissertation, Purdue University West Lafayette, Indiana.

Kongoli, F. 2016. Role of Science and Technology on Sustainable Development, Sustainable Industrial Processing Summit, SIPS, Montreal, 1–14.

Kurnaz, A., Özdoğan, O.N. 2017. İstanbul'da Yer Alan Yeşil Restoran İşletmeleri Hizmet Kalitesinin Grserv Modeli ile Değerlendirilmesi. Dokuz Eylül Üniversitesi İşletme Fakültesi Dergisi, 18(1), 75–99.

Legrand, W., Sloan, P., Simons-Kaufmann, C., Fleischer, S. 2010. "A review of restaurant sustainable indicators." In *Advances in Hospitality and Leisure*, edited by Joseph S. Chen, 167–183. Emerald Group Publishing Limited.

Lin, I.-H. 2010. Users' and Preparers' Perception of Sustainability Reporting and Corporate Sustainability. Report, Nova Southeastern University.

McKenzie, S. 2004. Social Sustainability: Towards Some Definitions. Hawke Research Institute Working Paper Series, 27, 1–31.

Mukumbi, K. 2013. Drivers of Investment in Corporate Sustainability Strategies of Retailers and Manufacturers in Developed and Developing Countries. Doctoral Dissertation, Michigan State University, ABD.

Namkung, Y., Jang, S. 2017. Are Consumers Willing to Pay More for Green Practices at Restaurants? Journal of Hospitality and Tourism Research, 41(3), 329–356.

Özdemir, G. 2018. Food Waste Management within Sustainability Perspective: A Study on Five Star Chain Hotels. Doctoral Dissertation, Institute of Social Sciences Gazi University, Ankara.

Paras, K.D. 2018. Measurements of Pm2.5, Pm1.0, and Black Carbon in Cooking and Non-Cooking Environments inside California Shopping Malls. Doctoral Dissertation, San Diego State University, ABD.

Passet, R. 1979. L'Economique et le Vivant. Petite Bibliotheque Payot, Paris (2nd Edition 1996) Economica, Paris.

Pimentel, D., Berger, B., Filiberto, D., Newton, M., Wolfe, B., Karabinakis, E., et al. 2004. Water Resources: Agricultural and Environmental Issues. BioScience, 54(10), 909–918.

Restaurant Azurmendi. 2018. Sustainable Azurmendi. Bilbao: Restaurant Azurmendi. https://azurmendi.restaurant/en/azurmendi-wins-sustainable-restaurant-award-worlds-50-best-restaurants/ (20.03.2021).

Restaurant Relae. 2016. Sustainability Report 2016. Kopenhag: Restaurant Relae. www.restaurant-relae.dk/wp-content/uploads/Sustainability-Report-2016_2.pdf(20.03.2021).

Şahin, Ü. 2004. Truva Atı Olarak Sürdürülebilir Kalkınma. Üç Ekoloji, 1(2), 9–30.

Salzberg, A.C. 2006. Adopting Sustainability Innovations in Restaurants: An Evaluation of the Factors Influencing Owner-Managers' Decisions in Richmond, Virginia. Doctoral Dissertation, Virginia Commonwealth University, ABD.

Sergio, M. 2003. Causes of Deforestation of the Brazillian Amazon. The World Bank, Working Paper, No 22. http://documents.worldbank.org/curated/en/7581714687688 28889/Causes-of-deforestation-of-the-Brazilian-Amazon (10.05.2021).

Shimokawa, S. 2016. Sustainable Meat Consumption in China. Journal of Integrative Agriculture, 14(6), 1023–1032.

Sprinkle, G.B., Maines, L.A. 2010. The Benefits and Costs of Corporate Social Responsibility. Business Horizons, 53(5), 445–453.

Steinfeld, H., Gerber, P., Wassenaar, T.D., Castel, V., Rosales, M., Rosales, M., de Haan, C. 2006. Livestock's Long Shadow: Environmental Issues and Options. Rome: FAO (Food & Agriculture Organization).

Szuchnicki, A.L. 2009. Examining the Influence of Restaurant Green Practices on Customer Return Intention. Master's Thesis, University of Nevada, ABD, Las Vegas.Thornton, P.K. 2010. Livestock Production: Recent Trends, Future Prospects. Philosophical Transactions of the Royal Society B: Biological Sciences, 365(1554), 2583–2897.

Turhan, A., Çakmak, B., Gökalp, Z. 2010. Türkiye'de Su Kaynakları Yönetiminin Değerlendirilmesi. Tarım Bilimleri Araştırma Dergisi, 3(1), 67–74.

Turhan, D.G. 2017. Unfolding Strategic Drivers of Corporate Sustainability Practices. İzmir: Doktora Tezi, Yaşar Üniversitesi Sosyal Bilimler Enstitüsü.

United Nations. (2015). Transforming Our World: The 2030 Agenda for Sustainable Development. New York: United Nations, Department of Economic and Social Affairs. https://sustainabledevelopment.un.org/content/documents/21252030%20Agenda%20for%20Sustainable%20Development%20web.pdf (17.03.2020)

Vanschenkhof, M. 2011. An Investigation of Water Usage in Casual Dining Restaurants in Kansas. Doctoral Dissertation, Kansas State University, ABD.

Vehkamäki, S. 2005. 2.2. The Concept of Sustainability in Modern Times. Sustainable Use of Renewable Natural Resources: From Principles to Practices, 34, 23–35. Helsinki: Helsingin yliopisto, metsäekologian laitos. https://researchportal.helsinki.fi/en/publications/theconcept- of-sustainability-in-modern-times (15.04.2021).

Veiga, J.B., Tourrand, J.F., Poccard-Chapuis, R., Piketty, M.G. 2003. Cattle Ranching in the Amazon Rainforest. XII World Forestry Congress, Quebec City, Canada.

Wang, Y.-F., Chen, S.-P., Lee, Y.-C., Tsa, C.-T. 2013. Developing Green Management Standards for Restaurants: An Application of Green Supply Chain Management. International Journal of Hospitality Management, 34, 263–273.

WCED. 1987. Our Common Future. United Nations: Oxford University Press.

Willie, P. 2019. Can All Sectors of the Hospitality and Tourism Industry Be Influenced by the Innovation of Blockchain Technology?. Worldwide Hospitality and Tourism Themes.

Yale School. 2019. Soy Agriculture in the Amazon Basin. Yale School of Forestry and Environmental Studies Global Forest Atlas. https://globalforestatlas.yale.edu (10.05.2021).

Yılmaz, Ş. 2014. An Assessment on the Link between Sustainability and Urban Form: The Case of Gaziantep. Master's Thesis, Middle East Technical University, Ankara.

Part III

CSR and Hospitality

11 Corporate Social Responsibility Perceptions of Undergraduate Level Students in Tourism Education

Cenk Murat Kocoglu and Omer Sarac

CONTENTS

11.1 INTRODUCTION

For businesses to continue their existence, they must be sensitive to the demands and needs of society and create a healthy economic environment. In addition to these, it has become one of today's indispensable obligations for businesses to protect the environment and support various projects to solve social problems (Özdemir 2009). Because in the enterprises' activities, only profit-oriented work without thinking about the social causes environmental and social issues to arise (Kahraman & Türkay 2014).

DOI: 10.1201/9781003138051-14

The imbalance between the economy and the environment lies at the root of the environmental and social problems that arise in many countries (Koçoğlu et al. 2020). In other words, only profit-oriented activities carried out by businesses harm sustainability. While humankind improves the quality of life economically with the rapidly developing science, technology, and industry, on the other hand, it harms nature and social life. Development activities carried out without balancing nature and social life, on the other hand, bring more harm than good. Because the economic gains that are tried to be obtained in the short term turn into losses in the medium and long time, causing regression and loss rather than contributing to the economy (Engin & Akgöz 2013). In this way, businesses that put economic benefits ahead of social and environmental benefits are excluded by society (Özgen 2007).

Ensuring that a business continues to be accepted in society depends not only on the awareness of society's problems but also on doing something about them. As the institutions grow, their commercial success and profitability increase, parallel to society's expectations. Because, apart from their economic responsibilities, businesses also have legal, ethical, and voluntary obligations (Engin & Akgöz 2013). Moreover, firms that try to fulfill all these responsibilities and are conscious of these issues reach a respected and appreciated business position in the society they operate in in the long term. Because the level of consciousness of consumers is increasing day by day, in this environment of conscious consumers, consumers take a stand against businesses that do not fulfill their corporate social responsibility (CSR) and turn their consumption activities to other parties (Kelgökmen 2010). In this context, CSR can be considered a fundamental strategic approach.

While CSR was carried out individually as a philanthropic activity, today, it is expressed as philanthropy, moral, economic, and legal responsibility. When it first emerged, Friedman (1970) explained the concept of CSR as companies fulfilling only their economic burdens. Afterward, it was pointed out that companies have economic and legal obligations and have different responsibilities toward society and other stakeholders (Stone 1976; Carroll, 1979; Frederick 1987). Thus, today, the concept of CSR is expressed as the fact that businesses are responsible to all their stakeholders and take them into account in all their decisions.

In light of CSR definitions, CSR programs should be problem-solving, and institutions should attempt to solve these problems by addressing a few national issues (Okay & Okay 2005). Because while 'sustainability' and 'corporate social responsibility' appear as concepts that complement each other, CSR plays a vital role in achieving sustainable development and corporate sustainability. One of the most important reasons for this is that the activities developed within CSR contribute to the environment, society, and economy. Panapanaan et al. (2003) examined the relationship between sustainability and social responsibility with a perspective expressed as a hierarchical approach. While the authors accepted business social responsibility as an intermediate goal in their studies, they considered business sustainability the goal.

Generally, the issue of CSR is perceived as the activities that industrial enterprises should do. However, the concept of CSR should be given importance by the tourism enterprises, the importance of which is increasing daily and should be conscious of such activities. Because in tourism activities, social life and the environment are neglected by considering the economic benefits, and sustainability is damaged. For example, the number of visitors to the Kaiping Observation Towers in China was wanted to be increased from 100,000 to 2 million. The aim is to generate an economic income of approximately 8 million dollars. In such a case, physical pressure applies to the structures due to excessive use, and future generations' use of the systems is harmed (CNN 2012). This situation causes the product to lose its positive image and its customers in the medium and long term. In tourism businesses where customer loyalty is more complex than other businesses, a tourism business acting with CSR awareness can increase its image in the eyes of consumers and at the same time establish customer loyalty.

CSR is highly effective in creating and developing not only the corporate image but also the brand image. Brand image is one of the factors that affect the preference of the product and service. Nowadays, all over the world, businesses that attach importance to CSR and make this understanding a part of their activities and thus develop their brand image are increasingly inclined to purchase their products and services. Therefore, brands that want to attract consumers to their side should act with an understanding of social responsibility (Özdemir 2009).

Intangible products are produced in tourism enterprises. Therefore, quality control is quite difficult. For this reason, the most important factor affecting consumers' purchase intention is the image of that product. In other words, the sustainability of tourism businesses depends on the positive image they create for their products. Therefore, it is essential to have a CSR culture in creating a positive image of a product (Vural & Coşkun 2011). To build a CSR culture in a tourism business, each department and all managers and employees that make up this department must perform activities following this social responsibility culture. From this point of view, future tourism business manager candidates need to be conscious about CSR in forming a corporate culture related to social responsibility. The research aims to measure the CSR perceptions of undergraduate students who study tourism in this context.

11.2 CONCEPTUAL FRAMEWORK

11.2.1 Corporate Social Responsibilities

CSR has emerged since the 1970s and has reached today by being defined in different ways. It can be said that CSR started in the modern sense with the book 'Social Responsibilities of business executives' written in 1953 by Howard B. Bowen, one of the pioneers of the concept of social responsibility. According to the definition made by Bowen (1953), social responsibility is defined as the behavior of managers following both the goals of the enterprise and the expectations and values of the society, determining policies that are compatible with these expectations and values, implementing them, making decisions and carrying out their activities.

After Bowen (1953), Carroll (1979) took the concept of CSR and divided responsibility into four categories: economic, legal, ethical, and philanthropic. In this study, Carroll stated that institutions fulfill their economic responsibility for themselves, and the concepts of legal ethics and philanthropy are the work carried out by the institution for others. Davis (1960), on the other hand, defined CSR as the decisions and behaviors of the businesses at a higher level than the economic interests. According to Kotler and Lee (2008, CSR is an obligation undertaken to improve the well-being of society through voluntary business practices and contributions from corporate resources.

Friedman (1970), on the other hand, defined the concept of CSR within legal boundaries and stated that businesses should only fulfill their economic responsibilities. Later, it was noted by many authors that companies do not have only economical and legal obligations but also have different responsibilities toward society (Davis, 1973; Stone, 1976; Carroll 1979; Frederick, 1987). As can be understood from the definitions, the concept of CSR refers to all internal and external stakeholders. These stakeholders can be listed as employees, customers, consumers, suppliers, competitors, shareholders, environment, state, and society. In the definition made by the European Commission, CSR is a concept that shows that businesses voluntarily bear social and environmental concerns in their activities and interactions with their stakeholders (European Commission 2002).

The social responsibilities of businesses are divided into three as economic, social, and environmental. CSR is defined as 'the contribution of the enterprise to sustainable economic development, its commitment to improving the quality of life of employees, their families and the whole society' (Kärnä et al., 2003). CSR has emerged as a result of Adam Smith's understanding of maximum profit. Businesses are production-oriented, and activities are viewed from efficiency and economy, with a sense of acting responsibly on society (Peltekoğlu 2001). The basic idea behind CSR is that businesses have to work for social improvement. It can be perceived as the voluntary decisions and steps taken by the business management to increase the welfare of the public and business employees. From this point of view, CSR (Kelgökmen 2010):

- It is not just a kind of philanthropy. It is a consistent policy that supports long-term goals.
- It is not just a project. It is a management approach that aims to identify social needs and issues.
- It is not some kind of expense. It is a recyclable investment.
- It is not an investment that is expected to bring profit. It is only an investment that will ensure and protect profitability.

11.2.2 Corporate Social Responsibility Components

Carroll (1991) stated that CSR has four dimensions: economic, legal, ethical, and philanthropic. Although these four different areas of responsibility are at certain levels in the social responsibility activities of businesses, the dimensions of ethics and philanthropy are increasing day by day. These elements are explained in more detail below (Carroll 1991).

Economic responsibilities: According to Carroll (1979), businesses are the first and foremost social responsibility of businesses as they survive by making a profit. These economic responsibilities are expressed as acting to increase the shareholders' earnings, maintain their competitive position, ensure continuity in profitability, turn to high profits, and continue the organization's operation with high efficiency (Carroll 1991; Ersöz 2007). Elements of economic responsibilities (Carroll 1991):

- It is essential for businesses to increase the number of earnings per share.
- It is essential to get the highest possible profit.
- It is essential to create a solid competitive position for the business.
- It is vital to achieving a high level of operational efficiency.
- To be a successful business, it is necessary to make a profit.

Legal responsibilities: It consists of the duties of the enterprises to act following the laws and regulations determined by the legal institutions while continuing their economic activities by making a profit. These responsibilities can be expressed as complying with the specified legislation, following national and local regulations, complying with minimum legal requirements in providing goods and services (Carroll 1991; Ersöz 2007). Elements of legal liability (Carroll 1991):

- It is essential to comply with the expectations of the state and the law. It is vital to comply with legal and institutional regulations.
- As an institution, it is vital to be a law-abiding citizen.
- A successful business fulfills legal requirements accurately and on time.
- It is essential to produce products/services that meet at least the minimum legal requirements.

While society accepts that businesses profit from their activities, it has not unconditionally approved this purpose. Therefore, the organization asks companies not to ignore specific legal controls while pursuing their economic activities. Community and business have agreed on the legal framework. The legal framework has established ethical principles for companies. The principles and values that the industry must comply with while maintaining its economic activities have been determined by lawmakers (Carroll 1991). The laws that companies must comply with can be divided into five: laws regulating competition, laws protecting the consumer, laws protecting the environment, laws providing equality and security, and laws regarding shareholders (Özgener 2004).

Ethical responsibility: Ethics, which can be defined as distinguishing between good and bad for society, appears as a frequently discussed concept and needs to be emphasized in scientific fields and daily life as part of social life (Ay & Aytekin 2005). Ethics comply with social rules and expectations even further than the laws (Coşkun 2010). Some of the ethical dimension components are being honest about the products or services produced by the business, not deceiving the other party in bilateral relations, complying with society's values, respecting the environment within the expectations of society (Carroll 1991; Öztürk 2013). Businesses have moral responsibilities toward their social stakeholders, who are groups that affect and are affected by their activities. These stakeholders include shareholders, investors, employees, consumers, suppliers, and competitors (Ay 2003). Business managers have to consider the ethical dimension of their decisions (Chryssides & Kaler 1999). Therefore, the necessity of ethical norms and ethical behavior in all activities is an important responsibility. Elements of ethical responsibility (Carroll 1991):

- It is essential to behave following social values and ethical norms.
- It is essential to recognize and respect new and developing norms in society.
- It is essential to avoid ethical norms that might hinder the achievement of the organization's goals.
- an excellent corporate citizen complies with social values and ethical norms.
- Being an honest institution and ethical behavior also brings along compliance with laws and regulations.

Philanthropy responsibility: It is expressed as businesses voluntarily feeling no legal and moral expectations without feeling under a specific obligation (Sığdı 2013). The purpose of this responsibility, which is at the top of the pyramid, is to carry out activities beneficial to the country, society, and the whole world as a good citizen. Businesses allocate some of their resources to educational, artistic, and social projects, indicating this responsibility (Lantos 2001). Elements of this responsibility (Carroll 1991):

- It is vital to behave following society's benevolence and philanthropic expectations.
- It is essential to support the arts.
- It is essential for employees and managers to engage in voluntary and social activities.
- It is vital to support education.
- While supporting social activities, the primary purpose should be to increase the quality of life.

Whether it is done voluntarily, ethically, or taking into account legal or economic dimensions, CSR studies are valued by the public, create a sense of trust toward the company, increase the social value of the company, add vitality and efficiency to advertising activities, strengthen relations with the media, and increase the social value of the company (Balta Peltekoğlu 2007). In addition, the increasing importance of cross-border trade, international companies, and global distribution networks, that the internet, mobile phones, and other personal digital devices make it easier to monitor and disseminate information about corporate activities, the increasing strength of nongovernmental organizations, consumers, and investors performing CSR has become very important with their support (Özdemir 2007). As seen in Figure 11.1 below, four dimensions make up Carrol's CSR pyramid.

11.2.3 Tourism Education

The continuous increase in the tourism industry's contribution to the country's economies (Keung 2000) increases the competition in the tourism market. It brings the need for human resources (Sem and Clements 1996). As it is known, although technological developments have advanced, jobs in the tourism sector are still produced and

FIGURE 11.1 Carroll's CSR pyramid.

Source: The CSR Journal (2021).

presented in a labor-intensive way. Therefore, these developments in tourism increase the need for a trained workforce even more (Mill 1990). In this context, tourism education should be given importance for tourism, which is labor-intensive and where automation is limited, to have a strong structure as a sector (Ünlüönen 2004) as long as there is no investment in human resources, physical, and technological equipment. Economic developments alone do not matter in increasing and improving the service quality (Seymen 2002).

Education contributes significantly to economic growth by developing a qualified workforce with the knowledge and skills required, especially the industry and service sector, and making employees more productive (Woodhall 1979). Furthermore, the necessity of ensuring the service quality required by modern tourism understanding and the realization of healthy and high-quality relations between tourists and those serving the tourist depends mainly on the high vocational and technical education levels of the workforce employed in the sector (Christou 1999; Alp 1992). In this context, education emerges as the primary way of achieving a high standard of living for individuals, developing and progressing societies, and being among modern countries (Hergüner et al. 2002).

Establishing the vocational and technical education system effectively and making it suitable for the demands and needs of the sector is among the main priorities of every developed country because a qualified workforce can only be provided by effective tourism education and training (Ünlüönen 2000). Tourism education is to contribute to the development of the tourism sector, give professional training to those working in the industry, provide knowledge and skills to those working in the tourism sector, train qualified tourism instructors, understand the importance of tourism in the economy, create a positive awareness of tourism in the society, and realize the objectives of training qualified employees and managers trained in the tourism sector

(Kızılırmak 2000; Sezgin 2001; Hacıoğlu 1992). In this direction, the primary purpose of tourism education institutions is to train staff who will work in the tourism sector, bring tourism awareness and philosophy to all educators, contribute to the development of the tourism sector, provide qualified personnel trained in the tourism sector (Mısırlı 2009) by teaching management techniques and adapt to the dominant, accepted understanding, and train senior tourism professionals who can comprehend new concepts, ideas, and technologies (Üzümcü & Bayraktar 2004).

11.3 METHOD

This study is aimed to measure the CSR perceptions of the students studying tourism at the level of undergraduate. Therefore, the quantitative data collection method was preferred in the study. Within the scope of the research, the population consists of the students of tourism management and tourism guidance departments at Karabük University Safranbolu Tourism Faculty. Using the survey technique, the research data were collected from the students studying in the fall semester of 2019–2020 between September 21, 2019, and December 15, 2019. The number of those who continue their education actively between these dates is 423. However, some students are absent. For this reason, the exact number could not be reached.

Data were collected from 414 students using the convenience sampling method, and 27 questionnaires were invalid in examining the obtained questionnaires. Invalid questionnaires were excluded from the evaluation, and analyses were carried out with the SPSS 22 package program over 387 questionnaires. It is stated in the studies that the sample size should be at least ten times the number of variables included in the scale used in the research (Kerlinger 1978; Hair et al., 1998; Kline 2011). Stevens (1996) stated that it suffices to add 15 times as much. The number is 180, which is 10 times the 18 statements in the questionnaire, and 270, 15 times more, were exceeded. On the other hand, since it has the power to represent a total population, 384 samples (Sekaran, 2003: 294) were also tried to increase the reliability of the study by exceeding it.

The 'Perceived Corporate Social Responsibility Scale' developed by Swaen and Chumpitaz (2008) was used in the study. The scale consists of two parts, and the first part includes 18 statements to measure the CSR perceptions of tourism students who have received undergraduate education. These statements were directed to the participants as 'strongly disagree,' 'disagree,' 'moderately agree,' 'agree,' and 'strongly agree' according to the 5-point Likert scale. In the second part, several demographic questions determine the respondents' age, gender, grade, and whether they have heard of CSR before.

11.4 RESULTS

11.4.1 Demographic Information

Table 11.1 includes the demographic characteristics of the students in the research. When the gender of the students participating in the study is examined, it is seen that the male participants constitute the majority. When the ages of the students were concerned, it was determined that more than half of them (229 people) were between

TABLE 11.1
Demographic Data

Gender	Frequency	Percentage
Female	168	43.4
Male	219	56.4

Age	Frequency	Percentage
18–21	146	37.7
22–25	229	59.2
26–29	12	3.1

Working Status	Frequency	Percentage
Yes	124	32
No	263	68

Grade	Frequency	Percentage
1st Grade	89	23
2nd Grade	133	34.4
3rd Grade	52	13.4
4th Grade	113	29.2

Internship Status	Frequency	Percentage
Yes	219	56.6
No	168	43.4

CSR Knowledge	Frequency	Percentage
Yes	281	72.6
No	106	27.4

the ages of 22–25 years. Looking at the students' class, the second-year students constitute the largest group with 34% (133 people). It is seen that 32% (124) of the students both studied and worked. When the internship status of the students was examined, it was determined that more than half of them (219 people) did internships. Finally, when the knowledge level of the students about CSR was examined, it was determined that 72% (281 people) knew CSR.

11.4.2 Explanatory Factor Analysis for CSR

Explanatory factor analysis was conducted to reveal the dimensional structures of the scale toward students' CSR attitudes and to determine its validity and reliability. Principal competent analysis (PCA), one of the factor analysis methods, and varimax, one of the orthogonal rotation types, were preferred for rotation. Kayser Mayer Olkin's (KMO) value was checked for suitability for factor analysis, and the Bartlett test was performed. A KMO value of 0.930 is excellent for factor analysis (Sharma 1996). According to the Bartlett test result, $X^2 = 4941.82$, $p < 0.05$ is suitable for factor analysis (Hair et al., 1998). Considering the factor loads, all of them are above 0.50, and Hair et al. (1998) are pretty good.

A reliability test (Cronbach Alpha) was conducted to measure the scale's structural validity and determine the scale's internal consistency. The Cronbach Alpha value shows the total reliability level of the questions under the factor. According to Nunnaly and Bernstein (1994), the scale is considered reliable when this value is 0.70 and above. Since the Cronbach alpha values of all dimensions that make up the scale are above 0.70, it can be said that the scale is reliable.

Explanatory factor analysis for CSR is included in Table 11.2. According to the Kaiser normalization, in the factor analysis made considering the factors with an eigenvalue greater than 1, it was determined that the scale related to CSR consists of four dimensions. The total variance percentage of the study was 72.99. Since this rate is higher than 50%, the analysis seems valid (Scherer et al., 1988). When the information in Table 11.2 was examined, the first factor (eight items) was named as activities

TABLE 11.2
Explanatory Factor Analysis Table for Corporate Social Responsibility Statements

Statements on Corporate Social Responsibility	Factor Load	Variance	α
Respect for employees		25.90	0.912
A socially responsible tourism business protects the rights of its employees	0.763		
A socially responsible tourism business ensures the health and safety of its employees	0.747		
A corporate socially responsible tourism business acts in compliance with applicable laws and regulations	0.728		
A corporate socially responsible tourism business treats employees well regardless of gender, ethnicity, or region	0.714		
A corporate socially responsible tourism business respects human rights in all countries where it operates	0.688		
A socially responsible tourism business creates employment	0.685		
A corporate socially responsible tourism business helps all employees who want to get more training	0.665		
A socially responsible tourism business does not operate in countries where human rights are violated	0.553		
Voluntary activities		19.45	.925
A corporate socially responsible tourism business supports philanthropy	0.814		
A socially responsible tourism business develops projects for developing countries	0.812		
A corporate socially responsible tourism business supports social and cultural activities	0.811		
A corporate socially responsible tourism business helps to develop countries	0.776		
Respect for consumers activities		15.51	.877
A corporate socially responsible tourism business treats consumers honestly	0.869		
A corporate socially responsible tourism business provides accurate information to consumers about its products	0.848		
A corporate socially responsible tourism business observes consumer rights (after-sales service, warranty)	0.846		
Environmental respect activities		12.12	.819
A socially responsible tourism business reduces the consumption of natural resources	0.815		
A tourism business with corporate social responsibility observes the ecological balance as much as possible	0.616		
A tourism business with corporate social responsibility implements environmentally friendly production practices	0.572		

Reliability analysis: .937; **Inference method:** principal component analysis; **Rotation method:** Varimax with Kaiser normalization, **Number of iterations:** 7; **Sum of variance:** 72.99; **KMO eligibility criterion:** .930; **Bartlett test of sphericity x^2:** 4941,82 p: 0.000.

TABLE 11.3
Averages for CSR

Dimensions	Mean	S. Deviation
Respect for consumers activities	3.92	0.92227
Respect for employees	3.68	0.87147
Environmental respect activities	3.64	0.86823
Voluntary activities	3.44	01.14472

of respect for employees, the second factor (four items) as voluntary activities, the third factor (three items) as activities of concern for consumers, and the fourth factor (three items) as activities of respect for the environment. It is seen that the internal consistency coefficient of each of these factors is between 819 and 925.

Table 11.3 includes the students' attitudes toward CSR. It is observed that the most positive attitudes of the students were realized in the dimension of 'activities to respect consumers' (3.92), followed by 'activities of respect for employees' (3.68) and 'activities of respect for the environment' (3.64), respectively. It has been determined that the dimension that students see less positively than other dimensions is 'voluntary activities.' When all averages are evaluated, it can be said that students of a tourism business treat consumers respectfully but voluntarily engage in relatively few philanthropic activities.

11.4.3 The Difference Between Students' Perceptions of CSR According to Internship and CSR Knowledge Variables

Analyzes were carried out to determine the difference between the CSR perceptions of the students according to whether they had an internship and whether they had CSR knowledge. This context checked whether the data were normally distributed, with skewness and kurtosis values. According to Tabachnick and Fidell (2013), if the skewness value is between –0.360 and –0.999, the normality assumption is provided if the kurtosis value is between –0.028 and 1.054. For this reason, the independent sample t-test was used as the difference test.

Table 11.4 shows the t-test table for the difference between the CSR perceptions of the students according to the variables of internship and CSR knowledge. First, when examining the perception of CSR dimensions according to the status of students' training or not, it was found that there is a difference in the variables of 'activities of respect for employees' and 'voluntary activities.' Considering the average of variables, it is seen that those who do not do internships perceive these dimensions more positively. The fact that students have sector experiences is effective in their negative perceptions. On the other hand, when examining the perception of CSR dimensions according to whether or not the students have CSR knowledge, it was determined that there is a difference in the dimensions of 'activities to respect consumers' and 'activities to respect the environment.' Looking at the average of the

TABLE 11.4
T-Test Table for the Difference between Students' CSR Perceptions According to Internship and CSR Knowledge Variables

Dimensions	Internship Status	Mean	t	p
Respect for employees	Yes	3.48	2.906	0.004
	No	3.78		
Voluntary activities	Yes	3.05	4.148	0.000
	No	3.62		
Dimensions	**CSR knowledge**	**Mean**	**t**	**p**
Respect for consumers activities	Yes	4.05	4.674	0.000
	No	3.57		
Environmental respect activities	Yes	3.74	3.969	0.000
	No	3.36		

variables, it was determined that those who had CSR knowledge perceived respect for consumers and activities of respect for the environment more positively. Since a student who knows the scope of the CSR subject will have a high expectation from tourism enterprises regarding these dimensions, it is evaluated that they see these dimensions more positively.

11.4.4 Correlation Analysis for the Relationships Between CSR Dimensions

Pearson correlation analysis was conducted to determine the relationships between the dimensions of Price Perception. In determining the relationship between variables in studies, generally, if $n > 100$ and $r > 0.70$, there is a 'strong relationship' between variables, 'moderate' if $r = 0.40$ to 0.70, 'weak relationship' if $r = 0.20$ and 0.40. It is accepted to be (Sökmen 2000).

Table 11.5 shows the correlation table for the relationships between the dimensions of CSR perception. Accordingly, a strong positive relationship between respect for employees and voluntary activities ($r = 0.707$), respect for consumers ($r = 0.403$), and activities of respect for the environment ($r = 0.633$) were found to be moderately positive. On the other hand, a weak relationship was revealed between voluntary activities concerning consumers ($r = 0.268$) and moderately positive relationships with activities of respect for the environment ($r = 0.564$). Finally, a moderate positive relationship was found between respect for consumers and the environment ($r = 0.520$). In this case, all dimensions have positive relationships is considered a remarkable result that an improvement in one size can also improve other dimensions.

11.5 CONCLUSION AND DISCUSSION

According to the factor analysis conducted in the study, in which the CSR perceptions of the students studying tourism at the undergraduate level were measured, four

TABLE 11.5
Correlation Analysis Between Variables

Dimensions	RCA	VA	RCA
Respect for consumers activities	1		
Voluntary activities	0.707**	1	
Respect for consumers activities	0.403**	0.268**	1
Environmental respect activities	0.633**	0.564**	0.520**

**p < 0.01.

dimensions were reached. However, when the studies in Turkey-based on the theoretical basis put forward by Carroll (1991) are examined; Aymankuy et al. (2016), Çalışkan and Ünüsan (2011), Özdemir (2007), and Koçoğlu (2018) found that CSR consists of four dimensions, as in this study, while Akdoğan and Bay (2012) found that CSR was five in the survey conducted by Avcı and Akdemir (2014), it was determined that CSR consists of three dimensions.

The CSR dimension with the highest perceptions of the students is the dimension of 'activities to respect consumers.' It can be said that the main reason for this is that they are also consumers, and they are sensitive about respecting their rights in the businesses they consume. The second dimension in which their perception is highest is the dimension of 'activities of respect for employees.' It can be said that the participants' working in hotels and the disrespect they face in the sector increase their sensitivity at this point. The third highest perception is the 'activities of respect for the environment' dimension. The perception rate of this dimension is close to the perception rate of the 'activities of respect for employees' dimension. In this case, it can be said that the participants are also sensitive to the environment. Finally, the 'Voluntary activities' dimension is where the participants' perceptions are the lowest. However, it still has a high perception level with an average of 3.44 (Özdamar 2003).

According to other studies measuring CSR perceptions, Lee et al. (2011) and Avcı and Akdemir (2014), while the order of importance of CSR is in the form of ethics, volunteering, legal, and economic responsibility, the order of importance of CSR by hardworking and Ünüsan (2011), it has been found in the form of economic, legal, ethical, and voluntary responsibility. The study of Koçoğlu (2018) revealed that the essential dimension of tourists is voluntary responsibility, followed by ethical, legal, and economic obligations, respectively.

Significant differences were determined as a result of the t-test conducted to determine whether the dimensions of 'respect for employees' and 'voluntary activities' differ according to the internship status of the participants. According to the test results, the perception levels of 'respect for employees activities' and 'voluntary activities' of the internship participants were lower than those who did not do an internship. This situation proves that tourism enterprises give less importance to CSR than expected. Furthermore, significant differences were determined due to the t-test conducted to determine whether the dimensions of 'activities to respect the consumer' and 'activities to respect the environment' differ according to the state of the participant's knowledge of the CSR concept. As a result of the test, the perception levels of the participants who have CSR knowledge are lower than those who do not have CSR concept knowledge. This situation reveals that it is necessary to provide training related to CSR while providing tourism education.

Correlation analysis was conducted to determine the relationship between the dimensions that make up the CSR scale. Significant differences were determined according to the results of the study. According to this result, all sizes are positively correlated with each other. In other words, any increase in any of the dimensions causes an increase in the others, and a decrease causes a decrease in the others. In this case, the necessary attention should be paid by considering not only one or a few dimensions of CSR but also all dimensions.

11.6 LIMITATION, RECOMMENDATION, AND FUTURE DIRECTIONS

The concept of CSR is gaining importance day by day. This concept is essential not only for industrial enterprises but also for service enterprises. The image that a business will need in its sustainability can be achieved with this concept. For this reason, it is vital to determine the level of CSR perceptions of future manager candidates. The most important limitation of this research is that although there are many tourism faculties in Turkey, the data were obtained only from Karabuk University tourism faculty students. Furthermore, although there are many data collection tools, only the survey technique was used in this study.

According to the research results, CSR perceptions of tourism faculty students have a high rate in all dimensions. Therefore, students with CSR knowledge perceptions must have a higher rate than those without CSR knowledge. In this direction, it can be recommended to increase CSR training in universities and concentrate on it. However, the CSR perceptions of the students who do internships are lower than those who do not can be evaluated as unfavorable. This indicates that tourism facilities have ineffective CSR policies and strategies. While this concept is so important, it can be suggested that tourism facilities make renewals for CSR policies and plans.

Researchers who want to work in this field in the future may be recommended to determine their perceptions of CSR for students of different applied sciences. Or, research can be conducted on the students of tourism faculties of various universities.

REFERENCES

Akdoğan, F. and Bay, E. 2012. İsteğe bağlı kurumsal sosyal sorumluluk faaliyetleri: Görünürde hayırseverlik, *Amme İdaresi Dergisi*, 45(1), 51–75.

Alp, T. 1992. *Türkiye'de turizm eğitimin yapısı, uygulanan politikalar ve sonuçları, turizm eğitimi, ankara, turizm bakanlığı turizm eğitimi genel müdürlüğü*, Yorum Basım Yayın Sanayi Ticaret Şirketi: 47.

Avcı, N. and Akdemir, İ. 2014. Konaklama işletmelerinde kurumsal sosyal sorumluluk algısının iş doyumu üzerindeki etkisi, *Ege Akademik Bakış*, 14(1), 125–135.

Ay, C. and Aytekin, P. 2005. Reklamda etik, *Öneri*, 6(24), 45–60.

Ay, Ü. 2003. *İşletmelerde etik ve sosyal sorumluluk*, Ankara: Nobel Yayınevi.

Aymankuy, Ş., Demirbulat, Ö. G. and Aymankuy, Y. 2016. Effect of social responsibility activities of the enterprises in accommodation enterprise preferences of potentıal domestic tourists, *Eurasian Academy of Sciences Social Sciences Journal*, 8, 110–134.

Balta Peltekoğlu, F. 2007. *Halkla ilişkiler nedir?*. İstanbul: Beta Yayınevi.

Bowen, H. R. 1953. *Social responsibility of the businessman*. New York, NY: Harpers and Brothers.

Çalışkan, O. and Ünüsan, Ç. 2011. Otel çalışanlarının kurumsal sosyal sorumluluk algısının iş tatmini ve işte kalma niyetine etkisi, *Anatolia: Turizm Araştırmaları Dergisi*, 22(2), 154–166.

Carroll, A. B. 1979. A three dimensional conceptual model of corporate performance. *Academic of Management Review*, 4(4), 497–505.

Carroll, A. B. 1991, The pyramid of corporate social responsibility: Toward the moral management of organizational stakeholders, *Business Horizons*, July–August, 34(4), 39–48.

Christou, E. 1999. Hospitality management education ın Greece: An exploratory study, *Tourism Management*, 20(6), 683–691.

Chryssides, G. D. and Kaler, J. H. 1999. *An introduction to business ethics*, London: International Thomson Publishing Inc.

CNN 2012. Tourism boom threatens China's Heritage Sites. [https://edition.cnn.com/2012/08/14/world/asia/china-heritagetourism/index.html] (Erişim 12 Ağustos 2020).

Coşkun, G. 2010. *Kurumsal pazarlama ve sosyal sorumluluk*. Ankara: Nobel Yayın Dağıtım.

Davis, K. 1960. Can business afford to ignore social responsibilities?. *California management review*, *2*(3), 70–76.

Davis, K. 1973. The case for and against business assumption of social responsibilities. *Academy of Management Journal*, 16, 312–322.

Engin, E., and Akgöz, B. 2013. Sürdürülebilir kalkınma ve kurumsal sürdürülebilirlik çerçevesinde kurumsal sosyal sorumluluk kavramının değerlendirilmesi. *Selçuk İletişim*, *8*(1), 85–94.

Ersöz, H. Y. 2007. *Türkiye'de kurumsal sosyal sorumluluk anlayışının gelişiminde meslek ve sivil toplum kuruluşları*. İstanbul: İstanbul Ticaret Odası Yayınları.

European Commission, 2002, Corporate social responsibility: A business contribution to sustainable development, Industrial relations and industrial change, Directorate-General for Employment and Social Affairs, Unit D.1, Manuscript.

Frederick, W. C. 1987. *Theories of corporate social performance*. In Sethi, S. P. and Falbe, C. M. (Eds.), Business and Society. Lexington, MA: Lexington Books.

Friedman, M. 1970. The social responsibility of business is to increase its profits. *New York Times Magazine*, 32(33), 122–126.

Hacıoğlu, N. 1992. *Yükseköğretimde mesleki turizm eğitimi geliştirme perspektifleri*, Turizm Eğitimi, Ankara, Turizm Bakanlığı Turizm Eğitimi Genel Müdürlüğü, Yorum Basın Yayın San. Ltd. Şti.: 92.

Hair, J. F., Anderson, R. E., Tatham, R. L., and Black, W. C. 1998. *Multivariate dataanalysis* (5th ed.), New Jersey: Prentice-Hall Inc..

Hergüner, G., Arslan, S. and Dündar, H. 2002. Beden eğitimi ve spor öğretmenliği bölümü öğrencilerinin okul deneyimi dersini algılama düzeyleri, *Pamukkale Üniversitesi Eğitim Fakültesi*, 11:44–58.

Kahraman, N. and Türkay, O. 2014. *Turizm ve çevre*, Ankara: Detay Yayıncılık.

Kärnä, J., Hansen E., and Juslin H. 2003, Social responsibility in environmental marketing planning, *European Journal of Marketing*, 37(5/6), 848–871. Research paper.

Kelgökmen, D. 2010. İşletmelerin kurumsal sosyal sorumluluk düzeylerinin belirlenmesine yönelik bir literatür taraması. *Ege Academic Review*, 10(1), 303–318.

Kerlinger, F. N. 1978. *Foundations of behavioral research*. New York, NY: McGraw Hill.

Keung, S. W. 2000. Tourist's perception of hotel frontline employees' questionable job-related behaviour, *Tourism Management*, 21(2): 121–134.

Kızılırmak, İ. 2000. Yüksekokulların turizm ve otelcilik programlarının turizm sektörünün beklentileri doğrultusunda değerlendirilmesi, *Milli Eğitim Dergisi*, 147: 54–60.

Kline, R. B. 2011. *Principles and practice of structural equation modeling* (3rd ed.). New York, NY: Guilford Press.

Koçoğlu, C. M. 2018. Otel işletmelerinde uygulanan sosyal sorumluluk faaliyetlerinin turistlerin satın alma niyeti üzerindeki etkisi: İstanbul örneği. *Mehmet Akif Ersoy Üniversitesi İktisadi ve İdari Bilimler Fakültesi Dergisi*, *5*(3), 615–631.

Koçoğlu, C. M., Saraç, and Ö. ve Batman, O. 2020. Safranbolu''da sürdürülebilir turizm gelişmesine yönelik yerel halkın tutumları, *Türk Turizm Araştırmaları Dergisi*, 4(1): 202–219.

Kotler, P. and Lee N. 2008. *Corporate social responsibility: Doing the good for your company and your cause,* Toronto, ON, John Wiley & Sons.

Lantos, G. P. 2001. The boundaries of strategic corporate responsibility, *The Journal of Consumer Marketing*, 18(7), 595–632.

Lee, Y. K., Kim. Y. S., Lee, K. H., and Li, D. 2011. The impact of CSR on relationship quality and relationship outcomes: A perspective of service employees, *International Journal of Hospitality Management*, 31(3), 745–756.

Mısırlı, İ. 2009. Akademik turizm eğitimi arama konferansı sonuç raporu, Muğla Üniversitesi, Bodrum.. Mill, R. C. (Ed.) (1990). *Tourism, the international business.* Englewood Cliffs, NJ: Prentice Hall.

Nunnally, J. C. and Bernstein, I. H. 1994. *Psychometric theory* (3rd ed.). New York, NY: McGraw-Hill.

Okay, A. and Okay, A. 2005. *Halkla ilişkiler kavram strateji ve uygulamaları*, İstanbul: Der Yayınları.

Özdamar, Ö. 2003. *Modern bilimsel araştırma yöntemleri*, Eskişehir: Kaan Kitabevi.

Özdemir, H. 2009. Kurumsal sosyal sorumluluğun marka imajına etkisi. *İstanbul Ticaret Üniversitesi Sosyal Bilimler* Dergisi, 8(15), 57–72.

Özdemir, Ö. H. 2007. *Çalışanların kurumsal sosyal sorumluluk algılamalarının örgütsel özdeşleşme, örgütsel bağlılık ve iş tatminine etkisi: Opet çalışanlarına yönelik uygulama.* İstanbul: Yayınlanmamış Doktora Tezi, Marmara Üniversitesi SBE.

Özgen, E. 2007. Kurumsal sosyal sorumluluk kavramı ve çalışan memnuniyetine etkisi. *Dicle Üniversitesi Ziya Gökalp Eğitim Fakültesi Dergisi*, 8, 1–6.

Özgener Ş. 2004. *İş ahlakının temelleri: Yönetsel bir yaklaşım*, Ankara: Nobel Yayınevi.

Öztürk, C. M. 2013. *Kurumsal sosyal sorumluluk kavramı ve gelişimi.* Canan Öztürk M. (Ed.), Eskişehir: Kurumsal Sosyal Sorumluluk, AÖF Yayınları.

Panapanaan V. M. 2003. Road mapping corporate social responsibility in Finnish companies, *Journal of Business Ethics*, 44, 133–148.

Peltekoğlu, B. F. 2001. *Hakla ilişkiler nedir?,* (2. Baskı), İstanbul: Beta Yayınları.
Scherer, R. Wiebe, F. A., Luther, D. C. and Adams, J. S. 1988. Dimensionality of coping: Factor stability using the ways of coping questionnaire, *Psychological Report*, 62, 763–770.
Sekaran, U. 2003. *Business research methods: A skill-building approach* (4th. Edition), New York, NY: John Wiley & Sons.
Sem, J. and Clements, C. 1996. Tourism and recreation management: Strategies for public lands, *Parks and Recreation*, 31(9): 92–105.
Seymen, A. O. 2002. Turizm işletmelerinde oryantosyon eğitiminin insan kaynakları yönetimi açısından önemi ve buna yönelik program modelinin oluşturulması. *Anatolia Turizm Araştırmaları Dergisi*, 13(1): 15–25.
Sezgin, O. M. 2001. *Genel turizm ve turizm mevzuatı*, Ankara: Detay Yayıncılık.
Sharma, S. 1996. *Applied multivariate techniques*, New York, NY: John Wiley & Sons Inc..
Sığındı, T. 2013. Kurumsal sosyal sorumluluk uygulamalarına ilişkin tüketici algılarının haritalandırma yöntemi ile incelenmesi. *International Journal of Social Science*, 6(5), 497–513.
Sökmen, A. 2000. *Ankara'da beş yıldızlı konaklama işletmelerinde örgütsel bağlılık ile işgören performansı arasındaki ilişkinin belirlenmesine yönelik ampirik bir araştırma,* Ankara: Yayımlanmamış yüksek lisans tezi, Gazi Üniversitesi.
Stevens, J. 1996. *Applied multivariate statistics for the social sciences*. Mahwah, NJ: Lawrence Erlbaum Associates.
Stone, C. D. 1976. Where the law ends: The social control of corporate behavior. *Business Horizons*, *19*(3), 84–87.
Swaen, V. and Chumpitaz, R. C. 2008. Impact of corporate social responsibility on consumer trust, *Resherche Et Applications En Marketing*, 23(4), 7–33.
Tabachnick, B. G. and Fidell, L. S., 2013. *Using multivariate statistics* (6th ed.) Boston, MA: Pearson.
The CSR Journal, 2021. Understanding the Four Levels of CSR, https://thecsrjournal.in/understanding-the-four-levels-of-csr/ Retrieved: 12.05.2021.
Ünlüönen, K. 2000. Turizm isletmeciliği öğretmenlik programlarının öğrenci beklentileri ve algılamaları açısından değerlendirilmesi, Gazi Üniversitesi Ticaret ve Turizm Eğitim Fakültesi *Dergisi*, 3: 218–238.
Ünlüönen, K. 2004. Turizm işletmeciliği öğretmenlik programlarının öğrenci beklentileri ve algılamaları açısından karşılaştırılması (1998–1999 ve 2003–2004 öğretim yılları), *Ticaret ve Turizm Eğitim Dergisi*, 1: 108–130.
Üzümcü, T. P. and Bayraktar, S. 2004. *Türkiye'de turizm otel işletmeciliği alanında eğitim veren yüksek öğretim kuruluşlarındaki eğitimcilerin turizm mesleki eğitiminin etiksel açıdan incelenmesine yönelik bir alan araştırması*, 3. Ulusal Bilgi, Ekonomi ve Yönetim Kongresi Bildiri Kitabı: 80.
Vural, Z. B. A. and Coşkun, G. 2011. Kurumsal sosyal sorumluluk ve etik. *Gümüşhane Üniversitesi İletişim Fakültesi Elektronik Dergisi*, 1(1), 61–87.
Woodhall, M. 1979. Education, work and employment ın developing countries—A synthesis of recent research. Education work and employment, a summary review, *International development research center manuscript reports*, Ottawa: IDRC: 34.

12 Hospitality Businesses in the Anthropocene Era

Recycling Practices

Nilgün Avci, Samet Can Curkan, and Hasan Tahsin Kokonalioğlu

CONTENTS

12.1 INTRODUCTION

It has become apparent that the world has been rapidly destroyed in the recent century. Global warming, greenhouse gases (GHGs), carbon emissions, and climate change have become part of the everyday life of ordinary people. Rarely does a day go by without the news of a climate disaster, loss of ice mass, flood, landslide, tornado, storm, excessive precipitation, excessive cooling, or extreme weather. These climate problems the world is facing emerged as a result of environmental changes. At the end of the 19th century, the world was accepted to have stepped into the Anthropocene Epoch, namely the age of human beings (Zalasiewicz et al. 2011). Anthropocene is the geological era dominated by recent global environmental changes based on humans' relationships and ecosystem. The reason why this era is called the human age is explained by the fact that the impact of human activities is beyond the self-renewal of the world.

DOI: 10.1201/9781003138051-15

Climate change was previously included only in the scientists' predictions. Still, now that all sectors face these changes, studies on climate change/studies on climate solutions have accelerated. Today, all sectors are in a struggle for determining their responsibility for the answer to act.

Following the data released by World Tourism Organization, the number of international tourists traveling around the world in 2019 increased by 4% compared to the previous year and exceeded 1.5 billion (World Tourism Organization 2021). In the same report, it was stated that tourism was listed in the third-export category in the world. The COVID-19 pandemic has affected the tourism and travel industry negatively and many other sectors. According to the data of the World Tourism Organization, in 2020, a 74% decrease was observed in the number of tourists due to the pandemic (UNWTO World Tourism Organization 2021). O'Callaghan-Gordo and Antó (2020) questioned in their studies 'if COVID-19 results from Anthropocene or not.' The study emphasized that the destruction of the natural habitat and species, capturing animals in unfavorable conditions, and marketing and consuming them paved the way for the pandemic conditions. These all were related to climate change and Anthropocene. We can predict that the Anthropocene may cause many more disasters in the world.

The decline in tourism due to the pandemic is an important fact that shows the fragility of tourism in the presence of the negativities experienced in the balance of nature. Reducing the vulnerability of the tourism sector in the face of crises and increasing its endurance are listed among the main targets. Mitigation and adaptation strategies are adopted under these circumstances. According to Dogru, Marchio, Bulut, and Suess, while the strategies to reduce the effects of climate change on the tourism sector include the improvement, restoration, creation, or protection of the existing standards to balance the inevitable consequences, adaptation strategies are the strategies aimed at changing the current standard to meet and adapt to the effects of the climate change (Dogru et al. 2019).

Tourism is one of the sectors both causing and getting affected by climate change and environmental problems. The most critical resources of the tourism sector are the natural beauties and climate of its geography. Although the resources in the world are not unlimited, damage to the environment and future generations occurs due to excessive and reckless usage of them. These damages, which are seen globally and affect all sectors, will significantly impact the tourism sector in the upcoming period. An increase in tourism activities increases energy use and waste. Transportation, one of the main components of tourism, is one of the essential carbon emission factors. According to the World Tourism Organization data, 59% of travel for tourism purposes is provided by air and 35% by land (World Tourism Organization 2021). This shows that vehicles using fossil fuels are the most preferred means of transportation. As another tourism component, accommodation establishments are the enterprises that have significant environmental impacts with the amount of energy they use, water consumption, and solid waste.

From a tourism perspective, sustainable tourism solves preventing the destruction of nature from reaching an irreversible point. Since tourism is a global phenomenon based on natural resources, sustainability in tourism in the Anthropocene age is significant. This study aims to determine the comprehension level of sustainable tourism of accommodation establishments, the essential pillar of hospitality businesses. In the study, the extent to which accommodation establishments adopted sustainable movements such as recycling, waste management, and eco-labels in the Anthropocene age and how they integrated into these movements are examined using a qualitative approach. The study consists of five parts. The first part consists of the introduction, the second part of the conceptual framework, the third part of the method, the fourth part of the findings, and the fifth part consists of the conclusion/recommendations.

12.2 LITERATURE REVIEW

12.2.1 Anthropocene and Tourism

Paul Crutzen first used the concept of Anthropocene in 2002 (Crutzen 2002). Although this concept has been used for about 20 years, it has not been officially adopted yet (Steffen et al. 2011). The Anthropocene defines a period of significant human impact on the planet's ecosystems, landforms, and global climate (Zalasiewicz et al. 2010). As a concept, Anthropocene refers to many forms of human-induced, global environmental changes such as climate change, losing biodiversity, and changes in the nutrient cycle (Moore 2015). Based on such geological and ecological events in which humankind is at the center, it would not be inappropriate to use the term 'Anthropocene' to describe the age we are living in. According to Crutzen, '*The Anthropocene could be said to have started in the late eighteenth century when analyses of air trapped in polar ice showed the beginning of growing global concentrations of carbon dioxide and methane.*'

Etymologically, the term Anthropocene is the combination of the words Anthropos (human) and cene (recent) in ancient Greek, and accordingly, the term Anthropocene implies that all humans induce geological fracture (Shoshitaishvili 2021). Thus, humankind's impact has been observed since its existence and will continue to be seen for long periods.

Human activities continue to increase day by day, and as a result of these increasing activities, people affect the environment they live in either positively or negatively. Furthermore, the size and continuity of these effects differentiate human beings from other species on earth. Thus, human has become a determining factor in the functioning of nature over time.

The concept of Anthropocene is derived from the idea that humankind wants to dominate the world it lives in. According to Crutzen and Stoermer, Anthropocene, the beginning of the new geological era, dates back to the Industrial Revolution, when the carbon dioxide and methane gas emission began to increase significantly compared to previous times (Crutzen and Stoermer 2000).

The increase in the world population has made urbanization inevitable. Today, the rapidly increasing world population has reached 7.7 billion. Humanity changed the planet at the same pace to meet the demands of this rapidly growing population. This population growth causes an increase in both energy and the economy. With population growth and resource utilization, humans have become a geological power changing the planet independently. The required amount of energy is bought by fossil fuels to a great extent. However, this fuel type causes very high levels of carbon emission.

Today, humankind has a feature disrupting, influencing the climate balance on our planet. Humanity uses these resources as if there is no limit and ignores the negative consequences. People's way of thinking about dominating nature has reached the point of destroying nature. Rapidly, increasing human activities are seen on earth and in the atmosphere. Global warming is entirely the result of human activities. In the Anthropocene age, fossil fuel consumption due to human, industrial, and agricultural activities cause global warming. Global warming occurs due to the excessive increase in GHGs such as carbon dioxide in the atmosphere and the temperature rise. With the rise of global warming, climate change happens. Climate changes bring about increases in meteorological events such as drought, floods, storms, and tornadoes. Global warming is expected to melt glaciers, water levels will rise, and many countries will submerge. Considering that 80% of all tourism is done in coastal areas, it is predicted that rising sea levels will pose a significant threat to tourism.

Unstable climate conditions have affected human life. All these conditions have also affected tourism and many other sectors. Mostafanezhad and Norum emphasize that just as tourism influenced the Anthropocene, the Anthropocene also reshaped tourism (Mostafanezhad and Norum 2019). Tourism contributes to the Anthropocene by restructuring the landforms for tourist transportation, accommodation, and entertainment. Tourism is accepted as one of the biggest threats and activities using wildlife and other natural areas (Duffy 2015). Tourism is a global activity with a significant capacity to change the environment, especially in developing destinations. According to Gren and Huijbens, our mission in the Anthropocene is no longer to modernize nature and society but to make the relations between the world and humanity ecological (Gren and Huijbens 2014). Resources must be used wisely so that future generations can use the same resources. Today, we need to handle the problems from the Anthropocene perspective and deepen the discussion of sustainability in tourism. Sustainability offers a stable approach to human-induced growth and the protection of the earth.

12.2.2 The Seventh Continent and Tourism

As stated in the previous part, humankind has stepped into a geological age that it has created on its own. Global warming is one of the most important effects of the Anthropocene. Global warming can be accepted as one of the most visible consequences of the Anthropocene Epoch. Another significant impact is the plastic waste pile found in the middle of the Pacific Ocean. Plastic wastes accumulated on the water surface due to their buoyancy and durability features and thus started to form islands. Plastic pollution is carried by prevailing winds and surface currents in the world's oceans (Eriksen et al. 2014). These accumulated plastic piles are called 'the seventh continent.' Plastic wastes continue to gather in the oceans at the micro-level. Plastic pollution will be one of the most challenging ecological threats for future generations. Plastic pollution in the sea will affect the whole ecosystem (Brach et al. 2018). The seventh continent reminds us that countries, people, and establishments must take the path of mitigating and stopping anthropogenic effects.

The central concept of the 16th Istanbul Biennial, held in İstanbul between September 14 and November 10, 2019, was the 'waste pile' as one of the most visible results of the Anthropocene. 'The Seventh Continent,' named after the vast mass of waste in the middle of the Pacific Ocean, is formed by 3.4 million square kilometers, 7 million tons of floating plastic piles (İstanbul Kültür Sanat Vakfı (İKSV) 2019). In the event (biennial) held in İstanbul, it was stressed that the accumulation of waste pollution on the seas was necessary for the entire world.

The Mediterranean faces extensive plastic pollution, just like the other seas. According to the Mediterranean Plastic Report presented by WWF in 2018, plastic materials compose 95% of the waste in the Mediterranean. In the same report, it was stated that there were 1.25 million plastic pieces less than 5 millimeters per square kilometer in the Mediterranean. Excessive use of plastics, inadequate waste management, and intensive mass tourism pose serious risks. The report indicated that 144 t of plastic waste from Turkey, 126 t from Spain, 90 t from Italy, 77 t from Egypt, and 66 t from France were disposed of in the Mediterranean daily. Furthermore, tourists visiting the Mediterranean coasts cause an increase of 40% in the wastes (Worldwide Fund for Nature (WWF) 2018).

Tourism is a significant industry that cooperates with many sub-sectors. The tourism movement continues to increase constantly. With this increase, the level of plastic and paper waste rises as well. In the study published in 2014, Pirani and Arafat compiled the research conducted in Toronto, New York, Los Angeles, the United Kingdom, Florida, Chicago, and Malaysia. They observed the waste measurements of accommodation establishments between 1990 and 2010. It was found in the study that the waste separated into paper, cardboard, and plastic was approximately equal to 29% of the whole waste (Pirani and Arafat 2014). Therefore, the amount of plastic waste can be reduced by decreasing plastics and waste production.

12.2.3 Sustainable Tourism

Anthropogenic effects have produced a visible impact on the world and Turkey. This is because the lives of all humanity depend on natural resources. Thanks to these resources, society has become a self-sufficient species that can produce, and in the absence of these resources, there will be nothing left in humankind's hands.

Natural resources are in constant transformation within the order set by nature. These resources, which exist in the cycle within nature, have renewed themselves for a certain period despite human intervention and excessive use. But, humanity is preventing this renewal from repairing the disruption. It is up to society to remove these obstacles and enable the world to renew itself. The essential instrument of humankind in fighting these negativities is sustainability. People are required to change their lifestyles and viewpoints of the world to adopt sustainability.

The World Commission used the concept of sustainability on Environment and Development (WCED) in the report titled 'Our common future, from one earth to one world,' published in 1987. In the report, sustainable development is defined as 'development that meets the needs of the present without compromising the ability of future generations to meet their own needs' (World Commission on Environment and Development 1987).

As a result of many mistakes made by humanity without considering sustainability, society has started a new age on its own; humanity itself will be able to save the world that has come to this point. This can only be achieved with the adoption of sustainability and the participation of all people. Because of all these reasons, today, understanding sustainability in tourism and other sectors is essential. The positive and negative effects of tourism are all associated with planning. It will be possible to reduce the harmful effects of tourism and increase its positive impacts on the environmental and socio-economic dimensions via sustainability. The actors in the value chain, suppliers, local community, and local governments should also be included in the process for sustainability.

The concept of sustainable tourism has been used since the 1980s. Sustainable tourism means ensuring continuity of the factors and assets that make up tourism without losing their quality and quantity (Gündüz 2004). This definition focuses primarily on the ecological sustainability of tourism rather than its potential contribution to long-term sustainable development. The World Tourism Organization defines sustainable tourism as 'Sustainable tourism development protects and enhances opportunities for the future while meeting current tourists and host regions' (UNWTO 2021).

The main target of the concept is to reduce GHG emissions, minimize environmental impacts, and reduce natural resource consumption to enable sustainable production and consumption of travel and tourism activities. Furthermore, sustainable tourism continues to increasingly explain the social and economic effects of tourism activities to maximize the tourism activities' positive economic and social contributions to the local communities.

The demand increasing and diversifying along with globalization shows that renewal and diversification will be called forth in tourism, as in most sectors. Today's tourism demand has gotten rid of the focus on the sea, sand, and sun and left its place to a more conscious understanding of tourism with the change of people's wishes and thoughts and the differentiation in the world. Each destination has its unique climate, geographical features, and attractiveness. Sustainable tourism has progressed due to the dissatisfaction of tourism demand with the existing tourism products, increasing environmental awareness among tourists, and cultural sensitivity. Tourism consists of several highly globalized and highly connected areas, each with its dynamics and perspectives such as travel, hospitality, recreation, etc.

By blending the emerging demand and the understanding of sustainability with the tourism sector, it has been tried to create a conscious tourism understanding that looks after all stakeholders' interests, aims to increase the local life quality, and protects the world.

The content of the sustainable tourism debate has expanded to include environmental and economic, social and cultural issues, political power, and social equity. Sustainable development advocates a holistic perspective; it can only be sustainable if considered within a global political, socio-economic, and ecological context. It is acknowledged that there should be national and international cooperation to facilitate sustainable tourism development policies. However, the industry's political structure and fragmented nature indicate that 'political systems dedicated to equitable development and resource use' are unlikely to emerge (Sharpley 2000). The World Tourism

Organization and United Nations Environment Programme suggest for sustainable tourism (United Nations Environment Programme (UNEP) and World Tourism Organization (WTO) 2005) to:

1. make the best of the environmental resources, the critical elements in tourism development, help protect the natural heritage and biodiversity by maintaining fundamental ecological processes;
2. respect the socio-cultural authenticity of the host communities, protect the established and living cultural heritage and traditional values, and contribute to intercultural understanding and tolerance;
3. provide long-term economic operations, including stable employment and income-generating opportunities and social services for host communities that deliver fairly distributed socio-economic benefits to all stakeholders and contribute to poverty reduction.

Accommodation establishments that have adopted sustainability must take on energy conservation, renewable energy use, water saving, food saving, waste reduction, waste decomposition, recycling, and reuse practices. Therefore, it is essential to raise awareness off and train the employees for these practices. In the same manner, the involvement of the guests in the process is also necessary. Moreover, the guests can be provided with sustainability education. Education can include the participation of guests in the energy production and consumption monitoring process at the hotel through a reward or bonus system, for instance, by setting up exercise bikes that generate electricity or developing collective point-scoring systems (Manniche et al. 2021).

The concept of sustainability, which can be interpreted in a wide range of ways in different sectors, is linked to a single typical result, which is a concern for the future. This understanding emerged with the strengthening of the effect of future anxiety on people. Humanity needs to leave the resources borrowed from future generations as they were to them and allow them to live. The pollution and wastes created by humankind have exceeded national and regional dimensions. Protection works without borders must be carried out for this borderless pollution, and in the same way, global involvement must be ensured. In a carbon-constrained global economy, much more consideration is required for the future of tourism development.

12.2.4 Eco-label Practices at Accommodation Establishments

Changes in consumer expectations changed the tourists' expectations as well. Tourists, who have experienced environmental changes in their lives, have preferred hotels with higher environmental sensitivity during their holidays. Thus, it is observed that responsible tourism and responsible tourist concepts have emerged together. Responsible tourists tend to minimize their impact on nature during their tourism behavior. These conscious tourists feel the necessity to compare the tourism establishments regarding their environmental sensitivities while making choices. Since it is difficult to measure the ecological practices of each hotel business, eco-labels offer essential solutions to this need.

Yücel and Emekçiler (2008) list the benefits of eco-labels as follows:

- help implement solutions for critical environmental issues, monitoring and reporting performance;
- reducing the costs by reducing the use of resources such as water, energy, and helping sales;
- contributing to the local economy by directing to the use of regional products;
- increasing awareness on environmental protection.

For hotels, it is essential to have an eco-label to ensure both attractiveness and environmental and social benefit. With the increasing interest in recycling and sustainability, until the 1990s, giving different awards and labels to touristic businesses based on the ecological activity and thus the initiation of certification programs became widespread (Kahraman and Türkay 2006).

The eco-labels used in the accommodation establishments are as follows:

ISO 14000 Environmental Management System Standards: It is the international standards series on environmental management. This standard considers all environmental issues related to air pollution, water and sewage problems, efficient use of resources, waste management, soil pollution, climate change, and adaptation. In addition, ISO 14000 provides a framework for developing and supporting environmental management system monitoring programs (International Organization for Standardization (ISO) n.d.).

Blue Flag: The certification program given by independent environmental non-governmental organizations in the member countries to beaches and marinas, which started to be shown in France in 1985 and has been put into practice in Turkey since 1993 (Türkiye Çevre Eğitim Vakfı (TÜRÇEV) n.d.).

Eco-label: Environmental label system that began to be issued by the European Union in 1992. It is an eco-label that considers raw material selection, production, consumption, and recycling phases (European Commission n.d.).

Green Star: Document issued by the Ministry of Culture and Tourism in Turkey to accommodation enterprises since 2008; it includes reducing the consumption of energy, water, and environmentally harmful materials and waste amount, increasing energy efficiency, promoting the use of renewable energy resources, planning and realizing the accommodation establishments to be environment-friendly as of the investment stage, the environmental adaptability of the facility, environment-enhancive regulation, and activities, ecological architecture, raising awareness on ecological consciousness, and providing education and making cooperation with the related institutions and organizations (T.C. Kültür ve Turizm Bakanlığı 2021).

Green Key: The award prepared by FEE shows that the accommodation establishments are compatible with nature. In Turkey, it has been given to accommodation establishments for one year by the Environment Foundation of Turkey since 2011 (Türkiye Çevre Eğitim Vakfı (TÜRÇEV) 2021).

White Star: It is a certification system initiated by the Turkish Hoteliers Federation (TÜROFED) to protect the environment and natural resources. It is started to be issued in 2008 and aims to reduce environmental damage by controlling water, electricity, energy, and solid waste.

Eco-labels ensure that accommodation establishments that have them are perceived as being environmentally sensitive, responsible, and understanding sustainability. Thus, it can create attractiveness for the tourists who adopt sustainability.

12.2.4.1 Waste Management in Accommodation Establishments

Economic activity is defined by a linear production and consumption model that assumes a take-make-waste model. It produces goods and services obtained through energy, labor, capital, and a single life cycle from natural resources (Rodríguez et al. 2020). By accepting the fact that resources are not limited, this take-make-waste model is being abstained from. Today, wastes have been considered a new source of production. Thus, instead of the linear output, it is switched to the circular economy. According to Ellen Mcarthur Foundation, 'A circular economy is reparative and regenerative as per its design and aims to keep products, components, and materials at the highest benefit and value at all times' (Ellen McArthur Foundation 2017). Tourism can be seen as a linear production economy that consumes water, energy, food, produces a lot of waste, and creates noise and air pollution. Converting tourism into a circular economy can be achieved by reducing waste and handling waste as a new source for production. This understanding is possible with the comprehension of sustainability.

Poor waste management can threaten the quality of our health and the environment and impose a burden on businesses and the national economy. Therefore, according to the studies of Manniche et al. (2021), it is emphasized that there is a need for more systematic and better-distributed information about current technological, social solutions, and best practices to reduce the environmental impact and increase the reuse and recycling of natural resources throughout the entire tourism supply chain.

The formation of public opinion regarding climate change and other serious environmental problems can be considered a sign that the tourist segment seeking sustainability in destination and accommodation facility selection is growing.

Today, solid waste management and recycling have become an issue that all hotels should emphasize. It has and will continue to have an important place in our lives due to environmental and economic reasons. Reasons such as rapid developments in the world, rapid industrialization, and increase in globalism have paved the way for decreasing people's resources and inadequacy.

The primary purpose of recycling is to obtain the raw material from the wastes and protect the new raw material. Recycling can be defined as the re-evaluation, reuse of wastes. Recycling is a resource recovery practice that refers to the collection and reuse of waste materials. Recycling supports the conservation of natural resources as it promotes the recycling and reuse of expired materials. Energy is saved by consuming less energy during these processes because old products are converted instead of new raw materials. Reducing the waste amount and recycling activities enable individuals, organizations, societies, and countries to invest in the future and the economy.

Accommodation establishments and businesses providing catering services create a lot of waste while using environmental opportunities. Because of the large number of employees and the people it provides services to, it is difficult to prevent this situation in accommodation establishments. The ideal solution to excessive raw material consumption and waste generation can be supplied by recycling. However, more waste turns into a bigger ecological footprint and thus causes more damage to the ecosystem. On average, a hotel generates about 1 kg of waste per guest overnight (International Tourism Partnership 2014a). Since millions of tons of trash are created annually in hotels worldwide, the tourism sector's waste management and recycling practices need to be stood over (Pirani and Arafat 2014). In their study conducted in hotels operating in Turkey, Kılınç Şahin and Bekar designated that 332 kg of food waste is generated in a hotel per day, and these wastes constitute 70% of the total waste (Bekar and Kılınç Şahin 2018). In the same study, it was determined that the main reasons for food waste were guests' taking much more than they could consume on their plates, oversized food portions, the staff's lack of education, and the preparation of meals with inferior quality products. 50–60% of hotel wastes are either recyclable or reusable wastes (Smith et al. 1993).

According to the report prepared by International Tourism Partnership on energy use in hotels and line with the information obtained between 2000 and 2007 from 300 four- and five-star hotels with 150–1000 rooms, 50% of the energy consumption of the hotels is electricity, 28% is gas or oil for heating, 10% water, 7% gas for kitchen, and 5% fuel (for vehicles, lawn mowers, etc.) (International Tourism Partnership 2014). In the same report, it was calculated that 22% of energy was used for the ventilation, heating, and cooling systems, 19% in guest rooms, 14% in other/unmeasured areas, 12% in kitchens, 8% in laundry, 8% in swimming pools, 8% was spent in elevators, 6% in F&B, and 2% in shared toilets. The hotel industry constitutes approximately 1% of global GHG emissions. Following the World Tourism Organization data, hotels and other accommodation establishments comprise 2%–5% of global CO_2 emitted by the tourism sector (World Tourism Organization (UNWTO) n.d.). In the Hotel Footprinting Tool program, the carbon footprint (tons CO_2e) of a 200-room hotel operating in Turkey is stated as 7,951 (Greenview 2020). These figures show that the hospitality industry must take recycling seriously to reduce its footprint.

Usually, at least 30% of the solid waste stream of a hotel can be spared for recovery and recycling (International Tourism Partnership 2014a). In their studies, Singh et al. (2014) ascertained that the potential impact of GHG on the environment was reduced through GHG reduction via recycling. It is known that separating and recycling the wastes decrease GHGs. Still, when they cannot recycle, they can contaminate groundwater by leaking to the soil, and the GHGs generated by it can cause damage.

Today, recycling procedures have been made relatively easy compared to previous times. Easy-to-reach recycling centers located in almost every destination help businesses. The most crucial step that can be taken toward modern development is to improve existing resources by recycling used and expired resources. A waste management program will help reduce waste generated and save materials, resources, and energy. Businesses that ensure their waste management healthily and efficiently make considerable savings in the long term. Waste management also creates a visible reduction in the carbon footprint produced for the hospitality industry.

Regarding the sustainability approach, the accommodation sector is developing from an environmental protection concept that focuses on reducing natural resource consumption and waste management to a more holistic approach that explains accommodation actors and activities' social and economic impact (Sorin and Sivarajah 2021). The most crucial evidence that the environmental awareness of accommodation businesses has increased in recent years is that many accommodation businesses worldwide have obtained eco-labels (Pirani and Arafat 2014). In the study conducted by Fabrice and Sivarajah in Scandinavian hotels, it was appointed that the circular economy applied at the hotels, and it was a source of value creation creating cost savings through waste management (Sorin and Sivarajah 2021). Concerning the circular economy in the tourism and hospitality industry, it is seen that water management, waste management, and energy monitoring are increasingly considered critical activities in an emerging strategy for sustainability management. A circular tourism economy can help ensure the sustainable use of resources, increase the efficiency of the tourism industry and provide sustainable development of tourism.

International Tourism Partnership offers four steps to reduce waste in waste management (International Tourism Partnership 2014a).

In the first step, it is primarily suggested not to buy unnecessarily. Thus, waste generation will be prevented. As the second step, waste collection and separation are offered for reusing or recycling. It will not be possible to reuse or recycle products that are not separated correctly. Hotel guests and employees should be motivated by raising awareness on this matter. The third step identifies that it is necessary to evaluate where certain items can be reused or the sale/donation of these items to organizations that can be used outside the hotel. Plans should be made regarding what resources can be reused within the hotel. If it cannot be used outside the hotel, sales of those sold, such as furniture, should be enabled. Those that cannot be sold can be donated to appropriate institutions or people through nongovernmental organizations. Cooperation and arrangement on food waste can be made for street animals with animal shelters. In the fourth step, it is recommended that besides the recycled wastes such as bottles, cans, cardboard, and paper, other wastes generated by the hotel, such as batteries, plastic bottles, wine cork, and frying oils, should also be taken into account for recycling. All products used in the hotel should be evaluated for their suitability for recycling or reuse.

This study aims to explore the practices that accommodation establishments are applying within the scope of sustainability. Therefore, measuring the awareness of accommodation establishments on sustainability and determining their practices and measures in this aspect are the research objectives.

12.3 METHODOLOGY

In this study, the qualitative research method is used. Since the qualitative research method is suitable for exploring, understanding, and interpreting the subject in-depth, it is ideal for understanding the sustainability perception of accommodation establishments and determining recycling practices (Yıldırım 1999).

Qualitative research gives importance to the subjective ideas of individuals with additional questions, while the researcher tracks the truth. It is especially preferred in the studies that discuss human and social phenomena. Qualitative methods allow direct talk with the participants, observe them in their natural environment, and understand them.

In the study, the phenomenological method was adopted in determining the sustainability understanding of accommodation establishments. The phenomenological approach is based on subjective human experiences and focuses on how they perceive the world (Creswell 2013). In this study, data were collected using the 'interview technique,' one of the most frequently used methods in qualitative research. The main reason for using the interview technique in the study is that, as Bogdan and Biklen (2006) emphasized in their work, interviewing is a compelling method to reveal people's perspectives, experiences, feelings, and perceptions. In this sense, six open-ended questions were determined following the purpose of the study. To test the reliability and validity of the interview form, it was sent to four faculty members who have previous studies in the field. In the light of the feedback, the final version of the interview form was shaped.

The open-ended questions of the interview form used in the study are as follows:

- What are the responsibilities of hotels for sustainable tourism?
- What do you think about the waste management practices of the hotels?
- What practices are applied in your hotel on waste management?
- Does your hotel have national or international eco-labels? (which ones)
- What is done as recycling practices in your hotel?
- What kind of support is provided from the environment to hotels to recycle?

While determining how many people will be interviewed during the field research, in other words, the number of participants, it is essential that the answers received from the participants and the emerging concepts and processes start to repeat each other. In literature, this situation is referred to as the 'saturation point' of the data. From this point of view, in this study, the researcher stopped collecting data by accepting that the data reached saturation when the participants' answers repeated each other. At determining the participants, managers at the administrative level of four- and five-star hotels providing service in Çeşme were selected. It was paid attention that managers were employees who took responsibility in the environment, ecosystems, waste management, recycling. The convenience sampling method was used to determine the participants. As in all social sciences studies, some difficulties were experienced during the data collection phase of this study. The most significant limitation of this study is that the data collection phase couldn't be carried out face to face as planned. The main reason for this is the COVID-19 pandemic that started in Turkey in March 2020. All data were collected by creating an online interview form because people were hesitant to participate in face-to-face activities and studies during the pandemic period. When the answers were deemed insufficient, an e-mail was sent to the same participant for an additional reply. Online surveys were sent to participants via e-mail in May and June 2020. The only advantage of the pandemic for the study was that employees at the administrative level in hotels quickly got back to the interview form due to the decrease in tourism movement.

The analysis process of the study started when the first answers of the participants were received. Then, the content analysis was applied to the data collected by the interview technique. Content analysis refers to any qualitative data reduction and interpretation attempts to determine fundamental consistencies and meanings by considering the qualitative material (Patton 2001). Firstly, the concepts and terms frequently used in the answers were noted and prepared for the next step. When the data reached a certain saturation point, the data collection process was completed. Then, the collected data were analyzed with MAXQDA 2020 Analytics Pro, a prevalent package software used in qualitative research. Lastly, the data were analyzed through the content analysis method, and codes identified categories and themes.

12.4 FINDINGS

The interview form prepared within the scope of the study could not be collected by face-to-face audio recording as planned due to the pandemic. Therefore, the interview forms were applied to the employees at the administrative level, who had knowledge about sustainability concepts (recycling, waste management, ecosystems, etc.) and followed the process in 11 hotels providing service in Çeşme in May and June 2020. Therefore, 11 'Hotels' analyzed in the study are coded as (H) while the 'Hotel Managers' were coded as (HM) from 1 to 11. Data of 11 hotels included in the scope of the study are shown in Table 12.1.

It is seen that the hotels included in the study are mainly of the five-star standard.

Seven of the hotels participating in the study area are five-star, three of them are four-star, and one of them is in the boutique hotel category.

As shown in Figure 12.1, the study is gathered under four main themes. These themes are hotel responsibilities, waste management, recycling, and external support (local governments).

TABLE 12.1
Information About the Hotels Included in the Scope of the Study

Hotels	Star of the Hotel	Room Number	Bed Capacity	Pension Type
H_1	4*	235	750	HD and UHD
H_2	5*	191	245	BB
H_3	5*	310	632	HB
H_4	5*	465	1200	HB
H_5	5*	312	630	BB, HB
H_6	5*	200	404	HB
H_7	5*	398	975	BB, HB
H_8	4*	138	298	HB, PLUS
H_9	4*	89	274	BB
H_{10}	5*	465	1000	HB
H_{11}	Boutique Hotel	20	45	BB

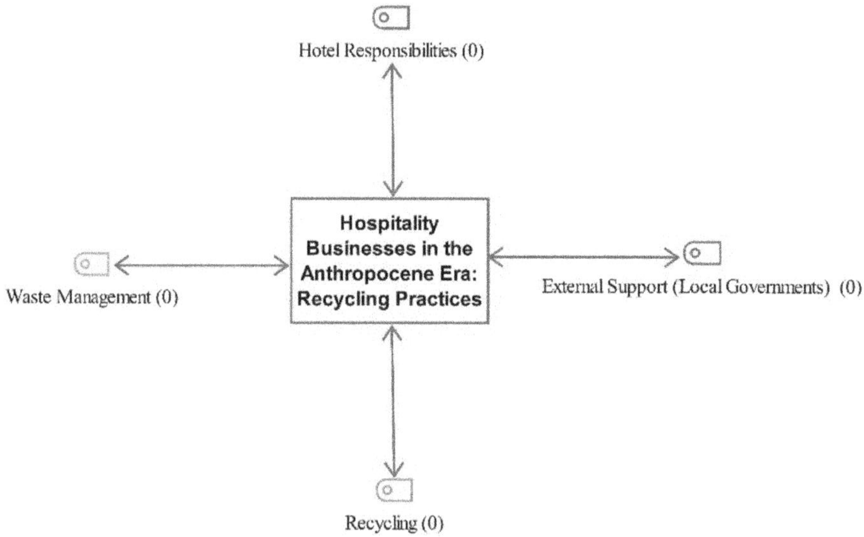

FIGURE 12.1 Main themes generated within the scope of the study.

12.4.1 Hotel Responsibilities

The study's first theme, 'Hotel Responsibilities,' is seen in the hierarchical code, sub-code, and partition model in Figure 12.2. The hotel responsibilities theme was coded by the participants under eight categories. These categories are as follows:

- Label systems;
- Encouragement;
- Qualified staff;
- Service quality;
- Cooperation;
- Staff education;
- Information;
- Efficient use of resources.

Some of the participants' statements about the codes are as follows:

> In terms of the location of the facility (country-city), it must bear traces of its location. The provided service must be of high quality.
>
> *HM_2—Service quality*

> We work with suppliers that have eco-labels. For instance, Migros, etc.
>
> *HM_4—Label systems*

> For example, the issue of personnel is very important. For the continuation of this sector, institutions providing education related to the sector must definitely

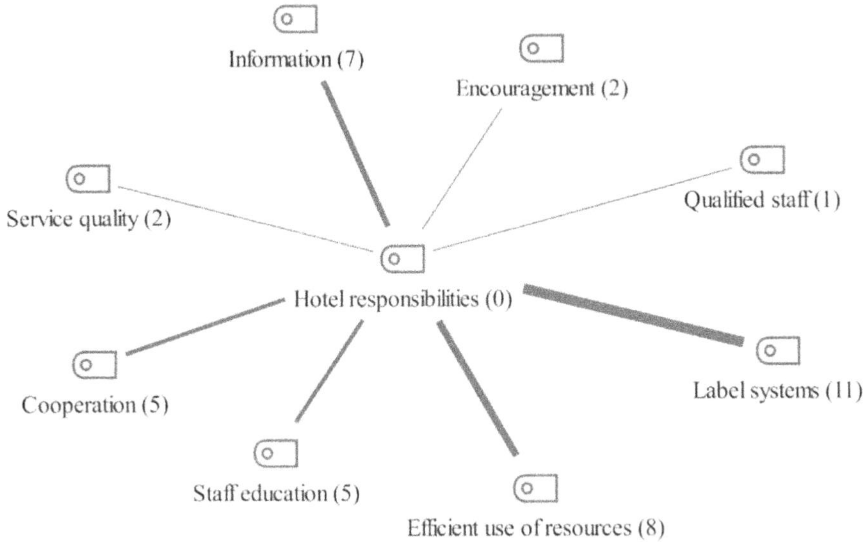

FIGURE 12.2 Hotel responsibilities theme code representation model.

be supported. The profession should be encouraged and employee rights should be at a high level. To evaluate our country, there has been a shortage of staff in recent years. Since this sector is a service sector, there won't be any hotels without staff. But I think that facilities are not aware of this fact. The students do not prefer Tourism Vocational High School anymore.

HM_2—Qualified staff

We separate recyclable wastes by placing Waste Separation containers in the guest and staff areas.

HM_5—Encouragement

This is a comprehensive subject. Facilities must work in cooperation with the local governments.

HM_2—Cooperation

HACCP documents, food safety programs, security programs, safety programs must be implemented.

HM_9—Label systems

To make waste management measurable by reducing energy, food and water consumption.

HM_{10}—Efficient use of resources

The participants mainly mentioned the label systems and efficient use of the resources. Information, cooperation, and the importance of staff education are the other most frequently coded statements.

12.4.2 Waste Management

The second theme of the study is waste management. The waste management process, as one of the most critical issues in sustainability that includes correctly separating, collecting, and transporting the waste, was composed of nine categories by hotel managers within the scope of the study. The code representation model of the waste management theme is shown in Figure 12.3.

When the participants' views on the waste management theme are examined, it is seen that the coding focuses mainly on the categories of decomposition and sensitivity. Some participants' answers to the types are as follows:

> Hotel decomposes garbage of plastic, paper, etc., and the food waste. Waste oils are collected and recycled. There is a separate collection area for the batteries. Thus decomposition of them is also enabled.
>
> *HM_1—Decomposition*

> Decomposition, information, guidance studies are carried out. Also, since the heating system is thermal, no liquid or solid waste is used
>
> *HM_4—Decomposition and sensitivity*

> The hotel chain we are affiliated with operates on an international scale, so additional efforts are made for waste management and recycling. Food waste is also sent to animal shelters.
>
> *HM_1—Recycling*

> Unfortunately, we live in a society where there is not enough information about waste management. In this sense, local government should give more support to this issue.
>
> *HM_{11}—Cooperation*

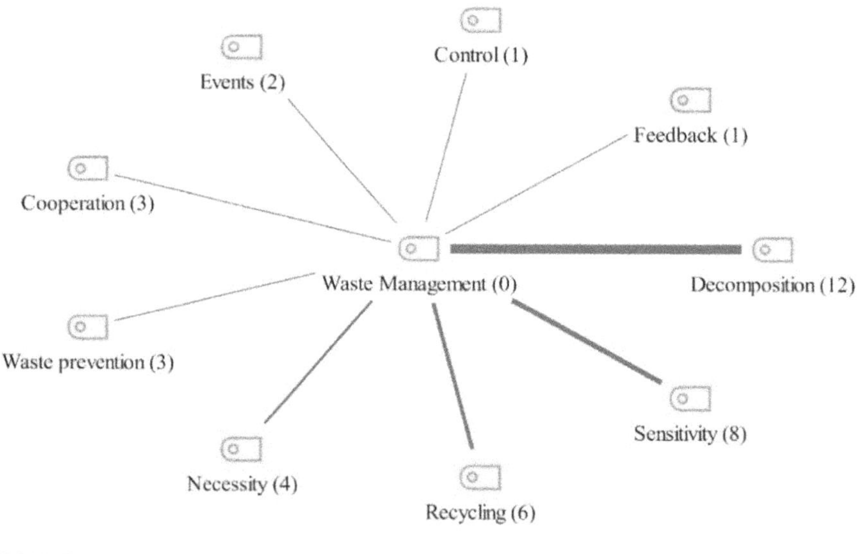

FIGURE 12.3 Waste management theme code representation model.

> Evaluations are made within the framework of reducing our waste in line with the Winnow waste management system.
>
> *HM_{10}—Sensitivity*

> We separate paper, plastic, and glass as recycling. We convert energy with tools that can be used or charged for a long time, such as batteries, lamps.
>
> *H_9—Decomposition*

12.4.3 External Support (Local Governments)

Another theme constituted within the scope of the study is external support. Since external support is coded with support provided by or expected to be provided by the local governments, it is named support from local governments. Three categories are generated under this theme. Figure 12.4 provides information about the categories.

Participants' answers to the categories generated under the external support theme are as follows:

> It is challenging for the hotel to maintain sustainability, to act alone for waste management or recycling. Therefore, the support of the local government and even the central government is critical at this point. The local government plays an active role in determining each item's destinations, the purpose of their use, and collecting the stored items from the hotel. Otherwise, the process cannot be expected to be healthy and sustainable; or requires a great effort.
>
> *HM_1—Waste Gathering*

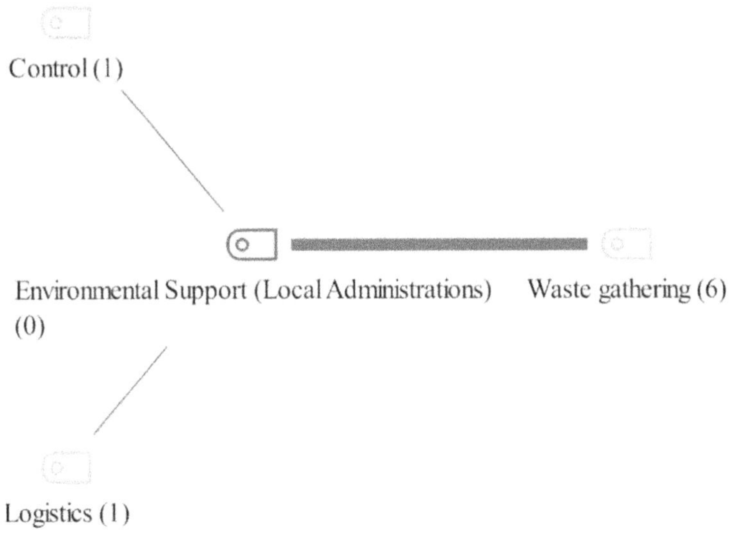

FIGURE 12.4 External support (local governments) theme code representation model.

> As far as I can see, the support of local governments is only limited to collecting waste decomposed by the hotels. If other local governments have other practices, I am not informed about the subject.
>
> *HM_2—Waste Gathering*

> They provide support for paper waste and food waste.
>
> *HM_4—Waste Gathering*

> Our waste food is delivered to the animal shelter every day through the local government.
>
> *HM_3—Waste Gathering*

> Companies contracted by the municipality collect oil wastes and plastic wastes. In addition, food waste is recycled at the municipality's animal shelter.
>
> *HM_{10}—Logistics*

12.4.4 Recycling

The last theme of the study is recycling. The recycling theme is associated with 'precision' and 'decomposition' categories. The code representation model of the recycling theme is shown in Figure 12.5.

Participants' answers to the categories generated under the recycling theme are as follows:

> In Turkey, mostly 20% of the hotels pay attention to this matter.
>
> *HM_6—Precision*

> Decomposition, information, guidance practices are applied. The decomposition process was started in 2007. Decomposed items must not be transported in the same container.
>
> *HM_4—Decomposition*

> We use durable, not disposable products. We choose cleaning products that do not harm nature and human health.
>
> *HM_{11}—Precision*

> We decompose plastic, paper, and glass. We are trying to deliver them to the institutions recommended by the Ministry.
>
> *HM_9—Decomposition and precision*

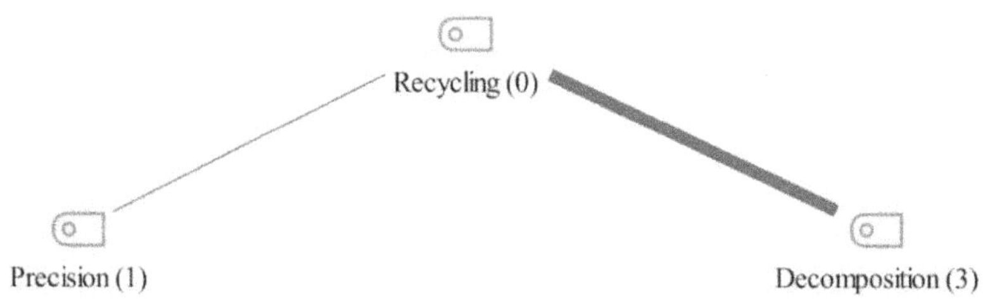

FIGURE 12.5 Recycling theme code representation model.

FIGURE 12.6 Cloud of codes.

Figure 12.6 consists of different codes based on the responses given by the participants. The most responses are, waste management, recycling progress, eco system, zero waste project.

12.5 CONCLUSION AND RECOMMENDATIONS

The primary purpose of this study is to explore the practices that accommodation establishments carry out within the scope of sustainability in the Anthropocene age. In line with the purpose of the study, interviews were done with the department managers of the accommodation establishments providing service in Çeşme and having practices within the scope of sustainability.

During the planning phase of the research, it was observed that only a tiny part of the hotels serving in Çeşme was conducting sustainable practices. Therefore, the first target of most hotels sensitive to sustainable movements is to be included in an ecosystem related to tourism. In the time, it was observed that awareness was created as the knowledge about the process increased.

When the themes generated within the scope of the study are analyzed, it is seen that hotels included in the research are involved in the process of waste management and recycling within the context of sustainability. When the answers given to the questions directed to measure the awareness on sustainable tourism are evaluated, it is seen that the hotels:

- show required sensitivity on the efficient use of resources;
- are included in the eco-label systems and work with the companies included in these systems while choosing their suppliers;
- inform their staff and guests on sustainable tourism.

Also, hotels encourage the staff and the guests regarding this issue. It is seen that some hotels are in cooperation with the local governments and the organizations and institutions in the region.

Another subject researched within the scope of the study is waste management, an essential issue in terms of sustainable tourism. Following the results of the study, the most common waste management practice in hotels is decomposition. Many hotels are meticulous about separating items such as garbage, battery, oil, and food. Also, it can be said that the hotel provides a suitable environment for staff and guests to throw their trash separately. Some hotels support the waste prevention program in this context by being included in the zero-waste project. The best example given to the 'sensitivity' category under the theme of waste management is that one of the hotels included in the study pays attention to using glass bottles instead of plastic bottles in the establishment. In addition, it is seen that hotels support recycling practices. Most of the hotels included in the study use wastewater to irrigate the gardens. In the same way, oils used in all hotels are accumulated for recycling. Hotels manage the process more professionally by cooperating with different companies and environmental consultants for recycling practices.

Hotel managers who participated in the study believe that the sustainability movement can achieve more success with cooperation. For this reason, it is emphasized that external (local government) support is necessary, especially in the collection and logistics of decomposed waste and ready for recycling. But when the answers are analyzed, it is seen that this support is insufficient. While we get the result that provided support is limited, the response of one participant supports our result. A participant with code O_4 stated that the municipality carried the items decomposed at the hotel in the exact vehicle and combined them in a single point. This move is a negative situation in terms of waste management. If the decomposed products' transport and storage processes are separated, it will be suitable for the purpose. Based on this result, it is recommended to organize informative meetings on sustainable understanding and cooperation for local administrations, institutions, organizations, NGOs, and chambers providing service in the region.

The biggest problem that Turkish tourism has experienced in recent years is that the tourists' per capita expenditure is not at the expected level. Based on the philosophy that qualified tourists are provided with qualified personnel, it is supported by the studies that hotels need and will need educated personnel who will adopt the understanding of sustainable tourism. One of the participants (OY_2) emphasizes that the young generation does not prefer the tourism sector. Still, it is required to educate employees who will adopt the sustainable tourism understanding. This can only be achieved by encouraging the profession and supporting institutions that provide tourism education. In the light of this result of the study, it is recommended to include a course that can convey the philosophy of sustainability to young generations besides the sustainable tourism course in the curriculum of institutions that provide tourism education at the high school and university levels. It is also believed that giving an elective sustainable tourism course as compulsory in many universities will be beneficial for students to raise awareness at an early age.

As stated in previous sections, supporting this study has some limitations and boundaries, with comparative analyses carried out in hotels that provide service in other coastal areas and city centers, and carrying out investigations in which quantitative and qualitative methods are used together will help to yield different results. Also, this study is conducted from the perspectives of the hotel managers. Therefore, studies to be carried out for the lower- and middle-level staff working at the hotel and the guests visiting the hotel will reveal different findings and results.

REFERENCES

Bekar, Aydan, and Songül K. Şahin. 2018. "Küresel Bir Sorun 'Gıda Atıkları': Otel İşletmelerindeki Boyutları (A Global Problem 'Food Waste': Food Waste Generators in Hotel Industry)." *Journal of Tourism and Gastronomy Studies* 6 (4): 1039–1061. doi:10.21325/jotags.2018.347.

Bogdan, Robert, and K. Biklen Sari. 2006. *Qualitative Research for Education: An Introduction to Theories and Methods*. 5th ed. London: Pearson.

Brach, Laurent, Patrick Deixonne, Marie-France Bernard, Edmée Durand, Marie-Christine Desjean, Emile Perez, Erik van Sebille, and Alexandra ter Halle. 2018. "Anticyclonic Eddies Increase Accumulation of Microplastic in the North Atlantic Subtropical Gyre." *Marine Pollution Bulletin* 126 (2018): 191–196. doi: 10.1016/j.marpolbul.2017.10.077.

Creswell, John W. 2013. *Qualitative Inquiry & Research Design Choosing Among Five Approaches*. 3rd ed. California: Sage Publications.

Crutzen, Paul J. 2002. "Geology of Mankind." *Nature* 415: 23.

Crutzen, Paul J., and Eugene, Filmor, and Stoermer. 2000. "The Anthropocene." *Global Change Newsletter* 41 (17). www.igbp.net/download/18.316f18321323470177580001401/1376383088452/NL41.pdf.

Dogru, Tarik, Elizabeth A. Marchio, Umit Bulut, and Courtney Suess. 2019. "Climate Change: Vulnerability and Resilience of Tourism and the Entire Economy." *Tourism Management* 72 (June). Pergamon: 292–305. doi: 10.1016/J.TOURMAN.2018.12.010.

Duffy, Rosaleen. 2015. "Nature-Based Tourism and Neoliberalism: Concealing Contradictions." Tourism Geographies 17 (4): 529–543. doi:10.1080/14616688.2015.1053972.

Ellen McArthur Foundation. 2017. "Circular Economy Overview." *Ellen McArthur Foundation*. www.ellenmacarthurfoundation.org/circular-economy.

Eriksen, Marcus, Laurent C. M. Lebreton, Henry S. Carson, Martin Thiel, Charles J. Moore, Jose C. Borerro, Francois Galgani, Peter G. Ryan, and Julia Reisser. 2014. "Plastic Pollution in the World's Oceans: More than 5 Trillion Plastic Pieces Weighing over 250,000 Tons Afloat at Sea." *PLoS One* 9 (12): 1–15. doi: 10.1371/journal.pone.0111913.

European Commission. n.d. "Environment." *European Commission*. https://ec.europa.eu/environment/ecolabel/.

Greenview. 2020. "Hotel Footprinting Tool." www.hotelfootprints.org/footprinting.

Gren, Martin, and Edward H. Huijbens. 2014. "Tourism and the Anthropocene." *Scandinavian Journal of Hospitality and Tourism* 14 (1): 6–22. doi:10.1080/15022250.2014.886100.

Gündüz, Fuat. 2004. "Çevre ve Turizmin Sürdürülebilirliği." *Planlama Dergisi*, no. 1: 58–67. www.spo.org.tr/resimler/ekler/3c04118df112c13_ek.pdf.

International Organization for Standardization (ISO). n.d. "ISO 14000 Family Environmental Management." *International Organization for Standardization* (ISO). www.iso.org/iso-14001-environmental-management.html.

International Tourism Partnership. 2014. "Envıronmental Management For Hotels, The Industry Guıde To Sustaınable Operatıon 2 Energy ." *International Tourism Partnership*. www.Environmental-Management-for-Hotels-2-Energy%20(1).pdf.

International Tourism Partnership. 2014a. "Envıronmental Management For Hotels, The Industry Guıde To Sustaınable Operatıon 4 Waste." *International Tourism Partnership*. www.Environmental-Management-for-Hotels-4-Waste%20(1).pdf.

İstanbul Kültür Sanat Vakfi (İKSV). 2019. "Yedinci Kıta." *16. İstanbul Bienali*. March. https://bienal.iksv.org/tr/16-istanbul-bienali/yedinci-kita.

Kahraman, Nusret, and Oğuz Türkay. 2006. *Turizm ve Çevre*. Ankara: Detay Yayıncılık.

Kültür ve Turizm Bakanlığı, T.C. 2021. "Çevreye Duyarlılık Kampanyası (Yeşil Yıldız)." T.C. Kültür ve Turizm Bakanlığı. https://yigm.ktb.gov.tr/TR-11596/cevreye-duyarlilik-kampanyasi-yesil-yildiz.html.

Manniche, Jesper, Karin Topsoe Larsen, and Rikke Brandt Broegaard. 2021. "The Circular Economy in Tourism: Transition Perspectives for Business and Research." *Scandinavian Journal of Hospitality and Tourism* 21 (3): 247–264. doi:10.1080/15022250.2021.1921020.

Moore, Amelia. 2015. "Islands of Difference: Design, Urbanism, and Sustainable Tourism in the Anthropocene Caribbean." *The Journal of Latin American and Caribbean Anthropology* 20 (3). doi: 10.1111/jlca.12170.

Mostafanezhad, Mary, and Roger Norum. 2019. "The Anthropocenic Imaginary: Political Ecologies of Tourism in a Geological Epoch." *Journal of Sustainable Tourism* 27 (4): 421–435. doi:10.1080/09669582.2018.1544252.

O'Callaghan-Gordo, Cristina, and Josep M. Antó. 2020. "COVID-19: The Disease of the Anthropocene." *Environmental Research* 187. doi: 10.1016/j.envres.2020.109683.

Patton, Michael Q. 2001. *Qualitative Research 6 Evaluation Methods*. 3rd Ed. California: Sage Publication.

Pirani, Sanaa I., and Hassan A. Arafat. 2014. "Solid Waste Management in the Hospitality Industry: A Review." *Journal of Environmental Management* 146 (December). Academic Press: 320–336. doi: 10.1016/J.JENVMAN.2014.07.038.

Rodríguez, Carlos, Carmen Florido, and Marta Jacob. 2020. "Circular Economy Contributions to the Tourism Sector: A Critical Literature Review." *Sustainability* 12 (11): 4338. doi: 10.3390/su12114338.

Sharpley, Richard. 2000. "Tourism and Sustainable Development: Exploring the Theoretical Divide." *Journal of Sustainable Tourism* 8 (1). doi: 10.1080/09669580008667346.

Shoshitaishvili, Boris. 2021. "From Anthropocene to Noosphere: The Great Acceleration." *Earth's Future* 9 (2): 1–11. doi: 10.1029/2020EF001917.

Singh, Nripendra, David Cranage, and Seoki Lee. 2014. "Green Strategies for Hotels: Estimation of Recycling Benefits." *International Journal of Hospitality Management* 43 (October): 13–22. doi: 10.1016/j.ijhm.2014.07.006.

Smith, Wayne, Marie, S. Hammer, and M. T. Jo. 1993. *Eco Purchasing Guide for Hotels and Motels*. University of Florida. www.greenbiz.com/sites/default/files/document/O16F6372.pdf.

Sorin, Fabrice, and Uthayasankar Sivarajah. 2021. "Exploring Circular Economy in the Hospitality Industry: Empirical Evidence from Scandinavian Hotel Operators." *Scandinavian Journal of Hospitality and Tourism* 21 (3): 265–285. doi: 10.1080/15022250.2021.1921021.

Steffen, Will, Jacques Grinevald, Paul Crutzen, and John McNeill. 2011. "The Anthropocene: Conceptual and Historical Perspectives." *Philosophical Transactions of the Royal Society A: Mathematical, Physical and Engineering Sciences* 369 (1938). doi: 10.1098/rsta.2010.0327.

Türkiye Çevre Eğitim Vakfi (TÜRÇEV). 2021. "Yeşil Anahtar Genel Bilgiler." *Türkiye Çevre Eğitim Vakfi (TÜRÇEV)*. www.turcev.org.tr/v2/icerikDetay.aspx?icerik_id=124.

Türkiye Çevre Eğitim Vakfı (TÜRÇEV). n.d. "Mavi Bayrak Türkiye." *Türkiye Çevre Eğitim Vakfı (TÜRÇEV)*. www.mavibayrak.org.tr/tr/Default.aspx.

United Nations Environment Programme (UNEP), and World Tourism Organization (WTO). 2005. *Making Tourism More Sustainable A Guide for Policy*. https://wedocs.unep.org/bitstream/handle/20.500.11822/8741/-Making%20Tourism%20More%20Sustainable_%20A%20Guide%20for%20Policy%20Makers-2005445.pdf?sequence=3&isAllowed=y.

UNWTO World Tourism Organization. 2021. "COVID-19 and Tourism 2020: A Year in Review." January. www.unwto.org/covid-19-and-tourism-2020.

World Commission on Environment and Development. 1987. "Our Common Future, From One Earth to One World." In *Report of the World Commission on Environment and Development: Our Common Future*, 10–27. New York, NY: Oxford University Press. https://sustainabledevelopment.un.org/content/documents/5987our-common-future.pdf.

World Tourism Organization. 2021. *International Tourism Highlights, 2020 Edition*. Madrid: World Tourism Organization (UNWTO). doi: 10.18111/9789284422456.

World Tourism Organization (UNWTO). n.d. "Hotel Energy Solutions (HES)." *World Tourism Organization (UNWTO)*. www.unwto.org/hotel-energy-solution.

Worldwide Fund for Nature (WWF). 2018. "Akdeniz Plastik Raporu'nu Yayımladı: Akdeniz'e En Çok Plastik Türkiye'den." June 7. www.wwf.org.tr/?7800/wwf-akdeniz-plastik-raporunu-yayimladi-akdenize-en-cok-plastik-turkiyeden.

Yıldırım, Ali. 1999. "Nitel Araştırma Yöntemlerinin Temel Özellikleri ve Eğitim Araştırmalarındaki Yeri ve Önemi." *Eğitim ve Bilim* 23 (112): 7–17.

Yücel, Mustafa, and Serkan E. Ümit. 2008. "Çevre Dostu Ürün Kavramına Bütünsel Yaklaşım; Temiz Üretim Sistemi, Eko-Etiket, Yeşil Pazarlama." *Electronic Journal of Social Sciences* 7 (26): 320–333.

Zalasiewicz, Jan, Mark Williams, Alan Haywood, and Michael Ellis. 2011. "The Anthropocene: A New Epoch of Geological Time?" *Philosophical Transactions of the Royal Society A* 369: 835–841. doi: http://doi.org/10.1098/rsta.2010.0339.

Zalasiewicz, Jan, Mark Williams, Will Steffen, and Paul Crutzen. 2010. "The New World of the Anthropocene." *Environmental Science & Technology* 44 (7): 2228–2231. doi:10.1021/es903118j.

Part IV

Case Studies

13 The Tourism-Led Growth Hypothesis Test Using Granger's Causality

A Case Study of Algeria

Abderrahmane Nadja Afifi, Sihem Touati, Ouahiba Chehat, Mohammed El Amine Abdelli, and Nadia Mansour

CONTENTS

13.1 INTRODUCTION

The economies of developing countries, tourism has become an indispensable source of wealth and growth, mainly because tourism is a leading sector that promotes economic growth, social welfare (Mohammed El Amine and Aied 2020), sustainable evolution, and penury reduction. However, the link between tourism, exchange rate, and economic development is not an automatic mechanism because growth is necessary but not sufficient to boost economic development. Tourism growth can even have perverse effects and ultimately turn out to be impoverishing growth if it does not lead to inclusive and sustainable development. In other words, this relationship can only exist if tourism creates new jobs, builds links with other economic sectors,

DOI: 10.1201/9781003138051-17

and stimulates the growth of basic infrastructure through construction, particularly of roads and port facilities and the airport. In addition, it contributes significantly to improving the global balance of payments deficit and successfully leads to foreign economic ties (Bouadam 2011).

Therefore, this link is only relevant if tourism generates growth and developing a training and effect contagion' to other economic sectors. Dritsakis (2004) announced that the 'development of tourism is a broad reference to the progressive evolution of the tourism sector, which became an essential determinant in the diversification of the economy. According to the annual report of UNWTO TOURISM (2017), the tourism industry became important internally and externally in the world's economic sectors, despite many challenges. This is because tourism accounts for 10% of the global GDP, 7% of international trade, and one in ten employments. For the next ten years, the International Tourism worldwide has increased by over 4% per year, up to 1.2 billion in 2016, a continuing growth rate that has not been seen since the 1960s. In Africa, Asia, and the Pacific, growth was most vital. As a result, tourism is one of the world's leading sectors.

The aim of this chapter is to analyze the relation between the real gross domestic product (RGDP), which represents dependent variable economic growth, the real international tourism earning (RITE), and the real exchange rate (RER) as independent variables to check for Engle and Engle and Granger (1987) causality analysis the validity of the tourism-led growth hypotheses (TLGH). Many experiments were carried out in the various economies of the world to test this hypothesis. Researchers in both studies have a large consensus on the effect of tourism on economic growth, concentrating on a single case country or those focused on several countries. To mention some studies that analyzed this topic, we note the Spanish economy studied by Balaguer and Cantavella-Jordá (2002), Dritsakis (2004); the Turkish case by Gunduz and Hatemi-J (2005), Katircioğlu (2010); for Cyprus Oh (2005); for Taiwan's economy was studied whether by Kim et al. (2006), Lee and Chang (2008); and Adnan Hye and Ali Khan (2013) for Pakistan. Thus, some of the literature was reviewed by Cohen et al. (2014), Brida et al. (2016), checking the hypothesis of tourism-led development (TLGH) on consumer actions in tourism. The results show that the economy is mainly driven by foreign tourism, where several studies using a dynamic panel data approach (Seghir et al. 2015) have found a positive relation that cointegrates the GDP with tourism spending. While several other studies show a clear relationship between these variables, the causality and conditionality of this interaction are different (Engle and Granger 1987). Also, Chulaphan and Barahona (2018) assessed that the evolution of international tourism played an important role in Thailand's economic growth and vice versa. Shahzad et al. (2017) used the quantile-on-quantile (QQ) approach and the recent tourist activity index incorporate the most used tourism variables. This strategy, recently added by Sim and Zhou (2015), provides a significant explanation for the relation between the growth of tourism and the economic development of a global dependence structure. Finally, Li et al. (2018) studied why the tourism sector is a critical factor in economic growth based on expectations of its economic impact capacities.

13.2 LITERATURE REVIEW

In the last few years, there has been a persistent failure in tourist literature to convey the sustainable growth to the theory of its maternal model, despite a significant consideration given to this idea by tourism academics and practitioners. Sustainable development is thus rarely discussed with tourism (Sharpley 2000).

A prominent feature of tourism is its power to build solid and various relationships. In fact, according to Grosso et al. (2007), on tourism in India, Brazil, and Indonesia, the tourism sector maintains much closer ties with other industries than most other sectors, confirming the stimulating effect tourism can have on the economy. Indeed, close intersectoral relations have a multiplier effect that generates many economic benefits for the country, produces jobs, and reduces poverty at the local level.

The TLGH in the first chapter has been published for over 16 years. According to Brida et al. (2016), many studies have been posted to study the temporal relationship between international tourism and economic evolution. Sometimes, the results in the same economy were conflicting. The various methods used to interpret these findings are essential explanations for the numerous analytical results achieved (Belloumi 2010).

Katircioğlu (2010) confirmed that tourism has proved its lack of new developments in research methods in econometrics such as cointegration and (Engle & Granger 1987) concept of causality. However, Engle and Granger (1987) showed that most economical time series are nonstationary. Therefore, failing to estimate such characteristics may cause misleading relations between the studied variables. In the 1990s, the extras of advances in time series analyses culminated in new approaches to assessing modeling and relationship between tourism and economic evolution through dual causality procedures based on both studies (Granger 1969, Sims 1972). However, these tests do not identify additional causal channels and may yield contradictory results (Belloumi 2010).

At the start of 2000, several empirical studies were carried out to examine the role of tourism revenues in economic growth using time series techniques. In line with the TLGH, Al-mulali et al. (2014), Balaguer and Cantavella-Jordá (2002) carried out the results for Granger's causality test in Spain (2005), showing that tourism unilaterally affects Spain's growth, confirming the results for the Turkish by Gunduz and Hatemi-J (2005), where studies have indicated bidirectional causality between tourism and economic growth in the foreign world. On the other hand, Dritsakis (2004) studied during the period 1960–2000 a strong link between tourism, RERs, and Greece's economic growth. At the same time, Oh (2005) found an utter difference by indicating a unidirectional Granger causality correlation in economic-driven tourism growth. In this case, the TLGH assumption was not achieved for the Korean economy. In proving the null hypothesis (Katircioğlu 2010), the results applied to the Turkish economy have supported those reached by Oh (2005), which confirms the opposite direction of the theory of economic-driven tourism development.

Lee and Chang (2008) have used a heterogenous panel method for cointegration because both OECD and non-OECD countries are related to international tourism and growth causal. The results show a higher effect on the economic growth of tourism development in non-OECD economies with a bidirectional relationship between variables, eventually. In contrast, the existence of a one-way causal relationship is confirmed by the increase in tourism to economic development in OECD countries (Engle and Granger 1987). In the same way, Mello-Sampayo and Sousa-Vale (2012) examined the more crucial economic growth effect of international tourism in southern and northern European economies by showing solid ties. Adnan Hye and Ali Khan (2013) reported that the relationship between tourism income and economic growth has led to economic development in Pakistan. Some of the literature has been reviewed by Cohen et al. (2014) about consumer behavior in tourism and the test of the theoretical economic background behind the hypothesis of TLGH (Brida et al. 2016). The empirical conclusion suggests that international tourism drives economic development. Some studies with a dynamic panel data approach found an essential way of integrating the relationship between economic growth and the cost of tourism (Seghir et al. 2015).

In contrast, some other studies using panel data announce the relationship between tourism and economic development (Engle and Granger 1987). Chulaphan and Barahona (2018) evaluated the weather development of international tourism has contributed to Thailand's economic growth and vice versa. Shahzad et al. (2017) used the QQ and a new composite tourism index, which contains the most widely used measures of visitors. Sim and Zhou (2015) provided the ideal context for capturing the general dependency structure between tourism and economic growth.

The application of the cointegration test was developed in the Bayer model (Bayer and Hanck 2013). Ohlan (2017) investigated the connections between tourism and economic growth in India. The findings of this study indicated a combination of tourism, industrial development, and financial gain. Finally, Li et al. (2018) review why the tourism industry is a crucial determinant of economic growth founded on perceptions of measuring its economic impact.

In the case of Algeria's economy, the empirical studies on the confirmation of the TLGH are less stringent, requiring precise empirical estimation of the direct impact of the RITE and the RER as independent variables, on the RGDP, which expresses economic growth as a dependent variable, using causality analysis to check the validity of this hypothesis (TLGH) in Algeria (Engle and Granger 1987).

13.3 METHODOLOGY

13.3.1 Data Description

This chapter focuses on exploring the complex relationship between the RER, international tourism earning, and economic growth in Algeria with the following variables:

LRGDP: 'Logarithm of Real Gross Domestic Product.'
LRITR: 'Logarithm of Real International Tourism Earning.'
LREXR: 'Logarithm of Real Exchange Rate.'

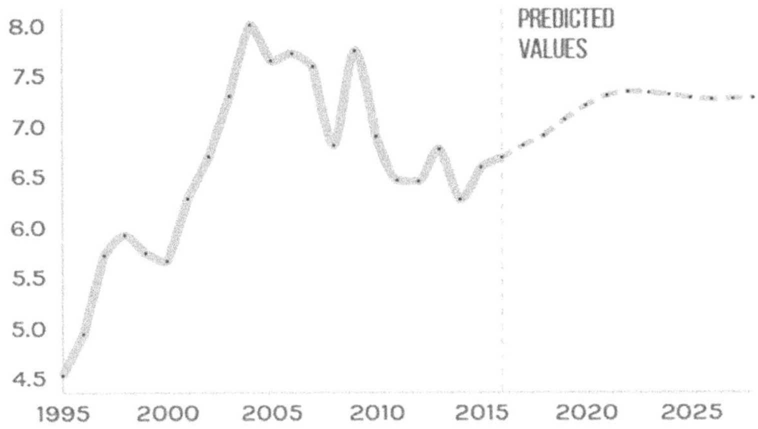

FIGURE 13.1 Total contribution the tourism to GDP in Algeria during the period 1995–2025.

The source for our study is from the World Bank, and we use some econometrics methods such as cointegration, error correction techniques, and causality test. The complete calculation consists of the following steps: first, the stationary monitoring of the unit root recognizable variables; this can be accomplished with the Augmented Dickey-Fuller (F-ADF) checking. The next step is testing whether a long-run combination of variables occurs (Johansen's 1988). Moreover, We use the vector error correction model (VECM) of Granger's if all the variables are combined with the order one (I (1)), but if there is no result, we must use the VAR form (Engle and Granger 1987).

13.3.2 Stationary: Graph, ACF Function, and Unit Root Test

13.3.2.1 Graph

A crucial first step in any econometric analysis is to examine the data visually; means, variance, and covariance of the process are constant over time. In addition, a stochastic process is said to be stationary covariance.

13.3.2.2 ACF Function

Another way to make the same point is to note that the series shown in Table 13.1 has a clear trend. However, the tight fit of the estimated model might fool a researcher into thinking the series is stationary around the cubic trend line shown in Table 13.1 because such trend lines are fit to make the observed residuals as small as possible.

Table 13.1 shows the ACF of the logarithmic of RGDP, natural logarithmic of REXR, and natural logarithmic of RITR. We can see that the ACF decays slowly. Thus, detrending the data does not seem to result in a stationary series. Nelson and Plosser (1982) could not refuse the null hypothesis of the unit root when they applied the Q test to the popular macroeconomic data (Schotman and Van Dijk 1991). However, to ensure a series is stationary, we use statistical tests such as the 'ADF test.'

TABLE 13.1
ACF Function

AC \ Variable	LRGDP	LRITR	LEXR
1	0.863	0.913	0.709
2	0.728	0.792	0.536
3	0.587	0.659	0.392
4	0.451	0.481	0.204

13.3.2.3 Unit Root Test

There are several statistical and economic reasons for inspecting whether a time series includes a unit root. Traditional methods of processing times series have proved insufficient to predict economic phenomena. They have grown significantly (Box et al. 2015) and the use of random processes of the ARIMA class (Slim 2017).

To test the presence of unit roots to prove the variables, we used the ADF test, depending on research (Dickey and Fuller 1979). The test is founded on the estimate of the regression follows, which contains a constant term and a trend:

$$\Delta y_t = a_0 + \gamma y_{t-1} + a_2 t + \sum_{i=2}^{p} \beta_i \Delta y_{t-i+1} + \varepsilon_t \tag{13.1}$$

The hypothesis is as follows:

$$\begin{cases} \gamma = 0; \text{ the series has a unit root and is not stationary.} \\ \gamma \neq 0; \text{ the series does not have a unit root and is stationary.} \end{cases}$$

Table 13.2 shows the results of the unit root test, the estimated values of γ for natural logarithmic of RGDP, natural logarithmic of RITR, and natural logarithmic of REXR statistically, they are not different from zero at all levels (0.01, 0.05, and 0.1).

Figure 13.2 shows that the three-time series (LRGDP, LREXR, and LRITR) during the study period 1995–2015 are originally nonstationary and increased.

When we take the first difference of all variables, we conclude that ADF statistic is more than critical values at these levels of significance to refuse the null hypothesis of the first-differenced variables. Therefore, the variables (LRGDP, LRITR, and LREXR) under consideration are I(1).

13.3.3 Lag Length Test

To assure consistency of the research findings with real economic situations and economic theories, appropriate lag length has been selected using the VAR framework

TABLE 13.2
Unit Root Test

Unit Root Test

Variables	LRGDP	LRITR	LEXR
Levels	11.005	0.764	–2.512
	P=(1.0000)	*P*=(0.8710)	*P*=(0.0149)
First difference	–3.848	–3.224	–2.933
	P=(0.0096)	*P*=(0.0028)	*P*=(0.0057)

for the cointegration test, VECM, and causality test. Table 13.3 shows the result of the lag length selection criterion, where we see that LR, FPE, AIC, SC, and HQ criterion suggested lag length 1.

13.3.4 Test of Cointegration

After confirming that all series are stationary and incorporated of the same order one I(1), the next step is to examine any long-run relationship between them. To do this, we apply Johansen's approach to test the presence of multiple cointegration relationships (***r***) (Johansen 1988).

The hypothesis is:

$$\begin{cases} H_0 : r \leq q \\ H_1 : q = r \end{cases}$$

Based on the trace statistics, λ trace is calculated thus:

$\boldsymbol{\lambda_{trace}(r) = -T\sum_{i+1}^{p} ln(1-\widehat{\lambda i})}$ $,/\lambda_{r+i}\ldots\lambda_n$ are the last values of eigenvectors (p–r).

Another test is the maximal eigenvalue test ($\lambda_{\max}$) which testes the following hypothesis:

$\begin{cases} H_0 : there\ are\ r\ cointegrating\ vectors \\ H_1 : there\ are\ (r+1)\ cointegrating\ vectors \end{cases}$; is calculated as follows:

$$\boldsymbol{\lambda_{max}(r, r+1) = -Tln\left(1-\hat{\lambda} r+1\right)}$$

Here we want to decide whether RGDP logarithm, real tourism earning logarithm, and RER logarithm are cointegrated. Cointegration shows how long-run equilibrium

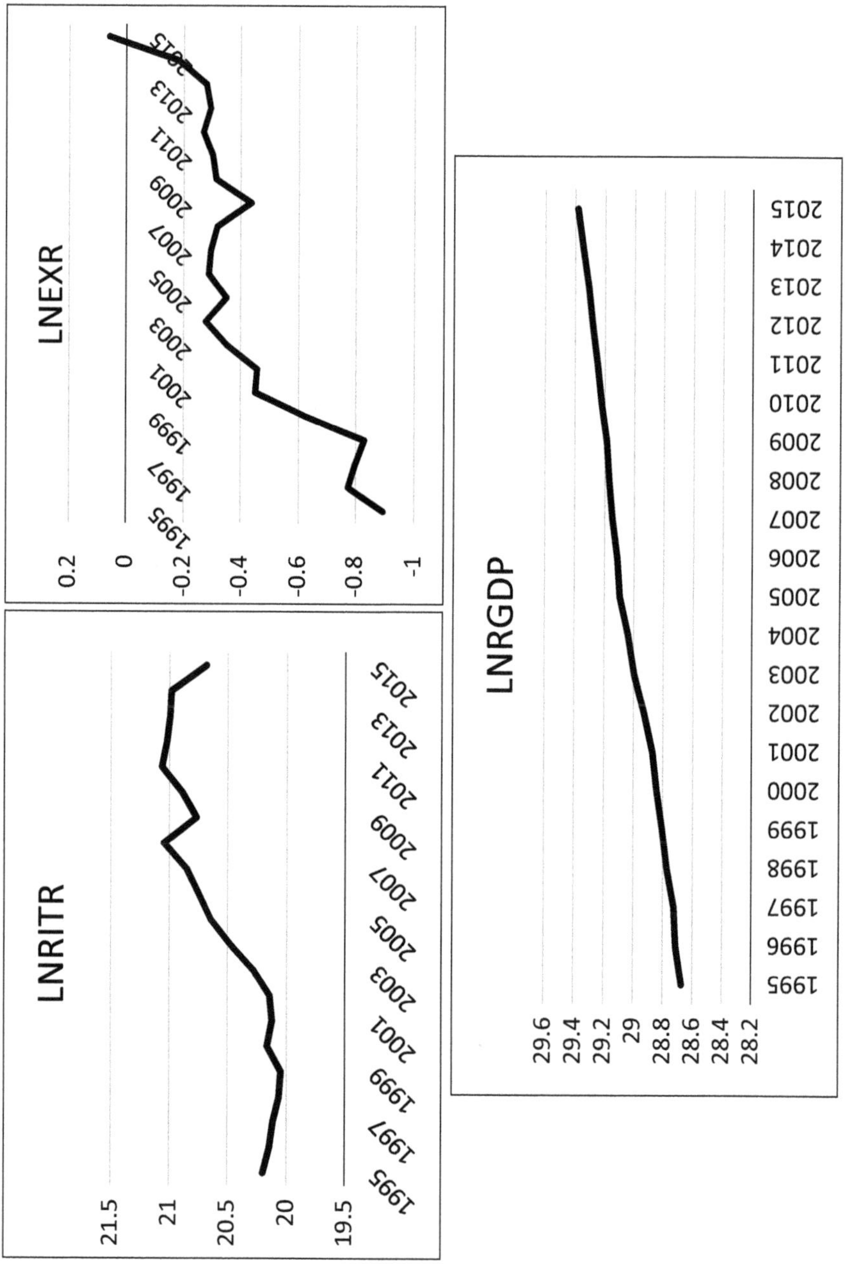

FIGURE 13.2 Graph of stationary.

TABLE 13.3
Lag Selection Based on VAR Lag Length Criterion

Lag	LogL	LR	FPE	AIC	SC	HQ
0	34.82192	NA	8.33e–06	–3.182192	–3.032832	–3.153035
1	106.7131	115.0259*	1.57e–08*	–9.471313*	–8.873874*	–9.354687*

TABLE 13.4
Test of Cointegration

Hypothesized No. of CE(s)	Trace Statistic	Max-Eigen Statistic
None*	47.939	33.896
At most 1	14.043	14.043

For the Trace test and Max-Eigen statistics, 1 cointegration equation(s) at 0.05 should be indicated.
*Statistical analysis with a Denotes hypothesis dismissal at 0.05 was conducted.

TABLE 13.5
Long-Run Equilibrium Relationship

Variable	Coefficient	Std. Error	*t*-Statistic	Prob.
C	22.46060	0.699236	32.12163	0.0000
LNRITR	0.330212	0.033302	9.915664	0.0000
LNREXR	0.487236	0.053775	9.060713	0.0000

performs a mix of economic variables. Some variables will be removed apart in the short run if they are combined. But in the long run, using economic forces, they can come closer to their equilibrium.

The results of the cointegration test are shown in Table 13.4. Trace test and Max-Eigen statistics indicate one (1) long-period equilibrium relationship between the variables. Therefore, the equation of the long-run relationships among the variables with the logarithm of RGDP as the dependent variable is as follows:

$$\boldsymbol{LNRGDP} = 22.460 + 0.3302\boldsymbol{INRITR} + 0.48\boldsymbol{LNEXR}$$

- Dependent variable: LRGDP

The result in Table 13.5 showed:

- The increase perpetual of 1% in real tourism earning will cause the RGDP to increase by 33.02%.
- A 1% rise in the RER will increase RGDP by 48.7%.

13.3.5 Vector Autoregressive Model with an Error Correction Mechanism (VECM)

After confirming the cointegration test between variables, this step develops models that embody the ECM concept. This term is used to perform the short-run adjustment dynamics of variables by indicating its speed in long-term equilibrium. For example, we can express the ECM derived from Johansen's (1988) test as follows:

$$\Delta x_t = \mu_x + \alpha_x ECT_{t=1} + \sum_{k=1}^{p} \beta_{xx,k} \Delta x_{t-k} + \sum_{k=1}^{p} \beta_{xy,k} \Delta y_{t-k} + \sum_{k=1}^{p} \beta_{xz,k} \Delta z_{t-k} + \varepsilon_{xt}$$

$$\Delta z_t = \mu_z + \alpha_z ECT_{t=1} + \sum_{k=1}^{p} \beta_{zx,k} \Delta x_{t-k} + \sum_{k=1}^{p} \beta_{zy,k} \Delta y_{t-k} + \sum_{k=1}^{p} \beta_{zz,k} \Delta z_{t-k} + \varepsilon_{zt}$$

$$\Delta y_t = \mu_y + \alpha_y ECT_{t=1} + \sum_{k=1}^{p} \beta_{yx,k} \Delta x_{t-k} + \sum_{k=1}^{p} \beta_{yy,k} \Delta y_{t-k} + \sum_{k=1}^{p} \beta_{yz,k} \Delta z_{t-k} + \varepsilon_{yt}$$

where *ECT* is the error correction term lagged one period, α is the short-run coefficient of the *ECT* in which ($-1<\alpha<0$), (*X*), (*Z*) and (*Y*) are the three endogenous variables in the model, and $\beta_{ij,k}$ reflect the impact of the (*k*) lagged value of the (*j*) on the current value of variable $i,j = x,y,z$. The ε_{it} are mutually uncorrelated white noise residuals.

This chapter analyzes the complex relationship between foreign tourist income, RER, and economic growth (DLRGDP) as the dependent variable. Table 13.6 shows the short-term effect. As the optimum lag duration was one, the results for one lag per variable are also provided.

The *ECT* coefficient of the RITR variable is not significant and negative (theoretically, it is expected to be between –1 and 0). Its significance indicates that any short-run shock diffused through the channel of GDP significantly touches the cointegrating relationship between GDP, tourism earning, and exchange rate. The results expose that tourist earning responds positively to GDP nonconsiderably. The RER responds positively and none significantly to GDP. This is for equation three below*. However, for equation 4**, the result is:

TABLE 13.6
The ECM Results

Dependent Variable D (LRITR)

Regressors	Coefficients	*t*-Value
D(LRGDP(–1))	–0.155	–5.581
D(LEXR(–1))	–0.512	–1.796
ECM	–0.356	–0.781

$$* D(LNRGDP_t) = a_1 D(LNRGDP_{t-1}) + a_2 D(LNRITR_{t-1}) + a_3 D(LNEXR_{t-1}) \quad (13.2)$$

$$** D(LNRITR_t) = b_1 D(LNRGDP_{t-1}) + b_2 D(LNRITR_{t-1}) + b_3 D(LNEXR_{t-1}) \quad (13.3)$$

The coefficient of the RITR variable error correction term is not relevant and harmful. The results show that GDP reacts negatively to tourist earnings and that the actual currency reacts negatively and not significantly to RITR.

13.3.6 Causality Test

The findings of the Causality Test are seen and analyzed in Table 13.7 using the vector error correcting model (Engle and Granger 1987). The analysis findings lead us to eliminate the null hypothesis since the RITE does not allow Granger to generate the RGDP as a dependent variable. On the other hand, Granger's causality is accepted as an alternative hypothesis from the RER toward RGDP. The combined impacts of both the RITE and the RER show that there is a significant effect on the RGDP as the null hypothesis is rejected. Nevertheless, the null hypothesis of RGDP does not cause an exchange rate, same as we cannot reject the null hypothesis of real tourism earning, which does not cause the RER.

TABLE 13.7
Causality Test Result

Dependent Variable: D (LNRITR)

Excluded	Chi-sq	df	Prob.
D (LNRGDP)	0.087986	1	0.7668
D (LNREXR)	0.020657	1	0.8857
All	0.128046	2	0.9380

Dependent Variable: D (LNRGDP)

Excluded	Chi-sq	df	Prob.
D (LNRITR)	3.533386	1	0.0601
D (LNREXR)	2.205312	1	0.1375
All	7.900979	2	0.0192

Dependent Variable: D (LNREXR)

Excluded	Chi-sq	df	Prob.
D (LNRITR)	0.002571	1	0.9596
D (LNRGDP)	0.525221	1	0.4686
All	0.923097	2	0.6303

13.4 CONCLUSION AND DISCUSSION

This research aimed to highlight and evaluate the short term. The long-term relationship between the RGDP, which reflected economic growth as a predictor, the RITE, and the RER as independent variables tests the validity of the tourism-led growth hippopotamus. This chapter used econometric approaches using the technique, stationary experiments, and the VAR model with the error correction function (VECM) (Johansen 1988). The Granger causality test was also used to determine the dynamic effect of tourism on the economic growth of Algeria.

The results showed that the RGDP, the RITE, and the RER are long-run linkages. We find that international tourism revenues positively impact Algeria's long-term economic growth, whereby an average 1% rise in global tourism earnings increases GDP by 33.02%. The same 1% increase in the RER increases RGDP by 48.7%. These findings show that Algerian GDP is growing more by channeling fiscal policy.

This confirms the findings for Greece (Dritsakis 2004), Turkey, and Tunisia (Belloumi 2010). Furthermore, for Pakistan (Adnan Hye and Ali Khan 2013), the TLGH was empirically improved, and Seghir et al. (2015) identified a significant way of cointegrating economic development and tourism expenditure from (49) economies. Moreover, Chulaphan and Barahona (2018) evaluated the contribution of expansion in the tourism sector in Thailand's economic development and vice versa (2017), examining ties between tourism development in India. Lastly, our findings are consistent with the results of Li et al. (2018), and tourism is a big impetus for economic development. In summary, these empirical findings further support the broad application of the TLGH.

The previous studies have had specific effects on the formulation of policies. First, the results refer to a single cause from foreign tourism earning to long-term economic growth. Therefore, governance needs to reestablish tourist installation and revenue allocation. Second, after it has been answered on the guess mentioned above in this study, we inferred that the positive gist in the long run of tourism on the Algerian economic emergence justifies the inevitability of government intervention to promote and increase tourism need, and, from another point of view, providing and fostering the maturation of tourism supply (Mohammed El Amine et al. 2020). However, the link between the RITE and the RER and the real economic growth (REG) is not an automatic mechanism because growth is necessary but not sufficient to boost economic development. Tourism growth can even have perverse effects and ultimately turns out to be impoverishing growth if it does not lead to inclusive and sustainable development. In other words, this relationship can only exist if tourism creates new jobs, builds links with other economic sectors, and stimulates the growth of basic infrastructure through construction, particularly of roads and port facilities, and airports, various equipment, etc. Therefore, this link is only relevant if tourism generates growth and develops a training and effect 'contagion' to other sectors.

REFERENCES

Al-mulali, Usama, Hassan Gholipour Fereidouni, Janice Y. M. Lee, and Abdul Hakim Mohammed. 2014. "Estimating the tourism-led growth hypothesis: A case study of the Middle East countries." *Anatolia* 25 (2):290–298. doi: 10.1080/13032917.2013.843467.

Balaguer, Jacint, and Manuel Cantavella-Jordá. 2002. "Tourism as a long-run economic growth factor: The Spanish case." *Applied Economics* 34 (7):877–884. doi: 10.1080/00036840110058923.

Bayer, Christian, and Christoph Hanck. 2013. "Combining non-cointegration tests." *Journal of Time Series Analysis* 34 (1):83–95. doi: https://doi.org/10.1111/j.1467-9892.2012.00814.x.

Belloumi, Mounir. 2010. "The relationship between tourism receipts, real effective exchange rate and economic growth in Tunisia." *International Journal of Tourism Research* 12 (5):550–560. doi: https://doi.org/10.1002/jtr.774.

Bouadam, Kamel. 2011. "The national strategy of tourism development in Algeria: issues, opportunities, and limitations." *Review of Applied Socio-Economic Research* 2: 23–37

Box, George E. P., Gwilym M. Jenkins, Gregory C. Reinsel, and Greta M. Ljung. 2015. *Time Series Analysis: Forecasting and Control*: John Wiley & Sons, USA.

Brida, Juan G., Cortes-Jimenez Isabel, and Manuela Pulina. 2016. "Has the tourism-led growth hypothesis been validated? A literature review." *Current Issues in Tourism* 19 (5):394–430. doi: 10.1080/13683500.2013.868414.

Chulaphan, Wanvilai, and Jorge F. Barahona. 2018. "Contribution of disaggregated tourism on Thailand's economic growth." *Kasetsart Journal of Social Sciences* 39 (3):401–406. doi: https://doi.org/10.1016/j.kjss.2017.07.012.

Cohen, Scott A., Girish Prayag, and Miguel Moital. 2014. "Consumer behaviour in tourism: Concepts, influences and opportunities." *Current Issues in Tourism* 17 (10):872–909. doi: 10.1080/13683500.2013.850064.

Dickey, David A., and Wayne A. Fuller. 1979. "Distribution of the estimators for autoregressive time series with a unit root." *Journal of the American Statistical Association* 74 (366a):427–431. doi: 10.1080/01621459.1979.10482531.

Dritsakis, Nikolaos. 2004. "Tourism as a long-run economic growth factor: An empirical investigation for Greece using causality analysis." *Tourism Economics* 10 (3):305–316. doi: 10.5367/0000000041895094.

Engle, Robert F., and C. W. J. Granger. 1987. "Co-integration and error correction: Representation, estimation, and testing." *Econometrica* 55 (2):251–276. doi: 10.2307/1913236.

Granger, C. W. J. 1969. "Investigating causal relations by econometric models and cross-spectral methods." *Econometrica* 37 (3):424–438. doi: 10.2307/1912791.

Grosso, Massimo G., Molly Lesher, and Enrico Pinali. 2007. "Services trade liberalisation and tourism development." doi: doi:https://doi.org/10.1787/244767010605.

Gunduz, Lokman, and Hatemi-J. Abdulnasser. 2005. "Is the tourism-led growth hypothesis valid for Turkey?" *Applied Economics Letters* 12 (8):499–504. doi: 10.1080/13504850500109865.

Hye, Adnan, Qazi Muhammad, and Rana Ejaz Ali Khan. 2013. "Tourism-led growth hypothesis: A case study of Pakistan." *Asia Pacific Journal of Tourism Research* 18 (4):303–313. doi: 10.1080/10941665.2012.658412.

Johansen, Søren. 1988. "Statistical analysis of cointegration vectors." *Journal of Economic Dynamics and Control* 12 (2):231–254. doi: https://doi.org/10.1016/0165-1889(88)90041-3.

Katircioğlu, Salih T. 2010. "International tourism, higher education and economic growth: The case of north Cyprus." *The World Economy* 33 (12):1955–1972. doi: https://doi.org/10.1111/j.1467-9701.2010.01304.x.

Kim, Hyun J., Ming-Hsiang Chen, and SooCheong (Shawn) Jang. 2006. "Tourism expansion and economic development: The case of Taiwan." *Tourism Management* 27 (5):925–933. doi: https://doi.org/10.1016/j.tourman.2005.05.011.

Lee, Chien-Chiang, and Chun-Ping Chang. 2008. "Tourism development and economic growth: A closer look at panels." *Tourism Management* 29 (1):180–192. doi: https://doi.org/10.1016/j.tourman.2007.02.013.

Li, Kevin X., Mengjie Jin, and Wenming Shi. 2018. "Tourism as an important impetus to promoting economic growth: A critical review." *Tourism Management Perspectives* 26:135–142. doi: https://doi.org/10.1016/j.tmp.2017.10.002.

Mello-Sampayo, Felipa de, and Sofia de Sousa-Vale. 2012. "Tourism and growth in European countries: An application of likelihood-based panel cointegration." doi: http://hdl.handle.net/10400.5/4419.

Mohammed El Amine, Abdelli, and Aied Malika. 2020. "The contribution of social responsibility to achieving a competitive moral advantage: A case study of sherhal sweets organization." In *Global Entrepreneurial Trends in the Tourism and Hospitality Industry*, edited by Batabyal Debasish, 217–236. Hershey, PA: IGI Global.

Mohammed El Amine, Abdelli, Mansour Nadia, and Nabila Smaili. 2020. "The engineering of territorial tourism study case of Algeria." In *Strategies for Promoting Sustainable Hospitality and Tourism Services*, edited by Korstanje Maximiliano Emanuel, George Babu and Nedelea Alexandru-Mircea, 122–139. Hershey, PA: IGI Global.

Nelson, Charles R., and Charles R. Plosser. 1982. "Trends and random walks in macroeconomic time series: Some evidence and implications." *Journal of Monetary Economics* 10 (2):139–162. doi: https://doi.org/10.1016/0304-3932(82)90012-5.

Oh, Chi-Ok. 2005. "The contribution of tourism development to economic growth in the Korean economy." *Tourism Management* 26 (1):39–44. doi: https://doi.org/10.1016/j.tourman.2003.09.014.

Ohlan, Ramphul. 2017. "The relationship between tourism, financial development and economic growth in India." *Future Business Journal* 3 (1):9–22. doi: https://doi.org/10.1016/j.fbj.2017.01.003.

Schotman, Peter C., and Herman K. Van Dijk. 1991. "On Bayesian routes to unit roots." *Journal of Applied Econometrics* 6 (4):387–401. doi: https://doi.org/10.1002/jae.3950060407.

Seghir, Guellil M., Belmokaddem Mostéfa, Sahraoui Mohammed Abbes, and Ghouali Yassine Zakarya. 2015. "Tourism spending-economic growth causality in 49 countries: A dynamic panel data approach." *Procedia Economics and Finance* 23:1613–1623. doi: https://doi.org/10.1016/S2212-5671(15)00402-5.

Shahzad, Syed J. H., Muhammad Shahbaz, Román Ferrer, and Ronald R. Kumar. 2017. "Tourism-led growth hypothesis in the top ten tourist destinations: New evidence using the quantile-on-quantile approach." *Tourism Management* 60:223–232. doi: https://doi.org/10.1016/j.tourman.2016.12.006.

Sharpley, Richard. 2000. "Tourism and sustainable development: Exploring the theoretical divide." *Journal of Sustainable Tourism* 8 (1):1–19. doi: 10.1080/09669580008667346.

Sim, Nicholas, and Hongtao Zhou. 2015. "Oil prices, US stock return, and the dependence between their quantiles." *Journal of Banking & Finance* 55:1–8. doi: https://doi.org/10.1016/j.jbankfin.2015.01.013.

Sims, Christopher A. 1972. "Money, income, and causality." *The American Economic Review* 62 (4):540–552.

Slim, C. 2017. "Nonstationarity modeling of economic and financial time series." *International Journal of Economics and Management Engineering* 11 (12):2773–2779. doi: https://publications.waset.org/pdf/10008340.

UNWTO TOURISM. 2017., Tourism Highlights.

Index

For Product Safety Concerns and Information please contact our EU
representative GPSR@taylorandfrancis.com
Taylor & Francis Verlag GmbH, Kaufingerstraße 24, 80331 München, Germany

www.ingramcontent.com/pod-product-compliance
Ingram Content Group UK Ltd.
Pitfield, Milton Keynes, MK11 3LW, UK
UKHW010957180926
475701UK00004B/422
* 9 7 8 0 3 6 7 6 8 5 5 4 6 *